Penguin Education

Sociolinguistics

Edited by J. B. Pride
and Janet Holmes

Penguin Modern Linguistics Readings

General Editor

David Crystal

Advisory Board

Dwight Bolinger
M. A. K. Halliday
John Lyons
Frank Palmer
James Sledd
C. I. J. M. Stuart

Sociolinguistics

Selected Readings

Edited by J. B. Pride and Janet Holmes

Penguin Books

Penguin Books Ltd, Harmondsworth,
Middlesex, England
Penguin Books Inc, 7110 Ambassador Road,
Baltimore, Md 21207, USA
Penguin Books Australia Ltd,
Ringwood, Victoria, Australia

First published 1972
This selection copyright © J. B. Pride and Janet Holmes, 1972
Introduction and notes copyright © J. B. Pride and Janet Holmes, 1972
Copyright acknowledgement for items in this volume will be
found on page 371

Made and printed in Great Britain by
Hazell Watson & Viney Ltd,
Aylesbury, Bucks
Set in Monotype Times

Contents

Part Four
Acquisition and Proficiency 267

Introduction

Sociolinguistics has been established as a distinct discipline for some years, comprehending the study of the structure and use of language in its social and cultural contexts. Courses in sociolinguistics rely to a large extent on articles published in a great number of heterogeneous periodicals, reflecting the variety of disciplines which have contributed to the development of the subject: linguistic, anthropological, sociological, psychological, educational journals – articles used to teach sociolinguistics can be found in all these. In this selection then we have tried to achieve these two goals: firstly, the majority of the articles have been drawn together from various periodicals and are ones which we have found useful in teaching an introductory undergraduate course in sociolinguistics; and secondly, there are also contributions which have not yet been published elsewhere, and which represent some part of the most recent work in this rapidly expanding field. Needless to say, any selection of Readings will inevitably reflect a personal view of what areas of study are crucial to the discipline concerned.

Many insights into the social meaning of language have been the result of sociolinguistic research into *bilingualism* and *multilingualism*. It is work of this sort that has revealed most clearly some of the ways in which linguistic variation serves to reflect and clarify socio-cultural values. Dialectal and stylistic variation will always tend to convey different social meanings, but it may on the whole be easier to identify the object of study in the case of languages as such, within bilingual or multilingual speech communities; moreover, bilingualism and multilingualism are far more characteristic of present-day societies than many monolingual speakers would suppose.

The study of the social meaning conveyed by different languages in a multilingual community can be undertaken at two levels, the one logically preceding the other. In the first place one can examine the way the languages are used on the macro-scale, using data from large-scale surveys to reveal community norms of language use. Then, against this background one can examine how the individual exploits his awareness of the society's norms in order to achieve particular effects. Many questions need answering in a description of multilingualism at the level of community norms: how does one abstract from the behaviour of individuals in order to isolate such norms; to what extent do they restrict the individual, or vary in different societies; can the same cultural values be expressed by different languages in different communities? Some of these questions are discussed in the first section of the book.

The sociolinguistic study of bilingual and multilingual speech communities assumes both formally linguistic and functional aspects. One of its main focal points concerns the intrinsic properties of *standard* languages. What is meant by a 'standard' language, by 'standardization', by a 'vernacular', and by other such closely related terms – 'colloquial' for example, 'dialect', even the term 'language' itself? Garvin (1959) some time ago stated that a standard language should exhibit both 'flexible stability' and 'intellectualization'; namely, responsiveness to culture changes, a degree of formal stability backed up by suitable codification, and a functional range which will embrace in particular what Ferguson (1968) has referred to as 'intertranslatability with other languages in a range of topics and forms of discourse characteristic of industrialized, secularized, structurally differentiated, modern societies'; furthermore, that the language should symbolize the unification, separateness and prestige of the community that uses it. One sees the central importance of each of these considerations in the study of sociolinguistics generally. There is its renewal of interest, for example, in what had been a main point of departure for modern linguistics, namely the relevance of language to the understanding of culture and vice-versa; and its attention to the fact that in so many parts of the world not only are there very many languages (sometimes hundreds) within given national boundaries, but also several (possibly competing) varieties of those languages – sometimes differing to the extent that neither their native users nor any linguist can confidently say '*this* is an example of *that* language'. Sociolinguistics also explores the difficulties – and considerable interest – involved in assessing the relative values of different functions performed by languages, functions which are by no means necessarily always headed by that of intellectualization. The need for a measure of uniformity in and among languages confronts, in other words, the need for cultural relativity and change, for some degree of dialectal diversity, and for the kind of functional power that allows 'the principal business of speech behaviour' to be, say, 'the manipulation of emotions by aesthetic devices' (Albert, 1964, on Burundi). A standard language is by no means what common usage would call a standardized language!

Standard languages which symbolize feelings of unification, separateness and prestige, sometimes qualify as *national* languages. Some of the recurrent aspects of this perplexing but important field of study are: what are or could be some of the roles of 'languages of wider communication' (such as English, or French, or Russian) not only as national languages but also as affecting other national languages? how can or should less widely used languages expand, both formally and functionally? what principles should govern the choice of languages at various levels in the educational system of a country? and so on.

Whether the community be bi- (or multi-) lingual or monolingual, variety within languages is the rule. What is meant therefore by the terms *dialect* and *style*? There is no simple answer. The question, for example, 'where (socially and structurally as well as geographically) does this dialect – or language – end and the next begin?' is both persistent and challenging. Criteria for decisions about this and about very many other associated problems are numerous and often contradictory in effect, nor is it easy to assign relative degrees of importance. There may be said, however, to be three main criteria: *linguistic structure, intelligibility*, and *social function*. Structural diversity (in both regional and social space) can often be so extreme as to force one to Zipf's conclusion that 'if a linguistic description has to be consistent it must be that of an idiolect' (i.e. the speech of one individual); one might add 'at one point in time'. Moreover isoglosses (structural boundaries) will by no means always coincide as between one level of analysis (grammatical, phonological, etc.) and another – or even between one system and another at a given level (sentence structure, word structure, etc.); and the problem of gradual transitions always remains. Measures of intelligibility may, or may not, provide a simple and reliable key to structural distance. But what is meant by intelligibility? How does one deal with evidence of 'non-reciprocal' intelligibility (Wolff, 1959)? Village dialects in India have been said to form 'a continuous chain from Sind to Assam, with mutual intelligibility between adjacent areas' (Gumperz, 1964) – but not between more distant areas. How important are beliefs about intelligibility as compared with the results of tests (see especially Haugen, 1966)? Social function is certainly not the least important criterion. Many factors can apply here: social class of various sorts (compare the caste system in India, for example, with socio–economic stratification elsewhere), topic (consider the linguistic choices involved in certain religions, or attaching to local or non-local topics, etc.), and so forth. One crucial factor is that of interpersonal relationship, reflected in styles of speaking or writing: what is meant by 'formality' in any given speech community, how are subjective feelings of status expressed, etc.? Dialectal variation is always likely to be closely bound up with stylistic variation, the one a function of the other. It is the potential range of this interrelationship that is conveyed by our selection in Part Three.

Any individual member of a community must acquire far more than the formal or structural features of his language(s). He must undergo a process of socialization; he must acquire a knowledge of the social and cultural values of his society, the constraints which the society imposes on behaviour

– including language behaviour. A knowledge of the different aspects of dialectal and stylistic variation examined in Part Three is part of the *communicative competence* which must be acquired by the ideal speaker–hearer in any speech community. Any measure of his linguistic proficiency will therefore involve consideration of his ability to speak appropriately in different social contexts, as well as his skill in manipulating the phonology and syntax of the different linguistic codes used in the speech community.

Before adequate methods of measuring communicative competence can be devised a logical prerequisite is detailed studies of the social environment in which the individual acquires language. In the past successful language acquisition has too often been regarded as an inevitable result of sufficient exposure to the language, without any attention to the kind of language the individual is being exposed to. Second-language teaching, in particular, has often been less successful than it might, as a result of the restricted variety of linguistic contexts with which students are provided.

Another aspect of successful language acquisition is the effect of the individual's motivation on the degree of proficiency he attains in the language. Psychological attitudes are often developed early in the socialization of the child and may well lead to discrimination on the part of the individual as to which codes he wants to acquire. Motivations of this sort seem to be of central importance to successful language learning.

Exposure to a rich variety of linguistic material is as important in first-language acquisition as in second-language learning. In any speech community however, social variables will inevitably influence the linguistic codes to which the individual is exposed. In rural areas of Tanzania, the child's contact with English, for example, may well be limited to the English taught in school. Even leaving aside the variation in linguistic competence of different English teachers, the child's proficiency in English will inevitably be restricted since his experience of English has been confined to only one social domain, very few role-relationships and a limited number of speech functions. His communicative competence in English will, therefore, be limited to the ability to manipulate the language in only very restricted social situations no matter how strong his motivation to acquire the language.

Opportunities to acquire a wide range of the linguistic codes used in a community may also be affected by its social structure. In some communities the social class to which an individual belongs determines the range of codes to which he is exposed. A member of the highest caste in India, for example, will generally control a wide range of linguistic codes; the social elite in Haiti can be defined as the 10 per cent who speak both Haitian creole and also standard French, compared with the 90 per cent who are monolingual in the creole. In monolingual English-speaking communities, too, the social class to which one belongs can affect the variety of linguistic styles with which one is familiar. The upper middle-class executive may feel linguistically inadequate in a working men's club. His communicative competence is restricted to the social contexts with which he is familiar. Similarly, an individual who has had only limited education may feel unable to express himself appropriately at a scientific congress, should he find himself there. In other words we are all confined, to some extent, to the styles we have acquired in the social situations within which we have been socialized. The influence of social factors on communicative competence is evident in all societies; various aspects of this area of sociolinguistics are examined in Part Four.

The areas examined in this selection of readings moves then from the generally macro-level of sociolinguistic study in Parts One and Two to the generally micro-level in Parts Three and Four in two related ways. Firstly, the emphasis moves from the social constraints on the use of codes which are imposed on the whole community to the social constraints on the individual's opportunity to acquire those codes. And secondly, there is more emphasis on code-switching between different languages in order to convey different social information in the earlier sections, while the later sections focus more on intra-language switching, i.e. switching between dialects or styles.

Finally, we are aware that there are areas of sociolinguistics which we have inevitably neglected, and can only plead limitations of space and hope that the selection we have made will prove an interesting introduction to the field which may whet the reader's appetite and encourage him to read further.

References

ALBERT, E. M. (1964), 'Rhetoric, logic and poetics in Burundi: culture patterning of speech behaviour', in J. J. Gumperz and D. Hymes (eds.), *The Ethnography of Communication, AmA*, vol. 66, no. 6, part 2.

FERGUSON, C. A. (1968), 'Language development', in J. A. Fishman, C. A. Ferguson and J. Das Gupta (eds.) *Language Problems of Developing Nations*, Wiley.

GARVIN, P. L. (1959), 'The standard language problem', in D. Hymes (ed.), *Language in Culture and Society*, Harper & Row.

GUMPERZ, J. J. (1964), 'Linguistic and social interaction in two communities', *AmA*, vol. 66, part 2, pp. 137–54.

HAUGEN, E. (1966), 'Semi-communication in Scandinavia', *Sociological Enquiry*, vol. 36, no. 2.

WOLFF, H. (1959), 'Intelligibility and inter-ethnic attitudes', in D. Hymes (ed.), *Language in Culture and Society*, Harper & Row.

Part One
Bilingualism and Multilingualism

The first article in this opening section is mainly theoretical. Fishman discusses the utility of the concept of 'domain' in abstracting from the behaviour of large numbers of individuals, in order to describe and analyse code-switching at the societal level (the term 'code' as used here comprehends language, dialect or style). Sankoff opens with a succinct description of three main trends in sociolinguistic analysis, and then shows how these can be used in the analysis of her own data from a multilingual community in New Guinea. Salisbury, Denison and Sorensen provide further empirical data on multilingual speech communities. Salisbury discusses the socio-cultural value of multilingualism and translation for certain New Guinea tribes. Denison is interested in the social variables which lead to the selection of one of three languages in an isolated Italian community. Sorensen presents a homogeneous culture area which is linguistically extremely heterogeneous and describes the many different combinations of languages which may feature in the repertoire of any one tribe.

1 J. A. Fishman

The Relationship between Micro- and Macro-Sociolinguistics in the Study of Who Speaks What Language to Whom and When

A revision of J. A. Fishman, 'Who speaks what language to whom and when', *La Linguistique*, 1965, vol. 2, pp. 67–88

The analysis of multilingual settings

Multilingual speech communities differ from each other in so many ways that every student of societal multilingualism must grapple with the problem of how best to systematize or organize the manifold differences that are readily recognizable. This paper is directed to a formal consideration of several descriptive and analytic variables which may contribute to an understanding of *who* speaks *what* language to *whom* and *when* in those speech communities that are characterized by widespread, and relatively stable, multilingualism. It deals primarily with 'within-group (or intragroup) multilingualism' rather than with 'between-group (or intergroup) multilingualism', that is, with those multilingual settings in which a single population makes use of two (or more) 'languages' or varieties of the 'same language' for internal communicative purposes (Fishman, 1967). As a result of this limitation mastery or control of *mother tongue* and *other tongue* (or, more generally, of the various languages or varieties constituting the speech community's linguistic repertoire (Gumperz, 1962) may be ruled out as an operative variable since the members of many speech networks could communicate with each other quite easily in any of the available codes or subcodes. It seems clear, however, that habitual language choice in multilingual speech communities or speech networks is far from being a random matter of momentary inclination, even under those circumstances when it could very well function as such from a purely probabilistic point of view (Lieberson, 1964). 'Proper' usage dictates that only *one* of the theoretically co-available languages or varieties *will* be chosen by particular classes of *interlocutors* on particular kinds of *occasions* to discuss particular kinds of *topics*.

What are the most appropriate parameters in terms of which these choice-patterns can be described in order to attain both factual accuracy and theoretical parsimony, and in order to facilitate the integration of small-group and large-group research rather than its further needless polarization? If we can solve the problem of how to describe language choice in stable within-group bilingual settings (where the limits of language mastery do not intrude), we can then more profitably turn (or return) to the problem of choice determinants in less stable settings such as those characterizing immigrant–host relationships and between-group multilingual settings more generally (Fishman, 1964).

A hypothetical example

American students are so accustomed to bilingualism as a 'vanishing phenomenon', as a temporary dislocation from a presumably more normal state of affairs characterized by 'one man, one language', that an example of stable intragroup bilingualism may help to start off our discussion in a more naturalistic and less bookish vein.

A government functionary in Brussels arrives home after stopping off at his club for a drink. He *generally* speaks standard French in his office, standard Dutch at his club and a distinctly local variant of Flemish at home.[1] In each instance he identifies himself with a different speech network to which he belongs, wants to belong, and from which he seeks acceptance. All of these networks – and more – are included in his overarching speech community, even though each is more commonly associated with one variety than with another. Nevertheless, it is not difficult to find occasions at the office, in which he speaks or is spoken to in one or another variety of Flemish. There are also occasions at the club when he speaks or is addressed in French; finally, there are occasions at home when he communicates in standard Dutch or even French.

Our hypothetical government functionary is most likely to give and get Flemish at the office when he bumps into another functionary who hails from the very same Flemish-speaking town. The two of them grew up together and went to school together. Their respective sets of parents strike them as being similarly 'kind-but-old-fashioned'. In short, they share many common experiences and points of view (or think they do, or pretend they do) and therefore they tend to speak to each other in the language which represents for them the intimacy that they share. The two do not cease being government functionaries when they speak Flemish to each other; they simply prefer to treat each other as intimates rather than as functionaries. However, the careful observer will also note that the two do not speak Flemish to each other invariably. When they speak about world affairs, or the worlds of art and literature, not to mention the world of government, they tend to switch into French (or to reveal far more

---

1. This example may be replaced by any one of a number of others: Standard German, Schwytzertütsch and Romansch (in parts of Switzerland): Hebrew, English and Yiddish in Israel; Riksmaal, Landsmaal and more local dialectal variants of the latter in Norway; Standard German, Plattdeutsch and Danish in Schleswig; French, Standard German and German dialect in Luxembourg, etc.

French lexical, phonological or even grammatical influence in their Flemish), even though (for the sake of our didactic argument) the mood of intimacy and familiarity remains clearly evident throughout.

Thus, our overall problem is twofold: (*1*) to recognize and describe whatever higher-order regularities there may be in choosing among the several varieties that constitute the repertoire of a multilingual speech community and (*2*) nevertheless, to provide the interpersonal fluctuation (lower-order societal patterning) that remains even when higher-order societal patterning is established.

Topic

The fact that two individuals who usually speak to each other primarily in *X* nevertheless switch to *Y* (or vacillate more noticeably between *X* and *Y*) when discussing certain topics leads us to consider topic *per se* as a regulator of language use in multilingual settings.

The implication of topical regulation of language choice is that certain topics are somehow handled 'better', or more appropriately, in one language than in another in particular multilingual contexts. However, this greater appropriateness may reflect or may be brought about by several different but mutually reinforcing factors. Thus, some multilingual speakers may 'acquire the habit' of speaking about topic *x* in language X, partially because that is the language in which they were *trained* to deal with this topic (e.g. they received their university training in economics in French), partially because *they* (*and their interlocutors*) may *lack the specialized terms* for a satisfying discussion of *x* in language Y[2] partially because *language Y itself may currently lack as exact or as many terms* for handling topic *x* as those currently possessed by language X, and partially because *it is considered strange* or inappropriate to discuss *x* in language Y. The very multiplicity of sources of topical regulation suggests that *topic* may not in itself be a convenient analytic variable when language choice is considered from the point of view of the larger societal patterns and sociolinguistic norms of a multilingual setting, no matter how fruitful it may be at the level of face-to-face interaction *per se*. What *would* be helpful for larger societal investigations and for inter-societal comparisons is an understanding of how topics reflect or imply regularities which pertain to

2. This effect has been noted even in normally monolingual settings, such as those obtaining among American intellectuals, many of whom feel obliged to use French or German words in conjunction with particular professional topics. English lexical influence on the language of immigrants in the United States has also often been explained on topical grounds. The importance of topical determinants is discussed by Haugen (1953, 1956) and Weinreich (1953), and, more recently, by Gumperz (1962) and Susan Ervin (1964). It is implied as a 'pressure' exerted upon 'contacts' in Mackey's description of bilingualism (1962).

the major spheres of activity in any society under consideration. We may be able to discover the latter if we inquire *why* a significant number of people in a particular multilingual setting, at a particular time, have received certain kinds of training in one language rather than in another; or *what it reveals* about a particular multilingual setting if language X *is* actually less capable of coping with topic *x* than is language Y. Does it not reveal more than merely a topic-language relationship at the level of face-to-face encounters? Does it not reveal that certain socio-culturally *recognized spheres of activity* are, at least temporarily, under the sway of one language or variety (and, therefore, perhaps under the control of certain speech networks) rather than others? Thus, while topic is doubtlessly a crucial consideration in understanding language-choice variance in our two hypothetical government functionaries, *we must seek a means of examining and relating their individual, momentary choices to relatively stable patterns of choice that exist in their multilingual setting as a whole.*

Domains of language behavior

The concept of domains of language behavior seems to have received its first partial elaboration from students of language maintenance and language shift among *Auslandsdeutsche* in pre-World War Two multilingual settings.[3] German settlers were in contact with many different non-German-speaking populations in various types of contact settings and were exposed to various kinds of socio-cultural change processes. In attempting to chart and compare the fortunes of the German language under such varying circumstances Schmidt-Rohr (1932) seems to have been the first to suggest that *dominance configurations* needed to be established to reveal the overall-status of language choice in various domains of behavior. The domains recommended by Schmidt-Rohr were the following nine: the family, the playground and street, the school (subdivided into language of instruction, subject of instruction, and language of recess and entertainment), the church, literature, the press, the military, the courts and the governmental administration. Subsequently, other investigators either added additional domains (e.g. Mak, 1935, who nevertheless followed Schmidt-Rohr in overlooking the work-sphere as a domain), or found that fewer domains were sufficient in particular multilingual settings (e.g. Frey, 1945, who required only home, school and church in his analysis of Amish 'triple talk'). However, what is more interesting is that Schmidt-Rohr's domains bear a striking similarity to those 'generally

3. The study of language maintenance and language shift is concerned with the relationship between change or stability in habitual language use, on the one hand, and ongoing psychological, social or cultural processes of change and stability, on the other hand (Fishman, 1964, 1966; Nahirny and Fishman, 1965).

termed' spheres of activity which have more recently been independently advanced by others interested in the study of acculturation, intergroup relations, and bilingualism (e.g. Dohrenwend and Smith, 1962).

Domains are defined, regardless of their number,[4] in terms of *institutional contexts* or *socio-ecological co-occurrences*. They attempt to designate the *major clusters of interaction situations that occur in particular multilingual settings*. Domains enable us to understand that *language choice* and *topic*, appropriate though they may be for analyses of individual behavior at the level of face-to-face verbal encounters, are, as we suggested above, related to widespread socio-cultural norms and expectations. By recognizing the existence of domains, it becomes possible to contrast the language of topics for individuals, or particular sub-populations, with the language of domains for a larger part, if not the whole, of the population.

The appropriate designation and definition of domains of language behavior obviously calls for considerable insight into the socio-cultural dynamics of particular multilingual speech communities at particular periods in their history. Schmidt-Rohr's domains reflect not only multilingual settings in which a large number of spheres of activity, even those that pertain to governmental functions, are theoretically open to both or all of the languages present, but also those multilingual settings in which such permissiveness is at least sought by a sizeable number of interested parties. Quite different domains might be appropriate if one were to study habitual language use among children in these very same settings. Certainly, immigrant–host contexts, in which only the language of the host society is recognized for governmental functions, would require other and perhaps fewer domains, particularly if younger generations constantly leave the immigrant society and enter the host society. Finally, the domains of language behavior may differ from setting to setting not only in terms of number and designation, but also in terms of level. Thus, in studying acculturating populations in Arizona, Barker, who studied bilingual Spanish Americans (1947) and Barber, who studied trilingual Yaqui Indians (1952), formulated domains at the level of *socio-psychological analysis*: intimate, informal, formal and intergroup. Interestingly enough, the domains defined in this fashion were then identified with domains at the *societal-institutional level* mentioned above. The 'formal' domain, e.g., was found to coincide with religious-ceremonial activities; the

4. We can safely reject the implication encountered in certain discussions of domains, that there must be an invariant set of domains applicable to all multilingual settings. If language behavior is reflective of socio-cultural patterning, as is now widely accepted, then different kinds of multilingual speech communities should benefit from analyses in terms of different domains of language use, whether defined intuitively, theoretically, or empirically.

'intergroup' domain consisted of economic and recreational activities as well as interactions with governmental—legal authority, etc. The inter-relationship between domains of language behavior defined at a societal-institutional level and domains defined at a socio-psychological level (the latter being somewhat similar to situational analyses discussed earlier) may enable us to study language choice in multilingual settings in newer and more fruitful ways.

The 'governmental administration' domain is a social nexus which brings people together *primarily* for a certain *cluster of purposes*. Further-more, it brings them together *primarily* for a certain set of role-relations (discussed below) and in a delimited environment. Thus, domain is a socio-cultural construct abstracted from topics of communication, relation-ships between communicators, and locales of communication, in accord with the institutions of a society and the spheres of activity of a speech community, in such a way that *individual behavior and social patterns can be distinguished from each other and yet related to each other*.[5] The domain is a higher-order abstraction or summarization which is arrived at from a detailed study of the face-to-face interactions in which language choice is embedded. Of the many factors contributing to and subsumed under the domain concept, some are more important and more accessible to careful measurement than others. One of these, topic, has already been discussed. Two others, role-relation and locale remain to be discussed. Role-relations may be of value to us in accounting for the fact that our two hypothetical governmental functionaries, who usually speak an informal variant of Flemish to each other at the office, except when they talk about technical, professional or sophisticated 'cultural' matters, are themselves not entirely alike in this respect. One of the two tends to slip into French more fre-quently than the other. It would not be surprising to discover that he is the supervisor of the other.

Domains and role-relations

In many studies of multilingual behavior the family domain has proved to be a very crucial one. Multilingualism often begins in the family and depends upon it for encouragement if not for protection. In other cases, multilingualism withdraws into the family domain after it has been dis-placed from other domains in which it was previously encountered. Little wonder then that many investigators, beginning with Braunshausen several years ago (1928), have differentiated *within* the family domain in terms of

5. For a discussion of the differences and similarities between 'functions of language behavior' and 'domains of language behavior' see Fishman, 1964. 'Functions' stand closer to socio-psychological analysis, for they abstract their constituents in terms of individual motivation, rather than in terms of societal institutions.

'speakers'. However, two different approaches have been followed in connection with such differentiation. Braunshausen (and, much more recently, Mackey, 1962; 1965; 1966) have merely specified family 'members': father, mother, child, domestic, governess and tutor, etc. Gross, on the other hand, has specified *dyads* within the family (1951): grandfather to grandmother, grandmother to grandfather, grandfather to father, grandmother to father, grandfather to mother, grandmother to mother, grandfather to child, grandmother to child, father to mother, mother to father, etc. The difference between these two approaches is quite considerable. Not only does the second approach recognize that interacting members of a family (as well as the participants in most other domains of language behavior) are *hearers* as well as *speakers* (i.e., that there may be a distinction between multilingual *comprehension* and multilingual *production*), but it also recognizes that their language behavior may be more than merely a matter of individual preference or facility but also a matter of *role-relations*. In certain societies particular behaviors (including language behaviors) are *expected* (if not required) of *particular individuals vis-à-vis each other* (Goodenough, 1965).

The family domain is hardly unique with respect to its differentiability into role-relations. Each domain can be differentiated into role-relations that are specifically crucial or typical of it in particular societies at particular times. The religious domain (in those societies where religion can be differentiated from folkways more generally) may reveal such role relations as cleric–cleric, cleric–parishioner, parishioner–cleric, and parishioner–parishioner. Similarly, pupil–teacher, buyer–seller, employer–employee, judge–petitioner, all refer to specific role-relations in other domains. It would certainly seem desirable to describe and analyse language use or language choice in a particular multilingual setting in terms of the crucial role-relations within the specific domains considered to be most revealing for that setting.[6] The distinction between own-group-interlocutor and other-group-interlocutor may also be provided for in this way when intergroup bilingualism becomes the focus of inquiry.

Domains and locales
Ervin (1964) and Gumperz (1964) have presented many examples of the importance of locale as a determining component of situational analysis.

6. These remarks are not intended to imply that *all* role—relation differences are necessarily related to language-choice differences. This almost certainly is *not* the case. Just which role-relation differences *are* related to language-choice differences (and under what circumstances) is a matter for empirical determination within each multilingual setting, as well as at different points in time within the same setting. In general, the verification of significantly different clusters of allo-roles (as well as allo-topics and allo-locales) (see below) is a prerequisite for the empirical formulation of domains.

If one meets one's clergyman at the race track the impact of the locale on the topics and role-relationships that normally obtain is likely to be quite noticeable. However, we must also note that domains too are locale-related in the sense that most major social institutions are associated with a very few primary locales. Just as topical appropriateness in face-to-face language choice is indicative of larger scale societal patterns, and just as role appropriateness in face-to-face language choice is similarly indicative, so the locale constraints and local appropriatenesses that obtain in face-to-face language choice have their large-scale implications and extrapolations.

The construct validity of domains

A research project dealing with Puerto Rican bilingualism in the Greater New York City Area has yielded data which may help clarify both the construct validity of domains as well as the procedure for their recognition. Since domains are a higher order generalization from *congruent situations* (i.e. from situations in which individuals interacting in appropriate role-relationships with each other, in the appropriate locales for these role-relationships, and discussing topics appropriate to their role-relationships) it was first necessary to test intuitive and rather clinical estimates of the widespread congruences that were felt to obtain. After more than a year of participant observation and other data-gathering experiences it seemed to Greenfield (1968) that five domains could be generalized from the innumerable situations that he had encountered. He tentatively labeled these 'family', 'friendship', 'religion', 'education' and 'employment' and proceeded to determine whether a typical *situation* could be presented for each domain as a means of collecting self-report data on language choice. As indicated below each domain was represented by a congruent person (interlocutor), place and topic in the self-report instrument that Greenfield constructed for high school students.

Domain	Interlocutor	Place	Topic
Family	Parent	Home	How to be a good son or daughter
Friendship	Friend	Beach	How to play a certain game
Religion	Priest	Church	How to be a good Christian
Education	Teacher	School	How to solve an algebra problem
Employment	Employer	Workplace	How to do your job more efficiently

Greenfield's hypothesis was that within the Puerto Rican speech community, among individuals who knew Spanish and English equally well,

Spanish was primarily associated with family and secondarily with friend-ship (the two, family and friendship constituting the intimacy value cluster); while English was primarily associated with religion, work and education (the three constituting the status-stressing value cluster).[7] In order to test this hypothesis he first presented two seemingly congruent situational components and requested his subjects firstly to select a third component in order to complete the situation and secondly to indicate their likelihood of using Spanish or English if they were involved in such a situation and if they and their Puerto Rican interlocutors knew Spanish and English equally well. Section 1 of Table 1 shows that Greenfield's predictions were uniformly confirmed among those subjects who selected congruent third components. Spanish was decreasingly reported for family, friendship, religion, employment and education, regardless of whether the third component selected was a person, place or topic.

However, as Blom and Gumperz (1968), Fishman (1968b) and others have indicated, seemingly incongruent situations frequently occur and are rendered understandable and acceptable (just as are the seemingly ungrammatical sentences that we hear in most spontaneous speech). Interlocutors reinterpret incongruencies in order to salvage some semb-lance of the congruency in terms of which they understand and function within their social order. Were this not the case then no seemingly con-gruent domains could arise and be maintained out of the incongruencies of daily life. In order to test this assumption Greenfield proceeded to present his subjects with two incongruent components (e.g. with a person from one hypothetical domain and with a place from another hypo-thetical domain) and asked them to select a third component in order to complete the situation, as well as to indicate their likelihood of using Spanish or English in a situation so constituted. Greenfield found that the third component was overwhelmingly selected from either one or the other of any two domains from which he had selected the first two components. Furthermore, in their attempts to render a seemingly incongruent situation somewhat more congruent, his subjects' language preferences left the relationship between domains and language choice substantially unaltered (directionally) regardless of whether person, places or topics were involved. Nevertheless, all domains became somewhat less different from each other than they had been in the fully congruent situations. Apparently, both individual indecisiveness as well as sociolinguistic norms governing domain regularity must be combined and compromised when incongruencies appear. Language choice is much more clear-cut and polarized in 'usual' situations governed entirely by sociolinguistic norms of communicative

7. For a discussion of the significance of value clusters in the study of diglossic societies see Fishman (1968b).

Table 1 **Spanish- and English-usage self-ratings in various situations for components selected by bilingual Ss,** Greenfield, 1968

1. Congruent situations: two 'congruent' components presented; S selects third congruent component and language appropriate to situation.

Congruent persons selected

	Parent	Friend	Total	Priest	Teacher	Employer	Total
mean	2·75	3·38	3·08	4·67	4·92	4·77	4·77
s. d.	1·67	1·22	1·15	0·68	0·30	0·44	0·38
n	12	13	13	12	12	13	13

Congruent places selected

	Home	Beach	Total	Church	School	Workplace	Total
mean	2·33	3·50	2·60	3·80	4·79	4·27	4·34
s. d.	1·11	1·37	1·14	1·57	0·58	1·39	0·99
n	15	6	15	15	14	15	15

Congruent topics selected

	Family	Friendship	Total	Religion	Education	Employment	Total
mean	1·69	3·33	2·64	3·80	4·78	4·44	4·38
s. d.	0·95	1·24	0·98	1·52	0·55	1·15	0·75
n	16	18	18	15	18	18	18

2. Incongruent situations: two 'incongruent' components presented; S selects any third component and language appropriate to situation.

All persons selected

	Parent	Friend	Total	Priest	Teacher	Employer	Total
mean	2·89	3·48	3·50	4·65	4·73	4·38	4·66
s. d.	1·41	1·21	0·73	0·63	0·42	0·74	0·57
n	13	13	13	13	13	8	13

All places selected

	Home	Beach	Total	Church	School	Workplace	Total
mean	2·63	3·86	2·77	3·71	4·39	4·42	4·10
s. d.	0·80	1·05	0·73	1·36	1·03	0·98	0·85
n	15	5	15	15	15	15	15

All topics selected

	Family	Friendship	Total	Religion	Education	Employment	Total
mean	2·88	3·81	3·26	3·07	3·65	3·81	3·49
s. d.	1·07	1·16	1·05	1·03	1·59	1·06	0·79
n	18	16	18	18	17	18	18

1 = all in Spanish; 5 = all in English

appropriateness than they are in 'unusual' situations which must be resolved by individual interpretation.

Greenfield's findings imply that the assumed relationship between face-to-face situations and larger-scale societal domains obtains for self-report data. However, it remained necessary for other investigators to determine whether the domains adumbrated in this fashion have more general validity in the speech community under study.

A language census conducted among all 431 souls in a two-block Puerto Rican neighborhood in Jersey City yielded the data shown in Table 2. Above and beyond examining the replies obtained to the individual census items the reader's attention should be directed to the results of the factor

Table 2 **Language census**

Item	Yes	Little	No	NP
1. Can understand Spanish conversation?	779	135	019	067
2. Can speak Spanish (conversation)?	833	077	016	074
3. Can read newspapers/books in Spanish?	397	049	318	237
4. Can write letters in Spanish?	390	030	339	241
5. Can understand English conversation?	571	176	183	070
6. Can speak English (conversation)?	536	181	216	067
7. Can read newspapers/books in English?	455	130	206	209
8. Can write letters in English?	387	063	327	223
	Spanish	*English*	*Both*	*NP*
9. First language understood (conversation)?	886	002	039	072
10. First language spoken (conversation)?	884	—	023	093
11. First language read (newspapers/books)?	401	—	297	302
12. First language written (letters)?	383	002	276	339
13. Most frequently spoken at home?	657	088	183	072
14. Most frequently read at home?	267	051	357	325
15. Most frequently written at home?	339	014	255	392
16. Most frequently spoken with fellow workers?	137	049	137	677
17. Most frequently spoken with supervisor?	046	009	264	680
18. Most frequently spoken with clients/customers?	032	014	035	919
19. Language of instruction in school?	339	237	167	257
20. Language liked most (conversation)?	362	285	186	167
21. Language of priest's/minister's sermon?	452	137	193	206
22. Language of silent prayer?	469	123	151	257
23. Language of church service?	427	160	193	220

Percentages carried to 3 places, decimals omitted

Source: Fishman (1968a)

On a re-interviewed sample of 124 cases the distributions obtained were practically identical to those shown above, indicating that the marginals reported above are quite stable.

The language replies to the census have been subjected to a factor analysis (verimax orthogonal rotation). The following five-factor solution appeared to be most revealing:

No.	Suggested factor name	Items (loadings)
1	Spanish: literacy	4(93), 3(92), 15(89), 12(88), 11(87), 19(71), 14(70), 20(54)
2	English (oral and written)	7(89), 6(88), 5(84), 8(82)
3	Spanish: oral	9(78), 1(71), 2(66), 10(63), 13(38)
4	Spanish: at work	18(79), 16(73), 17(55)
5	Spanish: in religion	21(93), 23(89), 22(40)

analysis (shown below the Table). If domains are more than the investigator's etic reclassification of situations then they should also become apparent from factor analysis which in essence, asks: which items tend to be answered in a consistent fashion. Of the five domains extracted from this analysis, all four domains considered appropriate for census questioning (language in the context of family, education, work and religion) appeared as separate factors, namely, 1. Spanish: literacy (=education), 3. Spanish: Oral (=family), 4. Spanish: at work, and 5. Spanish: in religion. In addition, an English factor also appeared indicating that although English is not specifically domain-associated for the population as a whole (it *is* so associated for children as we will soon see) it is also not displacively or transitionally related to Spanish. An orthogonal English factor indicates that (as in other speech communities marked by relatively stable and widespread bilingualism) there is no need for one language to be learned or used at the *expense* of the other in the population under study.

A third (and, for this presentation, final) indication of the construct validity of domains as analytic parameters for the study of large-scale socio-linguistic patterns is yielded by Edelman's data (1968). Here we note that when the word-naming responses of bilingual Puerto Rican children in Jersey City were analysed in accord with the domains derived from Greenfield's and Fishman's data reported above, significant and instructive findings were obtained. The most Spanish domain for all children was 'family' (Table 3a). The most English domain for all children was 'education'. The analysis of variance (Table 3b) indicates that not only did the children's responses differ significantly by age (older children giving more responses in both languages than did younger children), by language (English yielding more responses than does Spanish), and by domain (church yielding fewer responses than does any other domain), but that

Table 3a **Mean number of words named by young schoolchildren**

Age	Language	Domain Family	Education	Religion	Friendship	Total
6–8	English	6·2	8·2	6·6	8·3	7·3
	Spanish	7·6	6·2	5·8	6·4	6·5
	Total	6·9	7·2	6·2	7·4	6·9
9–11	English	11·7	12·8	8·7	10·9	11·0
	Spanish	10·5	9·4	7·2	9·7	9·2
	Total	11·1	11·1	7·9	10·3	10·1
Total	English	9·0	10·5	7·7	9·6	9·2
	Spanish	9·0	7·8	6·5	8·0	7·8
	Total	9·0	9·1	7·1	9·0	8·5

Table 3b **Analysis of variance of young schoolchildren's word-naming scores**

Source	Sum of squares	df	Mean square	F_{95}	F_{95}	F_{99}
Between subjects	1844·12	33				
C (age)	689·30	1	689·30	19·67*	4·17	7·56
D (sex)	15·54	1	15·54	0·44	4·17	7·56
CD	87·87	1	87·87	2·51	4·17	7·56
error (b)	1051·41	30	35·05			
Within subjects	1795·88	238				
A (language)	123·13	1	123·13	9·73*	4·17	7·56
B (domain)	192·54	3	64·18	8·51*	2·71	4·00
AB	65·12	3	21·71	11·67*	2·71	4·00
AC	16·50	1	16·50	1·30	4·17	7·56
AD	42·08	1	42·08	3·32	4·17	7·56
BC	61·54	3	20·51	2·72	2·71	4·00
BD	2·89	3	0·96	0·13	2·71	4·00
ABC	23·99	3	8·00	4·30*	2·71	4·00
ABD	6·70	3	2·23	1·20	2·71	4·00
ACD	14·62	1	14·62	1·15	4·17	7·56
BCD	13·53	3	4·51	0·60	2·71	4·00
ABCD	7·98	3	2·66	1·43	2·71	4·00
error (w)	1225·26	210				
$error_1(w)$	379·88	30	12·66			
$error_2(w)$	678·31	90	7·54			
$error_3(w)$	167·07	90	1·86			
Total	3640·00	271				

* Significant at or above the 0·01 level.

N = 34

Source: Edelman (1968)

these three variables *interact significantly* as well. This means that one language is much more associated with certain domains than is the other and that this is differentially so by age. This is exactly the kind of finding for which domain analysis is particularly suited. Its utility for inter-society comparisons and for gauging language shift would seem to be quite promising.

The integration of macro- and micro-parameters

The situational analysis of language and behavior represents the boundary area between micro- and macro-sociolinguistics. The very fact that a baseball conversation 'belongs' to one speech variety and an electrical engineering lecture 'belongs' to another speech variety is a major key to a even more generalized description of sociolinguistic variation. The very fact that humor during a formal lecture is realized through a *metaphorical switch* to another variety (Blom and Gumperz, 1968) must be indicative of an underlying sociolinguistic *regularity*, which obtained before the switch occurred, perhaps of the view that lecture-like or formal situations are generally associated with one language or variety whereas levity or intimacy is tied to another. Without such a view, without a more general norm assigning a particular topic or situation, as one of a class of such topics or situations, to one language rather than to another, metaphorical purposes could neither be served nor recognized.

As with all constructs (including situations, role-relationships and speech events), domains originate in the integrative intuition of the investigator. If the investigator notes that student-teacher interactions in classrooms, school corridors, school auditoriums, and in school laboratories of elementary schools, high schools, colleges and universities are all realized via H, as long as these interactions are focused upon educational technicality and specialization, he may begin to suspect that these congruent situations all belong to a single (educational) *domain*. If he further finds that incongruent situations involving an educational and a non-educational ingredient are, by and large, predictably resolved in terms of H rather than L if the third ingredient is an educational time, place or role-relationship, he may feel further justified in positing an educational domain. If informants tell him that the predicted language or variety would be appropriate in most of the examples he can think of that derive from his notion of the educational domain, whereas they proclaim that it would not be appropriate for examples that he draws from a contrasted domain, and, finally, *if the construct helps clarify and organize his data, and, particularly if it arises as a compositing feature of his data* – then the construct is as usefully validated as is that of situation or event – with one major difference.

Whereas particular speech acts can be apportioned to the speech events and social situations in which they transpired (Hymes, 1967), the same cannot be done with respect to such acts or excerpts in relationship to societal domains. Domains are extrapolated from the *data* of 'talk' rather than being an actual component of the *process* of talk. However, domains are as real as the very social institutions of a speech community and indeed they show a marked paralleling with such major social institutions (Barker, 1947). There is an undeniable difference between the social institution, 'the family', and any particular family, but there is no doubt that the societal norms concerning the former must be derived from data on many instances of the latter. Once such societal norms are formulated they can be utilized to test predictions concerning the distributions of societally patterned variation in talk across all instances of one domain *v.* all instances of another.

Thus, domains and social situations reveal the links that exist between micro- and macro-sociolinguistics. The members of diglossic speech communities can come to have certain views concerning their varieties or languages because these varieties are associated (in behavior and in attitude) with particular domains. The H variety (or language) is considered to reflect certain values and relationships within the speech community, whereas the L variety is considered to reflect others. Certain individuals and groups may come to advocate the expansion of the functions of L into additional domains. Others may advocate the displacement of L entirely and the use of H solely. Neither of these revisionist views could be held or advocated without recognition of the reality of domains of language-and-behavior in terms of *existing* norms of communicative appropriations. The high culture values with which certain varieties are associated and the intimacy and folksiness values with which others are congruent are both derivable from domain-appropriate norms governing characteristic verbal interaction.

There are several levels and approaches to sociolinguistic description and a host of linguistic, sociolinguistic and societal constructs within each (Figure 1). The choice among them depends on the particular problem at hand. This is necessarily so. Sociolinguistics is of interest to students of small societies as well as to students of national and international integration. It must help clarify the change from one face-to-face situation to another. It must also help clarify the different language-related beliefs and behaviors of entire social sectors and classes. It must be as useful and as informative to sociologists pursuing inter-societal and intra-societal topics as it is to linguists pursuing more contextualized linguistic description.

It would be foolhardy to claim that one and the same method of data collection and data analysis be utilized for such a variety of problems and purposes. It is one of the hallmarks of scientific social inquiry that methods are selected as a *result* of problem specifications rather than independently of them. Sociolinguistics is neither methodologically nor theoretically uniform. Nevertheless, it is gratifying to note that for those who seek such ties

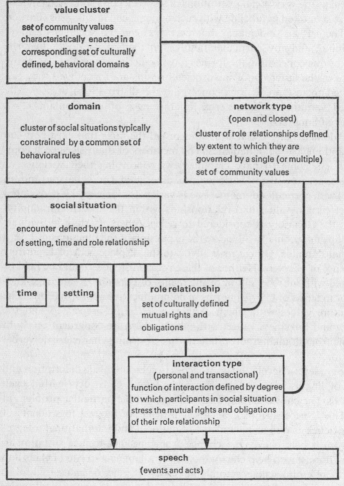

Figure 1 Relationship among some constructs employed in sociolinguistic analysis (Cooper, 1968)

the links between micro- and macro-constructs and methods exist (as do a number of constructs and methods that have wide applicability through the entire range of sociolinguistics). Just as there is no societally unencumbered verbal interaction so are there no large-scale relationships between language and society that do not depend on individual interaction for their realization. Although there is no mechanical part-whole relationship between them, micro- and macro-sociolinguistics are both conceptually and methodologically complementary.

References

BARBER, C. (1952), 'Trilingualism in Pascua; social functions of language in an Arizona Yaqui village', M A thesis, University of Arizona.

BARKER, G. C. (1947), 'Social functions of language in a Mexican-American Community', *Acta Americana*, vol. 5, pp. 185–202.

BLOM, J.-P. and GUMPERZ, J. J. (1968), 'Social meaning in linguistic structures: code-switching in Norway? in J. J. Gumperz and D. Hymes (eds.), *Directions in Sociolinguistics*, Holt, Rinehart & Winston (publ. 1972), pp. 407–34.

BRAUNSHAUSEN, N. (1928), 'Le bilinguisme et la famille', in *Le Bilinguisme et l'Education*, Bureau International d'Education, Généva-Luxembourg.

COOPER, R. L. (1968), 'How can we measure the roles which a bilingual's languages play in his everyday behavior?', *Proceedings of The International Seminar on the Measurement and Description of Bilingualism*, Ottawa Canadian Commission for Unesco.

DOHRENWEND, B. P. and SMITH, R. J. (1962), 'Toward a theory of acculturation', *Southwest J. of Anthrop.*, vol. 18, pp. 30–39.

EDELMAN, M. (1968), 'Word naming responses of bilingual Puerto Rican children', in J. A. Fishman (ed.), *The Measurement and Description of Language Dominance in Bilinguals*, Seventh Progress Report, Yeshiva University, N.Y.

ERVIN, S. M. (1964), 'An analysis of the interaction of language, topic and listener', *AmA*, vol. 66, part 2, pp. 86–102.

FISHMAN, J. A. (1964), 'Language maintenance and language shift as fields of inquiry', *Linguistics*, no. 9, pp. 32–70.

FISHMAN, J. A. (1965), 'Who speaks What Language to Whom and When', *La Linguistique*, vol. 2, pp. 67–88.

FISHMAN, J. A. (1966), *Language Loyalty in the United States*, Mouton.

FISHMAN, J. A. (1967), 'Bilingualism with and without diglossia; diglossia with and without bilingualism', *J. Soc. Issues*, vol. 23, no. 2, pp. 29–38.

FISHMAN, J. A. (1968a), 'Sociolinguistic analysis of census data', in J. A. Fishman, (Dir.), *The Measurement and Description of Language Dominance in Bilinguals* (Seventh Progress Report), New York: Yeshiva University (Mimeograph).

FISHMAN, J. A. (1968b), 'Sociolinguistic perspective on the study of bilingualism', *Linguistics*, vol. 39, pp. 21–49.

FREY, J. W. (1945), 'Amish (triple talk)', *Amer. Speech*, vol. 20, pp. 85–98.

GOODENOUGH, W. H. (1965), 'Rethinking "status" and "role"; toward a general model of the cultural organization of social relationships', in M. Banton (ed.), *Relevance of Models for Social Anthropology*, Praeger.

GREENFIELD, L. (1968), 'Spanish and English usage self-ratings in various situational contexts', in J. A. Fishman (ed.) *The Measurement and Description of Language Dominance in Bilinguals*, Seventh Progress Report, Yeshiva University, N.Y.

GROSS, F. (1951), 'Language and value changes among the Arapaho', *I.J.A.L.*, vol. 17, pp. 10–17.

GUMPERZ, J. J. (1962), 'Types of linguistic communities', *Anthrop. Linguistics*, vol. 4, no. 1, pp. 28–40.

GUMPERZ, J. J. (1964), 'Linguistic and social interaction in two communities', *Am.A*, vol. 66, part 2, pp. 137–54.

HAUGEN, E. (1953), *The Norwegian Language in America* (2 vols.), University of Pennsylvania Press.

HAUGEN, E. (1956), *Bilingualism in the Americas: A Bibliography and Research Guide*, University of Alabama Press.

HYMES, D. (1967), 'Models of the interaction of language and social setting', *Journal of Social Issues*, vol. 23, No. 2, pp. 8–28.

LIEBERSON, S. (1964), 'Language questions in censuses', in S. Lieberson (ed.), *Explorations in Sociolinguistics*, *I.J.A.L.*, vol. 33, no. 4, pp. 134–51.

MACKEY, W. F. (1962), 'The description of bilingualism', *Canadian J. Linguistics*, vol. 7, pp. 51–85.

MACKEY, W. F. (1965), 'Bilingual interference: its analysis and measurement', *J. Communication*, vol. 15, pp. 239–49.

MACKEY, W. F. (1966), 'The measurement of bilingual behaviour', *The Canadian Psychologist*, vol. 7, pp. 75–90.

MAK, W. (1935), 'Zweisprachigkeit und Mischmundart in Oberschlesien', *Schlesisches Jahrbuch für deutsche Kulturarbeit*, vol. 7, pp. 41–52.

NAHIRNY, V. C., and FISHMAN, J. A. (1965), 'Organizational interest in language maintenance', in J. A. Fishman (ed.), *Language Loyalty in the United States*, Mouton.

SCHMIDT-ROHR, G. (1932), *Die Sprache als Bilderin der Völker*, Munich.

WEINREICH, U. (1953), *Languages in Contact*, Linguistic Circle of New York (6th printing, 1968, Mouton).

2 G. Sankoff

Language Use in Multilingual Societies: Some Alternative Approaches[1]

The behaviour of multilinguals in communities where multilingualism is the norm, and communication regularly takes place in two or more codes, has received a considerable amount of attention in recent years. Rather than concentrating on the historical linguistic consequences of such heterogeneous situations, scholars have dealt instead with the network of communications itself, trying to elucidate, on the synchronic level, the systematic aspects of people's use of the various codes available to them. In this paper I intend to review some of the major trends in the analytical approaches which have been proposed and to illustrate with data I collected on the behaviour of multilinguals in New Guinea during 1966–7 and 1968.[2] It is not my intention to provide an exhaustive review of even the recent literature on multilingualism: rather, I wish to discuss several currents of thought within sociolinguistics, and to show their relevance to the study of speech behaviour in multilingual communities. The three main trends with which I shall deal can be summarized as (1) attention to the functions of speech; (2) attempts to specify the configuration of non-linguistic variables which result in the choice of particular linguistic options on the part of individual speakers; and (3) detailed examination of linguistic variation *per se*, and its correlation with non-linguistic variables.

Though the data with which I shall be dealing are drawn from a multilingual community, it is clear that the kind of linguistic behaviour involved (e.g. shifting, or switching, among the various codes available) is not specific or limited to multilinguals, that is, it does not differ qualitatively from the behaviour of monolinguals (shifting of style or level). Hymes, discussing bilingualism, puts it this way:

Cases of bilingualism *par excellence* . . . are salient, special cases of the general phenomena of variety in code repertoire and switching among codes. No normal

1. I wish to express my thanks to Norman Denison, John Gumperz and Dell Hymes, to whom I am much indebted for helpful comments on an earlier draft, read at the Canadian Sociology and Anthropology Association meetings, Winnipeg, 1970.

2. I wish to thank the Canada Council for support during both field work periods.

person, and no normal community, is limited in repertoire to a single variety of code . . . (1967).

And according to Gumperz:

In many multilingual societies the choice of one language over another has the same signification as the selection among lexical alternates in linguistically homogeneous societies (1968).

Both authors make the point that in every speech community there exist a variety of repertoires, of alternate means of expression. They go on to note that this fact has social implications, i.e. that in choosing among the various codes available to them, speakers indicate what might be called social meaning. A corollary of this is that speakers in any community share rules regarding language usage, which allow them to interpret the social meaning of alternate linguistic choices. Multilingual speech communities are, however, unique in one way: the fact that the alternates in question are (theoretically) discrete and easily identifiable (as separate languages) makes them particularly prone to certain types of sociolinguistic study.

Functions of speech

That speech has functions other than referential, and that stylistic and other shifts in the linguistic content of discourse often serve to mark off shifts in function is not a new idea in linguistics (Firth, 1935; Malinowski, 1935). The centrality of the question of linguistic function to linguistic theory was not dealt with in depth, however, until the more recent work of Jakobson (1960) and more specifically of Hymes (1962; 1970). In his most recent work on linguistic functions, Hymes (1970) notes that functions have often been treated in the linguistic and anthropological literature in a piecemeal way – anthropologists, for example, have noted special code varieties in the repertoires of some communities, such as differences in men's and women's speech (mainly North America) and in everyday v. respectful speech (mainly Oceania), and have then tried to discover and describe the social function served by the use of those varieties. Hymes proposes that a more balanced, global approach would proceed in the reverse direction, starting with social function (e.g. that respect will be expressed in every society) and seeking the linguistic means by which various functions are expressed. Ervin-Tripp (1967) notes that this is also the approach adopted by Geoghegan (1971) and Goodenough (1965).

It is easy to see the appeal of functional analysis to students of language behaviour in multilingual communities – shift in function appears a natural and highly useful way of explaining speech variation including code switching; conversely, to those interested in demonstrating function, multilingual societies often provide the most obvious or salient examples.

The perspective of examining the linguistic data in terms of the function of what is said implies that function be defined, in general, as the social effect of given forms or usages, and that the unit of analysis be defined in social terms. Hence the importance of the concept of speech event as a basic analytical unit. Taking the speech event as a starting point, one can either study the function the language used has for ongoing social interaction (an approach we shall later discuss as 'interpretive' in its analysis of the social meaning of language use), or one can take the reverse point of view and attempt to see to what extent the (broadly social) *factors* present in the communication situation influence what is expressed linguistically. To my knowledge, it was those authors concerned primarily with linguistic function (Jakobson, 1960; Hymes, 1962, 1964, 1967) who first presented systematic discussion of the components or factors in communicative events.

Factors and components

Taking now the alternation among various codes as a point of departure, we can point to a large number of studies which have attempted (at least implicitly) to predict language choices from a knowledge of the factors or components present in the communication situation. Summarizing her own discussion of types of formal statements or rules which could be made in sociolinguistics, Ervin-Tripp could well be speaking for numerous authors who have had the same general goals without necessarily attempting such a formal approach, when she says: 'The above description was primarily made from the standpoint of predicting a speaker's choice of alternatives in some frame' (1967).

A number of lists of types of factors which influence speech behaviour have been proposed, based broadly on those factors suggested by Jakobson (1960) and Hymes (1962). These lists usually include such factors as participants, topic, setting or context, channel, message form, mood or tone, and intentions and effects. 'Code' is generally also listed in theoretical discussions of the components of speech events (see also Hymes, 1967), but in descriptive and analytical work it is most often treated as the dependent variable, where certain combinations or configurations of the other factors are treated as independent. Of these, the three which have been discussed most widely, and which appear the most powerful in predicting language choice, are those involving participants, setting and topic (possibly in that order). This does not of course imply that the other factors can be neglected, and cases can readily be cited where factors such as speaker's intent or message form are clearly dominant.

With regard to the participants in a communicative event, a knowledge of their individual characteristics (extent of personal repertoires and competence in the various codes and speech varieties in question; class and ethnic identification) and of the relationships between participants can go a long way towards predicting their choices among alternate speech varieties, always *given a knowledge of the cultural definitions of appropriateness*. And particularly in situations where verbal repertoires are highly compartmentalized (see Gumperz, 1968), codes are often topic- and/or setting-specific.

Despite the hope expressed by some authors that careful, thorough and prolonged study of the factors involved in speech events might at some future date lead to the ability to completely predict or state rules specifying 'who speaks what language to whom and when' (Fishman, 1965), it now appears that such hopes are somewhat over-ambitious. This has become obvious through a number of detailed studies which, motivated at least in part by such a hope, have run into difficulty in two major ways:

1. Multi-code situations often appear to be marked by extremely frequent and rapid switching which, to put it bluntly, defies explanation, if by explanation one means accounting for every switch. Texts cited by Gumperz and Hernandez (1969) on Spanish–English bilinguals show this type of frequent switching very clearly.

2. In many cases, analysts have experienced difficulty in attributing segments to one code or the other. This is especially true in cases involving diglossia (e.g. a creole and a standard language), which have recently been recognized as displaying the characteristics of a continuum (DeCamp, 1968; St-Pierre, 1969). Labov (1970) cites a six-line text involving eighteen 'switches' to show the futility and arbitrariness of trying to identify segments as being one or other dialect of English. There may also be some cases where this problem arises in multilingual speech communities (e.g. Denison, 1970). Thus in any multi-code situation, it is important to remember not only that the codes in question often do not approximate to the monolingual standard (Gumperz, 1969), but that they may not display the property of discreteness. It is clear, however, that this second difficulty is more problematic in situations of diglossia than in cases of multi-lingualisms.

Linguistic variation

The third major trend I wish to outline is best exemplified in the work of Labov on English in New York City (1966) and more recently on non-standard Negro English (1969). Labov also takes the variability of linguistic data as a starting point, but instead of examining linguistic variants which can easily be identified as belonging to one speech variety or another, he has studied, in detail, specific linguistic variables, first in terms of their linguistic context, then in terms of their distribution within the speech community, correlating them mainly with characteristics of the speakers and of the situation (examining in particular the property of formality). In studying situations in which the salient linguistic variables form a continuum, he has argued, for example, that 'idiolects' show less system (internal consistency) than does the speech community taken as a whole, because individuals occupy or control particular ranges of variables whose total distribution (in social terms) must be known in order to understand the speech community as a system. Further, he is cautious of postulating the existence of a number of speech varieties or codes within a community if it cannot be shown that these constitute separate systems. To bring out his point, I shall quote at some length:

... we have the problem of deciding the place of this variation in linguistic structure. Current formal analysis provides us with only two clear options: (*1*) the variants are said to belong to different systems, and the alternation is an example of 'dialect mixture' or 'code switching'; (2) the variants are said to be in 'free variation' within the same system, and the selection lies below the level of linguistic structure. Both approaches place the variation outside of the system being studied. There are of course many cases which fall appropriately under one or the other of these labels. But to demonstrate that we have a true case of code-switching, it is necessary to show that the speaker moves from one consistent set of co-occurring rules to another . . . (Labov, 1970).

Labov has shown that certain types of variation previously conceived as 'free variation' (New York City case) and 'code switching' (non-standard Negro English case) are better analysed in terms of a single system, within which variation correlates highly with social and situational as well as linguistic constraints. But it is clear that similar types of constraints are also operative when linguistic behaviour involves choice among alternatives belonging to what we can safely identify as more than one code or speech variety. Further, there is another problem of considerable ethnographic interest which appears to be relatively intractable to Labov's methodology, i.e. the question of how the various speech variables combine to form clusters having particular social meaning as defined by members of the speech community (e.g. questions of styles, genres, appropriateness to particular social circumstances, etc.).

Labov himself specifies the two possible approaches (1966): one can either start with speech variables and examine their social distribution; or one can start with particular people and/or particular situations and examine the linguistic behaviour relevant to them. He prefers the former in giving a better idea of the linguistic system as a whole; if one is interested in the latter, however, it cannot be totally deduced from data collected within the framework of the former. This point will be raised again below in connection with the recent work of Gumperz, whose approach could be termed more ethnographic in the sense that he stresses this second line of inquiry.

Multilingual speech communities: the Buang case

To illustrate the analytical points I wish to discuss, I shall present a brief description of the language situation among the Buang of New Guinea. The main analytical questions to which I shall subsequently address myself are:

1. What are the relative merits of the various approaches I have presented and discussed in the first part of this paper in the analysis of speech variation in multilingual communities?

2. Is the assignment of segments to one or other speech variety or code an important problem, i.e. does it matter whether speech varieties are seen as one or several systems?

3. Independent of the type of approach chosen, how far can we reasonably go in accounting for code switching on the part of multilinguals?

The 2000-odd people who live in the seven villages of the headwaters region of the Snake River (Morobe District, New Guinea) identify themselves as being one of three Buang dialect groups. Informants explained that all the Buang speak one language, but that there are three dialects, of which one (lower Buang) is not well understood by them, although they communicate easily with speakers of the central dialect (for detailed discussion, including measures of language similarity and mutual intelligibility, see Sankoff, 1970, and 1968 chapters 4, 9 and 10).

Headwaters Buang is the native language of virtually all of these people (exceptions being a small number of foreign-born wives, mainly from central Buang). Almost everyone is fluent as well in Neo-Melanesian (New Guinea pidgin English). A few Buang men were exposed to Neo-Melanesian, beginning in about 1910, as indentured labourers conscripted to work on plantations in New Britain, and as carriers for various (mainly German) explorers. During the 1930s, knowledge of Neo-Melanesian became almost universal among Buang men, as they migrated in large numbers to work on the Bulolo goldfields. Subsequent generations have continued this trend of working away from home, so that at present virtually everyone under forty is fluent in Neo-Melanesian, as well as most men over this age. Tests indicate over 80 per cent of the population currently resident in the headwaters to have at least a good working knowledge of Neo-Melanesian, a proportion which would probably rise to 90 per cent if we were to consider the large numbers of Buang currently resident in towns.

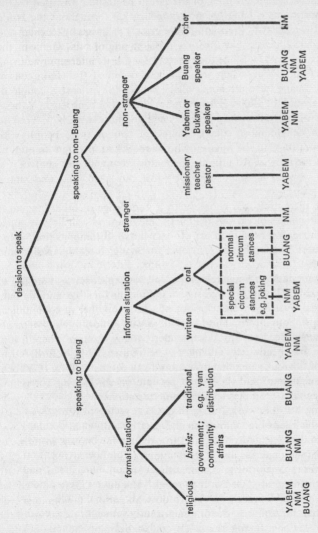

Figure 1 Factors constraining code choice for the Buang (NM = Neo-Melanesian, ... indicates optional distinction discussed on page 44)

A third language for many Buang is Yabem, also introduced during the 1930s by evangelists from the coast, themselves mainly native speakers of Bukawa, a language closely related to Yabem. Yabem, a language native to the Finschhafen area of the Huon peninsula, was used by the Lutheran mission as a language of evangelization throughout the Huon Gulf area. Evangelists to the Buang were closely followed by teachers and pastors, and it appears that the first mission school was set up in the headwaters area in 1936. Since then (except for a brief interruption during the Second World War, when the Japanese occupied the Huon coastal area), most Buang have attended village school for at least a couple of years, where, until the 1960s, instruction was carried out entirely in Yabem. Knowledge of Yabem is largely restricted to those who have been to school, although in most villages there are two or three people with special relationships to the mission who have picked up a fair amount of Yabem on their own. At present, probably about 80 per cent of the population between ages ten and forty-five can speak and understand Yabem.

Although there are some people with a knowledge of other languages (including languages of various neighbouring groups; English; and police Motu, the lingua franca of the Port Moresby area), communication within the headwaters Buang area is restricted to Buang, Neo-Melanesian and Yabem.

In collecting data on language usage, my first approach was simply to accumulate examples, in as exhaustive a manner as possible, and my data include notes, tapes and transcriptions of a large number of communication situations, both informal and formal, as well as normative statements about language use. I rapidly became alert to any instance where a language other than headwaters Buang was being used. This, in turn, led to a number of obvious generalizations about the contexts of use of Yabem and Neo-Melanesian, and the search became one of looking for refinements and counter examples to these generalizations.

In carrying out this work I was, in essence, trying to use a predictive model in which language choice on the part of individual speakers was taken as the dependent variable, and to account for choices in terms of social and situational variables. This attempt is summarized in Figure 1, which gives the major or gross constraints on code choice. Starting with the top of the diagram, 'Decision to speak', the model allows for choice between or among alternates having to do with various factors in speech events, so that, for example, the first factor has to do with the status of the interlocutor – is he a Buang or not? If yes, we examine the type of situation: if no, we check whether he is a stranger or not, and so on.

Notice, however, that the model does not present conditions which allow complete prediction of code choices. That is, more than one code possibility is listed as 'outcome' at the bottom of several branches. This is due to my rejection, during analysis of the material (Sankoff, 1968) of the 'predictive' approach as outlined in the section on 'factors and components' above. I realized that such factors could not be taken as predictive in the strict sense, and that they served rather to define certain types of situations in which particular code choices were normally acceptable, appropriate – even likely. As this may seem to many to be too weak a statement, I shall elaborate.

Grammatical rules for any one language describe the structure of possible strings in that language, but do not predict any particular surface realization of these rules by any particular speaker at any particular time; rather, they enable us to parse such surface realizations (i.e. to account for them in terms of the rules), as well as to identify some sentences as being ungrammatical. Similarly, sociolinguistic rules should enable us to interpret the social meaning or significance of choices or decisions (not necessarily conscious) on the part of speakers among alternates or variants carrying other than strictly referential meaning; they tell us which choices are acceptable ('grammatical'), which are inappropriate or unacceptable ('ungrammatical'), and may even give us gradations between these two (cf. Labov's 'variable constraints' (1970) which state probabilities of occurrence for certain linguistic forms given social as well as linguistic environment). To say that sociolinguistic rules are weak because they do not entirely predict which code a speaker will choose is analogous to saying that feature-specifying vocabulary selection rules are weak because they do not predict which word a speaker will choose (see Gumperz quotation, *supra*, p. 34).

Sociolinguistic rules can and do specify conditions under which certain kinds of choices are appropriate, whether the domain of choice be relatively restricted (use of honorifics or not; choice of terms of address in general; see Geoghegan, 1969) or very broad (choice of code over all occurring communication situations). In addition, they can be ordered in terms of generality or applicability. In the Buang case, for example, it would not have made sense to start with the variable 'tone' (e.g. joking) as the first factor to be considered in accounting for code choices, as it does not apply equally over all situations. Rather, I considered that facts having to do with the interlocutors were of primary importance and, as they apply in every case, placed this variable near the top of the tree for greater economy in the model. Next came situation-defining variables having to do mainly with setting and topic, followed by variables involving tone, channel, etc.

Notice also that the use of Buang constitutes what could be called the 'unmarked' case.[3] Thus unless the situation is specially marked as having a non-Buang interlocutor, or being formal, or containing special characteristics of tone, Buang is the language used. The fact that the use of Buang is unmarked also implies that when another factor not indicated in the diagram is added, the language used is still Buang. For example, we might consider 'channel' – the Buang are proficient yodellers, often calling across valleys to each other from distant ridges, and the only language they ever use for this is Buang. Nevertheless it is not necessary for the model to take yodelling into account, unless this channel must be marked for the use of other-than-Buang as is, for example, the written channel. Letters are written in Neo-Melanesian or Yabem.

To recapitulate the general argument: the model presented in Figure 1 defines certain general types of speech situation in which particular code usage is felt to be appropriate by the Buang. It does not predict which code will be used in any particular case. In fact, it defines certain situations in which *alternation* among the various codes is felt to be appropriate – formal meetings having to do with government affairs or economic development, for example.

One factor of great importance, particularly in formal situations where a speaker is addressing an audience is that which Hymes calls 'goals' or 'ends' (1967). Skill in oratory has often been described as one of the defining criteria of the Melanesian big man (e.g. Oliver, 1949), and I would contend that in a situation where several codes are available to a speaker, he manipulates them in many subtle ways in trying to harangue or convince his audience, choosing a particular turn of phrase in a particular language to drive home one point, switching languages and turning to another portion of his audience to make another. Use of code switching as creative rhetorical device by skilled orators was a marked feature of all formal public meetings among the Buang except those dealing with purely traditional topics. This behaviour was predictable in the sense that there existed a situational definition of when rapid code alternation would or could take place; one could not, however, predict what language a speaker would choose at any point in time. As I have argued elsewhere:

Particularly in the case of the leaders . . . realization that code switching and variation in language choice will still occur no matter how closely the sociolinguistic environment is specified, and that this variation itself is a crucial aspect of their position, as they conceive it, as the people conceive it, and as the analyst must conceive it, is more useful and meaningful than the attitude which prompts the construction of an elaborate deterministic model covering every possible instance of language choice (Sankoff, 1968).

3. For recent discussions of marking, see Geoghegan (1969) and (for an application to the language use of bilinguals) Gumperz and Hernandez (1969) and Gumperz (1970).

Gumperz and Hernandez take a similar position when they say:

It would be futile to predict the occurrence of either English or Spanish in the above utterances by attempting to isolate social variables which correlate with linguistic form. Topic, speaker, setting are common in each case. Yet the code changes sometimes in the middle of a sentence (Gumperz and Hernandez, 1969).

I feel that most students of multilingual, code-switching situations would agree with these two quotations regarding the futility of a complete predictive or deterministic model of code switching. What kind of analytical procedures can we then follow? Gumperz and Hernandez, in their perceptive analysis of code switching on the part of Spanish–English bilinguals, following an approach suggested in an earlier paper (Blom and Gumperz, 1967), propose that despite the unpredictability of code switching, code usage by multilinguals still carries social meaning. They suggest that cognitively oriented studies can indicate such social meaning, and propose that, following the cultural or social definitions of which language constitutes the unmarked usage in a particular situation, we can identify a speaker's strategies in using a language which is 'marked' in that situation to convey particular social meaning. Thus instead of trying to predict switches, they feel that it is more sensible to try to account for or interpret them in terms of social function.

Though I agree entirely with the thrust of their argument, and have used such an 'interpretive' approach myself (Sankoff, 1968), I have some reservations about whether it is always possible to identify one of the codes in question as being unmarked, and about whether in fact it is possible or feasible to attempt to interpret *every* switch. To justify these reservations, I shall summarize the material I have presented on the Buang in terms corresponding to those which they have used. Earlier, I noted that the use of Buang could be taken as the unmarked case. Rethinking in terms of Gumperz and Hernandez' discussion, however, it would seem more reasonable to attempt to specify which code is felt to be unmarked in the relevant, culturally defined situations. We can, however, see the diagram presented in Figure 1 as defining such situations, and each of the linguistic 'outcomes' as being unmarked for that particular situation. Thus, for example, to use Buang or Yabem in addressing a complete stranger would be marked as distinctly peculiar; to use Neo-Melanesian or Yabem to another Buang, in an informal situation, under 'normal circumstances' would imply a change in these 'normal circumstances', generally marking a joke, or a game or put-on.

What I am suggesting in analysing the Buang material is that the various factors in speech events can be ordered in accounting for code choices. Some of these factors (in the Buang case, participants, setting and topic, in that order) serve to define a number of situations in terms of appropriate (or unmarked) code usage. The model could be made more complicated by adding branches which would represent the influence of other factors (such as tone, ends, etc.), and I have illustrated this by the optional addition of 'joking' as a separate branch. It could, on the other hand, be made less complicated by removing, say, topic, from the situation-defining variables, treating foreign languages as unmarked for formal situations except when such situations are marked, by topic, as being ' + traditional'. Heuristically, however, it seems more satisfying to consider variables or factors having to do with individual speech strategies as constituting a marking of situations defined by the other variables. Thus the cut-off point between the situation-defining variables and the marking variables, which have to do with individual speech strategies, is not entirely arbitrary (see Figure 2). In terms of the first two approaches discussed in this paper, we

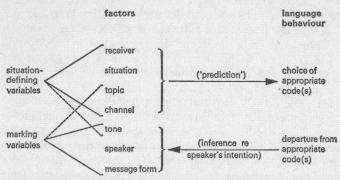

Figure 2 Tentative schematization ordering factors in speech events for code choices by the Buang

would thus be using the factors near the top of the list as in some sense predictive (in defining appropriateness or unmarked forms). Variation beyond this point would be analysed in terms of the 'functions' of using forms defined as marked, which in turn could be analysed, *post hoc*, as reflecting factors having to do with speakers' intentions.

'Receiver' or 'interlocutor' has to do with whether the receiver is a Buang, stranger, missionary, etc. 'Situation' can be either formal or informal, defined in terms of 'setting' – e.g. village square, church, etc. – and 'ends' or reason for speech event – e.g. report of local councillor. 'Topic' is qualified as being traditional, having to do with mission affairs or government business, etc. 'Channel' is either written or oral. 'Tone' refers to the speaker's intent to be serious, jocular, etc. 'Speaker' has to do not only with the person's linguistic competence in the various codes, but also with the impression he wishes to convey about himself. 'Message form' refers to the use of prayer, rhetoric, ordinary conversation, etc.[4]

As well as being a tentative formulation, Figure 2 is also a generalization and thus a simplification of reality. I have already noted that the choice of which variables to call 'situation-defining variables' and which to call 'marking variables' has been made in order to best account for a large number of cases, and is not to say that for some speech events, the factors cannot be ordered differently. With regard to the 'language behaviour', it is also true that a choice from among the codes regarded as appropriate can carry social meaning (not indicated in the diagram), that code choice including departures from the appropriate can alter the definition of the situation (as well as constituting a 'marking' of already defined situations), and so on. The schematization is presented as a convenient way of looking at a complicated situation.

Turning to my contention that, at least for the Buang case, there are situations which define alternation as appropriate (i.e. no one code can be analysed as unmarked), I present excerpts from a speech recorded at a village meeting. The topic was *bisnis* (Sankoff, 1969), more specifically, a village store for which the original capital had been contributed by several hundred people from several villages, some of whom now wanted their money back. The main village entrepreneur (and 'big man') was trying to convince people that he was running things properly and that people should leave their money in the enterprise.

(Neo-Melanesian is italicized and Buang is not; '. . .' indicates a very short portion of the speech not hearable on the tape: '#' indicates what I have analysed below as alternations, *not* any material omitted or break in the tape.)

Buang – Neo-Melanesian transcription

Olo ba kena, *trovel* ti vu Buweyew.
 # Orait, man bilong compaun, inoken
ripot long husat pepul bilong Ayayok,
Mambump, wonem hap. I mas ripot long
5 *olgeta long ples stret* (continuing
entirely in NM for 15 lines) *ikamap*
trovel o wonem, mi ken stretim olgeta
toktok. Orait. # Pasin ke ken be, *meni*
ti ken nyep la, su lok lam *memba* re,
10 olo ba *miting autim olgeta tok . . . moni*
ti ken nyep ega, rek mu su rek ogoko

4. John Gumperz (personal communication) has pointed out the importance of one factor omitted from this discussion, that which Harvey Sacks has labelled 'focus'.

nam be, ong *moni* rek, . . . *moni* ti ken
bak stua lam vu Mambump re, m nzom agon
Orait, bihain, bihainim bilong wok long
15 *bisnis, orait, moni bilong stua bai*
ibekim olgeta ples. Husat igat moni
paul na istap long buk bilong mi yet,
orait mi yet mi gat plantesin kopi, mi
ken bekim dinau bilong ol, Orait
20 *disfela tok em bilong pepul na ol ikirap*
gen orait pastaim kirap. # *Orait,* nga
ti ken be, vu, vu *as ples. Orait,* su
rek be *winim* ke, be *winim olgeta*
direkta, ga be *winim ol pepul,* olo ba
25 *kamap* vu bumbum re. # *Ino samting*
bilong masta na samting bilong kiap, em
i samting bilong mipela yet!

English translation

Next, there is a problem in Buweyew.
Now, men away at work shouldn't bring
grievances to just anyone from Ayayok,
Mambump, anywhere at all. They must
5 report to people from their *own*
villages (omitted) If any problem
comes up, I will be able to settle all
the arguments. O.K. This is the way –
the money that is there can't go back to the shareholders, and the
10 meeting brought up all these arguments . . . the
money that's there you won't take back,
your money will . . . this money from the
bulk store will come back to Mambump, and we'll hold on to it.
Now later, if we continue these business
15 activities, then the store money will
be repaid to everyone. Whoever's money
has gone astray, and it's registered in my book,
very well, I have a coffee plantation of my own – I can pay the
debts owing to them. Now this talk has to do with
20 the people, and if they want to bring
it up again, let them bring it up.
Now, this has to do with us, in the
villages. And it's not too much to handle for me, or for the
directors, or for the people, that it has to be

25   taken to the white man. It's not something to do with the white man or the
government officer – it's our thing!

If we count the actual number of switches, including isolated words, in
this text (which goes on in the same vein for about an hour), we arrive at
a total of twenty-nine, which does not tell us much. Looking more closely,
we can perhaps separate two kinds of tendencies. First, there is an alternation between sections of the speech which are basically Neo-Melanesian
and sections which are basically Buang. Line 1 is basically Buang, then
starting with 'orait' on line 2 and continuing to 'orait' on line 8 is Neo
Melanesian. Continuing from there through line 13 is again basically
Buang, with another entirely Neo-Melanesian section beginning on line 14
and continuing to 'kirap' on line 21. From 'orait' on line 21 to 're' on
line 25 is again basically Buang, with another Neo-Melanesian section
starting on line 25.

Thus in gross terms, we might say that in this test there are only five
alternations: Buang – NM – Buang – NM – Buang – NM. It is this gross
kind of alternation I am referring to when I say that both codes are
acceptable in the situation. It may be partly explicable as a stylistic,
rhetorical feature having to do with the importance of repetition and translation in Melanesian oratory (Salisbury, 1962). This speech, and others
like it, is certainly repetitive, but the speaker does not 'translate' what he
has just said into the other language as he goes along. Rather, he makes
one point in one language, then switches to the other to bring out a
different aspect of the argument.

The second tendency evident in this speech involves the very great
admixture of Neo-Melanesian words and phrases into sections of it which
are basically Buang (the reverse never occurs).[5] The most blatant example
of this is the negative construction, which in Buang involves *su* + predicate + *re*, starting with *su* on line 22 and finishing, after an almost entirely
Neo-Melanesian vocabulary in the predicate, with *re* on line 25 (other
Buang elements in the predicate include conjunctions, a future marker and
word 'I'). Although some of the words in question (e.g. *moni*) might be
the classed as loan words,[6] representing items or concepts for which there

5. Norman Denison's study of Sauris, a trilingual community in Italy (see Denison,
1968; 1971) also shows directionality in interference, and Denison (personal communication) has suggested that interference from 'H' to 'L' may be a 'near universal'.
In the present case, however, I would hesitate to classify the two speech varieties in
question as representing the type of 'H' *v*. 'L' distinction found in sociolinguistic
situations of diglossia as classically defined by Ferguson (1959).

6. For an interesting comparison with the Buang case, see texts presented in Laycock
(1966), involving heavy Neo-Melanesian borrowings into the Wosera dialect of
Abelam.

is no analogue in Buang, this is certainly not true for all, and there are many Neo-Melanesian words which could easily have been replaced (referentially) by Buang equivalents. Close examinations of these suggests tentative interpretations for some of them. For example, it seems that the Neo-Melanesian conjunction *orait* is being used stylistically, for greater emphasis, in place of the Buang conjunctions *olo ba* or *olo ga*. But for many other segments, there appears to be no very satisfying explanation in terms of the social meaning of that particular element, and I would argue that what carries weight in this 'marking' of Buang sections of the speech with extensive use of Neo-Melanesian is best analysed as a matter of degree, not in terms of showing what each element contributes. In addition, we are still faced with the problem that there does not appear to be any obvious way in which the larger segments in Neo-Melanesian differ from the basically Buang segments.

It is clear that this speaker's use of the two languages does carry social meaning. The use of Buang represents an identification with the people, shows that the speaker considers himself a part of the local community and is accepted as such. But he is also a valuable link with the modern, outside world, and his authority in this domain, his claim to understand *bisnis* (how modern economics works), to have outside contacts with urban businessmen (in this case, a Chinese merchant) and government officials are all substantiated by his use of Neo-Melanesian. That the speaker use both languages in this context is important – he keeps in touch with all segments of his audience by constant alternation. But exactly what he says in one language or the other is not in itself important.

For the Headwaters Buang, use of Neo-Melanesian is regarded as appropriate for people of power and authority, in contexts having a relationship to the broader colonial society, especially the domains of business and government. Its use in this context is not marked for leaders, or for people recognized as having had extensive contact with the outside world. But it easily becomes a joke when used by others. For example, Neo-Melanesian is often used, seriously, to give orders, as by a man at the village meeting assigning a work detail to a group of women, and in this context is perfectly acceptable (not necessarily to the women in question, who frequently disregard the orders). But for a child to tell his mother, in Neo-Melanesian, to do something, is definitely marked.

So far, I have discussed both the predictive and interpretive approaches in the analysis of language use in terms of the Buang data. I believe that the third type of analysis discussed at the beginning of this paper is also applicable. That is, it is possible to show that the extent of use of Neo-Melanesian (or of Yabem) forms a continuum which could be correlated with various social and situational variables, simply in terms of the relative proportion of Neo-Melanesian used. In terms of social stratification, for example, it seems clear that high status correlates with high frequency of use of Neo-Melanesian. One very gross comparison I did along these lines in analysing eight village meetings showed that, in thirty speeches by the two most eminent community leaders, Neo-Melanesian occurred twenty times, whereas it occurred only seventeen times in eighty-six speeches by all others present (Sankoff, 1968). (It might also be possible in such small communities to make status ratings in terms of folk categories – e.g. NM *bikpela man* ('big man') v. *rabis man* («Eng. 'rubbish', low-status man).)

Discussion

To summarize, I would like to return to the three questions posed on page 38. First, I think that each type of approach discussed has something to contribute to an understanding of the Buang case. With respect to predicting, i.e. the specifying of appropriateness in social-situational terms, I have suggested that the factors influencing speech events can be hier-archically arranged in terms of their relative weight in defining speech situations for the Buang, and that a good cutoff point would seem to be at the level where a speaker's intentions come into play. Again to illustrate with the example of a joke, I can think of no *a priori* way to predict when a speaker is about to make a joke or otherwise change the tone of the conversation. Thus it seems more reasonable, with this kind of factor, to do a *post hoc*, interpretive analysis, given that a joke has occurred, of its function and social meaning within the context of the conversation, and to state the linguistic means by which the utterance was marked as a joke (e.g. code switch).

An interpretive analysis of the social meaning of code choice would obviously give a great deal more depth to our understanding of language use by the Buang. I have given some suggestions as to the functions of some kinds of code choices: to justify my interpretation, it would be necessary to follow the type of methodology pioneered by Gumperz in working closely with informants in the analysis of recordings of conversations in which they actually participated. Such methods are well worth the time and effort involved.

Further evidence of the systematic aspects of code usage could be given by using the third approach, that is, the demonstration that it is possible to specify social and situational constraints according to which the relative frequency of code usage forms a continuum.

This brings us to the second question, i.e. whether it is necessary, given that the language behaviour demonstrates at least to some extent the properties of a continuum, to conduct the analysis in terms of one system. That code choice demonstrates systematic properties does not necessarily imply that there is only one code present. That is, in sociolinguistic terms, code choice is one aspect of a coherent sociolinguistic system; it is clear that, in the Buang case, each of the three codes in question is analytically separable from the others as a language.[7]

Regarding the third question (how well code-switching can be accounted for), it would appear that each of the three approaches has different goals. The last discussed approach is concerned rather with demonstrating tendencies than with the prediction of separate cases, and the predictive approach is, in my estimation, more useful in defining conditions of appropriateness. The interpretive approach, as exemplified mainly in the work of Gumperz and associates, would appear to be the most concerned with accounting for individual cases, although they too seem to be interested at least as much in making general statements about the kinds of social functions indicated by code choices. In other words, it would seem that the general focus of studies of code switching and code choice has been shifting towards an appreciation of the complexity of this behaviour as part of a sociolinguistic system. Ethnographies of speaking in multilingual communities can only profit by continued attempts to apply a variety of methodological and analytical approaches.

7. The phrasing of this paragraph, principally addressed to Labov's discussion quoted on p. 37 above, takes for granted the idea of levels within a sociolinguistic system (see discussion of this point by Hymes, 1970, pp. 125–6).

References

BLOM, J.-P. and GUMPERZ, J. J. (1967), 'Some social determinants of verbal behavior', Working Paper no. 4, Language Behavior Research Laboratory, Berkeley. (Revised version in D. Hymes and J. J. Gumperz (eds.), *Directions in Sociolinguistics*, Holt, Rinehart, Winston, 1972).

DECAMP, D. (1968), 'Toward a generative analysis of a post-creole speech continuum', paper read at the Conference on Pidginization and Creolization of languages, Mona, Jamaica, April. Mimeograph.

DENISON, N. (1968), 'Sauris – a trilingual community in diatypic perspective', *Man* (N.S.), vol. 3, pp. 578–94.

DENISON, M. (1970), 'Sociolinguistic aspects of plurilingualism', in *International Days of Sociolinguistics*, Istituto Luigi Sturzo, Rome.

DENISON, N. (1971), 'Some observations on language variety and plurilingualism', in E. Ardener (ed.), *Social Anthropology and Language*, Tavistock (see also this volume).

ERVIN-TRIPP, S. (1967), 'Sociolinguistics', Working Paper no. 3, Language Behavior Research Laboratory, Berkeley.

FERGUSON, C. A. (1959), 'Diglossia', *Word*, vol. 15, pp. 325–40.

FIRTH, J. R. (1935), 'The technique of semantics', *Transactions of the Philological Society*, pp. 36–72.

FISHMAN, J. A. (1965), 'Who speaks what language to whom and when?', *La linguistique*, vol. 2, pp. 67–88. (See also this volume).

GEOGHEGAN, W. (1969), 'The use of marking rules in semantic systems',
Working Paper no. 26, Language Behavior Research Laboratory, Berkeley.

GEOGHEGAN, W. (1971), 'Information processing systems in culture', in P. Kay
(ed.), *Explorations in Mathematical Anthropology*, M.I.T., Press.

GOODENOUGH, W. (1965), 'Rethinking "status" and "role": toward a general
model of the cultural organization of social relationships', in M. Banton (ed.),
The Relevance of Models for Social Anthropology, Praeger.

GUMPERZ, J. J. (1968), 'The speech community', in *International Encyclopedia* of
Social Sciences, vol. 9, pp. 381–6.

GUMPERZ, J. J. (1969), 'Communication in multilingual societies', in S. Tyler (ed.),
Cognitive Anthropology, Holt, Rinehart & Winston.

GUMPERZ, J. J. (1970), 'Verbal strategies in multilingual communication',
Monograph Series on Languages and Linguistics, Georgetown University, no. 23,
pp. 129–48.

GUMPERZ, J. J., and HERNANDEZ, E. (1969), 'Cognitive aspects of bilingual
communication', Working paper no. 28, Language Behavior Research Laboratory
Berkeley.

HYMES, D. (1962), 'The ethnography of speaking', in T. Gladwin and
W. Sturtevant (eds.), *Anthropology and Human Behavior*, Anthropological Society
of Washington.

HYMES, D. (1964), 'Introduction: toward ethnographies of communication',
AmA, vol. 66, no. 6, part 2, pp. 1–34.

HYMES, D. (1967), 'Models of the interaction of language and social setting',
J. Soc. Iss., vol. 23, no. 2, pp. 8–28.

HYMES, D. (1970), 'Linguistic theory and the functions of speech', in
International Days of Sociolinguistics, Istituto Luigi Sturzo, Rome.

JAKOBSON, R. (1960), 'Concluding statement: linguistics and poetics', in T. Sebeok
(ed.), *Style in Language*, Wiley.

LABOV, W. (1966), *The Social Stratification of English in New York City*,
Center for Applied Linguistics, Washington.

LABOV, W. (1969), 'Contraction, deletion and inherent variability of the English
copula', *Language*, vol. 45, pp. 715–62.

LABOV, W. (1970), 'The study of language in its social context', *Studium Generale*,
vol. 23, pp. 30–87 (see also this volume).

LAYCOCK, D. C. (1966), 'Papuans and pidgin: aspects of bilingualism in New
Guinea', *Te Reo*, vol. 9, pp. 44–51.

MALINOWSKI, B. (1935), *Coral Gardens and their Magic*, vol. 2, Allen & Unwin.

OLIVER, D. L. (1949), 'Human relations and language in a Papuan-speaking tribe
of southern Bougainville, Solomon Islands', Peabody Museum Papers, vol. 29,
Harvard University Press.

SALISBURY, R. F. (1962), 'Notes on bilingualism and linguistic change in New
Guinea', *Anthropological Linguistics*, vol. 4, no. 7, pp. 1–13 (see also this volume).

SANKOFF, G. (1968), 'Social aspects of multilingualism in New Guinea', Ph.D.
thesis, McGill University.

SANKOFF, G. (1969), '*Wok bisnis* and Namasu: a perspective from the village',
New Guinea Research Unit Bulletin no. 28, pp. 61–81.

SANKOFF, G. (1970), 'Mutual intelligibility, bilingualism and linguistic
boundaries', in *International Days of Sociolinguistics*, Istituto Luigi Sturzo, Rome.

ST-PIERRE, M. (1969), *Problèmes de diglossie dans un village Martiniquais*, thèse
de maîtrise, Université de Montréal.

3 R. F. Salisbury

Notes on Bilingualism and Linguistic Change in New Guinea

From R. F. Salisbury, 'Notes on bilingualism and linguistic change in New Guinea', *Anthropological Linguistics*, vol. 4, no. 7, 1962, pp. 1–13.

During anthropological fieldwork in the New Guinea Highlands in 1952–3 I made numerous observations on the prevalence of bilingualism and multilingualism. Not being a linguist I assumed that such observations were common in the linguistic literature, as many anthropologists have described similar situations to me in conversation. The scene in *The African Queen* of a multilingual church service is part of the folklore. Recent conversations with linguists have indicated that such situations have, in fact, been rarely described. As some historical information collected during a return visit to the area in 1961[1] connects these observations with evidence on linguistic change, I am presenting the data here so that they may be available for linguists and may indicate some of the research possibilities of the New Guinea area.

The ethnography of the Siane group of tribes has been outlined elsewhere (Salisbury, 1956, 1961a). For present purposes what is significant is that they are a congeries of culturally similar tribes, having no consciousness of an overriding political unity. Each tribe comprises several clans, and each clan is a sovereign political unit associated by ties of marriage, ceremonial interdependence and individual relations of friendship with all other neighbouring clans. Land was not scarce and warfare to extend tribal boundaries was unknown, although warfare over women, pigs or insults was endemic as part of the competition for prestige (Salisbury, 1961b). The same general culture, with local variations, continues both to east and west of the Siane, with no sharp discontinuities, and with non-Siane attending Siane ceremonies and vice-versa. Interaction between Siane and non-Siane is also the rule, and a statistical analysis of the marriage pattern indicates that marriages are random as between Siane and non-Siane. But the cultural and interactional homogeneity contrasts with the

1. This visit was supported by grants from the University of California Institute for International Studies and the National Institutes of Health (Grant No. M-4912). The earlier study was supported by the Australian National University. I am also indebted to my colleagues, Susan Ervin, John Gumperz and Dell Hymes, for comments on this paper.

linguistic situation. Siane is the westernmost language of the Siane-Gahuku-Bena family of languages (Salisbury, 1956; Wurm, 1961); across the divide to the west, people speak dialects of Dene (called by Wurm 'Chuave-Nomane') one of the Chimbu family of languages. Siane speakers themselves recognize three dialects of Siane – Komunku, Ramfau and Yaviyufa, while to the east and north there are slight transitions to the dialects of Kovena and Gahuku.

Diagram of linguistic relations near Emenyo tribe

CHIMBU-HAGEN FAMILY	SIANE-GAHUKU FAMILY
Chimbu-Dene sub-family	*Siane sub-family*

Sinesine language

Dene language	{ Mami-Duma dialect { Gai dialect { Siati dialect	*	Ono-Keto dialect ⎫ Komunku dialect ⎬ Siane Famfau dialect ⎭ language
			Yaviyufa language

Groupings are arranged in accordance with the spatial positions of the speech communities as well as in terms of linguistic classification. The position of Emenyo tribe is indicated. * A sketch map of the area is printed in Salisbury (1956, p. 449). Names used in Wurm (1961) have been modified for simplicity and to accord with native usage rather than with the names of Government Rest House sites.

Emenyo tribe, in one of whose villages I lived, speaks Komunku and borders on villages speaking Dene and Ramfau. I was struck by the number of Emenyo men speaking not merely Komunku and Ramfau dialects of Siane, but also various of the Dene dialects, from Duma to Siati which lies south of the Waghi River. Wives from all these language areas (except Siati where a story of original kinship with Emenyo linked the groups in a trade partnership) lived in the village. Conversations among the residents could often be trilingual, a Ramfau wife speaking in Ramfau to her son who replied in Komunku and who was supported by his wife speaking in Dene. Individuals often understood other languages but replied in their own, although on other occasions they might speak in different languages. I observed similar multilingualism in other western villages of Komunku tribe, or when accompanying Komunku tribesmen into Dene territory, but my observations were more detailed for Emenyo speakers of Komunku dialect and I shall restrict my discussion to them.

1. The type of bilingual conversations indicated above were most common when all speakers were at home in their own villages, at which time people

seemed tos peak whatever language was easiest for them, and others understood as best they might. The clearest example of this was provided by a
wife of Emenyo born in Ramfau, to whom I gave a series of psychological
tests involving repeated recall of a story. In a formal testing situation in
my own house she gave me a recall in Komunku dialect; the second recall
she gave me at her own house while the family dinner was in the oven and
she was nursing her baby, and it was in Ramfau dialect.

On the other hand, when there were visitors from Dene-speaking groups
or Komunku speakers were visiting in Dene areas, informal conversations
tended to be conducted in Dene with Emenyo bilinguals changing their
speech, although Emenyo monolinguals of course did not. Dene speakers
rarely changed to speaking Komunku. It is my impression that speech
adjustments were rarely made in informal conversations, when there was
visiting between Komunku and Ramfau dialect groups, but I did not
achieve sufficient fluency in Komunku dialect to be fully aware of dialect
variations until late in my stay.

More striking than the speech adjustments made in informal conversation were those made on formal occasions when ceremonies involved a clan
of Komunku speakers and a clan of another speech community. In such
situations each formal speech would be followed immediately by a translation of it into the other language. The same pattern is followed when
Administration officials speaking only pidgin, or when Lutheran missionaries speaking only the coastal Kate language, are present. In 1953 no
one seemed perturbed by a church service conducted in Komunku tribal
territory by a Dene catechist who had learned Kate, at which the Lutheran
missionary and I were present. The missionary addressed the congregation
in Kate, which the catechist translated into Dene, and an Emenyo translated the Dene into Siane. The catechist addressed me in pidgin and often
broke into pidgin in his Dene sermon. We Europeans spoke English
together. I noted that in Siane-Dene interactions it was more usual for
Emenyo bilinguals to deliver both translated speeches, from Siane into
Dene and vice versa, with Dene speakers rarely translating.

The distinction between informal conversations and formal speech-
making that I have used to contrast the environments in which different
patterns of bilingualism occur is somewhat imprecise, as the following
anomalous examples will show. One Emenyo man, Kaumfa, of whom
more details will be given below, spoke Dene on almost all occasions
within his own village. He was an important man and when speaking
publicly in Emenyo village he used Dene and was not translated; when
speaking publicly in any other Komunku-speaking village he used Dene
and was translated; when speaking privately with me when no one else
was about he used Siane, but when groups were present he used Dene and

it was translated to me. Another Emenyo man, the village tultul, Noimfanu, often spoke Dene and in 1961 (though not in 1953) he used somewhat the same pattern of linguistic alternation in conversations with me – Siane in private talk or when discussing general topics with a group around the kitchen fire, and Dene (with a translation by one of the audience) when he was telling me important matters or cultural generalizations. The village luluaï or headman often spoke to me without an intermediary in Siane (he could understand but did not speak pidgin), yet on many occasions he would not begin speaking until an audience was present, and after his speech would turn to a bystander and indicate that he should translate into pidgin before I could reply.

The obvious explanation, that translation is needed in a public situation to ensure unambiguous transmittal of information, would seem not to be applicable to such unnecessary translation as that shown by these examples. An even clearer case is provided by my replies to the luluaï's speeches, which were given in Siane. In fact in 1961 much stress was laid on my demonstrating that I had not forgotten Siane, and people refused to admit that they understood if I broke into pidgin and so they forced me to speak Siane the whole time. Even so, my replies to the luluaï were then repeated publicly (with elaboration it is true) in Siane to everyone within earshot. The gratuitous nature of the 'translation' is evident, for if my replies had not been clear, no translation could have been made at all. Instead we must interpret repetition and the translation of speeches as a linguistic means of emphasizing the importance and public nature of the discourse. The mechanism is deliberately used by speakers to distinguish the two linguistic environments, rather than its use being unconsciously determined by the speaker's finding himself in a particular social situation.[2] Bilingualism is thus a useful accomplishment for anyone who is likely to make public speeches and who wishes to be able to attract attention to the importance of what he says.

The prevalence of bilingualism also opens up the possibility of other manipulations of the language spoken on any one occasion. In any one locality there is a 'home' language where translation is not called for, and a 'foreign' one which calls for translation. The language a speaker chooses to use may thus symbolically indicate that he is 'at home' in a foreign area, that he wishes visitors to feel 'at home' in his area (or to feel they are 'foreigners'), that he wishes to flatter his hosts (or his guests) by assuming

2. This phenomenon is similar to the Chinook practice (French, 1958, p. 261) where a 'haranguer' could be hired to repeat a speaker's utterance and so make it public or 'non-casual'. French mentions interpretation as following the same pattern in Chinook; in Siane interpretation is more common than repetition as a mechanism for stressing importance.

that they are well-traveled men who need no translation. Which particular symbolic meaning is intended in any one instance cannot be definitively determined however, since the use of language in Siane is one of the many ploys used in the competitive one-upmanship involved in most spheres of social relationship.

2. The fact that there are more Emenyo bilingual in Dene, than Dene-speakers who are bilingual in Komunku is not associated with any feeling among the Emenyo that they are politically less important or that their language is inferior to Dene. Bilingualism is treated as a desirable accomplishment and their command of Dene makes them, if anything, superior to the Dene.

Emenyo actively cultivate bilingualism. A month after my arrival a group of labourers returned from indenture on the coast and raised the number of pidgin speakers in the village of 205 from three to twenty-three. Almost immediately a school began, in which the rest of the village males learned pidgin. A pidgin speaker would point to objects and make sentences such as 'This is a table; I put the comb on the table'; the circle of ten or fifteen students would repeat each phrase back. For two hours every evening one could hear the chant of phrase and response resounding through the village. Two youths utilized the presence of my servant, a Komunku speaker from an eastern group who spoke Gahuku, to learn a smattering of Gahuku. In 1961 most Emenyo could say the Lord's Prayer and the Creed in Kate, while at one church service conducted by the resident Kate catechist his renderings of the Bible into Siane were questioned by members of the congregation, who referred to the Kate version. A lively discussion regarding translation problems ensued during the service.

Another example of the prestige associated with the use of foreign languages is that provided by the use of songs. Of all the songs I transcribed in 1952–3, none were in the Siane language. When asked to translate the meaning of particular songs, informants would say that they did not know what the words meant, but they would give me a summary of what the songs were about. Thus an important song in the initiation cycle was said to be about the 'Mother of the Birds' calling all the various birds into her house and how they each made particular noises inside. This corresponds with the explanation given to the women for the sounds of the sacred flutes coming from the men's house. Two words were clearly intelligible to me – vire (the 'hornbill' in Siane), name (Gahuku and other Eastern languages for 'bird' which in Siane is nema); others seemed cognates of Siane words. Yet all Siane questioned denied that they could translate word-for-word. One day as I was walking for several hours with an Emenyo man, I realized he was singing the song to himself, and the words he was using were in Komunku dialect. I asked him to repeat so that I could copy them down. He said he did not know what the words meant and he repeated it to me in its unintelligible form. I had the same experience with a love song, sung at about 4 a.m. and narrating what happens when the cock crows, in the Ono-Keto dialect. I transcribed it in Ono, and later heard it sung privately in Siane, but could not get the Siane singer to admit he knew the words, except in unintelligible Ono. Though it may be desired to keep the initiation song officially secret (though it is sung publicly), the same reason could not be brought to explain the use of foreign language in a popular song, sung indiscriminately by boys on courting expeditions. It seems to be merely a mark of the sophistication and degree of travel of the singer, analogous with the singing of popular or folk songs in their original languages, rather than in well-established translations, as occurs in many Western countries.

3. Figures on the incidence of varying degrees of bilingualism were not collected in the field, but were compiled later from memory. They cannot claim 100 per cent accuracy, but the fact that trends appear despite the predominance of 'unknown' cases makes these trends more striking. They are indicative of what could be obtained by more intensive research.

Of the eighty-two adult males in the village in 1953, two spoke Dene more often than Komunku. One, Kaumfa, was the bosboi of a men's house mentioned above (cf. Salisbury, 1961a, pp. 28–30). He was one of the four most important men in the village, but died in 1960 before my return. He had been born in Emenyo, but his mother spoke Dene. His first wife was a Komunku speaker but he had also married, later in life, his brother's widow who spoke Dene. The second Dene speaker had migrated from a southern Dene tribe, where he had been born, to his mother's village in Emenyo some twenty years earlier. He had married a widow who had been born in the other clan-village of Emenyo tribe and had returned home on the death of her husband.

Two other men commonly spoke Dene, often acting as interpreters and sometimes using it in conversations with other Emenyo men. One of these was the village tultul, Noimfanu, both of whose parents spoke Komunku. His first wife was Dene-speaking and his second spoke the Ramfau dialect of Siane. He himself spoke both Siane dialects, Dene and fluent pidgin, although he had never worked outside Siane, where pidgin is required as a *lingua franca*. It was his use of Dene that first drew my attention to bilingualism. Soon after my arrival, discussion groups around my fire alternated between pidgin and Siane while I spoke only pidgin and tried to follow the Siane. After the first occasion on which I interjected into a Siane speech by Noimfanu and indicated I could now understand, a silence ensued. Later I noticed a three-way alternation of languages, with Dene being spoken especially by Noimfanu. I felt this was to keep me from understanding what was said. In 1961 Noimfanu used Dene more frequently, but when I jokingly taxed him with using it to hide things from me, he said that Dene was his real language. I shall discuss this statement later. The second frequent Dene speaker (although Komunku was his most used language) had been born in a Dene village of an Emenyo mother and had a wife from another Dene tribe. He had lived in Emenyo village for ten years before 1953, and had been one of the first indentured laborers from Emenyo. He spoke fluent but often inaccurate pidgin. He returned to his father's village in 1955 but addressed me in Komunku when he visited me in 1961.

I noted twelve other men as feeling called upon to translate Dene speeches to me on public occasions; nineteen men I can recall having heard speak Dene at some time; regarding forty-six men I have no recollections of their using any language but Siane; one I asked to translate but he denied that he understood Dene. The relationships between these degrees of bilingualism and the language of the speaker's mother and wife are summarized in Tables 1 and 2.

Table 1 **Degree of bilingualism observed in Emenyo men, and the linguistic affiliations of their parents' clans**

Degree of speaking of Dene	Parental languages				
	Komunku-Komunku	Komunku-Ramfau	Komunku-Dene	Komunku-Unknown	Total
Frequent Dene	1	—	3	—	4
'Translated' Dene	1	5	5	1	12
Some Dene	3	2	6	8	19
Unknown amount	11	13	13	10	47
No Dene	1	—	—	—	1
Total	17	20	27	19	82

The expectable relationship, that a man's fluency in Dene would be related to the fact that one of his parents spoke Dene, is confirmed. A comparison of those from Dene-Siane households with those from Siane households gives distribution of bilinguality that would occur by chance in less than 0·25 of cases ($\chi^2 = 4·14$, df 4). The low level of assurance for this relationship may be partly related to the number of 'unknown' cases. On the other hand a closer relationship may be discerned if those men born into families in which only one *dialect* was spoken by both spouses are compared with those men born into families in which the spouses spoke different dialects. Such a relationship would occur by chance in less than 0·20 of cases ($\chi^2 = 4·75$, df 4) and would seem to indicate that bilingualism among the Emenyo is not merely a case of individuals learning the languages of their parents, but of individuals brought up in a bilingual environment (regardless of the languages actually spoken) tending to be bilingual (even in other languages). A test of this relationship would have been possible if I had data on the degree of bilingualism in Ramfau dialect of Emenyo men. I was not sufficiently able to discern dialectical variations in normal conversation to obtain the necessary figures, however.

Table 2 **Degrees of bilingualism observed in Emenyo men and the linguistic affiliations of their first wife's clans**

Degree of speaking Dene	Wife's language			
	Komunku	Ramfau	Dene	Total
Frequent Dene	2	—	2	4
'Translated' Dene	4	4	4	12
Some Dene	7	7	5	19
Unknown amount	13	15	18	46
No Dene	1	—	—	1
Total	27	26	29	82

It is tempting to try to relate bilingual environment in childhood, and observed bilingualism, with general high status in the village. The figures are inadequate however, especially as the criteria for bilingualism are 'bilingualism as displayed publicly and observed by me'. Thus, the four frequent Dene speakers included two of the five most important men in the village; the twelve interpreters include nine younger men whose abilities came to my notice because they often accompanied me into Dene territory, but the other three were a bosboi and two lineage heads. The twenty whom I recollect speaking Dene on some occasion included the two other most important men and three lineage heads. All of these might have been expected to translate on some occasion when I would have heard them, but I did not in fact do so. Of those whose linguistic abilities I have classed as 'unknown', fifteen I knew quite well, and I feel I would have noticed if they did speak Dene, especially those who had Dene wives. The man who did not speak Dene was definitely of low status, and for other reasons I felt he was of low intelligence also. It seems likely that there is a relationship between high status and observed bilingualism, but such a relationship may well be due to high status (or nearness to me) giving more opportunity to display linguistic ability.

The data relating degree of bilingualism and the language of a man's wife would argue against interpreting my observations as reflecting merely the opportunities a man has for displaying linguistic skills. If this were true then it would be expected that there would be correlation between having a Dene wife and displaying linguistic competence in Dene. The relationship ($x^2 = 1\cdot67$, df 4), is in fact insignificant and could occur by chance in almost 80 per cent of cases. This lack of relationship also fails to confirm the common-sense hypothesis that a bilingual man would choose a foreign-language wife more commonly than a monolingual man would. Language does not seem to be a factor in wife-selection in Siane as appears from the close correspondence between the observed numbers of marriages with the three linguistic groups and the ratio to be expected on the assumption that marriage frequency is a function of the proximity of groups. The expected ratios would be ten marriages with Komunku speakers to eleven with Ramfau speakers and ten with Dene speakers. The same result appears from Table 3 where the language of a man's mother is correlated with his choice of spouse. In general the table shows that no relationship exists, although there is specific tendency for men with Dene mothers to choose Dene-speaking wives.

Table 3 **Linguistic affiliations of Emenyo men's parents and the linguistic affiliations of their first wife's clans**

Wife's language	Parental languages				
	Komunku-Komunku	Komunku-Ramfau	Komunku-Dene	Komunku-Unknown	Total
Komunku	5	8	7	7	27
Ramfau	6	9	6	5	26
Dene	6	3	13	7	29
Total	17	20	26	19	82

My recollection of the languages spoken by wives is not clear. I have already mentioned the shift of languages by a Ramfau-speaking wife. The tultul's Dene-speaking wife always spoke Dene with her husband in 1953 although her psychological test responses were all in Komunku. In 1961 she spoke Komunku much more frequently with her husband, although he then spoke Dene more frequently. It is my impression that wives usually spoke their native language but understood Komunku spoken by their husbands. As they remained longer in Emenyo village their use of Komunku increased.

Bilingualism seems to be disvalued among the women. In 1953 no Emenyo wife spoke pidgin, or appeared to understand it. An Emenyo sister who had married a foreign policeman and had lived in other districts of New Guinea, did return briefly on a visit and could speak pidgin. But her use of it occasionally in speaking to men seemed to cause much embarrassment and giggling among all the other women. In 1961 no woman except the tultul's second wife spoke pidgin, although I gained the impression that many could understand the language yet chose to deny it.

The degree of bilingualism in the community appeared to change between 1953 and 1961, as has been indicated. The figures given in Tables 1 and 2 are based on my notes and recollections from both periods of field work. Specific changes in the use of Dene by Noimfanu have been mentioned. On reflection I would say that three of the men listed as 'interpreters' would have been classed as 'occasional speakers' in 1953, while four 'occasional speakers' would have been classed as 'unknown' in 1953.

4. Most of the preceding analysis is based on observations made in 1953 in Emenyo village. Emenyo regarded themselves as speaking Komunku dialect, and observation suggested that the analysis of villages in a Komunku tribe would give comparable results. It is true that Emenyo claimed kinship with some Siati villages located south of the Waghi River and speaking a Dene language, but this kinship seemed fictitious or legendary. The separation of the Siati villages was explained by the following story:

A man of Emenyo had no sons, but had one daughter whom he dressed as a boy, and who grew up playing with boys. In due course it was time for her age mates to be initiated. Her father was sad and said 'To whom shall I show my sacred flutes? Who will look after them when I die?' He decided to show his daughter his flutes. He made a belt of woven cane which was so wide that when his daughter put it on, it completely hid her breasts. She went in and was shown the sacred flutes. By chance her belt slipped during the ceremony and she was noticed by some Komunku men who were present. The Komunku men were furious that the sacred flutes should be shown to a woman and they incited all the surrounding tribes to punish the Emenyo people. Everyone, from Komunku, Aranko, Ramfau, Duma, all came and fought Emenyo. They burned their houses and villages which stretched thickly all along the ridge where Pira Rest House now is, and all Emenyo fled. Some went singly to stay with kin; a group went together and travelled south for several days until they came to an area of virgin bush, south of the Waghi. 'At last,' they said, 'we are safe', and there they built villages and made gardens. Meanwhile the scattered Emenyo, who were living, one here, one there, like cassowaries, came back and built villages again on Emenyo territory. That is why there are some Emenyo here and some at Siati; that is why we visit each other (for trading purposes).

My queries attempting to put this story in a historical framework were met with the answer 'it happened in the time of the grandfathers' – and the term 'grandfather' is used generally for ancestors. On the basis of the language difference and the typical form of the story, I accepted it as a 'charter myth', possibly relating to some very distant past event.

In 1961, as I have said, more people spoke Dene and I challenged them as to why they were speaking Dene, saying that it was just to hide things from me. Several people replied, as noted previously, that Dene was their real language. Pressed further they repeated the story of the expulsion of Siati, and said that previously all Emenyo had spoken Dene. When the stragglers of Emenyo had come together again and rebuilt their villages they had taken up speaking Komunku, as Komunku tribe had then been the most powerful tribe in the area. This is not to say that they became subservient to Komunku, as conquest and absorption of other tribes is not practised in the Siane area, but that Komunku acquired prestige and Emenyo copied the prestigeful group. I again questioned this, pointing out that they could not give me any names of people, whom I could trace in my genealogies, and who had been alive then. They admitted this but said that if I had asked them this question in 1953 they could have answered, as at that time there had been one old man alive in Siati who had been born in Emenyo, speaking Dene, and had fled with the migrants. My attempts to elicit his age met with the response that he had been very old, as old as Rinawe's father would have been. Rinawe, one of the oldest men in Emenyo, had been about forty-five to fifty in 1933, when he had followed the advance party of the Taylor-Leahy expedition (see Salisbury, 1961a, pp. 113–14). His father would have been born probably about 1860, which is presumably the best estimate of the date of the linguistic change from speaking Dene to speaking Siane. Within one hundred years the boundary between the Chimbu and Gende-Gahuku-Siane families has moved several miles without there being any movement of peoples to explain the shift. This indicates that to use the existence of speech-communities as a proof of the existence of original political or ethnic communities is by no means always strictly valid.

The example, however, also shows that what appears in a classification as a radical change, involving the crossing of a boundary representing some three thousands of years of separate development (Salisbury, 1956; Wurm, 1961), in fact may involve little disruption in a community's speech behavior. Bilingualism on the scale found in both Emenyo and Komunku tribes would mean that a change in the 'official' language may only involve a dropping of interpretations of that language on public occasions and a slight change in the frequency of children learning that language at home. Communication can proceed as before. In fact, the example throws up the problem of how such multitudes of different speech communities could grow up in New Guinea and persist, if bilingualism is as common elsewhere in New Guinea, as my conversations with other anthropologists and with non-Highland natives would suggest it is. Should a difference between Siane and Dene involving 70 per cent of their basic vocabulary be considered as representing a 3000-year separation, especially in the light of the great prestige given to the borrowing of songs, etc., from other groups, and to the knowledge of numbers of languages, and in the light of the constant marriage across the linguistic boundary for well over a hundred years at the smallest estimate. Extensive linguistic borrowings would be expected (as can demonstrably be seen to occur from pidgin into local languages), and this would be expected to make the differences smaller than they are. A solution to this problem would be if, for New Guinea, a faster rate of linguistic differentiation were postulated than seems probable from the work of Swadesh and others on Indo-European (cf. Hymes, 1960). This example of Siane bilingualism and its prestigeful nature suggests a reason why such differentiation might occur.

If to know a foreign language is prestigeful, and situations exist where interpretation is a ceremonial device for the individual to show his knowledge, while at the same time stressing the importance of the occasion, then interpretation will be used more than is necessary to ensure communication. It is clearly pointless to interpret speeches to people of the same speech community, but if differences of speech are magnified so that it is possible to deny that the neighboring group speaks the same language, point is added to the making of interpretations. Innovations may be added to language with no fear of the language ceasing to be understandable, as one's own village are all aware of the innovation and can translate for strangers. In short, the counterpart of an emphasis on bilingualism and interpretation is an added intensity of local patriotism and ethnocentrism regarding the local dialect.

Linguistic differentiation and change would then be given added impetus by political rivalries between groups, while existing speech barriers are encouraged by individuals wishing to prove their ability to learn difficult, exotic languages.

These suggestions, of course, cannot be proved from the data to hand, though some confirmation comes from the way in which speakers say that people from other tribes say isolated words differently. Thus Ramfau speakers said that they used the word *kifa* for 'boy child', while Komunku speakers used the word *nifa*. (This is not a regular phonetic shift.) In fact Komunku speakers tended to use *nifa* to mean 'son, child' and *kifa* (generally combined as *kifa kevora*) for '(small) boy'. The suggestions are offered, rather, in the hope that they may induce more linguists to consider the laboratory conditions offered by New Guinea for the study of the phenomena of bilingualism and linguistic change.

References

FRENCH, D. (1958), 'Cultural matrices of Chinookan non-casual language', *I.J.A.L.*, vol. 24, pp. 258–63.

HYMES, D. H. (1960), 'Lexico-statistics so far', *Curr. Anthrop.*, vol. 1, pp. 1–30.

SALISBURY, R. F. (1956), 'The Siane language of the Eastern Highlands of New Guinea', *Anthropos*, vol. 51, pp. 447–80.

SALISBURY, R. F. (1961a), *From Stone to Steel: Economic Consequences of a Technological Change in New Guinea*, Cambridge and Melbourne University Presses.

SALISBURY, R. F. (1961b), 'Ceremonial economics and political equilibrium', in *Proceedings of the Sixth International Congress of Anthropological and Theological Sciences*, Paris.

WURM, S. A. (1961), 'The linguistic situation in the Highlands districts of Papua and New Guinea', *Australian Territories*, vol. 1, no. 2, pp. 14–23.

4 N. Denison

Some Observations on Language Variety and Plurilingualism

Excerpts from N. Denison, 'Some observations on language variety and plurilingualism', in E. Ardener (ed.), *Social Anthropology and Language*, Tavistock.

Historically speaking, Sauris (German: *die Zahre*) is a German linguistic island, in NE Italy, physically isolated until recently by its remote location high in the Carnian Alps (it lies between 1000 and 1400 m.) and, according to all the available evidence, separated for over 700 years by intervening Romance territory from its nearest German-speaking neighbour, Sappada (German: Pladen) (Bruniera, 1938; Hornung, 1960, 1964, 1967), which lies just south of the Austrian frontier and is itself virtually a linguistic island, since the high watershed of the Alps separates it from the Lesach valley in Austria.

The German dialect of Sauris (Denison, 1968; Hornung, 1960, 1964; Kranzmayer, 1956; Lorenzoni, 1938; Lucchini, 1882; Magri, 1941) has retained some archaic features of Southern Bavarian and has developed other specific features of its own, and these two characteristics combine to make it relatively inaccessible to other German speakers. As part of the province of Friuli, Sauris was severed from the Austrian empire and incorporated in the Italian state in 1866. Its political history has therefore been quite different from that of South Tyrol, from the eastern limits of which it is separated by some 50 km. of mountainous terrain, and its linguistic position reflects this difference. The linguistic evidence, in the absence of a documented history, makes it highly probable that Sauris was settled from the southernmost borderland between Carinthia and E. Tyrol, in the Lesachtal/Pustertal area, not much later than the year 1200 (Hornung, 1964, pp. 133–43, 1960, p. 10; Lorenzoni, 1938, pp. 10–19). The population of Sauris now stands at about 800, and seems unlikely ever to have been greatly in excess of that figure. Sauris is sociolinguistically remarkable in that in addition to their German dialect its inhabitants use two other languages in the course of their everyday lives: the national language, Italian, and a dialect of Friulian, the regional language, which is a Romance idiom distinct from, though closely related to, Italian.

Nowadays most children acquire Italian either as their first language, from their parents, or at kindergarten from the age of two. Lorenzoni (1938, p. 10) mentions the familiarity of some adult males with some form of standard German, acquired during periods of work in Austria or Germany. This is less common nowadays, especially in the fractions of Lateis and Sauris di Sotto, but there is some familiarity with other Italian dialects, especially Veneto, Triestino and Cadorino. [. . .]

Lest it be assumed that the use in Sauris of Friulian and Italian is of very recent date, it is interesting to note that 120 years ago Josef Bergmann (1849) gave German no chance of surviving there [. . .]. The German dialect is, however, still very much alive and spoken[1] in Sauris, even though it is still possible for a visitor to spend a whole day there during the summer and never hear a single word of German spoken.

Whatever the position may have been in 1919 (Magri, 1941, p. xviii) or in 1938 (Lorenzoni, 1938, p. 23), close and repeated observations[2] have revealed that language selection among adults in Sauris in the 1960s shows a high degree of correlation with situational categories: so that the three languages may indeed be regarded as diatypes.[3] Briefly, Italian correlates with the H end of the scale of situational categories and the German dialect with the L end, Friulian occupying the middle ground (M).[4] (For a

1. However, a generation of children is now reaching adolescence for whom Italian is the first and often the only active language; so that it really does now seem as if the years of survival of the German dialect (and, indeed, of Friulian also) are numbered.

2. I have made one or two study trips annually, for periods of up to six weeks, since 1964. Direct consultation with informants, whose accounts are cross-checked, supplements the analysis of taped material, some of it taped without the knowledge of all but one participant and without the author's presence, some of it taped without the knowledge of any participant.

3. Recent work (especially Fishman, 1967, 1968a, 1968b; Hymes, 1967a, b; Le Page, 1964) on the sociolinguistics of plurilingualism has shown that it can be most illuminatingly and economically treated within the same conceptual framework as diglossia (as originally put forward by Ferguson, 1959, and subsequently broadened by e.g. Fishman, 1967) and register. ('Register' was first used as a linguistic technical term by Reid, 1956, and given wider currency by Halliday and associates in e.g. Catford, 1965; Ellis, 1966; Halliday, McIntosh and Strevens, 1964; Gregory, 1967; Leech, 1966; Ure, 1967.)

These are all manifestations of language variety, and, more specifically, of what I prefer (with Gregory, 1967) to call diatypic variety. 'Diatypes' are varieties of language within a community, specified according to use (purpose, function), whereas dialects are specified according to groups of users. Like so many of the lines drawn in the social sciences, such distinctions are fuzzy at the edges, but they are no less serviceable for that. It is important to remember that in drawing them, one is not so much distinguishing between different bodies of material as between different ways of looking at the same material. People may (as Fishman, 1967 has pointed out) be bilingual or bi-dialectical with or without participation in diatypic (diglossic) situations: moreover, the same utterance may best be described dialectally to meet one particular explanatory aim, diatypically to meet another.

4. 'High' and 'low', as first put forward by Ferguson (1959) and developed in e.g. Fishman (1967). The values do of course form a continuous scale, but the attachment of identifiably distinct linguistic macro-structures to different parts of the scale

more detailed account, see Denison, 1968.) A number of facts of especial interest emerge. First, in order to retain the concept of separate languages functioning as diatypes, the language of a text must be defined as the language of its macro-structure: this is most relevant to the German dialect, for which 'macro' has to be particularly generously interpreted, in order to cope with Friulian and Italian intrusions of up to a sentence in length. Sharing of linguistic material in the diatypes is, ideally, undirectional: Italian material is available to Friulian for micro-structure, both Italian and Friulian are available to the German dialect for micro-structure; but German is not available to Friulian for micro-structure and neither German nor Friulian are available to Italian. Great pains are taken to avoid infringements in the direction L→H, and when they happen they are involuntary and minor. Almost the only intrusion of German into the other diatypes which is tolerated (because the villagers are unaware of it) is in suprasegmental phonology: Friulian speakers from the surrounding area say that people from Sauris speak with a 'characteristic lilt'. Segmental intrusions from German are very rare, and are greeted with extreme ridicule. The only examples that have come to my knowledge were produced by a deaf old woman (whose performance in Friulian and Italian was judged to be poor by her fellows) and a small child. The 'mistake' produced by the child was retailed to me by an adult informant as something he once heard a playmate say when the informant was a child. He still found it very funny. The deaf woman is one of the very few adults in Sauris who is not a competent trilingual. Another is a mentally retarded adolescent female, who is said to know only the German dialect. In each of these two cases my informants clearly considered the restricted diatypic access to be natural.[5] Interference of Friulian on Italian in Sauris is slightly more often encountered. [. . .]

---

does force a choice upon the speaker for each situation. In *di*glossic situations the two terms of the dichotomy correlate with H and L reaches of the scale. For the *tri*lingual system in Sauris we require an extra term: German is then L(ow), Italian is H(igh) and Friulian is M(id).

5. The choice of diatype for deaf people and imbeciles (often grouped together as one category) is interesting. In a German/Romansch bilingual community in Oberhalbstein, Grisons, Switzerland the only adult who knew no German was an imbecile. In Pöckau in the Slovene/German bilingual strip of Austrian Carinthia there is a mentally backward old man whose German is poor in the extreme, but whose house-to-house mimicry of the parson's Slovene sermon on feast-days assures him of a few days' splendid eating annually. On the other hand, a deaf middle-aged male in the same area knows no Slovene but only German. There has been a change here over recent decades from Slovene to German as the language spoken by most parents to their children. Hence, in all these cases, the language learned by imbeciles and the deaf is the language of the home, as one would expect. Yet in each instance the facts were explained to me by bilingual relatives or acquaintances of the individuals concerned, in terms of the alleged greater inherent simplicity of the language.

The functions of Italian are in the main eminently H: Italian is the language of organized religion (it has recently displaced Latin from most of the ritual part of this sphere), of school and of kindergarten. Most of the villagers can read and write no other language. Italian is used in speaking to outsiders (unless they are known as Friulian-speakers) and, more significantly, it is used between 'Saurians' when outsiders are present. The chief apparent breach in this H pattern is the now widespread use of Italian by parents in the home to their children of pre-school and school age. Many parents use only Italian with their children, so that, as a group, children in Sauris – at least in Lateis and Sauris di Sotto – constitute a monoglot anomaly in a trilingual community. This is not quite accurate, for most children have at least some degree of passive comprehension of Friulian and German as a result of their exposure to these languages: for although most adults address their children in Italian in the home, they continue to use German amongst themselves. The reason given by informants for this use of Italian is in almost all cases the desire to ease the path of their children at school; a few have mentioned the general usefulness of Italian as compared with the other languages (especially the German dialect), and one family recalled that they had been asked by the school teacher to use Italian with their children. In other words, Italian is used in order to teach it: the home is here an extension of school. Seen in this light, this is an H function like all the others. No parents professed to feel any conflict between this function and the dimension of intimacy, which among adults leads to the selection of German in the home, the intimate connotations of which they will explicitly acknowledge.

Any conflict which may have been felt initially has apparently been overcome in the very short time since German began to be displaced in the home in dealings with children – about twelve to fifteen years, judging by the present upper age limit of the almost monoglot Italian generation. The switch is not quite complete, even in Lateis and Sauris di Sotto; some families still speak German with their children, but the following remark made about one such child by the mayor's mother will illustrate the trend: *Povero bambino, non parla neanche friulano.* The child was two years old.

Here we seem to have an indication of the value placed by a community (in this case, both by the macro-community of the Italian nation and by the micro-community of the village) on a particular language-variety as a passport to 'better' things. Similarly, the use and teaching in English schools of a particular register for the formal imparting and acquisition of macro-community knowledge is an H activity which reflects the value which that community places on the transactions associated with that particular register. Many English parents address their children in an approximation to the 'school' register when they assume a particularly pedagogical or admonitory role, perhaps with the aim, conscious or otherwise, of acquiring the authoritative nimbus of the teacher. We may note that a common assumption amongst parents (and even some teachers) is that the 'school' register is *the* English language, and that all other registers (and dialects) are merely corruptions of it. Hence, where we note the pedagogical use of a particular diatype (or diatypes) in a community we may, by observing other, extra-linguistic, activities with which it correlates, make objective deductions about the value placed by a society (or an influential sector of it) on those activities. Where such values are in the process of (or in need of) rapid change, there may well be a time-lag before appropriate adjustments are made in the 'school' diatype; and it would be interesting to know, in a society such as exists in present-day Britain, whether any such sociolinguistic time-lag actually acts as a brake on social change. Conversely, if a change of diatypic function in a macro-community framework runs ahead of the needs of a particular micro-community (i.e. precedes any evidence of internal forces there tending in the same direction), then we must ask whether such a process may not in itself help to bring about or hasten conformist change in the micro-community, the linguistic end of the sociolinguistic innovation acting as a 'fifth column' or 'softening-up agent' for a more general acculturation (compare Fox 1968). It is in this light that we must view the language policies of nation-building in developing nations (see Le Page, 1964), and the resistance they often encounter.

The Carnian variety of Friulian (Bender, Francescato and Salzman, 1952; Francescato, 1967; Iliescu, 1964, in press; Marchetti, 1952; Pirona *et al.*, 1935) spoken in Sauris is used with acquaintances from the surrounding Friulian-speaking area, and also, in their presence, by Saurians to each help is Friulian *ajuuuut!*; and villagers hailing each other from a distance use Friulian – e.g. *Giovanin, van cà* even though they switch to German as soon as they are within normal talking range. The habitual use of Friulian for conversation within the group is a marker of those males in their twenties and thirties who have enjoyed the benefit of a secondary-school education in Ampezzo, also of the mayor and his family who lived for many years outside Sauris in a Friulian environment and now run a hotel, restaurant and bar at La Maina, the southernmost cluster of houses in the parish. Perhaps because it is the most accessible and the nearest part of Sauris to the outside world (though still some fifteen kilometres by a thought-provoking mountain road), Friulian appears to have become the predominant language at La Maina, though German is still in use between spouses in some of the families there. Friulian is commonly used for ordering drinks and for talk at the bar, not only in 'La Nuova Maina', run by the mayor's family, but elsewhere in Sauris too. However, there is apparently no automatic correlation between the language and this particular setting: as in general in Sauris, other ingredients in the situation, especially the roles of the participants, have greater priority than physical setting in diatypic selection (Denison, 1968, p. 583, 585). [. . .]

In general, there is far less *parole* recourse to specifically Italian elements in the Friulian of Sauris (though, being closely related languages, the two have quite a lot of structure in common anyway) than, say, in that of the environs of Udine, the provincial centre, where Friulian is the L diatype in a very complex three-term system with Veneto and Italian. Indeed, for Saurians, Friulian possesses the degree of integrity which goes with a modest dignity – less than they associate with Italian, but far more than they see in the German dialect. This is commensurate with the role which Friulian performs for them as a regional language, and also with its internal diatypic status mid-way between Italian and German. This has a curious consequence for transactions between the natives of Sauris and some of the middle-class citizens of Udine who drive up to Sauris for a weekend in the heat of August. For them, Friulian has decidely L connotations, and they tend to reserve it, so far as any attempt at sustained discourse is concerned, for rather patronizing dealings with the rural population. The rural population is in general well aware of this, and often defends itself by replying in Italian, the H connotations of which, although they do not conceal the inequality of status of the participants, nevertheless restore distance and a certain dignity to the transaction. I have noted many instances of this kind of sociolinguistic skirmishing in Friuli. A typical occurrence, which I was able unobserved to tape, was a consultation between building workers on a site near Ampezzo and the architect, who was from Udine. Only the foreman felt secure enough to respond consistently in Friulian to the architect's Friulian, the remaining workers frequently replied in Italian, though they carried on side discussions among themselves in Friulian. Now in Sauris, when middle-class Udinesi use Friulian with patronizing intent, or on patronizing assumptions, the operation misfires completely, leaving both sides happy after an exchange in Friulian, of which both sides have understood the primary semantics whilst retaining intact their divergent interpretations – L for the Udinesi, M for the Saurians – of the sociosemantics.

The following is a short sample of the German dialect of Sauris, extracted from a tape made, unobserved, of a highly unusual occurrence. One morning, a woman sent her husband, aged fifty to sixty, with the milk to the cooperative dairy in Sauris to make cheese. At 2 p.m. he had still not returned. The bar at 'La Nuova Maina' had just opened for the Easter season, and the cheese-maker had found his way there. Now, several glasses of schnaps later, he was conducting a quiet conversation with an old friend at one of the tables, when his wife – A – burst in and began to harangue him excitedly in German. Our extract begins just as she was slowing down to get her second wind, thus giving her husband – B – a chance to insert one or two half-hearted attempts at self-defence:

A: diər tsa gəla: ban ɛpas tuən man həlt zinte.
(It's a waste of time to believe anything you say.)

B: *ööö! no stà rabiàti, capîs-tu!*
(Oh, don't lose your temper, d'you understand!)

A: *eee*?! *no cor rabiàsi*! gɛa ha:m! vaspe:gn tuəʃt peisar.
(No need to lose my temper, indeed! Go home! You('d) do better, that's why.)

B: unt əxtər, dəha:me, bas tu:i?
(And then, at home, what do I do?)

A: beinst kʰa:n o·rbat əʃt, gɛəʃtə i:bər də bi:ze auf . . .
(If you've no work to do, you can take a walk up over the meadow . . .)

A: gea ha:m, əni gəzo:ţ, tuəʃt peisar.
(Go home, I said, you('d) do better.)

B: bein du: ʃaubəʃt mi ʃbərts ən, net . . .
(If you give me a black look, well . . .)

A: *ma*! miər məxʃtə a:n tsourn, bein də məxəšt zötəna kəmɛdias – *cjo* – i:beis-i net biə man tuən tsa gɛan in a burtshaus tsa neman-di di:. man mu:sn na·r – bis-net-bas-i: – in gaiʃt aufge:bn mu:səman.
(You make me angry when you play the fool this way. I don't know what it's coming to, to (have to) go into a pub like this to fetch you. It's enough to make a body – I don't know what – give up the ghost, it is.)

B: tuəʃt na·r tsbiə s i ba:rat a diəp . . .
(You act as if I were a thief . . .)

This text illustrates once more the low diatypic selective power of setting (as narrowly defined above) in Sauris, as compared with other factors in the situation. Even where there seems at first sight to be a high degree of correlation – as for instance with Friulian in bars, German in the home, Italian at church and in school, there turns out to be a more accurately predictive correlation with some other factor or factors present. Thus, in the case of Friulian at the bar, it is probably the semi-public nature of the primary transaction (ordering drinks, counting change, the frequent presence of outsiders) which is responsible, together, at 'La Nuova Maina', with the habitual use of Friulian by the landlord's family. For German in the home, one important condition is that the participants be adults. For Italian in church and at school, it is the highly institutionalized, formal (in church, ritual) nature of the activities which is most relevant, not the actual buildings.

I have elsewhere (1968, pp. 583–4) described how the formation of small groups (especially if for drinking) can effectively narrow and transform the total situation and lead to language-switching at 'La Nuova Maina'. The above text shows how anger can have the same effect, for the wife's voice was obviously louder than her husband's, felt appropriate for any language, especially German, given the other factors in the situation. This seems to have added to his embarrassment; at any rate, his own small part in the total exchange was at a very subdued decibel level. The most interesting point is the attempt made by the husband to shift the situation, bringing in the participation, and hence the support, of other males present, by the sudden switch to Friulian: *no stà rabiàti*. This was a true switch of diatype, not one of the many established Romance microstructural elements in the German dialect like *ma*, *kɔmɛdias* and *tjɔ* in our text, not a normal part of the code, but an act of creative *parole* improvization. At this point the husband lifted his head, which had hitherto been bent rather despondently over his glass, and looked for approval from the other males present. In the event, the ploy failed to get him off the hook by retrieving the situation from the domain – to use Fishman's term – of conjugal dispute and putting it back in the domain of good-natured talk in Friulian at the bar, in which all present would feel free to participate. For a moment, but alas! only for a moment, his wife was thrown off balance, and was constrained to make her immediate response – an ironic echo (note that it was not mere repetition) – in Friulian also. Here, as in the retaliatory use of Italian by Friulians, described above, we have an instance of the way in which individuals, by skilful manipulation of diatypes, seek to steer situations – or better, perhaps – to *create* situations to their own advantage. [. . .]

The almost exclusively L functions which macro-structure German performs in its spoken mode show a high degree of correlation with close participant relationships amongst adults, most regularly of all amongst female adults (regardless of topic). Non-rural technicality of topic makes for a greater incidence of Romance microstructure (lexis, grammar of short groups); as between Italian and Friulian micro-elements, the former are more, the latter less formally technical within an overall framework which belongs to the informal end of the scale so far as participant relationships are concerned. Rural topics, due allowance made for technological innovations, are among those which in Sauris correlate best with a high incidence of historically and synchronically 'German' microstructure and hence with a greater degree of homogeneity in L situations Other things being equal, the oldest speakers tend to show least, the youngest adults most, Romance microstructure in their German, females less than males age for age. Within such overall tendencies there is stylistic variation between individuals on this point, and the picture is further complicated by what amongst Saurians under fifty strikes one as being a almost incredibly random factor in linguistic transmission. Thus, of two males, close acquaintances aged about thirty, one knew and used the word *stiǝf pruǝdǝr* – 'stepbrother', whereas the other knew only (Ital.) *fratellaccio*. This second individual, however, knew and used *umǝgɔŋk*[h] 'procession', whereas the first used only (Friul.) 'procession' and thought he had heard the German word in the form *umǝdɔŋk*[h] (folk etymology!). Not infrequently one hears Saurians of this generation asking each other, or a senior, for an explanation of some item of German lexis which one of them has used, and of which one or more participants are ignorant. Apart from providing the investigator with an opportunity to establish a reputation for well-nigh divine omniscience (a temptation to be resisted, as anthropologists will appreciate), this may lead him to ponder with Hymes (1967b, p. 634) the case of Bloomfield's White-Thunder who 'speaks less English than Menomini, and that is a strong indictment, for his Menomini is atrocious. His vocabulary is small; his inflections are often barbarous; he constructs sentences of a few threadbare models...'. A young man in Sauris who failed to ask linguistic questions could easily become a White-Thunder so far as his German was concerned and there is evidence of a general impoverishment of the language, as a result, it seems, of the combined circumstances of its restricted diatypic function, its consequent low prestige (which reinforces the restriction of its diatypic function), and the random element in its diachronic transmission in these circumstances by a tiny community which never seems to have greatly exceeded 800 souls.

The survival in German amongst older, and some younger, Saurians of the general lexis of external church affairs such as processions, Christian feasts (Christmas, Easter, All Saints, All Souls) and verbs for 'pray', 'confirm', 'confess', is a reminder that Italian has assumed the H functions of religious observance within living memory. About fifty years ago a long line of native Saurian priests came to an end, and, with their succession by non-German-speaking priests from outside, sermons in German were discontinued. Up to about the same time German dialect explications (but Italian textbooks!) were used by the school teacher during the very brief exposure (one to three years) to formal schooling which children in Sauris then received. These facts, together with the recent penetration by Italian into relationships between parents and children in Sauris, show that what at first sight looks like a tolerably neat synchronic picture of diatypic distribution is none the less part of a rapidly shifting sociolinguistic scene.

At present, adults in Sauris may be said to inhabit three main diatypic spaces. It is likely that when the forefathers of the present population (better: *some* of the forefathers of *most* of the villagers) first settled their valley – which, on toponomastic evidence had no settled population before that time (Lorenzoni, 1938) – some twelve and a half centuries ago, these three 'worlds' were spatially delimited, and could have been adequately described by drawing three concentric half-circles to the south round ego, the first encompassing the village, the second the region (Friulian) and the third the great outside world (Italian).[6] Now that the region and the outside world are so unmistakeably represented inside the village and its daily activities, the diatypic spaces which now coexist there have become psychologically rather than physically distinct. When a Saurian, using German (*inzǝra ʃpro:xe*) says *biǝr* – 'we', he normally means himself and his fellow villagers. A visitor from the nearest town, Ampezzo, who may be in the next room, is spoken of and identified in German as *dǝr be:liʃe*, as are all other Italians, Carnians and Friulians. In German, a Saurian will today still speak of having worked *in vriaul* – 'in Friuli' – almost as though it were a foreign country. When our Saurian speaks Friulian, however, *noatris* refers to himself and his fellows as Friulians, or, at least, as Carnians, though it will more often than not exclude 'Italians'. When a villager speaks Italian he sees himself as part of the Italian nation: *Se non ci siamo noi*, – 'If we are not here' – said the deputy mayor, lamenting the depopulation trend in the high Alpine valleys, *chi è che diffende questi confini?* – 'who will defend these frontiers?'

Saurians are certainly not unique in having access to more than one social identity. However, it may be that by marking them off by such distinct diatypes adult Saurians constantly remind themselves that they cannot assume all their identities simultaneously. There are three ways of seeking unity in the phenomena of language . . . one peculiarly open to the sociolinguistic approach is to seek a unity in the future – to see the processes of sociolinguistic change that envelop our objects of study as underlain by the emergence of a world society' (Hymes, 1967b). In becoming trilingual, Sauris took a major step towards membership of a world society a far greater step than the world ever took towards Sauris. Today, in abandoning German and Friulian, the children of Sauris are being thrust even further towards a world society. In the process, they and world society are abandoning much of what was Sauris and much of what was Friuli. Let us hope that the bargain is worth its price.

6. Of course this is rather an oversimplification. The oldest Latin and Romance loan-words in Saurian German show that long before the Saurian migration the 'worlds' they inhabited were already beginning to merge. We are really concerned with a difference of degree here, but it is such a large degree of difference that it is easy to think of it as a difference of kind.

Summary

In this paper I have attempted to discuss within a general sociolinguistic framework samples of specific material from a particular trilingual case study. The following are some of the notions of more general scope and possibly wider application which I have sought to air:

1. In Sauris, different parts of the linguistic structure appear to be sensitive to different kinds of situational factors – macro-structure specifically to participant relationships and purpose, micro-structure specifically to topic and mood. This suggests that we should not be in too much of a hurry to generalize at too high a level of abstraction in the categorization of situational factors under such labels as formality, technicality, closeness, distance and the like. A detailed examination of the language in particular sociolinguistic situations will lead us to ask, more discriminatingly: formality in what respect? What kind of technicality, closeness, distance? Which factors in the situation correlate with which parts of the diatypic system?

The anthropologist or sociologist must be prepared to find that a given language bundles situational factors together in diatypic correlation in what may strike him as an arbitrary, and from his point of view a highly inconvenient, manner. Arbitrary it certainly will be, from a synchronic or logical point of view, in the same way as the connection between the English sound sequence [maind] and the senses 'object to' ('move or behave cautiously in respect of'), 'look after' and 'human thinking faculty' is arbitrary. (Incidentally, only the last of these senses is indifferent as regards register.) The bundling may be inconvenient, but it is infinitely better than none at all: it is the best starting point we have for the detection and scientific re-categorization of the particular factors bundled.

2. The assignment of linguistic material at the various primary levels of analysis, to particular diatypes, is not a simple matter. A number of different criteria may be useful here, including, for plurilingual communities; phonological evidence of assimilation of 'borrowed' lexis, frequency distribution of doubtful items according to situation category, substitutability or otherwise of loaned items by 'native' items in the sum of idiolects (with or without diatypic implications if a given substitution is made), statistically determined norm specifications as in Labov's work. We cannot shirk the *langue/parole* issue for specific occurrences of items if this is relevant for their sociosemantic effect. If it could be demonstrated for particular cases that their *langue/parole* status is sociolinguistically irrelevant, then, so far as this writer is concerned, there would be no need to pursue the matter for merely doctrinaire or theoretical linguistic reasons.

3. It is because there are sociolinguistic norms of expectation that partici-

pants are able to some extent to *create* social situations by skilful switching of diatypes. Some indication of the circumstances in which this may happen has been given above. Note, however, that a participant will be unable to impose a sociolinguistic situation if it is rejected as inappropriate by the others. To this extent the individual is no more a completely free agent sociolinguistically than he is linguistically in other respects, or in his social behaviour in general. In the words of Hymes (1971), the creativity of speakers is 'rule-governed creativity'.

4. In Sauris intra-diatypic influence and diachronic development is almost exclusively in the direction H → L. This is simply another dimension (and an illuminating one) of the well-known diachronic facts about the direction of linguistic influence between 'separate' communities of different cultural levels, or, as I would prefer to express it, of unequal prestige. Seen in this light, the synchronically arbitrary distribution of lexis according to register in English (most H words being of Latin or Romance origin, most L words being of Germanic origin), receives a diachronic 'explanation' in earlier periods (for an elite) of complete diglossia (Latin/English, later French/English) or even trilingualism (Latin/French/English) in diatypic function. Those who today possess all the relevant registers (especially at the H end of the scale) are the social heirs of those who were plurilingual, and exercised similar power by virtue of that fact. In terms of its methodological implications, this means that for communities whose history is not known, careful diatypic, synchronic analysis may enable a hypothesis to be framed about a probable historical profile of social contacts and influences, for comparison with, and supplementation of, the cultural-historical inferences which can be drawn from the well-tried method of comparative and historical linguistic analysis at the primary levels of linguistic structure, especially lexis. In this sense, the arbitrariness of sociolinguistic convention may to a certain extent be dispelled.

References

BENDER, B., FRANCESCATO, G., and SALZMAN, Z. (1952), 'Friulian phonology', *Word*, vol. 8, pp. 216–23.

BERGMANN, J. (1849), 'Die deutsche Gemeinde Sappada nebst Sauris . . .', *Archiv für Kunde österr. Geschichtsquellen*, vol. 3, parts 1 & 2, Akademie der Wissenschaften, Vienna.

BRUNIERA, M. (1938), 'Il dialetto tedesco dell'isola alloglotta di Sappada'), dissertation, University of Padua.

CATFORD, J. C. (1965), *A Linguistic Theory of Translation*, Oxford University Press.

DENISON, N. (1968), 'Sauris – a trilingual community in diatypic perspective', *Man* (NS), vol. 3, no. 4, pp. 578–94.

DENISON, N. (in press), 'Sociolinguistics and plurilingualism', in *Acts of the Tenth International Congress of Linguists*, pp. 551–9.

ELLIS, J. O. (1966), 'On contextual meaning', in C. E. Bazell *et al.* (ed.), *In Memory of J. R. Firth*, Longman.

FERGUSON, C. A. (1959), 'Diglossia', *Word*, vol. 15, pp. 325–40.

FISHMAN, J. A. (1965), 'Who speaks what language to whom and when?', *La Linguistique*, vol. 2, pp. 67–88. (See also this volume.)

FISHMAN, J. A. (1967), 'Bilingualism with and without diglossia; diglossia with and without bilingualism', *J. Soc. Iss.*, vol. 27, no. 2, pp. 29–38.

FISHMAN, J. A. (1968a), 'Sociolinguistic perspective on the study of bilingualism', *Linguistics*, vol. 39, pp. 21–49.

FISHMAN, J. A. (1968b), *Bilingualism in the Barrio*. Final Report, Contract No. OEC-1-7-062817-0297. US Dept. of Health, Education and Welfare.

FOX, R. (1968), 'Multilingualism in two communities', *Man* (NS), vol. 3, pp. 456–64.

FRANCESCATO, G. (1967), *Dialettologia Friulana*, Società Filologica Friulana, Udine.

GREGORY, M. (1967), 'Aspects of varieties differentiation', *J. Linguistics*, vol. 3, pp. 177–97.

HALLIDAY, M. A. K., MCINTOSH, A., and STREVENS P. D. (1964), *The Linguistic Sciences and Language Teaching*, Longman.

HORNUNG, M. (1960), 'Die Osttiroler Bauernsprachinseln Pladen und Zahre in Oberkarnien', *Osttiroler Heimatblätter*, vol. 98, pp. 1–14.

HORNUNG, M. (1964), *Mundartkunde Osttirols*, Akademie der Wissenschaften, Vienna.

HORNUNG, M. (1967), 'Romanische Entlehnungen in der deutschen Sprachinselmundart von Pladen', in *Mundart und Geschichte* (Kranzmayer Festschrift), pp. 41–69, Akademie der Wissenschaften, Vienna.

HYMES, D. (1967a), 'Models of the interaction of language and social setting', *J. Soc. Iss.*, vol. 27, no. 2.

HYMES, D. (1967b), 'Why linguistics needs the sociologist', *Soc. Res.*, vol. 34, part 4.

HYMES, D. (1971), 'Sociolinguistics and the ethnography of speaking', in E. Ardener (ed.), *Social Anthropology and Language*, Tavistock.

ILIESCU, M. (1964), 'Zu den in Rumänien gesprochenen friaulischen Dialekten', *Rev. Roum. Ling.*, vol. 9, pp. 68–78.

ILIESCU, M. (in press), 'Observations sur le bi- et multilingualisme des frioulans de Roumanie', in *Acts of the Tenth International Congress of Linguists*.

KRANZMAYER, E. (1956), *Historische Lautgeographie des gesamtbairischen Dialektraumes*, Academie der Wissenschaften, Vienna.

LEECH, G. N. (1966), *English in Advertising*, Longman, London.

LE PAGE, R. B. (1964), *The National Language Question*, Oxford University Press.

LORENZONI, G. (1938), *La Toponomastica di Sauris*, Istituto delle Edizioni Accademiche, Udine.

LUCCHINI, L. (1882), *Saggio di Dialettologia Sauriana*, Patronato di Udine.

MAGRI, G. (1941), 'Il dialetto di Sauris', dissertation, University of Padua.

MARCHETTI, G. (1952), *Lineamenti di Grammatica Friulana*, Societa Filologica Friulana, Udine.

PIRONA, G. A., CARLETTI, E., and CORGNALI, G. B. (1935), 'Ercole Carletti and Giovanni Battista Corgnali' in *Il Nuovo Pirona: Vocabulario Friulano*, Società Filologica Friulana, Udine.

REID, T. B. W. (1956), 'Linguistics, structuralism and philology', *Arch. L.* vol. 8, pp. 28–37.

URE, Jean N. (1967), *The Theory of Register and Register in Language Teaching*, University of Essex.

5 A. P. Sorensen Jr

Multilingualism in the Northwest Amazon

Revised version of A. P. Sorensen Jr, 'Multilingualism in the Northwest Amazon', *American Anthropologist*, vol. 69, 1967, pp. 670–84.

1. Field work for this report was done in the summers of 1959, 1960, 1962 and from June to December 1963. It was supported during much of this time by USPHS Research Grant MH–17,258. I wish to acknowledge the hospitality and cooperation extended to me by the Xaveriano missionary order in Colombia and the Salesian missionaries of the Brazilian Vaupés region. Various drafts of this paper were read by Drs Charles Wagley, Harvey Pitkin, Robert F. Murphy, and Dell Hymes. I am indebted to them for their criticisms and encouragement.

The cultural, social and linguistic units
Setting and culture area

In the central part of the Northwest Amazon, there is a large multilingual area encompassing many tribes, each possessing its own language, where almost every individual is polylingual – he knows three, four, or more languages well. The area of multilingualism coincides largely with the area in which the Tukano tribal language is a lingua franca. This area can be roughly defined as the Vaupés River and its tributaries. (The Vaupés flows into the Rio Negro, which in turn flows into the Amazon.) The region is the size of New England, or slightly larger. About half of it lies in Colombia and half in Brazil. The population is sparse, about 10,000.

Most tribes occupy a delimited, continuous stretch of a river; a few have a discontinuous settlement pattern. Altogether they form one large, homogeneous cultural group in the center of what is identified in the literature as the Northwest Amazon culture area (see Steward and Faron, 1959). There is historical as well as traditional evidence that some of these tribes may have originated outside of the Vaupés area, subsequently acculturating to the general central Northwest Amazon culture. Other tribes seem to have originated locally from proliferation by fission (Koch-Grünberg, 1909–10).

A couple of the larger tribes do not live in one continuous area, but in several areas. The numerous Tukano tribe occupies several continuous stretches of the Vaupés River and its principal tributaries, the Tikié and the Papurí, and also sites at the mouths of tributaries to these rivers. Historically, they have exerted a dominant influence in the area. The

Tukano tribal language serves as the *lingua franca* of the entire area. (Its use as a *lingua franca* antedates the appearance of other *linguae francae* in the region.) .

The various tribes making up this large, homogeneous cultural group contain about 90 per cent of the people in the area. The remainder consists of two ethnic groups. One is the Makú Indians, who live away from the rivers and are more or less nomadic. The other consists of the non-Indians, who call themselves *blancos* (in Spanish) or *brancos* (in Portuguese) and who number perhaps 1,500. Most of them live in the two or three airstrip towns.

Here, then, is a large culturally homogeneous area where multilingualism – and polylingualism in the individual – is the cultural norm. Anthropologically, this is a culture trait, and it is an outstanding culture trait of the area.

Social units

Social units of primary importance to the analysis of multilingualism in the central Northwest Amazon culture area are the nuclear family, lineage, sib, tribe, phratry; the longhouse group; the linguistic group; and the exogamy group. Secondarily important, as they represent aggregations from among the above, are the mission village and the nationality group. Although Indians claim that the tribe occupies the focal position in the structural articulations of all these groups, analysis indicates that it is the sib that really does. The tribe nevertheless identifies the linguistic unit.

Several nuclear families may be found in a lineage, and several lineages in a sib (or patrilineal clan), which is the named and localized unit of social organization. A tribe is a named political and ceremonial unit, consisting of several sibs; it has a separate history and is identifiable by a distinct language. Barring the few exceptions where some of its sibs belong to a different phratry from that of the majority, each tribe is aligned with one of five phratries. Each phratry is a named, exogamous group of sibs that marries into the other phratries in the area. A phratry is not a political or ceremonial unit *per se*.

The basic political and ceremonial unit of the Northwest Amazon is the longhouse group, which is also the basic unit of economic redistribution. (The nuclear family is the basic economic unit *before* redistribution.) A well-established longhouse group becomes, over a period of time, a cluster of lineages. A tribe is represented by a series of longhouses, located several hours' paddling distance apart from each other along a river and often situated at rapids for good fishing.

The tribe is co-extensive with the linguistic group, which is composed of those individuals who are expected to have used the language as their principal language when they were children in their nuclear family of orientation. The language that identifies the linguistic group is, then, at once the father tongue, the longhouse language, and the tribal language of each member; it is *not* the language that identifies the mother's linguistic group.

Linguistically, the name for the language is the name for the tribe in the plural possessive form, nominalized.

Some writers, such as Reichel-Dolmatoff (1963), have referred to the composite of all the Indian tribes (except the Makú) that share the same homogeneous culture and that participate in the system of exogamous phratries as the 'Tukano tribe'. (In this case, the language-bearing units of Tukanos, Desanos, Kubeos, Yurutís, etc., should probably be designated 'subtribes'.)

At present, however, Indians recognize the set of longhouses speaking the same father-language as the maximal unit, and this is the 'tribe' that is exogamous. The Indian identification of this exogamous, language-bearing unit as the maximal one is crucial in the analysis of multilingualism in the central Northwest Amazon. I shall use the term 'tribe' in accord with this identification.

The exogamic group is the phratry. Informants, however, claim that the unit of exogamy is the tribe. The few exceptional cases of tribes whose sibs belong to more than one phratry (e.g., the Kubeo) are well known and are taken for granted as minor exceptions to the state rule. This rule is expressed in a formula that one does not marry inside of one's own tribe-and-language group because one would then be marrying a sister or a brother. Although informants do not explicitly refer to it, they recognize exogamy at a phratry level, and all marriages conform to a rule of phratry exogamy as well as of tribal exogamy. Recognition of the multitribal composition of the phratry is expressed as: 'A Tukano will not marry a Baré because the Baré are brothers and sisters with the Tukanos.'

The exogamic phratry system is extended fictitiously to all tribes peripheral to and beyond the central Northwest Amazon area, even though members of these tribes may not themselves be aware that they fit into such a system.

A larger mission village is a unit that has been created by missionaries from two or more longhouse groups representing two or more tribes (hence linguistic groups) that have been required to tear down their longhouses, move together, and build separate adobe huts for each nuclear family. A larger mission village also contains a contingent of non-Indian missionaries and a boarding house of school children from nearby settlements. A smaller mission village is a single longhouse group that has been persuaded to tear down its longhouse and substitute a series of adobe huts, one for each nuclear family.

There are two nationality groups among the multilingual Indians described in this paper – the Colombian Indians and the Brazilian Indians (the periphery of the multilingual area may include some Venezuelan Indians) – and even the members of the longhouses in the zone most unacculturated to 'civilization' know whether they are Colombians or Brazilians. Also, Indians and non-Indians both agree that there are two clear-cut categories of people in the Vaupés: in Spanish these are called the *indígenas*, or Indians, and the *blancos*, or non-Indians (including Negros).

As for nationality-and-language, the Indians know that Spanish is the language of non-Indians on the Colombian side of the border and that Portuguese is the corresponding language on the Brazilian side of the border. Nationality has no bearing on exogamy.

Languages: degree and nature of relationships

The criterion used in this paper to differentiate languages is mutual unintelligibility. The Indians' identification of tribe with language was initially relied on to prepare a tentative list of languages, as the listing of 'tribes' was ostensibly also a listing of 'languages'. For the many informants asked, the criterion of tribal distinctiveness includes, by their own cultural definition, mutual unintelligibility between languages. The field procedure was to watch for occasions when an Indian would comment that he had not understood someone else in a discussion where more than one language was spoken, at which time I would inquire what were the languages concerned. I depended on an Indian commenting in Tukano to identify non-understanding situations, but I was also able to pick up cues of 'I don't understand' that I recognized in a number of the other languages. Thus I learned that such apparently closely related languages as Desano and Siriano, and even Tuyuka and Yuruti (see next two paragraphs), are mutually unintelligible. These and similar languages that are very closely related genetically make the central Northwest Amazon area an excellent one for close examination of the problem of language versus dialect (see Haugen, 1966b).

Several language families are represented in this multilingual area: Eastern Tukanoan, Arawakan, Indo-European, Tupí-Guaranían, and others that remain undetermined (cf. Mason, 1950; Noble, 1965). Of these, the family most widely represented and with the largest number of languages is the Eastern Tukanoan, a family that seems to be contained entirely within the Northwest Amazon. The following discussion of my impressions is limited to this family.

The degree of relationship among these Eastern Tukanoan languages cannot be rigorously stated yet, but it is my impression that the languages separated by commas in the list in the appendix are a little farther apart than are the languages in the Romance group or in the Scandinavian group. One can look at the Romance languages as a dialect chain, but in the Eastern Tukanoan language family the *intermediate* 'dialects' are missing, except perhaps for those languages in the appendix connected by 'and'. Central Algonquian languages (Bloomfield, 1946; Hockett, 1948) are more closely related than the Eastern Tukanoan languages seem to be. Approaching the problem from the opposite perspective, that is, from the point of view of reasonably demonstrated *dialects* within a language, the correspondences among the Eastern Tukanoan languages do not present the tightness or neatness that is so evident among those of the Karen dialects as drawn by Jones (1961).

Structural interrelationships are generally close among Eastern Tukanoan languages, but in the finer details of their similarities the languages do not coincide. In *broad* phonetic transcription, most of the Eastern Tukanoan languages share most of the same grid of phones, but the patterning of phonemes and the distribution of allophones vary from language to language.

The morphologies of these languages are generally similar, but they vary considerably on specific points. There can even be said to be an Eastern Tukanoan type, but each language still has its own distinctive differences. For instance, most Eastern Tukanoan languages have only two general forms for 'person' in the verbal paradigm, but not all: Piratuapuyo has three. The participal system seems to be more developed in some languages than in others. In lexicon, there is again general similarity, but not coincidence, between languages. In the exceptional area of kinship terminology, for example, more relatives may be distinguished in one language than in another, and what appear to be cognate terms in two languages may not refer to the same relative.

I have observed that when an Indian knows how to speak two closely related languages (of the sort connected by 'and' in the appendix), he carefully and even consciously keeps them apart. It has occurred to me that the exogamic and other cultural institutions to be discussed below may be exerting a force that makes a speaker want to render closely related languages farther apart, even to an artificial extent, but so far I have detected no linguistic innovations to this end. Here, however, I run the risk of overstating the dialect problem. As Weinreich has pointed out (1961: section 1.3), the learning of a new dialect presents the same situation as the learning of a new language.

The Eastern Tukanoan languages clearly share the same syntax. By this

I mean that they share the same types of multiword constructions. For example, they share a preference for a series of clauses in parataxis with a strong avoidance of hypotaxis; the same preferred (and not rigidly fixed) word order prevails (subject-object-verb); the same procedure is followed for developing a discourse topic, the sentence being prolonged by clauses in parataxis so as to provide more and more specificity to an original proposition stated in a main, and usually first, clause; listeners show the same pattern of response, attentively, politely, or disinterestedly repeating the last verb of the speaker's sentence; etc.

It is important for this discussion to point out that Indian speakers do not ascribe the Tukanoan type of syntax to Spanish. Neither is the full syntactic range of Spanish as used by Colombian non-Indian Spanish-speakers found in the Indians' Spanish. Further evidence comes from the response of Indians to metalinguistic questions. Monolingual Spanish-speakers, when quizzing Indians for forms in their language, typically ask for the forms one word at a time, following the order of the Spanish sentence (which may be phrased quite elegantly to ensure getting elegant Tukano). The translation process breaks down almost immediately; new Tukano forms for former Tukano forms are given as the Spanish sentence progresses, and the Spanish-speaker decides the Indian must be very indeterminate in whatever he says.

The actual manner in which an Indian normally translates from Spanish to Tukano is so regular that it can be stated almost as a rule: the Indian remains silent until the full statement has been made in Spanish, he waits then for a few seconds until apparently the way he would say it in Tukano comes to him, and then he restates it in a normal Tukano sentence that generally has a syntactic structure very different from that of the Spanish sentence. This suggests that most Indians may be 'coordinate' in their knowledge of Spanish and Tukano rather than 'merged' (Weinreich, 1953). Or, the cultural pattern may favor coordinate rather than merged control. This procedure can be enervating, culturally, to the monolingual Spanish-speaker, who expects to be replied to almost without audible pause between the end of his statement and the beginning of his responder's statement in rapid-fire repartee.

Anything said in Spanish is customarily repeated aloud in translation, even when all the Indians present already know Spanish. For the Indian, repeating a part of what a speaker says is a formal conversational device indicating understanding, assent (dissent if repeated with a negative suffix), and respect. In a formal gathering, as in the men's circle in the evening when the day's tasks are over, the amount of respect accorded to the older men who begin the session is indicated by how much the listeners repeat them. In the same setting, the remarks of a visitor speaking in another language are repeated in their entirety if someone present does not understand the language; as the conversation acquires more informal character and smaller conversation groups form, the repeating is dropped except for the respectful, assenting repeating of the last verbs of clauses and sentences; the visitor, indeed, may change to the language of the longhouse, if he knows it.

Repeating in translation something said in Spanish or Portuguese takes place in an interesting culture-contact situation. The encounter is rarely in a formal context for the Indian. It may be on a river bank, or on a trail, or on boats with the paddlers holding on to each others' boats and holding on to vines, or it may be on the street in a mission town. It almost never takes place in a formal gathering of Indians, as many situations calling for formal gatherings are discouraged by non-Indians. Nevertheless, many, or all Indians of the settlement may be present. The repeating is first of all a respectful recognition of the Spanish-speaking non-Indians, but there also seems at times to be an additional quality of defensiveness connected with the practice. The repeating seems to serve as a stalling device so that the Indians can evaluate something of the intentions of the non-Indians, as indicated by their demands, their mood, and their degree of tolerance of Indian habits (for example, whether they permit beer, or admonish women – and men – for going without upper garments). Most non-Indians issue orders and interrogate loudly, according to the Latin American stereotype of the way to speak to Indians, rather than 'converse' with them. The Indians, for various reasons, want to be sure that they have heard every question and order correctly. Consequently, repeating serves as a double-checking device, for corrections in translation are supplied unhesitatingly and immediately by other listeners following the translator. In sum, then, repeating is a formal conversational device indicating respect that also has an adaptive defensive function.

Certain formulaic communication styles – regardless of Indian language family – are probably the same throughout the area, particularly greetings on entering a new longhouse in traveling. I have witnessed and participated in many such situations where the longhouse language was unknown either to me or to some of my Indian traveling companions, and always the content of the initial sequence of bilingual statements was clear to all (namely, the assertion that one has arrived; from which direction – upriver or downriver – one has come, and from what named spot; how many days one has been traveling; and who one's father and mother and brothers and sisters are, and how they are faring). There are other occasional formulaic conventions, especially those involving repeating, that can help a novice gain familiarity with a language. Many languages also seem to share interjections. (In these respects the central Northwest Amazon area may constitute what J. Neustupny has termed a *Sprechbunde* (speech area). 'Semi-communication' (Haugen, 1966a) based on a partial knowledge of a language that is closely related to one already known may also occur.

Multilingualism

Because descent is patrilineal in the Northwest Amazon and residence is normatively and predominantly patrilocal, an individual belongs to his (or her) father's tribe, and to his father's linguistic group, which is also his own. Because of exogamy, his mother always represents a different tribe – tribal membership does not change for her upon marriage – and a different linguistic group. A woman invariably uses the language of the longhouse – her husband's language – when talking directly with her children. But she is usually not the only woman from her tribe in a long-house. In a longhouse of any size there are usually several women of her tribe, as well as groups of other women from other tribes; and during the course of a day, these several groups of women usually find occasion to converse with each other in their own original languages.

In addition to these multilingual contacts in the longhouse, others occur as a result of considerable traveling. Youths travel to investigate and evaluate available brides. A prospective bridegroom, if he does not know it already, learns his prospective wife's language from his prospective mother-in-law. Families also travel to visit relatives and affines. And there is travel for the sheer sake of travel.

A man's *mother's* language may be quite important because of the preferential-marriage system. There is a preference, though not an obligation, to marry his cross-cousin, particularly his mother's brother's daughter, real or classificatory. The kinship system is of Iroquoian type (Fulop, 1955). She will, of course, be of his *mother's* tribe and speak his *mother's* language. Therefore there is an added cultural incentive for a man to know his mother's language. If he has little opportunity to learn it – if she, for instance, is the only one of her tribe in the longhouse, and her tribe lives at a distance – his mother, nevertheless, will teach him lists of words in her language and how to say various things in it. Children are usually bilingual in both their father's and their mother's languages, but commonly use the former.

A child is frequently exposed to the other languages spoken in the long-house by the married women, who are ordinarily from more than one outside tribe, and by visitors. Visitors, especially, expose him to the lingua franca (which may also be the father's language or the mother's language for some individuals). Most children remain bilingual or trilingual in speech (with the lingua franca Tukano as the third language) until adolescence.

In the course of time, an individual is exposed to at least two or three languages that are neither his father's nor his mother's language. He comes to understand them and, perhaps, to speak them. I observed that as an individual goes through adolescence, he actively and almost suddenly learns to speak these additional languages to which he has been exposed, and his linguistic repertoire is elaborated. In adulthood he may acquire more languages; as he approaches old age, field observation indicates, he will go on to perfect his knowledge of all the languages at his disposal.

Each individual, then, has a personal repertoire of languages. Each longhouse, too, has its own characteristic language repertoire. Thus, the second longhouse up the Inambu River is a Tuyuka tribe longhouse that speaks Tuyuka; one third of the married women there are from the Barasana tribe, another third from the Desano tribe, and another third from the Tukano tribe. Careful field checking definitely corroborates that all individuals of this longhouse actually control at least these particular four languages within their individual repertoires. Most individuals know other languages besides these, but all share the basic longhouse inventory. The longhouse language, Tuyuka, is used to men and among men; women use the longhouse language with each other, but women who are classificatory sisters and hence from the same tribe have the option of using their own language when women from another tribe are not actually in the active conversation group, although other women (and men) within hearing understand it. All children use the longhouse language (i.e., their father's) to both their father and mother. As one continues up the river to the next longhouse, the proportion of Barasana women increases as the proportion of Desano women decreases, although the same four languages remain in a common longhouse repertoire shared by the individuals of that longhouse. Eventually a point will be reached where one of these languages will drop out of the longhouse repertoire, and perhaps another language (e.g., Tatuyo or Paneroa) will enter.

I must emphasize again that it is not just scattered individuals who know the various languages used in a given longhouse; but *all* the longhouse residents know them. In the mission villages, where what formerly were two, three, or more longhouses are now gathered together in one village of adobe huts, the linguistic picture resembles that of the single longhouse, but usually more than one father-language is present, for most missionary villages contain men from more than one tribe. (There seemed to be an incipient age-grading pattern between two father-tongues at one of the missions, but not at the others.)

Periodically, the missions have tried to prohibit the use of Indian languages, but these efforts were subsequently dropped. In aboriginal settings, in the mission compounds away from face-to-face contact with the missionaries themselves, and in any gathering of Indians, whether traveling, visiting or working rubber, no Spanish or Portuguese is used (except occasionally when Indians drink alcoholic beverages!). The field worker must rely upon a knowledge of at least one of the Indian languages in order to keep track of what languages are actually being spoken.

The Indians are quite unselfconscious about their multilingualism. They take it for granted. There is no development of cross-linguistic puns. There is no stylistic device of switching from one language to another or of interspersing one's conversation with quotes from another language. Conversations in two or more languages indeed occur on occasion, as in visiting, but no one takes special note of it. Each individual initially speaks in his own father-language during such a conversation in order to assert his tribal affiliation and identification, but after a while the junior persons change, without comment, to the longhouse language, to Tukano as the *lingua franca*, or to another language, whatever one is most convenient for the others. A person usually cannot enumerate how many languages he knows, and is perplexed at being asked to do so. The interviewer has to go over with him one by one the whole list of languages spoken in the area. But when approached, in this way, each individual definitely knows his own repertoire and can state what languages he speaks well, what ones he only understands but does not speak, etc.

I observed no tendency for people to claim knowledge of a language not actually known. I also observed that the Indians' terms for rating fluency, when translated into English, are *under*estimates. Thus when an Indian says he speaks such-and-such a language 'some', we would be more prone in English-speaking culture to say he speaks it 'quite well'. The unequally weighted rating scale used by informants in Tukano is perhaps best rendered by these English glosses and paraphrases: (*1*) 'none'; (*2*) 'hardly any' or 'just a few words'; (*3*) 'some, but not *well*' ('well' referring to pronunciation), or 'halfway'; (*4*) '*almost* all' or 'just a little lacks'; (*5*) 'all'. To an unqualified question, an informant usually gives his *speaking* fluency rating. He must be questioned separately for ratings on languages he understands but does not speak or 'hardly speaks'. All these observations make it appear that the Indians are indifferent or, perhaps, blasé about their multilingualism.

Their orientation to multilingualism is instrumental and practical, but not devious. The languages used in a given situation are not chosen with motives of concealment from others. Politeness leads visitors to use their hosts' language, if they know it. Reliance on one language as against another is not considered impolite, however, and only on rare occasions, when such a reliance is exaggerated insistently and provocatively, can it signal the expression of anything resembling a militant tribal rivalry. This may, but need not, occur during beer-drinking bouts, as at a formally arranged product-exchanging and friendship-renewing ceremony between two longhouses representing two tribes; but here it should be viewed as a means for expressing and releasing accumulated, and usually minor, tensions rather than as a product of the drunken brawl pictured by most non-Indians. Overt rivalry in most of these ceremonies seldom needs to go beyond the all-night competitive dancing of the separate rival troupes; and by the second day, the older men's chanting may end up entirely in the host-longhouse's language, while the younger men form one cooperative, consolidated dancing body. During the course of the ceremony, the women group according to their own tribal affiliations and sing as choruses in their own father-tongues. Married women alternate between singing in their original father-language, in their husband's language, and in the longhouse language of the hosts.

If neither one's father nor mother is Tukano, one nevertheless will speak Tukano as a lingua franca. Indirect evidence suggests that Tukano existed aboriginally, or at least early in the historic period, as a lingua franca, although its epicenter may have formerly been in the Lower Vaupés. The Tukano tribe may even have been the dominant group in a confederation or nation of sorts (Markham, 1910). At any rate, the Tukano are widely and strategically located and appear to have exerted a dominant influence in the whole area. The Tukano claim a mild prestige as the senior sibs of the area and regard all the other tribes as younger-brother sibs in a particular rank order (see Fulop, 1955); this ranking is accepted by the other tribes. Because the Tukano tribe is so widespread, almost every longhouse has at least one Tukano woman in it. Therefore, persons who do not have a Tukano for father or mother still have someone in their longhouse from whom they can absorb the correct pronunciation of Tukano.

Now, the Tukano language contains at least six dialects. As a *lingua franca* it is not pidginized but is learned in one or another of its tribal dialect forms, whatever one the learner is exposed to. Speakers for whom Tukano is not their father- or mother-language can still be identified as to regional dialect. Tukano, incidentally, is not an easy language to learn. It has a great many phonemes and an intricate tonal system; and apart from the tonal system, it has an intricate system of stress. This suggests the hypothesis that sheer intricacy may foster an all-or-none attitude toward learning to speak a phonologically elaborate language. Maintenance of Tukano as a *lingua franca* has probably been reinforced by there being some twenty-five or more language groups that it serves.

The Indians do not practise speaking a language that they do not know well yet. Instead, they passively learn lists of words, forms, and phrases in it and familiarize themselves with the sound of its pronunciation. The diverse and discrete phonologies of these languages and their dialects loom very prominently in the Indians' regard. They may make an occasional preliminary attempt to speak a new language in an appropriate situation, but if it does not come easily, they will not try to force it. One of the pre-conditions of language-learning in the area is a passive familiarity with lists of words (including inflected and derived forms) in languages likely to be learned. Much language-learning (especially of linguae francae) takes place within the peer group. Among closely related languages, a stage of 'semi-communication' (Haugen, 1966a) may be important in learning. Informants estimate that it takes them at least from one to two years to learn a new language fluently, regardless of language family. Most of them also estimate that it takes longer to learn Spanish than to learn Tukano or another Eastern Tukanoan language.

The early non-Indians who started coming into the area brought with them another language as *lingua franca*: Nheengatú (Ienkatú), also called Tupí, and also commonly referred to as *lingoa geral* (which means 'lingua franca' in Portuguese) or just *geral*. This is a Tupí-Guaraní language, and it is still spoken, even monolingually, along many portions of the Rio Negro by the detribalized Indian and White-Indian population, collectively known as *caboclos* (*cabucos* in 'Vaupense' Spanish).[2] Nheengatú spread as the lingua franca of the early rubber boom days, 1875–1920. When the rubber boom declined with the development of rubber plantations in Malaysia, the use of Nheengatú declined also. Now only some older people in the multilingual area described in this report know Nheengatú. Some younger people can repeat lists of words and forms in it, but they do not speak it. According to informants, it can be heard conversationally in the lower portions of the Vaupés, but I have not heard it used conversationally in the Middle Vaupés region. It was originally brought up the Amazon and to the Rio Negro by the Jesuits as the language of instruction; and it was well established there by the eighteenth century, when a contest with Portuguese began (Martius, 1867). Its grammar, originally adapted from a Latin model, was artificially built on a Tupí-Guaraní base similar to that of present day Guaraní.

After Nheengatú, Portuguese came in as another *lingua franca*. It is now the language of the non-Indians on the Brazilian side of the border and the language taught in the mission schools there.

2. See Rivera's powerful, authentic novel *La Vorágine* (1948) for Vaupense Spanish terms. The setting for much of this novel is the Colombian Vaupés region and the adjacent Casanare region (not dealt with, except indirectly, in this report). Rivera projected his morally and passionately torn protagonist, Arturo Cova, in ever-increasingly involved relief against the convoluted setting of the exploits of the notorious rubber barons. His Indians show up only as shadowy figures in the background – no doubt the way the rubber-gatherers, caught up in their own problems, saw them as they paused in dimly lit longhouses for their night's rest.

On the Colombian side, Spanish is the official lingua franca. There was much learning of Spanish in the rubber-gathering area during the rubber boom, and Spanish superseded Nheengatú as the dominant lingua franca there. The increasing importance of Spanish at the expense of Portuguese and the already fading Nheengatú coincided with a change in the rubber industry: to extract the *siringa* type of rubber, found in abundance in the Upper Vaupés River and Upper Apaporis River region of interior Colombia, instead of the less valuable but more widespread *balata* type found in both Colombia and Brazil. The stability of Tukano during this period of change probably enhanced its position as a lingua franca. The Upper Vaupés-Upper Apaporis region is just outside of the culture area being described in this paper, and it includes Indian workers who have come in from still other culture areas. While the knowledge of Spanish is spreading, via this rubber-gathering area, into the adjacent culture areas, the knowledge of Tukano is also spreading.

For about twenty years there has been a concerted attempt to teach Spanish to Colombian Indians in the schools. Perhaps one-third to one-half of the Indians already know Spanish as a second lingua franca. Many learned it when, as youths, they worked a few years in the rubber-gathering area. Theirs is good, understandable, and effective Spanish, although it may lack the subjunctive and certain other details of normative grammar. It cannot be called a 'broken Spanish'. At the missions, the insistence on using only Spanish has at times had an effect the reverse of the one desired and has invigorated Tukano and the other Indian languages. Along with measures to civilize the Indian linguistically and get him out of the long-house and into civilized villages, there have been attempts to detribalize the Indians by de-emphasizing exogamy. All these efforts, however, have only served to reinforce the persistence of the native languages.

Because this area is politically divided by the boundary between Colombia and Brazil, an Indian from Brazil who knows Portuguese finds that when he goes any distance into Colombia, Portuguese is not understood. Conversely Colombian Indians find they cannot use their Spanish in the interior of the Brazilian section. They then resort to their principal lingua franca, Tukano, which is understood on both sides of the border. And this situation obviously helps also in continuing Tukano as the main lingua franca.

Implications for some current issues

The one-language–one-culture image

Data from the central Northwest Amazon bear directly on the prevalent one-language–one-culture assumption, which, as Hymes (1964) and Gumperz (1961) point out, needs critical review. As I have shown, the multilingualism in the homogeneous culture of the central Northwest Amazon area serves to demarcate distinct, exogamous social units. Homogeneity of culture in this area does not mean homogeneity of language. And to speak of one language is not to speak of one entire culture. There is no one language that is father-language to all, nor is there any one language that is mother-language to everyone. What is father-language to some is mother-language to others and an unknown language to still others, all people who bear the same culture. The distribution of Tukano, as the lingua franca, does largely coincide with the extent of this culture area. But then the linguistic area of Tukano merges into the area of Nheengatú and thence into the area of Portuguese; the cultural areas of tribal Indians and of detribalized *caboclos* have perimeters that differ from those of the linguistic areas.

Implications for transformational linguistic theory

A number of details in the preceding description of the multilingual society in the central Northwest Amazon force some reconsideration of certain basic premises of transformational linguistic theory. Chomsky (1965, pp. 3–9) states that linguistic theory is concerned with the tacit knowledge of an ideally fluent monolingual speaker-hearer in a homogeneous speech community. An ideally fluent speaker-hearer in the central Northwest Amazon has to be someone who is *not* monolingual. There is also the question of what is to be considered a homogeneous speech community. A linguistic theory limited to one-language–one-group situations is inadequate to explain the actual linguistic competence of the people of the central Northwest Amazon.

Appendix: inventory of tribes and languages

1. Tribes and languages directly involved in multilingualism:

a Eastern Tukanoan language family, arranged in subgroupings suggested by a preliminary attempt at reconstruction by the comparative method (there are probably a few more languages to be documented in this group in subsequent field trips): Tukano, Tuyuka and Yurutí, Paneroa and Eduria, Karapana and Tatuyo, Barasana; Piratapuyo, Wanano; Desano and Siriano; Kubeo.

b Arawakan language family: Tariano; Baré. Most Tarianos now use Tukano as their household or father-language, and they marry Tukanos; many younger Tarianos do not know Tariano, although they are polylingual in other languages. The Baré along the Middle and Lower Vaupés use either Tukano or Nheengatú as their household or father-language, and very few speakers of the original Baré are left; the Baré are largely detribalized and *caboclo*ized.

(c) Several tribes-and-languages of various families of the Pirá-Paraná (Moser and Taylor, 1963) await direct checking in the field: Tabaino, Erulia (distinct from Eduria), Makuna, Yekuana, Datuana, and others. The status of some of these as dialects or languages also remains to be determined. The few Mirititapuyo of the Middle Tikié appear to use either Tukano or Desano as their household or father-language.

(d) Tupí-Guaranían language family: Nheengatú.

2. Tribes and languages bordering the multilingual area (many members of these tribes may be bilingual or even polylingual, but multilingualism is not widespread in a given tribe; many Indians of the multilingual area may include one or more of these languages in their repertoires):

(a) Arawakan language family: Kuripaka and Baniva. These are reported by some informants to be almost mutually intelligible.

(b) Undetermined language families: Karihona, Guayavero. I also have names, in Tukano only, of some dozen other languages spoken around the periphery of the area and along the Rio Negro.

3. Languages spoken in the multilingual area, but by speakers who do not possess multilingualism as a culture trait:

(a) Undetermined language family: Makú (Makú may be more than one language). A few Makú know Tukano or Desano or some other language, including Spanish or Portuguese, but most Makú do not; a few Tukanos Desanos, Piratapuyos, and Tuyukas know some Makú.

(b) Indo-European language family: Spanish, Portuguese, Italian. Two Colombian dialects of Spanish are found: Antioqueño, spoken by most missionaries, and Llanero, spoken by most rubber-gatherers. 'Vaupense' Spanish is basically Llanero Colombian Spanish with the addition of many Nheengatú and some Portuguese terms for things pertaining to the tropical rainforest.

(c) A special case is provided by languages neither spoken in the area nor represented there by groups of speakers. Small lists of words in Dutch can be obtained from older Indians on the Papurí, even though the former Dutch Montfortiano Fathers did not attempt to use Dutch with the Indians. Some Indians, moreoever, have learned a considerable amount of Latin.

Most names for languages and tribes in the literature are Nheengatú names, carried over into Spanish, Portuguese, German, English, etc.

References

BLOOMFIELD, I. (1946), 'Algonquian', in *Linguistic Structures of Native America*, *Viking Fund Publications in Anthropology*, no. 6, pp. 85–129.

CHOMSKY, N. (1965), *Aspects of the Theory of Syntax*, MIT Press.

FULOP, M. (1955), 'Noas sobre los términos y el sistema de parentesco de los Tukano,' *Revista Colombiana de Antropologia* vol. 4, pp. 121–64.

GOLDMAN, I. (1963), 'The Cubeo Indians of the Northwest Amazon', *Illinois Studies in Anthropology*, no. 2, University of Illinois Press.

GUMPERZ, J. J. (1961), 'Speech variation and the study of Indian civilization', *Am.A.* vol. 63, pp. 976–88.

HAUGEN, E. (1966a), 'Semicommunication: the language gap in Scandinavia', *Sociological Inquiry*, vol. 36, pp. 280–297.

HAUGEN, E. (1966b), 'Dialect, language, nation', *Am.A.*, vol. 68, pp. 922 35.

HOCKETT, C. F. (1948), 'Implications of Bloomfield's Algonquian studies', *Language*, vol. 24, pp. 117–31.

HYMES, D. (1964), 'Directions in (ethno-)linguistic theory', in A. Kimball Romney and R. G. D'Andrade (eds.), *Transcultural Studies in Cognition*, special publication, *Am.A.*, vol. 66,3, part 2, pp. 6–56.

JONES, R. B. (1961), 'Karen linguistic studies', *University of California Publications in Linguistics*, vol. 25.

KOCH-GRÜNBERG, T. (1909–10), *Zwei Jahre unter den Indianern. Reisen in Nordwest Brasiliens 1903-5*, 2 vols., Berlin.

MARKHAM, C. (1910), 'A list of the tribes of the valley of the Amazons', *J. anthrop. Inst.*, vol. 40, pp. 73–140.

MARTIUS, K. F. P. von (1867), *Beiträge zur Ethnographie und Sprachenkunde Amerikas zumal Brasiliens*, 2 vols., F. Fleischer, Leipzig.

MASON, J. A. (1950), 'The languages of South America', *BAE Bull.*, 143, vol. 6, part 4.

MOSER, B., and TAYLOR, D. (1963), 'Tribes of the Piraparana', *The Geographical Journal*, 129, part 4.

NOBLE, G. K. (1965), 'Proto-Arawakan and its descendants', *Int. J. Amer. Linguistics Publication* 38 (*IJAL* Vol. 31, no. 3, part 2).

REICHEL-DOLMATOFF, G. (1963), 'Review: Irving Goldman, The Cubeo: Indians of the Northwest Amazon', *Am.A.*, vol. 65, pp. 1377–9.

RIVERA, J. E. (1948), *La Vorágine*, Zigzag Press, Santigao.

STEWARD, J. H., and FARON, L. C. (1959), *Native Peoples of South America*, McGraw-Hill.

WEINREICH, U. (1953), *Languages in Contact*, 2nd edn., revised and enlarged 1962, Linguistic Circle of New York.

WEINREICH, U. (1961), 'Unilingualism and multilingualism', in A. Martinet (ed.), *Linguistique*, L'Encyclopédie de la Pléiade, Paris.

Part Two
Standard Language and National Language

Haugen provides a concise yet wide-ranging discussion of the various usages of the terms 'language' and 'dialect', from both structural and functional points of view; considers the relation of language and nation; and outlines the main properties of a fully developed or standard language. Ferguson, in an interim report on one aspect of the recent Language Survey of Ethiopia (part of the five-nation Survey of Language Use and Language Teaching in Eastern Africa), adds further descriptive detail to terms such as standard, vernacular, official, classical, colloquial, etc., and suggests ways in which the 'sociolinguistic profile' of a nation may be summarized. Tanner's discussion of the success of Indonesian as a national language and the functional differentiation and specialization of codes in Indonesia, starts out from an illuminating investigation of the speech resources and behaviour of a small group of Indonesian graduate students (an 'ethnic mosaic') in an American university – representative of the emerging Indonesian élite. Finally in this section, Hall's article (original to this volume) considers a wide range of problems connected with the standardization of pidgin and creole languages, with special reference to New Guinea pidgin English: which dialect is to be selected, what is to be the relationship between the spelling system adopted for a pidgin language and that of a dominant prestige-language, how efficient are these languages for conveying technological information, what might be their main uses, how might changes be brought about in their status, and so on.

6 E. Haugen

Dialect, Language, Nation[1]

E. Haugen, 'Dialect, language, nation', *American Anthropologist*, vol. 68 (1966), pp. 922–35.

The impossibility of stating precisely how many 'languages' or 'dialects' are spoken in the world is due to the ambiguities of meaning present in these terms, which is shown to stem from the original use of 'dialect' to refer to the literary dialects of ancient Greece. In most usages the term 'language' is superordinate to 'dialect', but the nature of this relationship may be either linguistic or social, the latter problem falling in the province of sociolinguistics. It is shown how the development of a vernacular, popularly called a dialect, into a language is intimately related to the development of writing and the growth of nationalism. This process is shown to involve the selection, codification, acceptance and elaboration of a linguistic norm.

The taxonomy of linguistic description – that is, the identification and enumeration of languages – is greatly hampered by the ambiguities and obscurities attaching to the terms 'language' and 'dialect'. Laymen naturally assume that these terms, which are both popular and scientific in their use, refer to actual entities that are clearly distinguishable and therefore enumerable. A typical question asked of the linguist is: 'How many languages are there in the world?' Or: 'How many dialects are there in this country?'

The simple truth is that there is no answer to these questions, or at least none that will stand up to closer scrutiny. Aside from the fact that a great many, perhaps most, languages and dialects have not yet been adequately studied and described, it is inherent in the very terms themselves that no answer can be given. They represent a simple dichotomy in a situation that is almost infinitely complex. Hence they have come to be used to distinguish phenomena in several different dimensions, with resultant confusion and overlapping. The use of these terms has imposed a division in what is often a continuum, giving what appears to be a neat opposition when in fact the edges are extremely ragged and uncertain. Do Americans

1. This paper was written as a contribution to the work of the Seminar on Sociolinguistics, held at the Indiana University Linguistic Institute in the summer of 1964, under the direction of Charles A. Ferguson. It has profited from extensive discussion with the members of the Seminar.

and Englishmen speak dialects of English, or do only Americans speak dialect, or is American perhaps a separate language? Linguists do not hesitate to refer to the French language as a dialect of Romance. This kind of overlapping is uncomfortable, but most linguists have accepted it as a practical device, while recognizing, with Bloomfield, 'the purely relative nature of the distinction' (1933, p. 54).

The two terms are best understood against the perspective of their history. In English both words are borrowed from French. *Language* is the older, having partially displaced such native words as 'tongue' and 'speech' already in Middle English. The oldest attestation in the OED is from 1290: 'With men þat onder-stoden hire langage.' The French word is itself late, being a popular derivative of Latin *lingua* with the probable form **linguāticum*, first attested in the twelfth century. *Dialect*, on the other hand, first appears in the Renaissance, as a learned loan from Greek. The oldest OED citation is from 1579 in reference to 'certain Hebrue dialectes', while the earliest French I have found (in Hatzfeld and Darmesteter's dictionary) is only sixteen years earlier and speaks of Greek as being 'abondante en dialectes'. A 1614 citation from Sir Walter Raleigh's *The History of the World* refers to the 'Aeolic Dialect' and confirms the impression that the linguistic situation in ancient Greece was both the model and the stimulus for the use of the term in modern writing.

There was need for some such term in Greece, since there was in the classical period no unified Greek norm, only a group of closely related norms. While these 'dialects' bore the names of various Greek regions, they were not spoken but written varieties of Greek, each one specialized for certain literary uses, e.g., Ionic for history, Doric for the choral lyric, and Attic for tragedy. In this period the language called 'Greek' was therefore a group of distinct, but related written norms known as 'dialects'. It is usually assumed that the written dialects were ultimately based on spoken dialects of the regions whose names they bore. These spoken dialects were in turn descended by normal linguistic divergence from a Common Greek language of an older period, which can be reconstructed by comparison of the dialects with each other and with their Indo-European kinsmen. In the post-classical period, however, the Greek dialects disappeared and were replaced by a rather well-unified Greek norm, the *koiné*, essentially the dialect of Athens. So, in the Hellenistic period 'Greek' became the name of a norm that resulted from a linguistic convergence. The differences among the dialects were eliminated in favor of a single, triumphant language, based on the dialect of the cultural and administrative center of the Greeks.

The Greek situation has provided the model for all later usage of the two terms 'language' and 'dialect'. Much of the unclarity in their application stems from the ambiguities present in that situation. This has become evident with their extension to other countries and with their adoption into the technical terminology of linguistics. In a descriptive, synchronic sense 'language' can refer either to a *single* linguistic norm, or to a *group* of related norms. In a historical, diachronic sense 'language' can either be a common language on its way to dissolution, or a common language resulting from unification. A 'dialect' is then any one of the related norms comprised under the general name 'language', historically the result of either divergence or convergence.

Since this historical process can be indefinitely repeated, the two terms are cyclically applicable, with 'language' always the superordinate and 'dialect' the subordinate term. This is also clear from the kind of formal structures into which they can be placed: 'X is a dialect of language Y,' or 'Y has the dialects X and Z' (never, for example, 'Y is a language of dialect X'). 'Language' as the superordinate term can be used without reference to dialects, but 'dialect' is meaningless unless it is implied that there are other dialects and a language to which they can be said to 'belong'. Hence every dialect is a language, but not every language is a dialect.

In addition to the ambiguities provided by the synchronic and diachronic points of view distinguished above, increasing knowledge concerning linguistic behavior has made the simple application of these two contrasting terms ever more difficult.

In French usage a third term developed, *patois*, which applied primarily to the spoken language. The term *dialecte* is defined in the dictionary of the Academie Française and other French dictionaries as *variété régionale d'une langue*. Littre (1956) explicitly requires that a dialect 'include a complete literary culture' (*comportant une complète culture littéraire*). As pointed out by André Martinet (1964), this usage reflects the special French situation, in which there were a number of regional written standards, which were then superseded by the written standard of Paris. The French dialects were regional, like the Greek, and literary, but not functionally distinguished like the Greek. When the dialects ceased to be written, they became *patois*: 'Après le XIVe siècle, il se forma une langue littéraire et écrite, et les dialectes devinrent des patois' (Littré). Even more succintly, Brun (1946) writes: 'Un patois est un dialecte qui s'est degradé.' A patois, then, is a language norm not used for literary (and hence official) purposes, chiefly limited to informal situations. Thus Provençal might be considered a French dialect, but its local, spoken varieties are all *patois*. This distinction introduces a new dimension in our discussion: the social functions of a language. In terms of the language-dialect distinction, we may say that a patois is a dialect that serves a population in its least prestigious functions. The distinction of patois-dialect is therefore not one between two kinds of language, but between two functions of language. The definition in Littré (and others like it) clearly suggests a pejorative attitude toward the patois, since it no longer carries with it 'a complete literary culture'.

In English the term 'patois' has never been seriously adopted in the description of language, and 'dialect' has carried the full burden of both scientific and popular usage. Older writers, cited in the OED, often used it for any specialized variety of the language, e.g., 'the lawyer's dialect'. Samuel Butler (*Hudibras*, 1663) railed against 'a Babylonish dialect, which learned pedants much affect'. General usage has limited the word largely to the regional or locally based varieties, such as 'Lancashire dialect' or 'Irish dialect' in reference to varieties of English. It is less customary to speak of 'London dialect' or 'Boston dialect', except in reference to the lower-class speech of those cities. Nor is it common to speak of 'British dialect' in reference to cultivated English speech, and Americans are generally resentful of being told they speak 'American dialect' when reference is had to the speech of educated people. Martinet is therefore beside the mark when he writes that in America 'the term denotes every local form of English but without any suggestion that a more acceptable form of the language exists distinct from the dialects' (1964). It is quite different with the word 'accent': an American may inoffensively be described as having a 'New England accent' or a 'Southern accent,' and, of course, all Americans speak of the English as having an 'English accent'. 'Dialect' is here as elsewhere a term that suggests informal or lower-class or rural speech. In general usage it therefore remains quite undefined whether such dialects are part of the 'language' or not. In fact, the dialect is often thought of as standing outside the language: 'That isn't English.' This results from the *de facto* development of a standard language, with all the segregation of an elite and the pyramidal power structure that it has usually implied.

As a social norm, then, a dialect is a language that is excluded from polite society. It is, as Auguste Brun (1946) has pointed out, a language that 'did not succeed'. In Italy, Piedmontese is from every linguistic point of view a language, distinct from Italian on the one hand and French on the other, with a long tradition of writing and grammatical study. But because it is not Tuscan, and Tuscan became the standard language of all Italy, Piedmontese is only a 'dialect', yielding ground to Italian with every generation and kept alive only by local pride and linguistic inertia (Clivio, 1964). Only if a 'dialect' is watered down to an 'accent' – that is, an intonation and a set of articulations, with an occasional lexical item thrown in for color – does it (say in Germany or Italy or England) become *salon-*

fähig. As a complete structure it is out in the cold limbo of modern society. In America the stigma is placed not so much on local dialects, since these are few and rarely heard, as on 'bad' English, which is quite simply lower-class dialect. The language of the upper classes is automatically established as the correct form of expression. They cannot say only, 'L'état, c'est moi,' but also 'Le langage, c'est le mien'.

In trying to clarify these relationships, linguistic science has been only moderately successful. Even in the Renaissance if was perfectly clear to serious students of the subject that the term 'language' was associated with the rise of a nation to conscious unity and identity. George Puttenham wrote in his book *The Arte of English Poesie* (1589): 'After a speech is fully fashioned to the common understanding, and accepted by consent of a whole country and nation, it is called a language.' This kind of historical development, by which convergence was achieved at the expense of deviating varieties, was familiar to the men of that age. But the arbitrary tower-of-Babel approach to linguistic divergence was dispelled by the discovery, in the early nineteenth century, of historical regularity. The realization that languages have resulted from dialect-splitting gave a new content to the terms and made it possible to begin calling languages like English and German 'dialects' of a Germanic 'language'.

But in the mid-nineteenth century, when scientific study of the rural and socially disadvantaged dialects began, a generation of research was sufficient to revolutionize the whole idea of how a dialect arises. The very notion of an area divided into a given number of dialects, one neatly distinct from the next, had to be abandoned. The idea that languages split like branches on a tree gave way to an entirely different and even incompatible idea, namely, that individual linguistic traits diffused through social space and formed isoglosses that rarely coincided. Instead of a dialect, one had a *Kernlandschaft* with ragged edges, where bundles of isoglosses testified that some slight barrier had been interposed to free communication. Linguistics is still saddled with these irreconcilable 'particle' and 'wave' theories; this in effect involves the differing points of view from which any linguistic structure can be seen: as a unitary structure (a 'language'), or as one of several partially overlapping structures (the 'dialects').

Without going into the problems raised by this conflict, we may simply state that the 'particle' theory of language as a unified structure is a fruitful hypothesis, making it possible to produce an exhaustive and self-consistent description. But it excludes as 'free variation' a great many inconsistencies within the speech of any informant, and it fails to account for the fact that communication is possible between users of identifiably different codes.

Comparative grammar succeeded in reconstructing the common structure from which 'dialects' could be derived. Contrastive grammar has tried to program the differences between languages in order to ease the learner's task or, on a higher theoretical plane, to arrive at a linguistic typology. But there is still no calculus that permits us to describe the differences between languages in a coherent and theoretically valid way.

Our discussion has shown that there are two clearly distinct dimensions involved in the various usages of 'language' and 'dialect'. One of these is *structural*, that is, descriptive of the language itself; the other is *functional*, that is, descriptive of its social uses in communication. Since the study of linguistic structure is regarded by linguists as their central task, it remains for sociologists, or more specifically, sociolinguists, to devote themselves to the study of the functional problem.

In the *structural* use of 'language' and 'dialect', the overriding consideration is genetic relationship. If a linguist says that Ntongo has five dialects, he means that there are five identifiably different speech-forms that have enough demonstrable cognates to make it certain that they have all developed from one earlier speech-form. He may also be referring to the fact that these are mutually understandable, or at least that each dialect is understandable to its immediate neighbors. If not, he may call them different languages, and say that there is a language Ntongo with three dialects and another, Mbongo, with two. Ntongo and Mbongo may then be dialects of Ngkongo, a common ancestor. This introduces the synchronic dimension of comprehension, which is at best an extremely uncertain criterion. The linguist may attempt to predict, on the basis of his study of their grammars, that they should or should not be comprehensible. But only by testing the reactions of the speakers themselves and their interactions can he confirm his prediction (Voegelin and Harris, 1951; Hickerson, Turner and Hickerson, 1952). Between total incomprehension and total comprehension there is a large twilight zone of partial comprehension in which something occurs that we may call 'semicommunication'.

In the *functional* use of 'language' and 'dialect,' the overriding consideration is the uses the speakers make of the codes they master. If a sociolinguist says that there is no Ntongo language, only dialects, he may mean that there is no present-day form of these dialects that has validity beyond its local speech community, either as a trade language or as a common denominator in interaction among the various dialect speakers. A 'language' is thus functionally defined as a superposed norm used by speakers whose first and ordinary language may be different. A 'language' is the medium of communication between speakers of different dialects.

This holds only within the limits established by their linguistic cognacy: one could not speak of Ntongo as a dialect of English just because its speakers use English as a medium of intercommunication. The sociolinguist may also be referring to the fact that the 'language' is more prestigious than the 'dialect'. Because of its wider functions it is likely to be embraced with a reverence, a language loyalty, that the dialects do not enjoy. Hence the possibility of saying that 'Mbongo is only a dialect, while Ngkongo is a language'. This means that Ngkongo is being spoken by people whose social prestige is notoriously higher than that of people who speak Mbongo. When used in this sense, a dialect may be defined as an undeveloped (or underdeveloped) language. It is a language that no one has taken the trouble to develop into what is often referred to as a 'standard language'. This dimension of functional superiority and inferiority is usually disregarded by linguists, but it is an essential part of the sociolinguist's concern. It becomes his special and complex task to define the social functions of each language or dialect and the prestige that attaches to each of these.

What is meant by an 'undeveloped' language? Only that it has not been employed in all the functions that a language can perform in a society larger than that of the local tribe or peasant village. The history of languages demonstrates convincingly that there is no such thing as an inherently handicapped language. All the great languages of today were once undeveloped. Rather than speak of undeveloped languages as 'dialects', after the popular fashion, it would be better to call them 'vernaculars', or some such term, and limit 'dialect' to the linguist's meaning of a 'cognate variety'. We are then ready to ask how a vernacular, an 'undeveloped language', develops into a standard, a 'developed language'. To understand this we will have to consider the relation of language to the nation.

The ancient Greeks and Romans spread their languages as far as their domains extended, and modern imperialists have sought to do the same. But within the modern world, technological and political revolutions have brought Everyman the opportunity to participate in political decisions to his own advantage. The invention of printing, the rise of industry, and the spread of popular education have brought into being the modern nation-state, which extends some of the loyalties of the family and the neigborhood or the clan to the whole state. Nation and language have become inextricably intertwined. Every self-respecting nation has to have a language. Not just a medium of communication, a 'vernacular' or a 'dialect', but a fully developed language. Anything less marks it as underdeveloped.

The definition of a nation is a problem for historians and other social scientists; we may accept the idea that it is the effective unit of international political action, as reflected in the organization of the United Nations

General Assembly. As a political unit it will presumably be more effective if it is also a social unit. Like any unit, it minimizes internal differences and maximizes external ones. On the individual's personal and local identity it superimposes a national one by identifying his ego with that of all others within the nation and separating it from that of all others outside the nation. In a society that is essentially familial or tribal or regional it stimulates a loyalty beyond the primary groups, but discourages any conflicting loyalty to other nations. The ideal is: internal cohesion – external distinction.

Since the encouragement of such loyalty requires free and rather intense communication within the nation, the national ideal demands that there be a single linguistic code by means of which this communication can take place. It is characteristic that the French revolutionaries passed a resolution condemning the dialects as a remnant of feudal society. The dialects, at least if they threaten to become languages, are potentially disruptive forces in a unified nation: they appeal to local loyalties, which could conceivably come into conflict with national loyalty. This is presumably the reason that France even now refuses to count the number of Breton speakers in her census, let alone face the much greater problem of counting the speakers of Provençal. On the other hand, a nation feels handicapped if it is required to make use of more than one language for official purposes, as is the case in Switzerland, Belgium, Yugoslavia, Canada and many other countries. Internal conflict is inevitable unless the country is loosely federated and the language borders are stable, as is the case in Switzerland.

Nationalism has also tended to encourage external distinction, as noted above. In language this has meant the urge not only to have one language, but to have one's own language. This automatically secludes the population from other populations, who might otherwise undermine its loyalty. Here the urge for separatism has come into sharp conflict with the urge for international contact and for the advantages accruing both to individual and nation from such contact. Switzerland is extreme in having three languages, no one of which is its own; Belgium has two, both of which belong to its neighbors. The Irish movement has faltered largely under the impact of the overwhelming strength of English as a language of international contact. The weakness of the New Norwegian language movement is due to the thorough embedding of Danish in the national life during four centuries of union; what strength the movement has had is derived from the fact that Danish was not one of the great international languages.

Whenever any important segment of the population, an elite, is familiar with the language of another nation, it is tempting to make use of this as the medium of government, simply as a matter of convenience. If this is also the language of most of the people, as was the case when the United

States broke away from England, the problem is easily solved; at most it involves the question of whether provincialisms are to be recognized as acceptable. But where it is not, there is the necessity of linguistically re-educating a population, with all the effort and disruption of cultural unity that this entails. This is the problem faced by many of the emerging African and Asian nations today (Le Page, 1964). French and English have overwhelming advantages, but they symbolize past oppression and convey an alien culture. The cost of re-education is not just the expense in terms of dollars and cents, but the malaise of training one's children in a medium that is not their own, and of alienation from one's own past.

The alternative is to develop one's own language, as Finland did in the nineteenth century, or Israel did in the twentieth. Different languages start at different points: Finland's was an unwritten vernacular, Israel's an unspoken standard. Today both are standards capable of conveying every concept of modern learning and every subtlety of modern literature. Whatever they may lack is being supplied by deliberate planning, which in modern states is often an important part of the development process.

It is a significant and probably crucial requirement for a standard language that it be written. This is not to say that languages need to be written in order to spread widely or be the medium of great empires. Indo-European is an example of the first, Quechua of the Inca Empire an example of the second (Buck, 1916). But they could not, like written languages, establish models across time and space, and they were subject to regular and inexorable linguistic change. It is often held that written language impedes the 'natural' development of spoken language, but this is still a matter of discussion (Zengel, 1962; Bright and Ramanujan, 1964). In any case the two varieties must not be confused.

Speech is basic in learning language. The spoken language is acquired by nearly all its users before they can possibly read or write. Its form is to a great extent transmitted from one generation of children to the next. While basic habits can be modified, they are not easily overturned after childhood and are virtually immovable after puberty. The spoken language is conveyed by mouth and ear and mobilizes the entire personality in immediate interaction with one's environment. Writing is conveyed by hand and eye, mobilizes the personality less completely, and provides for only a delayed response. Oral confrontation is of basic importance in all societies, but in a complex, literate society it is overlaid and supplemented by the role of writing.

The permanence and power of writing is such that in some societies the written standard has been influential in shaping new standards of speech. This is not to say that writing has always brought them into being, but rather to say that new norms have arisen that are an amalgamation of speech and writing. This can of course take place only when the writing is read aloud, so that it acquires an oral component (Wessén, 1937). There is some analogy between the rise of such spoken standards and that of pidgin or creole languages (Meillet, 1925, p. 76; Sommerfelt, 1938, p. 44). The latter comprise elements of the structure and vocabulary of two or more languages, all oral. They have usually a low social value, compared to the oral standards, but the process of origin is comparable. The reawakening of Hebrew from its century-long dormant state is comprehensible only in terms of the existence of rabbinical traditions of reading scripture aloud (Morag, 1959). Modern Hebrew has shown a rapid adaptation to the underlying norms of its new native speakers, so that it has become something different from traditional Hebrew. Similarly with the standard forms of European languages: one is often hard put to say whether a given form has been handed down from its ancestor by word of mouth or via the printed page. 'Spelling pronunciations' are a well-known part of most oral standards, even though purists tend to decry them.

While we have so far spoken of standard languages as if they were a clear and unambiguous category, there are differences of degree even among the well-established languages. French is probably the most highly standardized of European languages, more so than, for example, English or German. French, as the most immediate heir of Latin, took over many of its concepts of correctness and its intellectual elaboration. French in turn became a model for other standard languages, and its users were for centuries nothing loth to have it so considered. When English writers of the eighteenth century debated whether an English academy should be established to regulate the language, the idea of such an institution came from France. The proposal was rejected largely because the English did not wish to duplicate what they regarded as French 'tyranny'.

In France, as in other countries, the process of standardization was intimately tied to the history of the nation itself. As the people developed a sense of cohesion around a common government, their language became a vehicle and a symbol of their unity. The process is reasonably well documented in the histories written for the older European languages. But the period since the French Revolution has seen a veritable language explosion, which has been far less adequately studied. In many countries a process that elsewhere took centuries of effort on the part of a people and its writers has been compressed into a few short years or decades. In a study of the new standards developed since 1800 for Germanic languages, Heinz Kloss has suggested that there may be a typical profile for what he has called the *Ausbau* of a new language (Kloss 1952, p. 28). First comes its use for purely humorous or folkloristic purposes. Then lyric writers may adopt it, followed by prose narrators. But it has not reached a crucial stage of development until success is achieved in writing serious expository prose, or what he calls *Zweckschrifttum*. Beyond this comes the elaboration of the language for purposes of technical and scientific writing and government use. Each of these 'domains' (as Fishman (1964) has called them) constitutes a challenge for the language in its attempt to achieve full development.

While making a survey of the world's standard languages, Ferguson proposed (1962) to classify them along two dimensions: their degree of standardization (St. 0, 1, 2) and their utilization in writing (W 0, 1, 2, 3). Zero meant in each case no appreciable standardization or writing. St. 1 meant that a language was standardized in more than one mode, as in the case, for example, with Armenian, Greek, Serbo-Croatian, and Hindi-Urdu. He also included Norwegian, but it is at least arguable that we are here dealing with two languages. St. 2 he defined as a language having a 'single, widely accepted norm which is felt to be appropriate with only minor modifications or variations for all purposes for which the language is used'. W 1 he applied to a language used for 'normal written purposes', W 2 to one used for 'original research in physical science', and W 3 to one used for 'translations and résumés of scientific work in other languages'.

These categories suggest the path that 'underdeveloped' languages must take to become adequate instruments for a modern nation. The 'standardization' to which Ferguson refers applies primarily to developing the form of a language, i.e., its linguistic structure, including phonology, grammar and lexicon. We shall call this the problem of *codification*. Ferguson's scale of 'utilization in writing' applies rather to the *functions* of a language. We shall call this the problem of *elaboration*, a term suggested by a similar usage of Bernstein's (1962) and corresponding to Kloss's *Ausbau*. As the ideal goals of a standard language, codification may be defined as *minimal variation in form*, elaboration as *maximal variation in function*.

The ideal case of minimal variation in form would be a hypothetical, 'pure' variety of a language having only one spelling and one pronunciation for every word, one word for every meaning, and one grammatical framework for all utterances. For purposes of efficient communication this is obviously the ideal code. If speakers and listeners have identical codes, no problems of misunderstanding can arise due to differences in language. There can be none of what communication engineers call 'code noise' in the channel (Hockett, 1958, pp. 331–2). This condition is best attained if the language has a high degree of stability, a quality emphasized by many writers on the subject (e.g., Havránek, 1938). Stability means the slowing down or complete stoppage of linguistic change. It means the fixation forever (or for as long as possible) of a uniform norm. In practice such fixation has proved to be chimerical, since even the most stable of norms inevitably changes as generations come and go. At all times the standard is threatened by the existence of rival norms, the so-called 'dialects', among its users. It is liable to interference from them and eventually to complete fragmentation by them.

Apparently opposed to the strict codification of form stands the maximal variation or elaboration of function one expects from a fully developed language. Since it is by definition the common language of a social group more complex and inclusive than those using vernaculars, its functional domains must also be complex. It must answer to the needs of a variety of communities, classes, occupations, and interest groups. It must meet the basic test of *adequacy*. Any vernacular is presumably adequate at a given moment for the needs of the group that uses it. But for the needs of the much larger society of the nation it is not adequate, and it becomes necessary to supplement its resources to make it into a language. Every vernacular can at the very least add words borrowed from other languages, but usually possesses devices for making new words from its own resources as well. Writing, which provides for the virtually unlimited storage and distribution of vocabulary, is the technological means enabling a modern standard language to meet the needs of every specialty devised by its users. There are no limits to the elaboration of language except those set by the ingenuity of man.

While form and function may generally be distinguished as we have just done, there is one area in which they overlap. Elaboration of function may lead to complexity of form, and, contrariwise, unity of form may lead to rigidity of function. This area of interaction between form and function is the domain of *style*. A codification may be so rigid as to prevent the use of a language for other than formal purposes. Sanskrit had to yield to Prakrit, and Latin to the Romance languages, when the gap between written and spoken language became so large that only a very few people were willing to make the effort of learning them. Instead of being appropriate for 'all purposes for which the language is used', the standard tends to become only one of several styles within a speech community. This can lead to what Ferguson (1959) has described as 'diglossia', a sharp cleavage between 'high' and 'low' style. Or it may be a continuum, with only a mild degree of what I have called 'schizoglossia', as in the case of English (Haugen, 1962). In English there is a marked difference between the written and spoken standards of most people. In addition, there are styles within each, according to the situation. These styles, which could be called 'functional dialects', provide wealth and diversity within a language and ensure that the stability or rigidity of the norm will have an element of elasticity as well. A complete language has its formal and informal styles, its regional accents, and its class or occupational jargons, which do not destroy its unity so long as they are clearly diversified in function and show a reasonable degree of solidarity with one another.

Neither codification nor elaboration is likely to proceed very far unless the community can agree on the *selection* of some kind of a model from which the norm can be derived. Where a new norm is to be established, the problem will be as complex as the sociolinguistic structure of the people involved. There will be little difficulty where everyone speaks virtually alike, a situation rarely found. Elsewhere it may be necessary to make some embarrassing decisions. To choose any one vernacular as a norm means to favor the group of people speaking that variety. It gives them prestige as norm-bearers and a headstart in the race for power and position. If a recognized elite already exists with a characteristic vernacular, its norm will almost inevitably prevail. But where there are socially coordinate groups of people within the community, usually distributed regionally or tribally, the choice of any one will meet with resistance from the rest. This resistance is likely to be the stronger the greater the language distance within the group. It may often be a question of solidarity versus alienation: a group that feels intense solidarity is willing to overcome great linguistic differences, while one that does not is alienated by relatively small differences. Where transitions are gradual, it may be possible to find a central dialect that mediates between extremes, one that will be the easiest to learn and most conducive to group coherence.

Where this is impossible, it may be necessary to resort to the construction of a new standard. To some extent this has happened naturally in the rise of the traditional norms; it has been the aim of many language reformers to duplicate the effect in new ones. For related dialects one can apply principles of linguistic reconstruction to make a hypothetical mother tongue for them all. Or one can be guided by some actual or supposed mother tongue, which exists in older, traditional writings. Or one can combine those forms that have the widest usage, in the hope that they will most easily win general acceptance. These three procedures – the comparative, the archaizing, and the statistical – may easily clash, to make decisions difficult. In countries where there are actually different languages, amounting in some African nations to more than a hundred, it will be necessary either to recognize multiple norms or to introduce an alien norm, which will usually be an international language like English or French.

Finally, a standard language, if it is not to be dismissed as dead, must have a body of users. *Acceptance* of the norm, even by a small but influential group, is part of the life of the language. Any learning requires the expenditure of time and effort, and it must somehow contribute to the well-being of the learners if they are not to shirk their lessons. A standard language that is the instrument of an authority, such as a government, can offer its users material rewards in the form of power and position. One that is the instrument of a religious fellowship, such as a church, can also offer its users rewards in the hereafter. National languages have offered membership in the nation, an identity that gives one entrée into a new kind of group, which is not just kinship, or government, or religion, but a novel and peculiarly modern brew of all three. The kind of significance attributed to language in this context has little to do with its value as an instrument of thought or persuasion. It is primarily symbolic, a matter of the prestige (or lack of it) that attaches to specific forms or varieties of language by virtue of identifying the social status of their users (Labov, 1964). Mastery of the standard language will naturally have a higher value if it admits one to the councils of the mighty. If it does not, the inducement to learn it, except perhaps passively, may be very low; if social status is fixed by other criteria, it is conceivable that centuries could pass without a population's adopting it (Gumperz, 1962, 1964). But in our industralized and democratic age there are obvious reasons for the rapid spread of standard languages and for their importance in the school systems of every nation.

The four aspects of language development that we have now isolated as crucial features in taking the step from 'dialect' to 'language', from vernacular to standard, are as follows: (a) selection of norm, (b) codification of form, (c) elaboration of function, and (d) acceptance by the community. The first two refer primarily to the form, the last two to the function of language. The first and the last are concerned with society, the second and third with language. They form a matrix within which it should be possible to discuss all the major problems of language and dialect in the life of a nation:

	Form	Function
Society	Selection	Acceptance
Language	Codification	Elaboration

References

BERNSTEIN, B. (1962), 'Linguistic codes, hesitation phenomena and intelligence', Language and Speech, vol. 5, pp. 31–46.

BLOOMFIELD, L. (1933), Language, Holt, Rinehart & Winston.

BRIGHT, W., and RAMANUJAN, A. K. (1964), 'Sociolinguistic variation and language change', in Proceedings of the Ninth International Congress of Linguists, Mouton.

BRUN, A. (1946), Parlers Régionaux: France Dialectale et Unité Française, Didier.

BUCK, C. D. (1916), 'Language and the sentiment of nationality', Amer. Polit. Sc. Rev., vol. 10, pp. 44–69.

CLIVIO, G. (1964), *Piedmontese: a Short Basic Course*, mimeographed, Center for Applied Linguistics, Washington, D.C.

DICTIONNAIRE DE L'ACADÉMIE FRANÇAISE (1932), Paris, 8th edn.

FERGUSON, C. A. (1959), 'Diglossia', *Word*, vol. 15, pp. 325–40.

FERGUSON, C. A. (1962), 'The language factor in national development', *AL*, vol. 4, no. 1, pp. 23 7.

FISHMAN, J. A. (1964), 'Language maintenance and language shift as a field of inquiry', *Linguistics*, vol. 9, pp. 32–70.

GUMPERZ, J. J. (1962), 'Types of linguistic communities', *AL*, vol. 4, no. 1, pp. 28–40.

GUMPERZ, J. J. (1964), 'Hindi-Punjabi code switching in Delhi', in *Proceedings of the Ninth International Congress of Linguists*, Mouton.

HATZFELD, A. and DARMESTETER, A. (1920), *Dictionnaire Général de la Langue Française*, Paris, 6th edn.

HAUGEN, E. (1962), 'Schizoglossia and the linguistic norm', *Monograph Series on Languages and Linguistics*, Georgetown University, Washington, no. 15, pp. 63–9.

HAVRÁNEK, B. (1938), 'Zum Problem der Norm in der heutigen Sprachwissenschaft und Sprachkultur', in J. Vachek (ed.), *A Prague Reader in Linguistics*, Bloomington, Ind.

HICKERSON, H., TURNER, G. D., and HICKERSON, N. P. (1952), 'Testing procedures for estimating transfer of information among Iroquois dialects and languages', *IJAL*, vol. 18, pp. 1–8.

HOCKETT, C. F. (1958), *A Course in Modern Linguistics*, Macmillan.

KLOSS, H. (1952), *Die Entwicklung Neuer Germanischen Kultursprachen von 1800 bis 1950*, Pohl, Munich.

LABOV, W. (1964), 'Phonological correlates of social stratification', in J. J. Gumperz and D. Hymes (eds.) *The Ethnography of Communication, AmA*, vol. 66, no. 6, part 2, pp. 164–76.

LE PAGE, R.B. (1964), *The National Language Question: Linguistic Problems of Newly Independent States*, Oxford University Press.

LITTRÉ, E. (1956), *Dictionnaire de la Langue Française*, Paris.

MARTINET, A. (1964), *Elements of General Linguistics*, University of Chicago Press.

MEILLET, A. (1925), *La Méthode Comparative en Linguistique Historique*, Institute for Sammenlignende Kulturforskning, Oslo.

MORAG, S. (1959), 'Planned and unplanned development in modern Hebrew', *Lingua* vol. 8, pp. 247–63.

J. A. H. Murray *et al.* (ed.), *Oxford English Dictionary* (1888 ff.), Oxford University Press.

SOMMERFELT, A. (1938), 'Conditions de la formation d'une language commune', *Actes du IV Congrès International de Linguistes*, Copenhagen.

VOEGELIN, C. F., and HARRIS, Z. S. (1951), 'Methods for determining intelligibility among dialects of natural languages', *Proceedings of the American Philosophical Society*, vol. 95, pp. 322–9.

WESSÉN, E. (1937), 'Vårt riksspråk: Nagra huvudpunkter av dess historiska utveckling', *Modersmalslärarnas Förenings årsskrift*, pp. 289–305.

ZENGEL, M. S. (1962), 'Literacy as a factor in language change', *AmA*, vol. 64, pp. 132–9.

7 C. A. Ferguson

The Role of Arabic in Ethiopia: A Sociolinguistic Perspective

C. A. Ferguson, 'The role of Arabic in Ethiopia: a sociolinguistic perspective', *Languages and Linguistics Monograph Series*, no. 23, 1970, pp. 355–68.

Abstract. First, the language situation in Ethiopia is summarized in a national sociolinguistic profile formula with commentary. Second, the major kinds of variation in Arabic as used throughout the world are characterized briefly. Then the main section of the paper examines the use of Arabic in Ethiopia as mother tongue, lingua franca, religious language and trade jargon. Finally, a report is given on attitudes toward Arabic on the part of users of the language in Ethiopia, based on impressionistic observations and the replies to about 100 questionnaires.

As I understand the purpose of my paper in this discussion of second language learning in formal education contexts, it is to call attention to the wide variety of multilingual situations in which bilingual education may take place.[1] It seems clear that hypotheses or conclusions about second language acquisition will be affected by such factors as the nature of the linguistic environment, the relative dominance of the relevant languages in the society, their degree of standardization – indeed by the whole range of issues involving the respective roles of the languages and their means of acquisition outside the educational system. Some of the other speakers at this Round Table have already emphasized the variety of multilingual situations, but the presentation of one particular setting – Arabic in Ethiopia – may still be of value, since the kinds of decisions needed for the teaching of Arabic in the schools of Ethiopia are different in many respects from those needed in more familiar situations.

1. This paper is in the nature of an interim report on one subproject of the Language Survey of Ethiopia. The Survey is part of the five-nation Survey of Language Use and Language Teaching in Eastern Africa supported by the Ford Foundation. This paper was presented in preliminary form at the Conference on Ethiopian Languages held in Addis Ababa, October 1969. Even in its present form it provides very little information not already well-known to many Arabists and specialists in Ethiopian affairs. What merit it may have probably lies in the attempt to communicate this information in such a way that it can be readily assimilated by social scientists, linguists, or interested laymen and can thereby serve as the basis for more extended research or policy making.

National sociolinguistic profile formulas

One method of presenting the sociolinguistic setting of a language is to include it in a formula representing the sociolinguistic profile of a nation or other political entity (Ferguson, 1966; Uribe Villegas, 1968). This method differs from others in that it selects a political entity rather than any other demographic, societal, cultural, or psychological framework, and in that it uses a particular taxonomy of language types and functions (Stewart, 1968). This method makes no strong claims for predictive value and omits important sociolinguistic data relevant for assessment of the 'roles' of languages in a nation; it does, however, offer a convenient way of making gross sociolinguistic comparisons among nations and it seems to have considerable heuristic value in suggesting lines of investigation and data collection often overlooked in the establishment of national language policies.

Briefly summarized, the method consists of (*1*) identifying the number of major and minor languages and languages of special status in the nation and (*2*) representing them in an additive formula using capital and lower case letters standing for language types and functions respectively. A third, more informative, expansion of the formula specifies the languages by name, so that a separate key can provide information on degree of linguistic distance among them and dialect diversity within them; if necessary, information can be added on the diversity of writing systems used. A sample national profile formula in alternative expansions might read:

1. 2Lmaj + 6Lmin + 1Lspec
2. (Sow + Sei) + (5Vg + Sge) + Crl

Formula (*1*) states that in the nation in question there are two major languages, six minor languages, and one language of special status. Expanded formula (*2*) specifies the major languages as two Standard languages (S) one of which is official (o) and also serves as an important lingua franca within the country (w) and the other is used extensively in education (e) and serves as the nation's means of communication with other countries (i). It further specifies the minor languages as five vernaculars (V) which primarily serve to identify their speakers as members of particular ethnic or other sociocultural groups (g) and one standard language which not only serves this function but is also used in education. Finally, it specifies the language of special status as a Classical (or dead Standard) language used chiefly for certain religious (r) and literary (l) purposes. Further details of the method, with more precise defining criteria for the various categories, can be found in the articles cited.

Language situation in Ethiopia

Like many other nations of Africa, Ethiopia is a highly multilingual country, although it differs from most other African nations in having an indigenous language constitutionally recognized as its official language. The currently available body of data is not adequate for definite identification of the major and minor languages of the country, but an approximation can be made on the basis of the present estimates of the Language Survey of Ethiopia, subject to correction as more extensive and accurate information becomes available.

The Ethiopian profile formula reads:

1. 5Lmaj + 13Lmin + 3Lspec
2. (3S + 2V) + (13V) + (1C + 1S + Arabic)
2a. (Sowe + Sie + Sgw + Vgw + Vg) + (13Vg) + (1Cr + 1Sw + Arabic)

L maj (in approximate order of sociopolitical importance)

Sowe	Amharic	(Ethio-) Semitic
Sie	English	Indo-European (Germanic)
Sgw	Tigrinya	(Ethio-) Semitic
Vgw	Galia	E. Cushitic
Vg	Somali	E. Cushitic

L min (in alphabetical order)

V_1g	Afar	E. Cushitic
V_2g	Anyuak	Nilo-Saharan
V_3g	Beja	N. Cushitic
V_4g	Chaha Guarage	(Ethio-) Semitic
V_5g	Derasa	E. Cushitic
V_6g	Gumuz	Nilo-Saharan
V_7g	Hadiyya	E. Cushitic
V_8g	Janjero	Omotic
V_9g	Kefa	Omotic
$V_{10}g$	Kembata	E. Cushitic
$V_{11}g$	Sidamo	E. Cushitic
$V_{12}g$	Tigré	(Ethio-) Semitic
$V_{13}g$	Wellamo	Omotic

L spec

Cri	Geez	(Ethio-) Semitic
Sw	Italian	Indo-European (Romance)
Arabic	Arabic	Semitic

Amharic is a standard language, with a writing system of its own (the Geez syllabary with a few additions) and literature going back to the fourteenth century; it serves as the medium of instruction in all government primary schools, the primary language of oral and written communication in the government and the armed forces and the only Ethiopian language whose function as a lingua franca is national in scope; it is declared in the Constitution of 1965 as the official language of the Empire.

English is the medium of instruction in all government secondary schools and higher education; it is an important spoken and written medium in government communication; it is the language of upward socioeconomic mobility. It has been publicly recognized by the government as the nation's second language, and serves as its chief medium of communication with other countries.

Tigrinya is a standard language, using essentially the same writing system as Amharic; it has a small literature, and the publication of newspapers in Tigrinya antedates that of Amharic. Formerly the medium of instruction in primary schools in the Eritrea region, in which role it is being replaced by Amharic, it still serves as a lingua franca in many parts of that area.

Galla is a vernacular with considerable dialect diversity which does not seem to be moving toward standardization; it is not normally written but is spoken as a mother tongue by more people than any other language in Ethiopia. In certain parts of the country it serves as a lingua franca.

Somali is a vernacular spoken over a large but sparsely settled area. It has considerable dialect diversity, but mutual intelligibility is high among them and there is some trend towards standardization. It has a large oral literature but is rarely written; in neighboring Somalia where it is the mother tongue of 90% of the country, Arabic or European languages are used for writing (Andrzejewski, 1962).

The minor languages are all vernaculars used by ethno-linguistic communities of at least 100,000 members. Most are clearcut languages, but several, e.g. Wellamo (-Gofa-Gemu-Kullo- ...) and Gumuz (-Sese-Disoha-Dakunza-Sai- ...) might be regarded as dialect clusters. Afar is often considered together with the closely related language Saho. Chaha Gurage may not be spoken by 100,000, but it is included as probably the most important representative of the cluster of languages called Gurage which taken together may have nearly a million speakers.

Geez is a classical language known from inscriptions as far back as the fourth century B.C.; its periods of literary flowering were between the seventh and thirteenth centuries, long after it had ceased to be a spoken language. Today it serves as the liturgical language of the Ethopian

Orthodox Church; it is the vehicle of traditional Ethiopian ecclesiastical and historical literature and is still used for the composition of poetry. Geez uses a syllabary of some 250 characters derived from the writing system of South Arabic inscription.

Italian has no official or publicly recognized status in the nation, but there are several thousands for whom it is their mother tongue and there is a fairly active Italian press. In its standard form (with some dialect differences brought from Italy) it serves as a lingua franca among some sections of society, particularly in the Eritrea area. In a pidginized form it serves as a lingua franca at a different level in scattered areas of Ethiopia. The use of Italian seems to be declining in favor of English and Amharic.

Varieties of Arabic

Arabic, as a great world language spoken by some hundred millions of people over the enormous area from Morocco to the Persian Gulf and attested in literature for nearly a millennium and a half, offers a bewildering range of variation. First there is the Classical written language extending from pre-Islamic poetry to modern technical journals: this variety shows essentially the same sound system and morphology but with considerable variation in vocabulary, syntax, and forms of discourse. Next there is Colloquial Arabic, the chain of regional dialects which constitute the Arabs' mother tongue today. The extent of variation among these dialects is greater than that between what are recognized in other circumstances as separate languages (e.g. Norwegian and Swedish), but the speakers of these dialects have a strong sense of linguistic unity, and a speaker of Arabic recognizes that speakers of other dialects are also speaking Arabic. These two varieties, Classical and Colloquial, exist side by side in the Arabic speech community in a diglossia relationship (Ferguson, 1959a; Gumperz, 1962; Fishman, 1968).

Among the regional dialects some may be regarded as 'prestige dialects' (cf. Johnstone, 1967, pp. xxix–xxx), notably those of important urban centers such as Cairo, Beirut-Damascus-Jerusalem, Baghdad (Muslim variety) and northern Moroccan cities. Arabic speakers, within the areas of influence of these prestige dialects, may in the course of their lives adjust their own dialect in the direction of the prestige dialect or even be bidialectal (e.g. Blanc, 1964).

Intermediate between the two varieties or sets of varieties, relatively 'pure' Classical and Colloquial, there are many shadings of 'middle language'. These intermediate forms, some highly fluctuating and transitional, others more stable, represent two tendencies: classicization, in which a dialect is modified in the direction of classical, and koineization, in which dialects are homogenized by the modification or elimination of features which are felt to be especially distinctive of a particular regional dialect (Blanc, 1959).

Some of these intermediate varieties may be viewed collectively as a 'pan-Arab koine' (cf. Johnstone, 1967, pp. xxv–xxx), and indeed the Arab world seems to be developing such a koine for at least the third time in its known history (pre-Islamic poetic koine, koine of early centuries of the Muslim era, modern koine; cf. Ferguson, 1959b).

Finally, in certain areas and under certain social conditions where Arabic has been used for limited purposes by people of other mother tongues, it has developed pidginized forms in which the lexicon and overt grammatical categories of the language have been drastically reduced. The best-known examples are the Turku of the Lake Chad area and Central Africa, and the 'Bimbashi' Arabic which spread southward from the Sudan (Heine, 1968, and references).[2]

Arabic in Ethiopia

Having reviewed the method of sociolinguistic profile formulas, the general language situation in Ethiopia, and the nature of sociolinguistic variation within Arabic, our task is now to identify the kinds of Arabic and their respective functions in Ethiopia in such a way that this information can be represented in the total profile formula for the nation.

Since at least as far back as the fourth millennium B.C. there has been traffic and communication across the Red Sea, between southern Arabia and the coast of eastern Africa including the Ethiopian area. And since at least the seventh century of the Christian era, this has involved the appearance of speakers of Arabic (as opposed to South Arabian languages) on African soil. This process of temporary and permanent immigration of Arabic speakers from Yemen and the southern coast of Arabia has continued into the nineteenth and twentieth centuries. The immigrants have brought both language and religion, and Arabic and Islam have spread to African populations, partly separately and partly in close connection.

Also, peoples further south along the East African coast and inland who

2. The entire range of linguistic variation in Arabic has been studied chiefly by descriptions of 'pure' varieties and studies of local variation in a given dialect area. (For a summary of the research see Abboud, in press.) Studies of variation in some kind of social context have been extremely rare (e.g. Blanc, 1960 and 1964; Mitchell, 1957). We are certainly far from having sociolinguistically sophisticated studies of verbal interaction of small groups, studies of the sociolinguistic patterns of whole communities such as villages or social institutions, or large-scale studies of whole nations or the whole Arab world. It may be hoped that the new generation of Arab linguists will undertake studies which will utilize such fruitful sociolinguistic constructs as domain, network, social situation, role relationship, and interaction type (Fishman, 1968).

have become Muslim, as a result of influence from Yemen and southern Arabia, have moved northward, bringing with them the use of Arabic for various purposes within their basically non-Arabic-speaking-society. The best example may be the constantly expanding population of Somali tribes, all of whom have been Muslim since the beginning of the sixteenth century.

Since at least as far back as the second millennium B C, there has been traffic and communication between Egypt and the Ethiopian area. With the coming of Christianity into Ethiopia in the fourth century, religious ties with the church in Egypt formed a special line of communication, and in medieval times a large part of the literary production in Geez consisted of translations from Arabic works used by the Coptic Christians of Egypt. In the nineteenth century, Egyptian political influence extended down the Red Sea on to the Eritrean lowlands and the city-state of Harar, and this also directly affected the spread of Arabic and Islam, separately and together.

Finally, since at least the nineteenth century there has been movement of Arabic-speaking Muslims from the Sudan into Ethiopia. In addition to groups of Arabic mother tongue, many have been speakers of other languages who used Arabic as a lingua franca.

This rapid and drastically oversimplified historical account of the spread of Arabic into Ethiopia cannot do justice to the complex story, which deserves research and study in itself, but it can give some indication of the varied strands of influence involved in the present-day use of Arabic in the nation. One aspect of Arabic influence on Ethiopian language – the presence of Arabic loanwords – has received treatment in a number of studies by Leslau (e.g. Leslau, 1957).

Arabic as mother tongue

It is not possible to estimate with any high degree of accuracy the number of native speakers of Arabic resident in Ethiopia, although it must run in the tens of thousands. The total number is, however, relatively small, and by this criterion Arabic cannot be included in the *L min* of the formula.

The varieties of Arabic in use by the mother-tongue speakers are roughly comparable to those in use in other parts of the Arabic-speaking world, i.e. there is a diglossia situation in which the speakers acquire the Colloquial in childhood and then superpose some amount of Classical Arabic for written and formal oral use. The kinds of Colloquial in use in Ethiopia seem to cluster around two norms, one of which may be labeled 'Yemeni', the other 'Sudanese'. Neither of these two varieties is homogeneous in Ethiopia and there is fluctuation and use of intermediate varieties, but Arabic speakers generally recognize the existence of the two major types, which differ in pronunciation, certain details of morphology, and in a considerable number of lexical items, including some items of basic vocabulary. The two varieties in any case are to a high degree mutually intelligible.

As an illustration of the nature of the difference, we may cite material elicited from two Ethiopian speakers of Arabic. Both had essentially the same sound system, but differed, for example, in their reflexes of Classical / qðθ/:

Classical	'Yemeni'	'Sudanese'
/q/	/q/	/g/
/ð/	ð, d/	/d/
/θ/	θ, t/	/t/

In matters of morphology, for example, the 'Sudanese' had the ending -ta for the first and second person singular of the past tense while the 'Yemeni' had -t for both, but in some styles of speech used -tu for the first person and -ta for the second. Or, the equivalent of *this* was *da* after the noun for the 'Sudanese' and *haða* before the noun for the 'Yemeni'. On the standard 100-word list of basic vocabulary used in the Survey, the two informants had different words on about thirty items, although this may be misleading, since for a number of these the other word would also have been familiar either as a synonym or from Classical use. Examples of the differences:

	Yemeni	Sudanese	Classical
'foot'	xuff	riǰil	riǰl
'man'	raǰul	zōl	raǰul
'sit'	ǰalas	gaᶜad	ǰalisa, qaᶜada
'water'	mōya (masc.)	mōya (fem.)	māʼ
'what'	ʼēš	šunu	mā

Arabic as a religious language

Every Muslim in the world, regardless of mother tongue, learns at least a few expressions in Arabic, such as greetings (e.g. some version of *Assalāmu ʼalaykum* 'Peace be on you'), invocations (e.g. *Bismillāh* 'in the name of God'), a statement of faith ('There is no god but God, and Muhammad is God's messenger') and prayers, including the Fātiha, the opening *surah* of the Qurʼan. Additional study of Islamic precepts requires memorization of further Arabic material, especially the Qurʼan, and ideally the mastery of Arabic to read the traditional works of theology, jurisprudence, ethics, traditions of the Prophet, and so on.

In Ethiopia there are great differences from one region to another, one ethnic background to another, and one individual to another, in the amount of Arabic a Muslim acquires for primarily religious reasons. The mastery of a few greetings and so on is relatively insignificant in the total language economy of Ethiopia, but certain aspects of the religious use of the language deserve special attention. In the first place, many thousands of Muslims every year become literate in Arabic by studying with a traditional teacher (*mucallim*) or attending some kind of traditional school (*madrasa*);[3] typically this is their initial (or, in some cases, only) acquisition of literacy since it normally takes place before entry into a 'modern' government or private school. Secondly, there may be more than a hundred thousand Muslims in Ethiopia who do not speak Arabic well, but who make use of Arabic to the extent of reciting long passages from Arabic works, carrying on stereotyped conversational exchanges in a religious context, or following to some extent a sermon or exhortation in Arabic.

Arabic as lingua franca

More important than the preceding two points, in terms of extent of active use of Arabic in Ethiopia, is the widespread use of Arabic as a means of oral communication between speakers of different languages. There is no doubt that Amharic is the most important lingua franca in Ethiopia as a whole, but a number of other languages serve as lingua francas in limited areas, not only major languages like Tigrinya and Galla as mentioned above but even quite minor languages such as Wetawit (Berta) in the Beni Shengul region of western Ethiopia. The use of Arabic as a lingua franca only partially follows regional lines; it tends to coincide more with religious boundaries. Arabic is used as a lingua franca mostly among Muslims of various mother tongues. Some indication of the range of use of Arabic as a lingua franca is given by the questionnaire replies of twenty freshmen at Haile Selassie I University who claimed knowledge of Arabic (October 1969). These twenty students, of about twenty-one years of age, came from six different provinces, and represented ten different tongues. Twelve of the students claimed to speak Arabic 'fluently', six 'with difficulty', and two 'only a little'. While we cannot assume that these findings are representative of the users of Arabic throughout the country, they clearly show that Arabic can function widely as a lingua franca.

There are of course many Muslims in Ethiopia who are unable to converse in Arabic, so that the latter cannot be regarded as a normal secondary

3. Of twenty university freshmen who claimed knowledge of Arabic (Addis Ababa, October 1969), all but three claimed some reading knowledge. Fourteen reported having learned to read in a *madrasa*, which they reported having attended for periods ranging from two to eight years (mean five).

language for Muslims, but it is probably true that hundreds of thousands (as high as a million?) Muslims in the country are able to use some kind of spoken Arabic as a means of oral communication, whereas the number of non-Muslims able to do so is very small. The kind of Arabic spoken in this way tends to cluster around 'Yemeni' and 'Sudanese' norms, but it often fluctuates more than mother tongue Arabic, mixes regional dialects, and incorporates features of Classical Arabic. Finally, we must take note of the fact that an indeterminate (although fairly small) number of Muslims who cannot use Colloquial Arabic as a means of conversation have learned enough Classical Arabic in *madrasa*, mosque, radio, and reading to be able to use it to a limited extent as a lingua franca, and with some hesitation we may add 'w' also to the 'C' part of Arabic in the formula: Crlw:Vgw.

Arabic as trade jargon

Many of the Arabic-speaking immigrants to the Ethiopian areas through the centuries have been merchants, and Arab traders, shopkeepers, and small merchants can be found in many parts of Ethiopia. In communication between Arab merchant and customer, often a rudimentary, pidginized form of Arabic is used, and this use of Arabic is not so strongly limited to Muslims as the more general lingua franca use just described. Although there has been as yet no systematic study of this kind of Arabic, impressionistic observation notes some of the usual features of pidginized Arabic, such as the m. sg. for all persons of the verb, and so on. Some indication of the use of Arabic in trade transactions is given in the freshman student responses. Of the twenty students, eighteen checked 'usually use Arabic' or 'may use Arabic' in the market, in shops, or both (one student did not answer the question). Next to religious use (prayers, preaching), the trade use (market, shops) was most often checked in the 'usually use Arabic' column (religious use: twelve checks; trade use: nine checks).

Arabic in the Ethiopian formula

The material presented above on the types and functions of Arabic in Ethiopia may be summarized by an entry for Arabic in the national profile formula as:

Crlw: Vgw: (Pt)

This formula is to be interpreted as follows: there is a Classical form of the language which serves religious and literary purposes and is in a diglossia relationship with vernacular varieties of the language, the use of which serves as a mark of social group identity (i.e. Islam); both forms of the language, as well as the intermediate varieties characteristic of diglossic languages, serve as a lingua franca in the country. Less certain is the existence of a pidginized form of the language used primarily as a trade jargon.

Attitudes toward Arabic

We may assume that every community has some shared beliefs about language and attitudes toward language. In multilingual countries we can assume that some of these beliefs and attitudes will be about the appropriateness of the use of particular languages for different purposes as well as about esthetic and moral values inherent in one language and its uses in comparison with another. In order to understand fully the role of Arabic in Ethiopia, it would be desirable to have information on the attitudes of Ethiopians toward Arabic and its use in comparison with their attitudes toward other languages.

Previous studies of attitudes toward Arabic (Ferguson, 1959; Nader, 1962) have been based on participant observation in communities of Arabic mother tongue, and studies of the role of Arabic in a multilingual society have been concerned with Arabic as a national language in relation to a European former colonial language (e.g. Gallagher, 1968) or to a local minority language (e.g. Jernudd, 1968). Accordingly, there is little precedent for a study of attitudes toward Arabic in a nation where it serves as a secondary lingua franca and religious language. A few predictions might be hazarded on the basis of the description above but field investigation is required for any dependable conclusions.

Some meagre indications of the attitudes toward Arabic held by users of the language in Ethiopia can be found in the results of the questionnaire. To the question 'What languages would you like your children to know?' the twenty university freshmen and the seventy Dire Dawa respondents gave overwhelming preference to English, Arabic, Amharic, and French (82, 81, 61, 57 votes respectively), the other languages named being mostly mother tongues. This at least testifies to the importance they attach to knowledge of Arabic. The responses to the questions about which languages seemed most pleasant and most unpleasant gave preference to Arabic and English as the most pleasant, and apart from 17 votes for Gurage gave no clear pattern of languages regarded as unpleasant (scattered votes or no language named). Again, this gives some indication of a favourable attitude toward Arabic.

The answers to a complex question on language preferences for different uses give some slight additional information. Arabic was not consistently preferred to English, mother tongue, or Amharic for any use, although the largest number of top preference votes for use of Arabic was for talking about religion. This suggests that the use of Arabic as a lingua franca is not out of some kind of preference for that language, but because it is favoured by the existing language competences of the people communicating.[4]

Finally, the answers to the questions about the use of Arabic in government schools and on the radio are of interest. The votes were overwhelmingly in favor of the teaching of Arabic as a subject in government schools, the use of Arabic in broadcasting to Ethiopians, and the recitation of the Qur'an over the Ethiopian radio. The vote was indecisive on the question of teaching the Qur'an in the schools (8 yes, 9 no, 3 no vote). Whatever else may be their attitudes about Arabic, the students seemed to want more use of Arabic under government auspices.

This very little bit of information about language attitudes is tantalizing, and points to the need for a broader investigation with other techniques. Even with fuller information on the attitudes of Ethiopians who use Arabic as a secondary language, any attempt at characterizing the position of Arabic in the nation or predicting future trends would fail without investigation of the attitudes of those in the country who have Arabic as their mother tongue as well as the attitudes of the vast majority of Ethiopians who have little or no knowledge of Arabic at all.

4. The preferences for other languages are of some interest. English was the most strongly preferred for the largest number of uses: 15 out of the 20 gave it top preference for seeing movies and reading books for fun, and 11 and 13 respectively for reading newspapers and listening to news broadcasts. Amharic was not consistently given preference above mother tongue or English for any use, but was preferred by five respondents for talking during sports or for writing letters. As might be expected, the mother tongue was strongly preferred for listening to songs; more surprising was the vote on talking about religion, in which mother tongue preferences exceeded Arabic.

References

ABBOUD, P. F. (1969), 'Arabic dialects', in A. Sebeok et al. (eds.), Current Trends in Linguistics, vol. 5: Southern Asia and North Africa, Mouton.

ANDRZEJEWSKI, B. W. (1962), 'Speech and writing dichotomy as the pattern of multilingualism in the Somali Republic', in Colloque sur le Multilinguisme, Brazzaville.

BENDER, M. L. and COOPER, R. L. (1969), 'The prediction of between-language intelligibility', mimeograph, Addis Ababa.

BLANC, H. (1960), 'Stylistic variations in spoken-Arabic: a sample of interdialectal educated conversation', in C. A. Ferguson (ed.), Contributions to Arabic Linguistics, Harvard University Press.

BLANC, H. (1964), Communal Dialects in Baghdad, Harvard University Press.

FERGUSON, C. A. (1959a), 'Diglossia', Word, vol. 15, pp. 325–40.

FERGUSON, C. A. (1959b), 'The Arabic Koiné', Language, vol. 35, pp. 616–30.

FERGUSON, C. A. (1966), 'National sociolinguistic profile formulas', in W. Bright (ed.), Sociolinguistics, Mouton.

FERGUSON, C. A. (1969), 'Myths about Arabic', Languages and Linguistics Monograph Series, vol. 12, pp. 75–82, Georgetown University.

FISHMAN, J. A. (1968a), 'Societal bilingualism: stable and traditional', in *Bilingualism in the Barrio*, US Office of Education. Revised version of 'Bilingualism with and without diglossia; diglossia with and without bilingualism', *J. Soc. Iss.*, vol. 23, part 2, pp. 29–38, 1967.

FISHMAN, J. A. (1968b), 'Sociolinguistic perspective on the study of bilingualism', in *Bilingualism in the Barrio*, Washington, D.C., US Office of Education.

FISHMAN, J. A. (1968c), 'The relationship between micro- and macro- sociolinguistics in the study of who speaks what language to whom and when[1] (in this volume).

GALLAGHER, C. F. (1968), 'North African problems or prospects; language and identity', in J. A. Fishman *et al.* (eds.), *Language Problems of Developing Nations*, Wiley.

GUMPERZ, J. J. (1962), 'Types of linguistic communities', *AL*, vol. 4, part 1, pp. 28–40.

HEINE, B. (1968), 'Afrikanische Verkehrssprachen', *Infratest Schriftenreihen zur empirischen Sozialforschung*, Bd. 4, Köln.

JERNUDD, B. (1968), 'Linguistic integration and national development', in J. A. Fishman *et al.* (eds), *Language Problems of Developing Nations*, Wiley.

JOHNSTONE, T. M. (1967), *Eastern Arabian Dialect Studies*, Oxford University Press.

LESLAU, W. (1957a), 'The phonetic treatment of the Arabic loanwords in Ethiopia', *Word*, vol. 13, pp. 100–23.

LESLAU, W. (1957b), 'Arabic loanwords in Amharic', *BSOAS*, vol. 19, pp. 221–44.

LESLAU, W. (1957c), 'Arabic loanwords in Argobba', *JAOS*, vol. 77, pp. 36–9.

LUKAS, J. (1936), 'The linguistic situation in the Lake Chad area in Central Africa', *Africa*, vol. 9, pp. 332–49.

MITCHELL, T. F. (1957), 'The language of buying and selling in Cyrenaica; a situational statement', *Hesperus* vol. 44, pp. 31–71.

NADER, L. (1962), 'A note on attitudes and the use of language', *AL*, vol. 4, part 6, pp. 25–9.

STEWART, W. A. (1968), 'A sociolinguistic typology for describing national multilingualism', in J. A. Fishman (ed.), *Readings in the Sociology of Language*, Mouton.

TRIMINGHAM, J. S. (1952), *Islam in Ethiopia*, Cass.

URIBE VILLEGAS, O. (1968), 'Instrumentos para la presentación de las situaciones sociolingüísticas', *Revista Mexicana de Sociologia*, vol. 30, pp. 863–4.

8 N. Tanner

Speech and Society among the Indonesian Elite: a Case Study of a Multilingual Community

Excerpts from N. Tanner, 'Speech and society among the Indonesian elite: a case study of a multilingual community', *Anthropological Linguistics*, vol. 9, no. 3, 1967, pp. 15–39.

Within a large American university town in the spring of 1962 was a small community of twenty-six members made up of Indonesian graduate students, their wives, and their children.[1] Their residences clustered within an area three blocks long and one block deep. With one or two exceptions, all members knew each other, and many of the men were in daily contact in the classroom and library. Those whose residence or academic schedule placed them outside the bounds of frequent chance encounter with fellow Indonesians seldom allowed more than a few days to pass without actively seeking out other group members for shopping expeditions, weekend or holiday excursions, and Indonesian student organization activities such as group dinners, tennis matches, and displays during the campus International Week. They helped each other find apartments, learn to drive, buy cars and other goods and pack for home, and they lent each other money when necessary.

This small, somewhat encysted, closely-knit group encompassed and integrated, although not without strain, a considerable degree of diversity. The group, although small in number, was an ethnic mosaic, made up of thirteen Javanese, five Minangkabau, two Sudanese, four mixed Javanese-Sudanese, one Mandailing Batak, and one Chinese, thus giving a fair representation of some of the larger ethnic groups of Indonesia. Eleven members had a strong Islamic heritage, while fifteen had secular or syncretic religious backgrounds. Ten had business or professional class backgrounds and fourteen had aristocratic backgrounds (no data on two members). There were thirteen men, six women, and seven children.

1. Findings have been checked and in some cases amplified during subsequent field research in Indonesia during 1963–6 under the sponsorship of a Foreign Area Fellowship Program grant. This paper was written while I was in Indonesia and rewritten during 1966–7 while I was a Carnegie Fellow with the Committee for the Comparative Study of New Nations at the University of Chicago. Thanks are due to John Gumperz and Dell Hymes for encouraging me to write this article, as well as to June Rumery for editing the first version of it, and to Jakub Isman, Roger Paget, Daniel Lev, and Clifford and Hildred Geertz for their constructive criticisms at various stages of the writing.

It was the very heterogeneity of this highly educated group which made it representative of the emerging Indonesian elite. Indonesia is an island republic, a cultural as well as a geographic archipelago. At one level the nation can be conceptualized as consisting of a series of localized ethnic segments. Each segment contributes a portion of its most able members to the overarching urban elite who govern the nation, become its scholars, run the major enterprises, symbolize national unity, and provide models for changing behavior.

The community was multilingual, as is the larger Indonesian elite which it typified. Its speech resources included not only the languages of its constituent ethnic groups, i.e., the vernaculars or regional languages, but also the national language, Indonesian, as well as the foreign languages English and Dutch and, in addition, certain commonly recognized varieties of some of these languages. How these speech resources were utilized for what Hymes has called 'the specialization of particular languages or varieties to particular situations or functions' (Hymes, 1962) is one of the special emphases of this paper.

Table 1 lists the code resources of the group as a whole. Code, as the term is used in this paper, refers to any form of speech whether named or unnamed that the society in question differentiates from other forms. The concept code thus includes both what we commonly understand by the term language, and intra-language distinctions that I call varieties, that is, speech levels, dialects, and styles. In Table 1, languages but not varieties are listed according to apparent frequency of use within the group. The number of speakers of each language and variety is given at the right of each. For those varieties where there was disagreement on number of speakers I have included both the highest and lowest counts. A distinction has been made between those languages and varieties used within the group and those potentially available, that is, known and perhaps spoken outside the group by some members, but not currently utilized within this group. [. . .]

It is interesting to note that in the early interviews the codes mentioned by informants generally had the status of languages. However, as research progressed I found that increasingly finer distinctions were made particularly for the most frequently used languages.

No one member of the group commanded this full range of codes, yet each of them had a 'speech repertoire' including several of them. Focusing on these repertoires and their interplay is helpful for understanding the internal relations of the community, and suggests some possibilities for the study of communication in multilingual communities generally. Just as an individual can play many roles, so can he adjust his code to a particular role. The patterns will differ between communities whose members

Table 1 **Languages and varieties known to group members and number of speakers of each**

Languages	No.	Used in group	No.	Potentially available	No.
Indonesian	26	standard (*bahasa Ind. resmi*)	21		
		daily (*bahasa Ind. sehari-hari*)	26		
		'Djakarta slang'	19/14		
		other regional 'slangs'	?		
		special styles: individualized and very intimate 'slangs'	?		
Javanese	20	high (*krama*)	15/9	very high (*krama inggil*)	15/4
		low (*ngoko*)	20		
Minangkabau	5	daily	5		
Dutch	20	standard	5/4		
		familiar	11/10		
		broken	10/9		
English	24	standard	24		
Sudanese	8	daily	7	high (*lemes/halus*)	2
		broken	1	low (*kasar*)	?
Batak	1			Mandailing Batak	1
				Toba Batak	1
Chinese	1			standard (Mandarin)	1
Palembang	1			Palembang	1

have diverse speech repertoires, and communities in which they are the same for all. Within a community, the position of an individual with an extensive repertoire will differ substantially from that of an individual with a limited one. Another subject for study is the process of linguistic socialization and the extent to which codes are internalized by individuals, [. . .]

Four important characteristics of the speech repertoires of the Indonesian elite became apparent during interviews with group members. First, in many cases the ethnic or regional language was not the exclusive language of the home – a fact doubtless contributing to what seems to be a remarkable linguistic flexibility among the Indonesian elite and lack of intense emotional commitment to a 'mother tongue'.

Second, the inclusion of the same language in informants' speech repertoires was no guarantee that the same 'meanings' were attached to that language by these informants. Individual patterns of language socialization varied considerably, resulting in diverse attitudes to the various codes in their speech repertoires. These differences are a matter of emotional connotation and of habitual association of a particular code with a particular type of situation as well as a matter of fluency.

Third, for all informants codes had specialized uses, a topic which will be discussed in more detail later. Although the childhood speech patterns of informants in some sense foreshadowed those of the adult, they did not determine them. Patterns of code specialization vary with circumstances and must be viewed as an on-going adaptive process. For these informants it is the principle of code specialization that is the important characteristic of childhood linguistic experience, not the pattern of code specialization itself. Not one person interviewed reported a static linguistic history in this respect. For each, not only were new codes added at various stages in life, but the range of use of each code perceptively narrowed or broadened with changing environment and circumstances.

Fourth, the simple fact that all of the informants' speech repertoires intersected in a minimum of one language – their national language, bahasa Indonesia – cannot be too highly stressed. Bahasa Indonesia, in modern Indonesia's complex society, functions as a sort of linguistic highest common denominator. Despite differences in mode of acquiring Indonesian, whether at home or at school, as an infant or in middle age, it is an almost universally known code among educated, travelling, or urban Indonesians. This is due to many factors: Malay, the language from which Indonesian developed, was used as an auxiliary language at lower government levels by the Dutch colonial government; Indonesian was adopted as one of the symbols of the early nationalist movement ('one people, one homeland, one language') and given exclusive official status and strong encouragement during the Japanese occupation during the Second World War, a policy that was continued by the Indonesian government after independence. Interestingly, Indonesian never had a serious competitor for its place as the national language, a fact attesting to the wisdom of the early nationalist leaders and the self-restraint of the Javanese, Indonesia's dominant ethnic group. It is this one fact – that Indonesian is not the vernacular of any one prominent Indonesian ethnic group – that has given it its great advantage and which has made it acceptable to all Indonesians, whatever their vernacular. Indonesia's attainment of widespread use in less than a generation since it was first exclusively used as the official language during the Japanese occupation is also a credit to the rapid extension of mass education. It is perhaps also due to the fact that Indonesian is an easy language to learn. Its use by inter-ethnic married couples among the urban elite may have also contributed to its spread. Whatever the reasons, Indonesia is outstanding among the newly independent multilingual nations in having a truly successful national language.

This small society, then, can be characterized as one that possessed a wide range of code resources but one in which the speech repertoires of individuals were never identical and often varied considerably. Given the limitations to code choice imposed by the points of intersection of participants' speech repertoires, both situational and motivational factors served further to guide code selection in any linguistic encounter between group members. The work of Brown and Ford (1961) and of Rubin (1962) stresses social distance as a particularly significant situational variable. My informants also mentioned social distance, as measured by several complex factors, as an important situational variable, but they stressed other factors as well, such as setting and content of verbal exchange.

Settings of 'performances' recognized by this group included meetings, parties, classes, and informal gatherings and excursions of the bachelors. While standard Indonesian was the proper code for meetings of the campus Indonesian organization, it would have been ludicrous to use it during an informal gathering of 'the boys'. The restraint and relative seriousness of the former contrasted with the carefree style of 'Djakarta slang', the most common code for the latter. This type of informal gathering was a strictly masculine performance, and should a woman enter the scene, both topic and certain aspects of style were likely to require immediate modification. This points to an additional consideration that the character of the situation is influenced not only by the relationship between the immediate participants but also by the presence of others who provide an audience for the performance. Who else is there is an important aspect of the setting of an encounter.

Parties and classes were also mentioned as being relevant settings for interaction among group members. Parties seem to require some use of intimate codes, but because they bring together people between whom there may be considerable social distance the extremely familiar styles generally have little place. The classroom setting parallels that of the meeting, but since classes were conducted in English, and most of the other students were American, the Indonesians in these classes addressed each other in standard English rather than in standard Indonesian. In such cases it was the performance itself – the meeting, the class, or whatever – that was conducted in the aforementioned codes; conversation preceding or following the performance might take place in different codes. This is a significant point, for it emphasizes the importance of a recognized setting, or performance, as an independent factor in code selection. Supporting examples from the Indonesian scene include that of Djakarta school children using Indonesian in class but switching to Djakartanese as soon as the recess bell rings, and that of Parliament members speaking Javanese or Dutch before and after the session but using the national language, Indonesian, during the session itself.

Content, or topic, also influenced code selection in the case study group in at least two instances. Discussions concerning their field of study uniformly included profuse use of English terminology and, especially among the Ph.D. candidates, were often carried out almost entirely in English. Discussions about women, on the other hand, were not language specific, or even, strictly speaking, style-specific but did always utilize some sort of familiar stylistic variations which included what they called 'dirty slang'. In Indonesia, topic also influences code choice; for example, Geertz (1960) reports that the Javanese speak of modern politics in Indonesian but about traditional Javanese culture, particularly religion, in Javanese.

Social distance, the third situational variable influencing code selection, can be differentiated into 'vertical' and 'horizontal' dimensions. In other words, there are two types of questions relevant to the determination of social distance – first whether someone is 'above' or 'below' oneself and secondly 'how close' (Brown and Gillman, 1960). The vertical measure is essentially a means of placing people on a respect–disrespect continuum while the horizontal one refers to a formal–intimate continuum. In this group, age, class background and marital status were vertical dimensions, while degree of friendship, sex, ethnic background (and sometimes religious background), educational background in terms of the university one came from, field of study and proximity of current residence were horizontal dimensions.

As might be anticipated, social distance – being a composite of so many potentially conflicting elements – was not always a clear guide to code choice for participants in an encounter. This had given rise to an increasingly common rule of thumb: 'when in doubt, use Indonesian'. The following example serves to illustrate this point. When asked what language he usually spoke to his friend's Javanese wife, a young Javanese man answered, 'It's a little unusual, with most of the other Javanese I speak *ngoko* (low Javanese, a symbol of easy-going familiarity among equals when used reciprocally). But with her I speak Indonesian. Actually, I have tried speaking *ngoko* with her, but she answers in Indonesian. Perhaps she feels that we aren't so close yet.' In this case, the language repertoires of both are similar, although the man knows Dutch, can use Djakarta slang, and a little Sundanese, while the woman's repertoire is more limited. However, they both know low and high Javanese (*ngoko* and *krama*), standard and everyday Indonesian (*bahasa Indonesia resmi* and *bahasa Indonesia sehari-hari*) and English. They are both young adults of nearly the same age, good friends, neighbours, and are both university educated. In addition they are both sincere Moslems, quite religious by Javanese standards, and thus have an additional tie of 'closeness' (although the woman was considered to be 'more religious' than the man). Social distance is minimized in all these respects. However, they are of the opposite sex and both married, factors which tip the scales toward constraint, and more importantly, are of differing class backgrounds. The woman comes from a family that may be characterized as bourgeois while the man is a descendant of the old Javanese aristocracy. Use of *ngoko* (low Javanese) with him would plunge her into a degree of familiarity that would seem inappropriate to one reared to show respect to the nobility. Yet, use of *krama* (high Javanese) would seem incongruous to a friend and neighbor so similar in age, education and religious philosophy.

In such ambiguous situations, where participants are social equals in terms of one value scale, but in a subordinate-superordinate position according to another, individuals can avoid the difficulties and embarrassment involved in either proclaiming their equality or acknowledging their superiority or inferiority, by communicating with one another in Indonesian. By so doing they indicate neither respect, disrespect, nor unwanted familiarity, but at the same time can avoid 'stiffness' by use of everyday Indonesian rather than standard or 'schoolbook' Indonesian. In Indonesian public life, where there is an ever-increasing ambiguity as to whether to rank members of the new elite in terms of achieved or ascribed status, the Indonesian language provides a noncommittal mode of communication.

Indonesian is also a good neutral starting point in initial conversations with new acquaintances. It is a safe first choice, giving participants an opportunity to gather adequate information about each other so they can make a transition to another more appropriate code. The dynamics of code shifting is of interest in itself. Any attempt on the part of one participant to move from the safety and neutrality of linguistic exchange in Indonesian can be rebuffed by the other party by ignoring the code shift and answering in Indonesian. Thus, the party who contemplates changing from Indonesian to some more intimate code, whether a vernacular, a slang such as 'Djakarta slang', or Dutch, often tests out the other by inserting into the discussion a few words of the code to which he wishes to shift. If the other responds in kind, the transition is usually rapidly completed. If not, the former need never acknowledge that any such change of code was even considered.

Setting, content, and social distance, along with the participants' speech repertoires are, then, the situational factors influencing code selection in an encounter. [. . .]

Motivational as well as situational factors influence code choice. A party to an encounter has his own interests to consider. He may feel it more beneficial to either downplay or emphasize any or all considerations of social distance. He may try to structure the situation in such a way that a certain performance and not another will be carried out. He can certainly always change the subject. Even the consideration of speech repertoire, which has so far been treated as a given, is not immune to manipulation. One can pretend not to know certain codes or to know much more of them than is actually the case.

Given the fact of the functional specialization of code usage among the Indonesian elite, a topic which will be discussed in more detail shortly, participants to an encounter can manipulate the symbolic value of various codes according to their own purposes. If it is to an actor's advantage to emphasize ethnic solidarity, he may use the ethnic language; if it is not, another code can be used. A code suitable among good friends may be used because the participants want to convince each other and/or their audience that they are good friends regardless of whether they really are or not. If one is determined to practise a code, he may doggedly use it with everyone he meets that knows it, regardless of other situational factors. If he, on the other hand, dislikes speaking in a certain code, he may refuse to speak it no matter how well he knows it or how appropriate its use may be. Codes that are incongruous for the setting of the encounter may be used for jokes; those that are improper because of the degree of social distance between the speakers may be used for insult. A code that is little known to other participants may be used in order to impress them, or two or more participants may use such a code in order to exclude a third or keep certain information from him. Purpose, thus, takes its place as a selective factor among those of speech repertoire, social setting, content, and social distance, and helps us to understand the functions of any particular code in an encounter under analysis.

I now shift to a discussion of the overall uses of the various codes in this group and in Indonesia in general. Codes have been divided into three categories: national, regional, and foreign, and will be discussed in that order. In most cases, the unit of discussion will be a language, but for the most commonly used languages – Indonesian and Javanese – I will make finer distinctions, differentiating the uses of several varieties as well.

The range of uses, or functional range, of a language is the product of the uses to which its specialized varieties can be put. The languages utilized by this group have noticeably different functional ranges. This finding conflicts with the currently popular assumption that all languages are functionally equivalent and opens the door to a further useful type of cross cultural comparison. It must, however, be emphasized that such differences in range are in no way fixed and do not reflect differing potentials of the languages concerned. For example, certain gaps in the functional range of Indonesian are rapidly being filled as the language accommodates itself to the increasing burden of popular use. This expansion of range proceeds as more specialized varieties are differentiated within the language and as established forms of speech come to be considered appropriate to additional or different uses. Correspondingly the ranges of some of the ethnic languages and of Dutch are in the process of contraction as certain varieties fall into disuse, or come to have fewer functions. With these comments in mind, let us now compare the varieties of Indonesian used within the group.

Daily or ordinary Indonesian is the usual, informal, everyday conversational variety of Indonesian. It is the style of Indonesian spoken in most face-to-face encounters between acquaintances and friends of different ethnic groups. As such its range of use is so broad as to make it difficult to list the special functions. Daily Indonesian is contrasted with the Indonesian which is taught in school, a style some people called *bahasa resmi*, or standard language. Structural differences between daily Indonesian and standard Indonesian include shortening of words, omission of words, changes of word order, some word substitution, and minor differences in pronunciation and rhythm. The difference between the standard language and its ordinary, conversational style is the difference between *Marilah kita turun kebawah* and *Ajok kebawah*. In English, the first is 'Let us go down(stairs)', while the second can be expressed by saying, 'Come on', and gesturing to indicate downstairs. Another example of the difference between standard and daily Indonesian is the contrast between *Apakah jang dia katakan?* and *Apa dia bilang?*. The substitution of the Javanese word bilang for the Indonesian root 'kata' is an important aspect of the contrast between the two phrases. *Apa katanja?* is a commonly used phrase on the borderline between standard and daily Indonesian, combining the virtues of both. All become simply 'What did he say?' in English.

In Indonesia, standard Indonesian is used for elementary, high-school and university instruction, radio broadcasts, speeches, newspaper and magazine articles, official letters, and in general for all purposes for which 'good', 'correct', standard Indonesian is appropriate. As such it has undergone and is continuing to undergo a particularly rapid vocabulary expansion. Vocabulary growth is so rapid that students returning to Indonesia after a few years abroad sometimes jokingly comment that they can no longer read the newspapers – a statement which is only a partial exaggeration. Terms are borrowed from both foreign and regional languages, and are constructed from the consolidation of initial letters or syllables selected from already existing terms. Partially because Indonesian is expanding so rapidly, it is rather difficult to define the boundaries of each of its styles. Some would doubtless differentiate the more conservative 'schoolroom Indonesian' from the faster changing and sometimes rather confusing newspaper Indonesian, which many consider to be substandard. However, despite differences within the broad category which I call standard Indonesian, this style has an identity of its own as a 'formal', 'educated' mode of speech or writing that can be contrasted to daily, conversational Indonesian.

In the area of polite expression Indonesian is considered less rich than some of the ethnic languages, particularly Javanese and Sundanese. Over and over again, the people that I interviewed told me, 'Oh yes, we may speak Indonesian, but in speaking to our older relatives it is not so polite.' Or they would say, 'Yes, I can speak Indonesian to the Consul (the Indonesian consul who was stationed in a nearby metropolis was Javanese), but it is nicer if I speak high Javanese.' Nevertheless standard Indonesian can and does serve as an adequately respectful speech style in the many situations where the participants are not of the same ethnic group.

Indonesian in general, whether the official or the daily variety, is regarded as a neutral, democratic language. A speaker of Indonesian need not commit himself to any particular social identity, nor need he impute one to those with whom he converses.

All educated Indonesians know Indonesian; nevertheless even for members of this group (most strongly for those who are Javanese) and more so for the less cosmopolitan, Indonesian carries the unmistakable connotation of a public language. It is a language in which many find it somewhat difficult to be either properly polite to their elders and social superiors or appropriately intimate with family and good friends.

The gap at the intimate end of the scale is partially filled by slang expressions borrowed from various regional codes. As one Indonesian expressed it, 'to some extent the dialects enrich the Indonesian language, to make it more intimate, to fill a certain lack'. [. . .]

The expressive or functional range of Indonesian is expanding along several dimensions. The aspects of this expansion stressed by informants were that:

1. Standard Indonesian shows signs of becoming more acceptable for polite speech – as indicating respect and social distance,

2. Slangs based on regional codes are being incorporated into daily Indonesian in order to make it 'swing', to mute its public, utilitarian, colourless and stiff connotations, and transform it into a flexible, informal style capable of promoting sub-group solidarities.

3. Through vocabulatly expansion it has begun the process of becoming an adequate vehicle for technical discussions and for advanced as well as elementary education.

The Javanese numerically dominated the group as they do the nation, and Javanese was by far the most commonly spoken ethnic language. The ethnic languages have similar ranges of use, ranges that contrast with Indonesian, on the one hand, and with the foreign languages, Dutch and English, on the other. Javanese, however, also has its own special characteristics. In particular, variety differences are far more strongly marked in Javanese than in Indonesian, the other ethnic languages, Dutch, or English. Whereas in these latter languages one finds diffuse ranges of stylistic variations, in Javanese a set of relatively distinct levels has crystalized. These levels are utilized in such a way as to indicate fine shades of relative rank, with the 'higher' speaker using a 'lower' (less respectful, more intimate) form of speech to his subordinate than the subordinate, in turn, uses to his superiors.

The varieties are ordered in a series of some three to six levels from very low to very high (Geertz, 1960, pp. 248–60). One Javanese group member listed and attempted to translate the levels from lowest to highest as follows: *ngoko* ('impolite'), *krama ngoko* ('half polite'), *krama madya* ('polite') and *krama inggil* ('high polite'). He said that ngoko and krama madya were the basic forms and the other forms were but elaborations; other group members generally referred simply to ngoko and krama, and sometimes to krama inggil. Within this group only ngoko and krama were used, but krama inggil was sometimes used with high Indonesian officials stationed in the United States and with visiting dignitaries.

As Geertz illustrates so well in his discussion of Javanese etiquette and linguistic levels (1960), it is the configuration or combination of levels used in an interaction that is important. The many possible combinations provide a wide range for the indication of status and social distance. It is significant that, within the group itself, only two of the many possible level configurations were utilized, and that both were strictly reciprocal: ngoko-ngoko and krama-krama. Both parties to an encounter were careful to return the same degree of respect and formality (krama) or intimacy (ngoko) as was shown towards them. This attenuation of level use is primarily a function of group composition, that is, all were of approximately the same educational level and had similar social positions as university instructors in Indonesia, and thus in terms of these criteria at least were of roughly equal status. Age and degree of friendship became the major determinants of social distance in this case.

For familiar parlance between very close friends and in the intimacies of family life, the Javanese described three different patterns of code use. Among most of the older Javanese of the group, both ngoko and a familiar form of Dutch were used to fulfill this function. That Dutch as well as low Javanese should be so used among them is not surprising since most of them were Dutch educated, and Dutch was also usually one of the languages of their homes. The remainder of the Javanese adults seemed to regard ngoko as the only code entirely appropriate for expressing familiarity. This also is understandable, for these younger members were part of a transitional generation, a generation which was still young when Dutch lost its place as the language of upper class homes and schools, but for whom Indonesian had not yet gained entrance to the home. Among the children of the group a third pattern is emerging. Everyday Indonesian and a little English, as well as ngoko, are used in these Javanese homes. The teenage daughter of one family also used some Djakarta slang at home, the major code of her Djakarta peer group, although her parents tried to discourage it for they regarded it as kasar sekali ('very crude'). For this younger generation the number of potential intimate codes is again expanding. However, Javanese parents expressed some concern over the likelihood of their children growing up deficient in the higher forms of Javanese, krama and krama inggil. They were especially worried about this lack as it affected the relations of their children with non-urban older relatives, for according to traditional patterns of propriety, Javanese children should show varying degrees of linguistic respect with kin depending upon relative generational level (Geertz, 1961).

An intriguing bit of information given by one Javanese informant was that different levels could be used with the same relatives, depending on the social context. In her case, privately she and her parents used ngoko reciprocally, but in public she switched to krama, showing the proper degree of respect to them when there were others around to notice. Clifford Geertz has commented that he believes this pattern is very common in Java, but that it is hard to get data on it because they will not do it when you are there to listen, nor are they usually willing to admit they do it (personal communication, 1966). This is the sort of example to delight the hearts of all proponents of the Goffman approach to role theory, for it illustrates that after all, a performance is not much use without an audience (Goffman, 1963). It also brings to our attention once again the fact that social distance is not the only important situational variable in code selection. In this case, setting is the determining factor. Depending on the type of performance, that is, on the setting, the degree of social distance portrayed by mode of speech may expand or contract.

The case of the Javanese language is unique because of its particularly clearly marked levels and the elaborate etiquette governing their use.

Nevertheless, the range of functions of Javanese is similar to that of Indonesia's other regional languages. It is the vehicle of the traditional culture and social life of an ethnic group but not of the activities of a modern nation. As such, social interaction along traditional lines such as with non-urban older relatives, or cultural activities specific to that ethnic group such as traditional drama and literary forms, finds the vernacular the most appropriate medium of expression, while modern education, business, government, and art forms such as the movies and the modern novel, do not. [. . .]

Dutch occupied a peculiar position among the codes used in this group. It is the language of Indonesia's previous rulers. As such it was used widely by the former Indonesian elite, an educated, westernized, and bureaucratized nobility. The most privileged sent their children to the special schools provided for Dutch children, while the slightly lower ranking attended the Dutch language schools for Indonesians. Prior to the period of Japanese rule (1942–5), at which time Indonesian became the official language, Dutch was the language of government (although Malay was also used as an auxiliary language at lower governmental levels), the major language of education, and above all the language of prestige. During colonial days it was even spoken in the homes of the most Western-oriented Indonesians. There are thus, today, some Indonesians for whom Dutch is as much, or more, their native tongue as is their ethnic language. Among such older people Dutch is still used as a familiar mode of communication and still functions as an 'in-language' among the Djakartan political elite, although its official use in government has lapsed and English and Indonesian have largely replaced it in the academic world, at least as far as university lectures and textbooks are concerned. Intellectual discussions among older scholars, however, are still frequently carried on in Dutch. A reading knowledge of Dutch is also still necessary in fields specifically related to Indonesia such as history, ethnology and customary law. It seems doubtful that Indonesian or English can replace Dutch completely in these fields, for although the process of translating important Dutch works is well under way, translation can never make 350 years of documentation entirely available. (. . .) Within the case study group Dutch had two main functions:

(1) as a familiar clique code similar in function to the informal varieties of the vernaculars, but with the differing social connotations mentioned above, and

(2) as an important source of supplementary vocabulary, especially in the provision of terms for material objects and academic concepts. It is probable that even the second utilitarian use of Dutch shares in the first function. (. . .)

N. Tanner 137

English has a particularly specialized range of uses. In Indonesia, English as well as Indonesian is an acceptable language of instruction at the university level and scholars make considerable use of English sources. It is important in many international aspects of business and politics. As a medium of paperbacks, magazines and movies it is popular among teenagers and young adults. Many expressions derived from these sources are utilized in the flirtations carried out among modern youth as part of the 'new date' complex. Among those young people who are moderately fluent whole conversations may be carried out in English because most of them would feel constrained and awkward were they to flirt in their ethnic language or even in Indonesian. English has become the language of romance for some segments of Indonesia's youth.

Some informants felt that English is rapidly becoming the mark of the well-educated man, a symbol of the new elite, as Dutch was of the old. To them English is a useful international language, one that is largely free from the invidious connotations of Dutch. However, as yet English hardly carries the degree of prestige that Dutch once did, is not yet widely used as an intimate language as Dutch still is, nor is it spoken with anything approaching the same frequency.

For group members, the uses of English were even more restricted than they were in Indonesia. All members were fluent in English and some used it as much as Indonesian as far as total talking time was concerned. However, save for the exceptions below, English was seldom used within the group itself. Rather it was the group's language for dealing with outsiders – Americans and other foreign students. As such, it was constantly used with faculty, fellow students, friends, clerks, mechanics, landlords, doctors and salesmen. It was the language of lectures, exams, and term papers; TV, movies, and novels; call girls, car lots, and wholesale houses; and most were well able – imperfectly to be sure – to vary their style appropriately according to these differing contexts. English was used whenever Americans were present, although not necessarily to the exclusion of Indonesian, the vernaculars, or Dutch. But within the group, the use of English generally shrank to a handful of words and phrases inserted into conversations dominated by other codes. The major exception to this generalization was with regard to discussions carried on among a few of the men about their field of study. As one man commented, 'It's not just that we want to show off, but the terms are English, we studied it in English, and it's easier to talk about the concepts in English.' A second exception lay in the realm of verbal play. Relative newcomers to the group were sometimes teased with phone calls from oldtimers speaking in English and pretending to be the newcomer's faculty adviser, or they were roused from a sound sleep early in the morning by a friend purposely speaking

English as a sort of challenge or test of the other's proficiency at an unguarded moment. Another type of exception was exemplified by the woman who reported that she and her husband preferred to argue in English. This paralleled the comment of another woman that she liked to swear in Dutch more than in Indonesian or her vernacular 'because it doesn't sound so rough'.

What has been said about code specialization can be summarized as follows: the regional languages, although they contrast both in types of variety differentiation and the uses to which the varieties are put, nevertheless have similar ranges of use in the total Indonesian linguistic scheme – whether the frame of reference be Indonesia in general or this group in particular. Speaking in a vernacular with another of the same ethnic background indicates intimacy and ethnic solidarity. With kin, save in certain urban settings (mainly Djakarta and Medan, Indonesia's two largest cities), the vernacular is the appropriate vehicle of both intimacy and respect. Similarly, particularly for the Javanese and Sundanese, the ethnic language is the most adequate instrument for expressing fine shades of respect and social distance with members of the same ethnic group, and they feel especially constrained to use it with important older people. [. . .]

Indonesian, Dutch and English contrast with the vernaculars in that they are neither regionally nor ethnically limited in their use. Although each of these languages can be used to indicate some degree of both familiarity and respect, they are used with different categories of people than those with whom the vernaculars are used. Indonesian is used within the group and the nation first and foremost during ethnic interaction, while English is largely reserved for interaction with outsiders. The position of Dutch has changed drastically. Its former official functions are now filled by Indonesian; its previous educational uses are now largely filled by Indonesian plus English. English has almost completely replaced it in its prior function of relating Indonesia to the rest of the world in politics and business, as has Indonesian in inter-ethnic communication. Dutch retains its usefulness only in certain academic disciplines and as an intimate code among the upper class, especially among the middle-aged and older.

Indonesian is of course proving to be a far more effective vehicle than Dutch ever was for inter-ethnic communication, politics, education and other public purposes. It is far more widely used in magazines, newspapers, and radio (not to mention the newly inaugurated TV) than was Dutch, and is also used for some public purposes – such as speeches in the mosque in some areas – where Dutch would never have been used. Indonesian's rapidly increasing use goes hand in hand with the great increase in elementary education and the increasing national orientation of the masses as well as of the elite. In addition, since Indonesian cannot be used to indicate extremely fine distinctions of rank as can Javanese, it is regarded as a more suitable linguistic vehicle for the newer, more democratic national ideology.

For the case study group, Indonesian functioned much as do the vernaculars on the broader Indonesian scene, serving to mark off the Indonesians from American society much as the ethnic languages mark off Javanese or Minangkabau or Batak or Sundanese or any other ethnic group as distinct in its own right from the larger Indonesian society. Indonesian was not only a convenient way for Indonesians of different ethnic backgrounds to talk with each other, but it also symbolized their common group membership. [. . .]

This paper has presented the case of a particular multilingual community – that of a group of Indonesian graduate students, their wives and their children, in the USA. It is an interesting and complex case and has special value for the light it sheds upon the success of Indonesian as a national language and the functional differentiation and specialization of codes in Indonesia. Presenting something of the richness, complexity, and patterning of language usage among the Indonesian elite has been a goal in itself. I have tried to reconstruct on paper the character of the group which served as my sample and of its individual members, and to make the case live by giving examples and using quotations.

But the significance of this case lies not only in the detail given about code use in Indonesia, but also in the concepts which have been utilized to present the raw material and in the theoretical approach, the framework in which the content finds its meaning. Concepts such as those of the total code resources of a society, speech repertoires, the functional differentiation and specialization of codes, and the functional range of a language should prove useful to further research along these general lines. Further, the usefulness of an activity frame of reference, of a concentration on speech and society, on a community and the linguistic behavior of its members, has been shown and some of the components of this type of analytical approach have been presented (Hymes, 1964). In this approach, an interaction unit, the linguistic encounter, becomes the starting point of analysis. In code selection the points of intersection of the actors' speech repertoires provide the possibilities for code use in that encounter. If, as often occurs, several codes are common to the speech repertoires of participants to the encounter code, selection is further determined by situational and motivational factors. Setting or performance, and content or topic, take their place alongside the frequently mentioned factor of social distance as important situational variables. Motivational factors are many, for actors are active agents, manipulating the character of situations in which they participate according to their own intents. Code selection, it is stressed, is a dynamic process, which often involves the preliminary use of a neutral code – in this case bahasa Indonesian – while information necessary to code choice is gathered; and informal 'testing' of a code that an actor hypothesizes is probably appropriate by inserting words or phrases of the proposed code into the conversation, and noting the other actor's response before risking a complete shift of code.

This paper, then, has attempted to exemplify an ethnographic or sociological approach to linguistic anthropology. There is a great wealth of largely untapped data that can be readily described and analysed if the relations between 'language and culture' are conceptualized in terms of the use of symbols in interaction rather than of the formal relations between symbolic products.

References

BROWN, R. W., and FORD, M. (1961), 'Address in American English', *J. abnorm. Soc. Psychol.*, vol. 62, pp. 375–385.

BROWN, R. W., and GILMAN, A. (1960), 'The pronouns of power and solidarity', in T. A. Sebeok (ed.), *Style in Language*, Wiley.

GEERTZ, C. (1960), *The Religion of Java*, Free Press.

GEERTZ, H. (1961), *The Javanese Family*, Free Press.

GOFFMAN, E. (1963), *Behavior in Public Places*, Free Press.

GUMPERZ, J. J., and HYMES, D. (eds.) (1964), *The Ethnography of Communication*, *AmA.*, vol. 66: 6, part 2.

HYMES, D. (1962), 'The ethnography of speaking', in T. Gladwin and W. Sturtevant (eds.), *Anthropology and Human Behaviour*, Anthropological Society of Washington.

HYMES, D. (1964), Introductions to Part 5 and Part 7, in D. Hymes (ed.), *Language in Culture and Society, A Reader in Linguistics and Anthropology*, Harper & Row.

RUBIN, J. (1962), 'Bilingualism in Paraguay', *AL*, vol. 4, pt 1, pp. 52–68.

9 R. A. Hall Jr

Pidgins and Creoles as Standard Languages

R. A. Hall Jr, 'Pidgins and creoles as standard languages', original paper.

A pidgin language is, by definition, one whose structure and lexicon have been drastically reduced, and which is native to none of those who use it. A creole, likewise by definition, is a pidgin language which has become the native language of a speech-community (cf. Jespersen, 1922, chapter 12; Bloomfield, 1933, pp. 471–5; Hall, 1965, pp. 10–14). Both pidgins and creoles have clearly definable and describable grammatical structures, which, however, differ markedly from those of the 'full-sized' source-languages from which they are historically derived.[1] Melanesian Pidgin English (Neo-Melanesian),[2] for instance, has only four bound forms, all of which are traceable to English sources, but have shifted so far from English that they have changed their meaning and have no direct functional equivalents in English (see Table 1). Similarly, the verbal system of Haitian and other French-based creoles shows, not tenses indicated by

Table 1 **Melanesian Pidgin English bound forms**

MPE bound form	Function in MPE	English source	Function in English
-fela	adjectival suffix	fellow	noun
-fela	pronominal plural-suffix	fellow	noun
-im	verbal transitive suffix	(h)im	object pronoun
i-	third person predicate-marker	(h)e	subject pronoun

Source: Hall, 1943, pp. 20–21

1. I shall use the term 'source-language' for, say, English in relation to the various kinds of Pidgin English; French in relation to Haitian and other creoles (e.g. those of Martinique, Guadeloupe, Mauritius); or Spanish in relation to Papiamentu. In so doing, I am not making a stand on the theory of monogenesis versus polygenesis or on that of 'relexification' (cf. Thompson, 1961; Taylor, 1961, 1965; and Whinnom, 1965; and, for counter-arguments, Hall, 1965, pp. 120–3).

2. Abbreviations for language-names frequently cited: CPE=Chinese Pidgin English: HC=Haitian Creole; MPE=Melanesian Pidgin English. For the last-mentioned, I once suggested (Hall 1954, p. 91) the term *Neo-Melanesian*, which, however (as pointed out by Capell, 1969), does not seem to have achieved any great popularity.

suffixes, but aspects indicated by prefixes. Thus, HC/ap(è)-/ is from the French preposition *après* 'after', but means 'be . . . -ing, *être en train de* . . .', as in /mwẽ ap-mǎže/ 'I am eating', and /fèk-/, though from French (*ne*) *fait que* 'does . . . only . . .', means 'have just . . . -ed', as in /li fèk-rive/ 'he has just arrived'.

Similarly, the vocabularies of pidgins and creoles manifest extensive shifts in meaning. Many of these changes are the result of the inevitable broadening of reference involved in pidginization. If a given semantic field has to be covered by a few words rather than many, each word must of course signify a wider range of phenomena. Two pidgin examples out of many: CPE *spit* means 'eject matter from the mouth', by both spitting and vomiting; MPE *gras* means 'anything that grows, blade-like, out of a surface', as in *gras bilong hed* 'hair', *gras bilong maus* 'moustache', *gras bilong fes* 'beard'. The vocabularies of creole languages are normally extended by borrowing from the source-languages or others, but their basic lexicon often shows the type of semantic extension just discussed for pidgins, as in Guiné Crioulo /əəbi/ 'hear, understand' < Port. *ouvĩ* 'hear'; /fiiju/ 'off-spring, fruit' < Port. *filho* 'son'; /kaloor/ 'heat, sweat' < Port. *calor* 'heat'; /algiŋ/ 'person' < Port. *alguem* 'some-one' (cf. the parallel semantic development in MPE *samting* 'thing' < Eng. something) (Wilson, 1962).

Until relatively recently, the tongues of preliterate, prestigeless groups have received, in general, little attention in comparison with languages which serve as the vehicles of culture and civilization. In the case of pidgins and creoles, this disfavour is increased by the ease with which speakers (native or non-native) of the source-languages can recognize the extensive dislocation, grammatical and semantic, which we have just discussed. The contempt and hostility thus engendered is at the base of such derogatory terms as 'mongrel jargon', 'bastard lingo' and the like, applied to pidgins and creoles (discussed at length in Hall 1955a, page 14).[3]

In modern times, however – roughly since the beginning of the twentieth century – the increasing autonomy and democratization of many formerly colonial areas has brought with it a corresponding advance of those regions' languages to the status of standards. This process has taken place (not without a certain resistance in some quarters) in the case of a number of pidgins and creoles as well. It began as early as the turn of the century in what was then Kaiser Wilhelms Land (German New Guinea, the Bismarcks, and the northern Solomons) with MPE. Since experience with

3. This feeling is not limited to speakers of prestige-languages, but is apparently common to all who come in contact with what seems to them an unjustifiably reduced version of their native tongue, comparable to children's talk. In Port Moresby, I was told that speakers of Motu have this same attitude towards the pidginized Police Motu.

problems of standardization involving pidgins and creoles has been longer in New Guinea than elsewhere, our references to this area will be correspondingly frequent.

The problems connected with the establishment of a standard language are of three kinds: the choice of a variety to be preferred above others; the areas of human activity in which it is to be used; and the achievement of recognition for the new standard. In the normal slow rise of West European standard languages over several centuries, these problems present themselves in relatively mild form, and in such a way that they are resolved without excessive difficulty. They slot into an on-going, crystallized *Questione della Lingua* only when the political, economic and social factors involved remain stagnant, as was the case in Italy from the sixteenth to the nineteenth century (cf. Hall, 1942). In the sudden twentieth-century acceleration of the development of new standards, however, these problems present themselves all at once, calling for immediate resolution even when, as in some instances, not all the relevant factors are known or have reached a definitive condition (cf. Ray, 1963).

A standard behaviour-pattern – whether linguistic or non-linguistic – is usually regarded as necessarily unitary, admitting of relatively little deviation. There have been a few exceptions to insistence on a single linguistic norm, but they are found, in general, in artificial situations, involving particular literary genres. In Old Provençal lyric poetry, forms and phonetic developments from several different dialects were in free alternation (cf. Grandgent, 1905, pp. 3–4). In ancient Greece, different dialects were used for different types of literary productions (cf. Buck, 1933, pp. 20–21), and in Middle Indic drama, members of each caste spoke the appropriate variety of Sanskrit or Prakrit (cf. Gray, 1939, p. 37). The simplest type of linguistic variation is regional, and hence the choice of standard has usually been made among local dialects of any given language. (Since pidgins and creoles are used, in general, only by groups on the lowest socio-economic level, questions of social prestige have normally not arisen in their case.) This problem has usually been settled by choosing the dialect of the administrative centre of the region involved.

Thus, in the early twentieth century, the German administration in New Guinea had its capital at Rabaul, and recruited its native 'police-boys' from that region. Hence the MPE of the Rabaul area, with its characteristic phonological and lexical features carried over from Kuanua, the native language of Rabaul and the Gazelle peninsula (e.g. *balus* 'bird > aeroplane'), was carried by the police-force to all parts of Kaiser Wilhelms Land. The Australians, on taking over this territory after the First World War, found this situation existing as a *fait accompli*, and had no choice but to continue and extend it (cf. Hall 1955, pp. 37–8). Similarly, in

Haiti, the heavily Gallicized usage of Port au Prince has been, in recent years, gaining over the 'purer' Creole of the country districts, despite some opposition from the *authentiques* who favour linguistic and other patterns free from French influence (cf. Efron, 1954). A drive for some type of standard is absent only from areas where the pidgin or creole has, as yet, received no official recognition, due to the unquestioned dominance of an immensely more prestigious language, as is the case with English in the British Solomons (cf. Hall, 1955b) and in Hawaii (cf. Reinecke, 1969), or with French in Guadeloupe and Martinique.

Closely connected with the question of a single standard is the problem of orthography (cf. Turner, 1960, and Hall, 1959 and 1965, pp. 39–48). In general, spelling systems designed for serious use have been developed for pidgins and creoles through the efforts of non-governmental groups, particularly missionaries. On occasion, rival missionary organizations have prepared somewhat differing orthographies, to which they have clung with irrational emotional attachment. The most notorious instance of such unnecessary differentiation was the use of $<\eta>$ by Lutherans and $<\mathrm{ng}>$ by Roman Catholics for the voiced velar nasal continuant in MPE. Intelligent collaboration between formerly rival groups, and resultant unification of orthographies, has fortunately been on the increase, as in Suriname, where three groups have agreed on a single spelling system for Sranan (cf. Donicie, 1967, p. 11), and in New Guinea, where Protestant and Roman Catholic missionaries and the government established a unified spelling for MPE.

It is not possible to set up a universally valid ideal for 'reducing' a pidgin or creole to writing, any more than for any other language, because there are too many possible variant factors that can be involved. We may summarize these under three types of relationship: to the locally-based standard, to other varieties of the language, and to whatever prestige language is dominant in the area. At least in theory, the orthography should reflect, as accurately as possible, the phonological system of the dialect on which the standard is based: Rabaul for MPE, Paramaribo for Sranan, and so forth. If the situation warrants it, morphophonemic alternations can also profitably find representation. In MPE, for instance (as in Commonwealth Standard English in general)[4] morpheme-final /-r/ is automatically lost (after /a ə o/) or becomes /ə/ (after /u ʊ i ɪ e ɛ/), but reappears before a suffix beginning with a vowel (e.g. -*im* transitive; cf. Table 1). Thus we have the alternations shown in Table 2. In the Alexis-

4. I am distinguishing between two main varieties of Standard English: North American (United States and Canada) and Commonwealth (all the other English-speaking areas, almost all of which are, or were, part of the British Empire, later Commonwealth).

Table 2 **Morphophonemic alternations involving /r/ in Melanesian Pidgin English**

Morpheme-final	Before suffix	Alexishafen orthography	Current official orthography
[sə′piə] 'spear'	[sə′pɪrɪm] 'to spear'	spir, spirim	sipia, sipirim
[′fajə] 'fire'	[′fajrəp] 'to fire'	fair, fairap	faia, faiarap
[′nəmbə] 'number'	[′nəmbərɪm] 'to number'	nambar, nambarim	namba, nambarim

hafen Catholic Mission's orthography, this final -r was written everywhere in the more phonetically oriented system which was finally adopted for general use, it is written only where a vowel follows in a suffix.

In theory, also, an orthography should represent as much of a compromise as possible between various, somewhat divergent, dialects. Again in MPE, the contrast between <p> and <b>, <t> and <d>, <k> and <g> represents the voiceless, voiced contrast for virtually all speakers of English and for many Melanesians. For other Melanesians, in whose languages this contrast is not present, these same pairs of letters serve to indicate the oppositions between non-prenasalized and prenasalized consonants: e.g. *tabak* ['taᵐbak] 'tobacco' v. *hipimap* ['hipᵒ 'hibɪməp] 'pile up'. In other languages, this may perhaps not be possible, and speakers of one dialect may have to learn to adopt the pronunciation of another, or else accept a discrepancy between their speech and the orthography.

The two problems just discussed arise in connection with the designing of an orthography for any language. With pidgins and creoles, however, the situation is complicated still further by the (often extremely strong) pressure exerted on their users to conform wholly or in part to the spelling systems of a dominant prestige-language. In its extreme form, this pressure leads to the use of conventional spelling for all words which seem in any way similar to those of the source language (English, French, etc.). For others, a rough and ready adaptation is made. We therefore find – especially in the notations made by travellers and others unskilled in any kind of linguistic analysis – such representations of MPE sentences as *S'pose me stop here* (F. Coombe, writing in 1911, quoted in Hall, 1955, pp. 94–5). One of the earliest attempts to use HC as a literary language was made by George Sylvain in his poems (Sylvain, 1901), with spellings of the kind evidenced in these lines:

Atò, té g'ain gnou chòguiè
Avec gnou ti pòtt-en-tè.

'Then, there was a kettle and a little earthenware pot' (p. 25).

Even when a reasonably accurate orthography has been developed, there is a strong temptation for native speakers of the source-language (who have usually been trained to regard its spelling as more definitive than any pronunciation) to introduce new or unfamiliar words in their conventional spelling. We therefore find such incongruities as *council* where the normal spelling would be *kuunsil*, parallel to *kuuntim* 'count' or *maunten* 'mountain'. Similar incongruities were of course widespread in the spelling of Greek and Latin loan-words in Western European languages during the Renaissance and afterwards (cf. Baugh, 1935, pp. 255–6; Cohen, 1947, pp. 163–6, or virtually any other history of English or French). In earlier times, such learned spellings carried prestige and served to distinguish scholarly users of the language from the great mass of unlettered speakers, according to Veblenian principles of conspicuous and prestigious waste (cf. Hall, 1960). It is questionable, however, whether similar inconsistencies should be intentionally introduced and allowed to cause confusion in newly developed orthographies, since all they do is to disorient the naïve speaker of a pidgin or creole (cf. Gudschinsky, 1951, p. 12; Hall, 1965, pp. 45–6).

A different problem presents itself when literacy in the pidgin or creole is expected to serve as a stepping-stone to the learning of the dominant language, whether this latter be directly related historically or not. In some instances, the orthography of the dominant language is reasonably regular, at least in certain respects, so that an adjustment can be made in the way the pidgin or creole is written, to make transition to literacy in the dominant language easier. On this principle, the McConnell-Laubach orthography[5] for HC used *ou* for /u/, *ch* for /š/, and *j* for /ž/, since these graphemes are used wholly consistently in French. McConnell-Laubach also used the circumflex to represent nasalization, as in *mâjé* /mãže/ 'to eat', for both consistency and ease of use with typewriters having French keyboards. The alternative procedure, of writing nasalized vowels with vowel-letter plus *n* or *m* (e.g. *manjé, mangé*), advocated by Charles-Fernand Pressoir, had the advantage of being closer to French orthography, but the disadvantage of being farther from the actual phonology of both French and Creole, and of necessitating some artificial way of representing

5. Valdman (1968, pp. 321–7, and 1969, pp. 179–80) is wrong in denying the status of an orthography to the McConnell-Laubach way of writing HC. The difference between McConnell-Laubach, and Pressoir's adaptation thereof, lies only in the fact that the latter is based on the strongly French-influenced speech of the upper classes in Port au Prince, whereas McConnell-Laubach reflects the phonology of the non-Gallicizing masses of the people. That the phonemes of HC are simply a sub-set of those of French (Berry, 1969) is untrue; cf. Hall (1970). The basic defect of most recent studies of HC is their limitation to the usage of socially powerful but linguistically unrepresentative urban upper-class bilinguals.

a non-nasalized vowel-phoneme followed by a nasal consonant, e.g. the insertion of a hyphen or the addition of a mute *e* to show that the letter *n* or *m* stood for an actual sound, as in *mou-n* or *moune* /mun/ 'person'.

Ever since ancient times, it has been thought by many that, for a language to have the status of a standard, it had to be 'given rules' in a grammar, and have the meanings of its words defined in a dictionary. This has been the function of the various language academies founded during the Renaissance and Baroque eras in Europe (cf. Hall, 1964, chapter 62), and in more recent times in such countries as Indonesia. For some pidgins and creoles, grammars and dictionaries have been provided in recent decades, some by linguists (e.g., for MPE, Hall, 1943; for HC, Sylvain 1936, Hall, 1953, d'Ans, 1968; for West African Pidgin English, Schneider 1966) and others by non-linguists (e.g., for MPE, Murphy, 1943, Mihalić, 1957, Steinbauer, 1969; for HC, McConnell and Swan, 1945; for Martiniquais Creole, Jourdain, 1956a, 1956b). In general, the direct effect of the linguistically-based descriptions in conferring prestige on the languages described has been minimal, and that of the more popularly oriented grammars and dictionaries has not been much greater. No academies or similar normative institutions have as yet been founded in this field.

In the use of pidgins and creoles, we must first of all distinguish between humorous and serious functions. Speakers of prestigious European standard languages are wont to regard non-standard varieties as fit only for non-serious purposes: anecdotes (often with real or supposed characteristics of dialect-speakers as the butt of the joke), stories, or humorous poems, often somewhat less than elegant.[6] Such narratives or poems are sometimes done in imitation of some well-known literary work, and occasionally achieve a certain artistic merit of their own.[7] As a result of such use, however, non-standard varieties, and especially pidgins and creoles, are frequently thought of as unfit for serious functions.

The first step towards overcoming such prejudices is usually taken in connection with practical needs, and often by unofficial or semi-official bodies. With most pidgins and creoles, these needs have been perceived first by missionary groups in connection with evangelization. Literacy has been a goal, for such organizations, primarily as a means for enabling converts to read the Bible and other edifying material. Orthographies (cf. above) are often first developed in this connection. At first, portions of the Bible are paraphrased[8] or translated, and subsidiary reading matter is prepared, normally by Europeans who have learned the pidgin or creole

6. e.g. the 'erotic poem' in MPE quoted in Hall (1943, p. 83).

7. e.g. the paraphrase of Longfellow's *Excelsior* in CPE, once very popular with 'old China hands', reproduced in Hall (1944, pp. 112–13).

8. As in the *Liklik Katolik Baibel* (Alexishafen, 1946, and later editions).

involved. More extensive and thorough Bible translations come later.[9] Often, Europeans who are ignorant of the grammatical and semantic structure of the pidgin or creole interpret such material only in the light of the humorous uses mentioned earlier, and make merry over such expressions as MPE *Yesus i pikinini bilong God* 'Jesus is the Son of God', or *God i urs bilong olgeda samting* 'God is the source of everything'. Nevertheless, the use of a pidgin or creole in the missionary context is often its first step on the way to recognition and function as a standard.

Beyond evangelization lies the problem of elementary education in general. It is generally recognized in informed circles that the most efficient and effective way to educate youngsters is to make them literate in their native tongue first, and then to teach any other language – no matter how much more prestigious it may be – as a foreign idiom. This principle holds for a creole as well as for any other language that is native to a speech-community. In some areas like New Guinea, a great number of languages are spoken,[10] many of them only in small communities of a few hundred speakers. On the other hand, by now a large proportion of the population[11] know and use a pidgin as a lingua franca, and find it considerably easier to learn than a 'full-sized' foreign language. Under such circumstances, it is clearly advisable to make use of the pupils' already existing knowledge of the pidgin as a foundation on which to attain initial literacy and to impart basic instruction. Unfortunately, many observers and policy-makers are ignorant of these elementary principles, and are not willing to make use of the already existing language-skills which native children or adult learners bring to school with them.[12] On occasion we even find that – as is reported from Mauritius and Réunion – the local population, although speaking a creole all the time, holds it in such low esteem that parents are unwilling for their children to become

9. As in the *Nupela Testamen* (Canberra and Port Moresby: British and Foreign Bible Society, 1969).

10. The exact number of tongues spoken in New Guinea is not known; estimates vary from several hundred to a thousand or more. Laycock (1969, p. 37) speaks of 'approximately 700 distinct languages estimated to exist in the New Guinea region (including West Irian)'.

11. In 1954 it was roughly estimated that over half the male population, and a considerably smaller number of the females of New Guinea spoke MPE; the proportion of pidgin-speakers has undoubtedly increased since then.

12. For instance, a severe, but not fatal, setback was given to the use of pidgin in making New Guinea children literate by the uninformed and pretentious, but influential, pronouncement of a United Nations committee in 1953 that 'Melanesian Pidgin is not only not suitable as a medium of instruction, but has characteristics derived from the circumstances in which it was invented which reflect now outmoded concepts of the relationship between indigenous inhabitants and immigrant groups' (quoted in Hall, 1955, p. 101).

literate in it, preferring for them to be taught in a prestige-language (English or French, respectively) of which the children do not know a word when they enter school.

Despite their lack of prestige, pidgins and creoles have been shown to be completely satisfactory media for conveying technological information. Manuals have been prepared, using multicolor techniques of reproduction, for such fields as medicine, carpentering and automobile repair. In this type of material, incidentally, there is some justification for at least giving the spelling of a technical term in the prestige-language of the region, as well as in a phonologically accurate orthography (e.g. *heart* alongside of *hart*), because technicians, medical assistants and others are likely to come across such spellings on labels, in captions for illustrations, and the like.

In connection with literacy campaigns and elementary education, many informal pidgin and creole newspapers have been published for shorter or longer periods. At the outset, they are usually mimeographed; later, they are often printed. They are normally put out either by missionary groups or by governmental education agencies. They contain local news, somewhat simplified world news, and announcements of various kinds. Religiously-oriented papers frequently feature original compositions by native converts describing their experiences; similarly, accounts of trips, adventures, and the like are published in non-religious newspapers. A similar function is fulfilled, in oral communication, by radio broadcasts with news, informative talks and songs (see below).

Once a pidgin or creole has been used to a certain extent for semi-official purposes such as those just discussed, informal use of its written form is likely to take root and spread. Not only casual notes, but fairly long letters, are sent from one portion of the territory to another, especially where, as in New Guinea, men are separated hundreds of miles from their families to labour on plantations. From this kind of writing to free compositions, narrating folk-tales and adventures is only a short step. Popular songs – either unaccompanied or with guitar or other accompaniment – are widespread in many pidgin- and creole-speaking communities.

However, as has been noted by various observers, the definitive seal of approval as a fully recognized standard is dependent on the use of a language in two functions: fully official (governmental) and bellettristic.[13] In these respects, also, MPE has been more advanced than many other pidgins or creoles. Since 1965, when the Territory of Papua and New Guinea became semi-autonomous under the Australian mandate, and the House of Assembly was established, MPE has been recognized as an

13. cf. the remarks of Voorhoeve (1967, p. 105); 'I think that only the poets can really convince the general public that these languages are worth sincere admiration.' For the general background of the situation in Suriname, cf. Rens (1953).

official language for use in parliamentary discussion alongside of English (cf. Hull, 1968). It has been increasingly used as a vehicle for literary composition, beginning with the present writer's efforts to retell various traditional European stories (e.g., the legends of Troy, Roland, the Cid, Tristan and Isolde) in pidgin.[14] Even more ambitious efforts have been made in Haiti, with works like Félix Morisseau Leroy's adaptation of the *Antigone* to the Haitian scene, and in Suriname and Curaçao.

The major difference between a pidgin or creole and any other indigenous language, in achieving recognition as a standard, lies in its relation to the prestige-language of the region in which it is used, especially if this latter is its source-language. Any non-standard language has to combat prejudice with regard to its use, as opposed to that of a more firmly established variety, whether on the local, the regional, or the national level. A pidgin or creole, in addition to questions of simple social standing, has to confront the widespread opinion that it is a 'debased' or 'corrupted' variety of some other language, whether that language be the dominant prestige-tongue of the region or not. As long as no political considerations are involved, pidgins or creoles have little or no chance of achieving recognition on the basis of intrinsic merit, or even usefulness, alone.

The only factor, apparently, which can bring about a change in the status of a pidgin or creole is political, i.e., pressure effectively exerted by or on behalf of the population which uses it, for its recognition. Such pressure has been exerted, in recent years, on the local and regional level in many areas, including Sierra Leone, New Guinea, Haiti, Suriname, and the islands of the Netherlands West Indies (Curaçao, Aruba, Bonaire).[15] In an independent country, the major example to date of a language originating as a trade jargon and achieving the status of national standard is Indonesian, an outgrowth of Bazaar Malay (cf. Kahin, 1952). The correlation between political factors and status-achievement, for pidgins and creoles, is so close that we may expect to see other such languages rise to the status of standards only where the areas where they are spoken gain political independence or autonomy, and use the local tongue as a symbol of nationality.

14. cf. Hall (1955c). Some of these stories were mimeographed and circulated in New Guinea by the Department of Education.
15. cf. the remarks of Valkhoff (1966, pp. 144–5).

References

BAUGH, A. C. (1935), *A History of the English Language*, Appleton-Century-Crofts.
BERRY, P. (1969), 'Literacy and the question of Creole', in R. P. Schaedel (ed.), pp. 204–80.
BLOOMFIELD, L. (1933), *Language*, Holt, Rinehart, Winston; and Allen and Unwin.

BUCK, C. D. (1933), *Comparative Grammar of Greek and Latin*, University of Chicago Press.

CAPELL, A. (1969), 'The changing status of Melanesian pidgin', *La Monda Lingua-Problema*, vol. 1, pp. 107–15.

COHEN, M. (1947), *Histoire d'une Langue: le Français*, Éditions Hier et Aujourd'hui (later edns by Éditions Sociales).

D'ANS, A.-M. (1968), *Le Créole Français d'Haïti: Étude des unités d'Articulation, d'Expansion et de Communication*, Mouton (Janua Linguarum, Series Practica, no. 106).

DONICIE, A. (1967), *De Creolentaal van Suriname: Spraakkunst* (Derde druk), Radhakishun & Co., Paramaribo.

EFRON, E. (1954), 'French and Creole patois in Haiti', *Caribb. Q.*, vol. 3, pp. 199–214.

GRANDGENT, C. H. (1905), *An Outline of the Phonology and Morphology of Old Provençal*, Heath.

GRAY, L. H. (1939), *Foundations of Language*, Macmillan.

GUDSCHINSKY, S. (1959), 'Recent trends in primer construction', *Fundamental and Adult Educ.*, vol. 11, no. 2, Appendix B.

HALL, R. A., Jr (1942), *The Italian Questione della Lingua: an Interpretative Essay*, University of North Carolina Press (UNCSRLL, no. 4).

HALL, R. A., Jr (1943), *Melanesian Pidgin English: Grammar, Texts, Vocabulary*, Linguistic Society of America.

HALL, R. A., Jr (1944), 'Chinese pidgin English: grammar and texts', *J. Amer. Orient. Soc.*, vol. 64, pp. 95–113.

HALL, R. A., Jr (1953), *Haitian Creole: Grammar, Texts, Vocabulary*, American Anthropological Association Memoir no. 74.

HALL, R. A., Jr (1954), 'The status of Melanesian Pidgin', *Australian Q*, vol. 26, no. 2, pp. 85–92.

HALL, R. A., Jr (1955a), *Hands Off Pidgin English!*, NSW, Pacific Publications Pty Ltd.

HALL, R. A., Jr (1955b), 'Pidgin English in the British Solomon Islands', *Australian Q.*, vol. 27, no. 4, pp. 68–74.

HALL, R. A., Jr (1955c), 'The provision of literature in Neo-Melanesian', *South Pacific*, vol. 7, pp. 942–4.

HALL, R. A., Jr (1959), 'L'ortografia delle lingue pidgin e créole', in *Ioanni Dominico Serra ex munere laeto inferiae*, Linguori, Naples, pp. 205–13.

HALL, R. A., Jr (1960), 'Thorstein Veblen and linguistic theory', *American Speech*, vol. 35, pp. 124–30.

HALL, R. A., Jr (1964), *Introductory Linguistics*, Chilton.

HALL, R. A., Jr (1965), *Pidgin and Creole Languages*, Cornell University Press.

HALL, R. A., Jr (1970), Review of d'Ans (1968), *Am.A*, NS, vol. 72, pp. 685–6.

HULL, B. (1968), 'The use of pidgin in the House of Assembly', *J. Papua-New Guinea Soc.*, vol. 2, no. 2, pp. 22–5.

JESPERSEN, O. (1922), *Language: Its Nature, Origin, and Development*, Allen and Unwin, Macmillan.

JOURDAIN, É. (1956a), *Du Français aux Parlers créoles*, Klincksieck.

JOURDAIN, É. (1956b), *Le Vocabulaire du Parler Créole de la Martinique*, Paris. Klincksieck.

KAHIN, G. M. (1952), *Nationalism and Revolution in Indonesia*, Cornell University Press.

LAYCOCK, D. C. (1963), 'Why study New Guinea languages?', *Kilvung*, vol. 2, no. 1, pp. 36–41.

McCONNELL, H. O., and SWAN, E., Jr (1945), *You Can Learn Creole*, Port au Prince, Imprimerie de l'État.

MIHALIĆ, F. (1957), *Grammar and Dictionary of Neo-Melanesian*, The Mission Press, Illinois.

MURPHY, J. (1943), *The Book of Pidgin English*, W. R. Smith and Paterson Pty Ltd.

RAY, P. S. (1963), *Language Standardization: Studies in Prescriptive Linguistics*, Mouton (Janua Linguarum, Series Minor, no. 29).

REINECKE, J. E. (1969), In *Language and Dialect in Hawaii*, S. M. Tsuzaki (ed.) University of Hawaii Press.

RENS, L. L. E. (1953), *The Historical and Social Background of Surinam Negro-English*, North Holland Publishing Co.

SCHAEDEL, R. P. (1969) (ed.), *Research and Resources of Haiti*, Research Institute for the Study of Man.

SCHNEIDER, G. D. (1966), *West African Pidgin-English*, G. D. Schneider.

STEINBAUER, F. (1969), *Concise Dictionary of New Guinea Pidgin (Neo-Melanesian)*, Kristen Press, Medang.

SYLVAIN, G. (1901), *Cric? Crac!*, Chez l'Auteur, Port au Prince.

SYLVAIN, S. (1936), *Le Créole Haïtien: Morphologie et Syntaxe*, Chez l'Auteur, Port au Prince and Imprimerie De Meester, Wetteren.

TAYLOR, D. M. (1961), 'New languages for old in the West Indies', *Comparative Studies in Sociology and History*, vol. 3, pp. 277–88.

TAYLOR, D. M. (1963), 'The origin of West Indian creole languages: evidence from grammatical categories', *AmA*, NS, vol. 65, pp. 800–814.

THOMPSON, R. W. (1961), 'A note on some possible affinities between the Creole dialects of the Old World and those of the New', *Creole Language Studies*, vol. 2, pp. 107–13.

TURNER, G. W. (1960), 'Written pidgin English', *Te Reo*, vol. 3, pp. 54–64.

VALDMAN, A. (1968), 'Language standardization in a diglossia situation: Haiti', in J. A. Fishman, C. A. Ferguson, and J. Das Gupta (eds.), *Language Problems of Developing Nations*, Wiley, pp. 313–26.

VALDMAN, A. (1969), 'The language situation in Haiti'.

VALKHOFF, M. (1966), *Studies in Portuguese and Creole, with Special Reference to South Africa*, Witwatersrand University Press.

WHINNOM, K. (1965), 'The origin of the European-based Creoles and pidgins', *Orbis*, vol. 14, pp. 510-27.

WILSON, W. A. A. (1962), *The Crioulo of Guiné*, Witwatersrand University Press.

Part Three
Dialectal and Stylistic Variation

In this section the writers examine the ways in which intra-language variation can convey social information. Bright and Ramanujan explore the relevance of such factors as caste, formality and literacy to linguistic diversity and innovation in South Asia, while Geertz, and Labov, discuss relationships between status and familiarity in dialects of Javanese and American English respectively. Like these, Gumperz is concerned with code-switching behaviour but within the context of small group interaction. The last four writers describe particular functions of language. Ervin-Tripp and McIntosh indicate the social significance of address usage; Andrzejewski outlines the functions and stylistic characteristics of oral literature in Somali; and Frake describes the sociolinguistic rules governing a particular social event, and ways in which high social status is reflected in the participants' linguistic competence.

10 W. Bright and A. K. Ramanujan

Sociolinguistic Variation and Language Change

W. Bright and A. K. Ramanujan, 'Sociolinguistic variation and linguistic change', in *Proceedings of the Ninth International Congress of Linguists*, Cambridge, Mass., 1964.

Introduction

It seems probable that no language is as monolithic as our descriptive grammars sometimes suggest; wherever sufficient data are available, we find diversity within languages on all levels – phonological, grammatical, and lexical. Such diversity can be studied along three synchronic dimensions – geographical, social, and stylistic. The geographical dimension is, of course, the main one which has occupied the attention of dialectologists and which has been presented in dialect atlases. Other types of variation within languages, however, have received less attention. What is here termed the social dimension of linguistic variation is correlated with the socially established identity of the speaker and/or the person addressed or mentioned. Examples are the special linguistic forms used in Nootka to speak to or about children, fat people, dwarfs, hunchbacks, etc. (Sapir, 1915); cases of separate men's and women's speech, as in Koasati (Haas, 1944); and the cases, familiar from our own society, where speech differences are correlated with the speaker's social status. The term 'sociolinguistic variation' may be applied to cases such as these, and in addition to those where linguistic variation is correlated not with the identity of persons, but with other factors in the social context. These are the factors we have called stylistic. Linguistic styles determined by such factors range from the special war-path speech of the Chiricahua Apache (Opler and Hoijer, 1940) to the written styles appropriate to particular literary contexts in societies like our own. Included here also are differences between formal and informal styles of speaking. Although these occur, perhaps, in most languages of the world, some speech communities such as those of Arabic and Modern Greek show such a marked difference between formal and informal style as to produce a kind of bidialectism which Ferguson (1959) has named *Diglossia*.

The study of all these varieties of sociolinguistic variation has proved especially fruitful in the South Asian area (India, Pakistan, Ceylon), and a volume recently published (Ferguson and Gumperz, 1960) has dealt with several aspects of the subject. On the one hand, clear-cut social dialects are found to be associated with the caste system of Hindu society, and these 'caste dialects' constitute one important field for investigation. On the other hand, many Indian languages have formal and informal styles which are differentiated to the point of diglossia. However, since most published works on South Asian languages concentrate on high-caste dialects or formal style, adequate data on differences of caste dialect and on diglossia, as well as on relationships between the two phenomena, are still lacking.

In the Dravidian languages of South India, we find sociolinguistic factors organized into at least two contrasting patterns. In Tamil and Kanarese (and probably also in Telugu and Malayalam), there are classic cases of diglossia. The formal or literary style is used by educated persons in writing and in public address; it varies only slightly with the social class or place of origin of the person using it. Contrasting with this is an informal or colloquial style, showing much greater internal diversity. Differences correlated with the regional and caste background come to the fore in this informal style, although the speech of the educated may be somewhat more uniform that that of the uneducated. An entirely different pattern is found in the Tulu speech community, occupying a small area on the western coast of South India, and probably also in the area of the Kodagu or Coorg language, farther inland. Here we find Hindu societies comparable to those in the rest of South India, but lacking a tradition of written literature in the native tongue. The social functions which are elsewhere served by a formal style of the local languages are here served by the formal variety of Kanarese. Tulu is, to be sure, sometimes written in Kanarese script for informal purposes, but the language is not the customary medium either for education or for a literary tradition. Dialect divisions corresponding to regional differences and caste differences do occur in Tulu, however, just as in the informal styles of Kanarese or Tamil.

The question then arises: What processes have operated to bring about the differences that exist between modern caste dialects? If forms of the present-day dialects are compared with earlier forms of Dravidian speech, it is apparent that some modern forms represent retentions of earlier ones, while others represent innovations. It has been claimed that linguistic innovation in general comes from the lower social levels; thus a recent paper speaks of *la langue populaire, riche en innovations, qui a pour elle le grand nombre, et la langue des classes aisées, qui est plus conservatrice* (Schogt, 1961, p. 91). On the other hand, it has also been argued that phonetic change, and perhaps linguistic change in general, are initiated by the upper social strata, in order to 'maintain a prestige-marking difference' from the lower strata (Joos, 1952, p. 229). The lower class is said to narrow the gap again by imitation, forcing the upper class to innovate still more. Thus language change is viewed as a 'protracted pursuit of an elite by an envious mass, and consequent "flight" of the elite' (Fischer, 1958, p. 52). The information available on Indian caste dialects can be used to test such views. Two years ago, an investigation of material from Kanarese, and to a lesser extent from Tulu (Bright, 1960a, 1960b) reached the following conclusions:

1. It is inadequate to operate simply in terms of 'change'; changes must be classified as phonological, grammatical, or lexical, and as involving loan materials or native materials.

2. In a comparison of a Brahmin dialect of Kanarese with a middle-caste Non-Brahmin dialect (the abbreviations B and NB will be used hereafter), the B dialect showed innovation on the more conscious levels of phonological and lexical borrowing and of semantic change, while the NB dialect showed changes on the less conscious levels of native phonology and morphology.

3. However, in a similar study of Tulu, B and NB dialects showed phonological change in similar degrees; the data then at hand were insufficient for the study of other types of change in Tulu.

In an effort to account for the difference between the Kanarese case and the Tulu case, it was hypothesized that it might be due to the existence of a separate formal style in Kanarese, especially as actualized in the written language. That is, the greater literacy of Kanarese Brahmins was seen as a force counteracting tendencies to change in their dialect – the 'frozen' phonology and grammar of the literary language serving to retard the unconscious processes of change to which speech is normally subject. Tulu Brahmin speech, on the other hand, having no written Tulu tradition to affect it, has been subject to changes of the same type that have operated in the NB dialects of Tulu. In more general terms, it is suggested that literacy, wherever it is present in human societies, acts as a brake on processes of linguistic change. This suggestion has recently been supported by a study of Latin legal terminology over a 2000-year period. This study finds an unusually high retention rate in legal vocabulary, and concludes that 'since these materials have been selected within an area where total literacy is a primary and integral necessity in the communicative process, it seems reasonable to conclude that it is to be reckoned with in language change through time and may be expected to retard the rate of vocabulary change' (Zengel, 1962, pp. 138–9).

It is clear that further study of South Asian caste dialects is desirable in order to establish more clearly the role of literacy in linguistic change. To this end, we have now examined data on caste dialects of Tamil, a language with an exceptionally long literary tradition; at the same time, an expanded body of Tulu data has been taken into consideration. The following sections present our findings on these two language communities.

Tamil

The majority of publications on Tamil deal exclusively with the formal style of the language, as manifested in the writing system. Colloquial Tamil, in its various geographical and social dialects, has received attention in publications of Vinson (1895), Matthews (1942) and Jothimutthu (1956); but these works suffer from lack of organization, and they fail to give clear geographical and social identifications of their data. More systematic discussions have been presented by Bloch (1910), Shanmugam Pillai (1960), Zvelebil (1959, 1960, 1961), and the present authors (1962). The work done to date, however, has barely scratched the surface of the subject, and generalizations about Tamil dialectology are still risky.

With these qualifications in mind, we have nevertheless attempted to find general features distinguishing B from NB dialects of Tamil, and to ascertain which social group plays the innovating role in each case. B data have been obtained from Ayyangar and Ayyar informants; NB data have been obtained from members of Vellala, Nadar, Chettiar and Christian communities. The historical perspective is provided by considering the Literary Tamil form (which is usually, though not always, historically prior to the colloquial form), the cognates in other Dravidian languages (by reference to Burrow and Emeneau, 1961), and the forms which loanwords have in their source languages. The comparisons made are divided into those involving vocabulary, phonology, and morphology; syntactic comparisons are yet to be carried out.[1]

Caste differences in Ta. vocabulary may be classified into two types. In the first type, one caste has a loanword and the other has a native word, e.g. B jalõ 'water' (Skt. jala-), tīrtõ 'drinking water' (Skt. tīrtha-), taṇṇi 'water not for drinking' (native), as against NB taṇṇi 'water in general'. In most of the cases noted, it is B which has innovated by introducing the loanword; a contrary case occurs, however, in Bãmbadeyã 'husband', NB puruṣē (Skt. puruṣa-). In a second type of vocabulary, both castes have native terms, e.g. B tūngu, NB orangu 'sleep'. The B form also has the meaning 'hang' (intransitive), which is apparently the original sense; cf. the corresponding transitive tūkku 'lift', and Ka. tūgu 'weigh'. The NB form reflects L Ta. uranku and other Dravidian forms meaning 'sleep'. Here B has innovated through semantic shift where NB has not; our sample

1. Abbreviations used are Ta. for Tamil, LTa. for Literary Tamil, Ka. for Kanarese, P Dr, for Proto-Dravidian and Skt. for Sanskrit.

contains no cases of the opposite possibility. There are, however, cases where the two dialects differ without evidence that one has innovated more than the other, e.g. B *alambu*, NB *kaḷuyu* 'wash'; both apparently descended without change of meaning from PDr. stems.

Phonological comparisons of B and NB again may be classified into two types. The first type is that of loanwords, in which B frequently preserves non-native phonology, while NB assimilates them to the native pattern, e.g. B *svāmi*, NB *sāmi*, *cāmi* (Skt *svāmin-*). At the same time, B is prone to hypercorrections in loanwords, such as *jīni* 'sugar' (NB *cīni*, from Hindi *cīni*), and *krāfu* 'haircut' (NB krāppu, from English 'crop'), where the foreign sounds /j/ and /f/ are erroneously introduced. The second type of phonological comparison involves native words, where the differences found between caste dialects are most clearly typified by the cases where B has /ṛ/ while NB has /r/ inconsistently varying with /y/ (in northern areas) or /ḷ/ (in southern areas); e.g. B *vāṛepparo* 'banana' as against NB forms like *vāṛeppoḷo*, *vāḷepparo*, and *vāḷeppaḷo*. The overall picture thus shows B as innovator in the introduction of foreign phonemes, sometimes in etymologically unpredictable places. NB, on the other hand, innovates in native material, although the result (at least for educated speakers) is often free variation between older and newer forms, rather than complete replacement of the older.

Morphological differences between B and NB mostly involve varying shapes of morphemes, not all of which can be explained by the regular phonemic correspondences. An example is B -du, NB -ccu 'it' (subject of verb), as in B *vandudu*, NB *vanduccu* 'it came' (LTa. *vantatu*). In this case it appears that the NB form represents an analogic extension of the ending found in both B and NB *pōccu* 'it went', *āccu* 'it became' (LTa. *pōyiṛṛu*, *āyiṛṛu*). In this, as in other examples, NB plays the innovating role. In some other examples, to be sure, B and NB seem to have innovated equally, but in different directions, as when the present tense marker (LTa. -kiṛ) becomes -h in some NB dialects, but -r in B; e.g. B *paṇra*, NB *paṇṇuhā* 'he does' (LTa. *paṇṇukiṛāṇ*). But no clear case has been noted in which B has innovated while NB remains conservative.

The examination of Tamil materials which has been carried out so far shows a situation similar to that previously noted for Kanarese. Neither dialect has a monopoly of innovations in any part of the structure, and yet tendencies are discernible: on the part of B, toward greater use of foreign vocabulary, foreign phonology and semantic shifts; on the part of NB, toward shifts in native phonology and in morphology.

Tulu

Published data on Tulu are found in Brigel (1872), Ramaswamy Aiyar (1932a, 1932b, 1936) and Krishnamurti (1958). These sources do not, unfortunately, distinguish regional dialects, so that there is difficulty in separating regional variations from social variations. This problem has been solved in part by checking with three Tulu speakers.

The comparisons between B and NB dialects of Tulu can be classified as were those of Tamil. Thus we have: vocabulary differences involving loanwords, such as B *puruse* 'husband' (Skt. *puruṣa-*), NB kaṇḍane (cognate with Ta. *kaṇṭan*, Ka. *gaṇḍa*); vocabulary differences involving native words, such as B *jōvu, jēvu* 'girl', NB poṇṇu. The B form means 'child' in some NB dialects, and can be compared with Parji cēpal, Ollari sēpal 'boy'; the NB form is cognate with Ta. *pen* 'woman, girl'. A semantic shift is evident in the B usage. In both these types of correspondence only the B dialect is found to innovate, either by loans from Sanskrit, Hindi, or Kannada, or by semantic shifts of native terms.

Phonological correspondences are also of two types. (1) Some cases involve loan phonology, as when B aspirated stop corresponds to NB unaspirated stop. Some of these cases are loans from Indo-Aryan, e.g. B, *gandha* NB *ganda* 'fragrance' (Skt. *gandha-*). In other cases, however, B forms with aspiration may be traced to PDr., which had no distinctive aspiration: e.g. B *chaḷi*, NB *caḷi* 'cold' (cf. Ta. *caḷi*). The B aspiration in such cases presumably originates as a hypercorrect pronunciation. (2) Other cases involve native phonology, such as B /s/, NB /t/ from PDr. *c, as in B *sikk-*, NB *tikk-* 'be obtained' (cf. Ta. *cikku*). The B form may be regarded as the more conservative, especially since PDr. *c probably included sibilant allophones (as in many modern Ta. dialects). Five other sound correspondences have been noted in which NB shows greater innovation. But we also have a smaller number of cases where the opposite is true, such as the correspondence of B /ē/ to NB /yā/ where PDr. appears to have had *yā, as in B *ēnu*, NB *yānu* 'I' (cf. Ta. *yāṉ*). It thus appears that both B and NB have innovated in phonology, with the NB dialect showing the greater number of innovations. The B dialect, however, shows one special kind of innovation, the introduction of the foreign element of aspiration.

Morphological correspondences between B and NB Tulu are more difficult to deal with historically, since we have no writing system to reflect older forms, and no full reconstruction of PDr. morphology has yet been made. Certain correspondences do yield to investigation, however, such as the one between B -no, NB -da, genitive suffix with 'rational' nouns; thus we find B *āṇu-no*, NB *āṇu-da* 'of the boy' (cf. Ta. *aḷ-iṇ*, with cognate stem). With 'irrational' nouns Tulu has B -nte, NB -da; apparently NB has generalized the dental suffix so as to apply to all types of noun. On the other hand, we find a correspondence between B -i, NB -a, present participle marker, as in B *barpi*, NB *barpa* 'coming'; the NB form agrees with other Dravidian languages, as in Ta. *varu-kiṇr-a*, Ka. *bar-uv-a* 'coming'.

In the morphological comparisons, as in the phonological ones, both B and NB are found to innovate. In summary, the Tulu evidence shows the Brahmins as chief innovators in the more conscious varieties of change – semantic shift, lexical borrowing, and phonological borrowing. In the less conscious processes of phonological and morphological change involving native materials, both B and NB dialects innovate.

Conclusion

We feel that the evidence so far examined supports the hypothesis that upper and lower class dialects innovate independently of one another, and in two ways, here labelled conscious and unconscious. Of these types of change, the more conscious variety is regularly the mark of the upper-class dialect. The less conscious changes apparently may affect both upper and lower dialects, as seen in the Tulu case; but in Kanarese and Tamil, where there is widespread literacy among Brahmins, the formal written style seems to have retarded the less conscious processes of innovation. A study of the Kodagu language, which like Tulu lacks a literary tradition, would be extremely valuable for the further testing of this hypothesis.

The importance of sociolinguistic factors in language history has recently been pointed up by Hoenigswald (1960, p. 55) and by Schogt (1961). We feel that further investigation of social dialects in the South Asian context can contribute much to understanding the mechanisms of linguistic change.

Discussion
Haugen:

The terms 'informal' or 'colloquial' style have recently been replaced by 'casual' (*v.* 'non-casual' for 'formal') by Voegelin. In my recent studies on this subject I have arrived at the point of suggesting that 'private' style might be a better term when looking at the problem from a social point of view. The opposite would then be 'public' style, the style used when one person speaks to a public. These would be the two ends of a continuum.

The conclusion that literacy inhibits linguistic change is a familiar one in traditional histories of language. But of course it has not been properly tested, and evidence in its behalf is always welcome. A recent straw in the wind was the extraordinarily conservative showing of Icelandic in a recent critique of glottochronology published in *Current Anthropology* by Bergsland and Vogt. Icelanders have been literate during most of their thousand-year history, and this may be part of the explanation.

The terms 'conscious' and 'unconscious' as applied to innovation are somewhat slippery, unless carefully defined. Perhaps they could be associated with the terms used by some of 'surface' *v.* 'depth' grammar; the B changes are superficial, resulting from borrowing, while the N B changes are deep, resulting from language drift.

Fischer:

The Tulu data of Dr Bright may be of special value in determining the social position of the originators of linguistic change, since the complicating factor of the literacy of the Brahmins as opposed to the non-Brahmins is absent or weak in this case. Evidence of the sequence of innovations in the language which are shared by both Brahmin and non-Brahmin dialects would be of great interest.

One word of caution, however: it is my opinion that the actual dynamics of linguistic change are to be found within communities of face-to-face speakers. If the barriers to social contact and communication between Brahmins and non-Brahmins in this part of India are firm and strict enough, then the élite *within* each lower caste or group of communicating castes may be more important as a sociolinguistic model than the next higher caste. I think some sort of elite is always involved as a 'pursued and fleeing model' in linguistic change, but I do not think it is always a formally recognized political, economic, or religious elite. If in fact *intra*-caste elites are dynamically the most important as models in this part of India, then imitation of higher-caste speech by the lower would be much weakened, though I would not expect it to be entirely absent. I suspect that in investigating caste barriers to communication, the earlier years of life, through adolescence, may prove most critical.

Sjöberg:

The patterns you have described for Tamil and Kannada certainly hold for Telegu as well. Highly educated Telegu speakers use both a formal and an informal style, depending on the social situation. But the pattern is most prominent among Brahmins, excluding strongly Westernized ones in recent years. From your discussion now, I have the impression that you believe there are two separate systems–Brahmin–non-Brahmin dialects and formalinformal styles. But with Telegu speakers the 'Brahmin dialect' includes at least two styles, formal and informal. Speakers of non-Brahmin dialects would include a few having a formal and informal style, but many with just a single style, the informal or colloquial. The chart does not make this overlapping of the two systems clear. Furthermore, the diagram does not include *un*educated persons, whose speech would diverge considerably from the most informal style of Brahmins and even middle-class persons.

References

BLOCH, J. (1910), 'Castes et dialectes en Tamoule', *Mémoires de la Société de Linguistique*, vol. 16, pp. 1–30.

BRIGEL, J. (1872), *A Grammar of the Tulu Language*, Bangalore.

BRIGHT, W. (1960a), 'Linguistic change in some South Indian caste dialects', in C. A. Ferguson and J. J. Gumperz (eds.), (1960), pp. 19–26.

BRIGHT, W. (1960b), 'Social dialect and language history', *Curr. Anthrop.*, vol. 1, pp. 424–5.

BRIGHT, W. and RAMANUJAN, A. K. (1962), *A Study of Tamil Dialects*, Committee on South Asian Studies, University of Chicago, mimeograph.

BURROW, T. and EMENEAU, M. B. (1961), *A Dravidian Etymological Dictionary*, Oxford University Press.

FERGUSON, C. A. (1959), 'Diglossia', *Word*, vol. 15, pp. 325–40.

FERGUSON, C. A. and GUMPERZ, J. J. (1960), *Linguistic Diversity in South Asia*, Indiana University Research Center in Anthropology, Folklore and Linguistics, publication no. 13.

FISCHER, J. L. (1958), 'Social influences in the choice of a linguistic variant', *Word*, vol. 14, pp. 47–56.

HAAS, M. R. (1944), 'Men's and women's speech in Koasati', *Language*, vol. 20, pp. 142–9.

HOENIGSWALD, H. (1960), *Language Change and Linguistic Reconstruction*, University of Chicago Press.

JOOS, M. (1952), 'The medieval sibilants', *Language*, vol. 28, pp. 222–31.

JOTHIMUTTHU, P. (1956), *A Guide to Tamil by the Direct Method*, Madras.

KRISHNAMURTI, B. (1958), 'Proto-Dravidian *z', *Indian Linguistics*, vol. 19, pp. 259–93.

MATTHEWS, G. (1942), 'The vulgar pronunciation of Tamil', *Bull. Sch. Oriental Stud.*, vol. 10, pp. 992–7.

OPLER, M. and HOIJER, H. (1940), 'The raid and war-path language of the Chiricahua Apache', *AmA*, vol. 42, pp. 617–34.

RAMASWAMY AIYAR, L. V. (1932a), 'Tulu prose texts in two dialects', *Bull. Sch. Orient. Stud.*, vol. 6, pp. 897–931.

RAMASWAMY AIYAR, L. V. (1932b), 'Tulu initial affricates and sibilants', *Q. J. Mythic Soc.* (Bangalore), vol. 22, pp. 259–73.

RAMASWAMY AIYAR, L. V. (1936), 'Materials for a sketch of Tulu phonology', *Indian Linguistics*, vol. 6, pp. 385–439.

SAPIR, E. (1915), 'Abnormal types of speech in Nootka', *Geological Survey of Canada, Memoir 62, Anthropological Series, no. 5*, Ottawa.

SCHOGT, H. G. (1961), 'La notion de loi dans la phonétique historique', *Lingua*, vol. 10, pp. 79–92.

SHANMUGAM PILLAI, M. (1960), 'Tamil – literary and colloquial', in

C. A. Ferguson and J. J. Gumperz, *Linguistic Diversity in South Asia*, Indiana University Research Center in Anthropology, Folklore and Linguistics, publication no. 13, pp. 27–42.

VINSON, J. (1895), 'Les variations phonétiques de la prononciation populaire Tamoule', *Centenaire de l'Ecole des Langues Orientales Vivantes*, pp. 115–26, Paris.

ZENGEL, M. S. (1962), 'Literacy as a factor in language change', *AmA*, vol. 64, pp. 132–9.

ZVELEBIL, K. (1959), 'Dialects of Tamil, 1–2', *Archiv Orientálni*, vol. 27, pp. 272–317, 572–603.

ZVELEBIL, K. (1960), 'Dialects of Tamil, 3', *Archiv Orientálni*, vol. 28, pp. 414–56.

ZVELEBIL, K. (1961), 'Some features of Dindigul Tamil', *Te. P. Mī, Manivirā Malar* (T. P. Meenakshisundaram Commemoration Volume), pp. 424–6, Coimbatore.

11 C. Geertz

Linguistic Etiquette

Excerpt from C. Geertz, *The Religion of Java*, Free Press, 1960.

The entire etiquette system is perhaps best summed up and symbolized in the way the Javanese use their language. In Javanese it is nearly impossible to say anything without indicating the social relationship between the speaker and the listener in terms of status and familiarity. Status is determined by many things – wealth, descent, education, occupation, age, kinship, and nationality, among others, but the important point is that the choice of linguistic forms as well as speech style is in every case partly determined by the relative status (or familiarity) of the conversers. The difference is not minor, a mere *du* and *Sie* difference. To greet a person lower than oneself (or someone with whom one is intimate) one says *Apa paḍa slamet*, but one greets a superior (or someone one knows only slightly) with *Menapa sami sugeng* – both meaning 'Are you well?' *Pandjenengan saking tindak pundi?* and *Kowé seka endi?* are the same question 'Where are you coming from?', in the first case addressed to a superior, in the second to an inferior. Clearly, a peculiar obsession is at work here.

Basically, what is involved is that the Javanese pattern their speech behavior in terms of the same *alus* to *kasar* axis around which they organize their social behavior generally. A number of words (and some affixes) are made to carry in addition to their normal linguistic meaning what might be called a 'status meaning'; i.e., when used in actual conversation they convey not only their fixed detonative meaning 'house', 'body', 'eat', 'walk', 'you', 'passive voice', but also a connotative meaning concerning the status of and/or degree of familiarity between the speaker and the listener. As a result, several words may denote the same normal linguistic meaning but differ in the status connotation they convey. Thus, for 'house' we have three forms (*omah, grija, dalem*), each connoting a progressively higher relative status of the listener with respect to the speaker. Some normal linguistic meanings are even more finely divided (*kowé, sampéjan, pandjenengan, pandjenengan dalem*, for ascending values of 'you'), others less (*di-* and *dipun-*) for the passive voice; but most normal meanings, taking the vocabulary as a whole, are not divided at all. Thus the word for 'table' is *medja* no matter to whom one is speaking.[1]

A further complication is that status meanings are communicated in speech not only intentionally in terms of word selection *within* the speaker's dialect but unintentionally in terms of the dialect he uses as a whole. Not only are there 'levels' of speech within the dialect which are ranked in terms of their status (or *alus/kasar*) connotations; the various dialects in the community as a whole are also ranked in terms of the *alus* to *kasar* spectrum, this latter sort of ranking being characteristic, of course, of any stratified society.

In order to clarify the relationship between the intra-dialect and inter-dialect systems of status symbolization, one voluntary and one involuntary, I offer the accompanying three charts depicting paradigmatically how a single sentence alters within each of the dialects and among them. Table 1 shows the speech range in status terms for what I would call the non-*prijaji* but urbanized and at least slightly educated group, which would include the better educated *abangans*, most urban *santris*, and even some of the lower *prijajis*, particularly when they are mixing with people outside their own immediate circle. It is, then, the most common dialect in the town. Table 2 shows the dialect of most peasants and uneducated townsmen, which is the most common style of all in terms of sheer numbers of users. Table 3 depicts the *prijaji* dialect, which, although spoken by a relatively small group of people, provides an ideal model of correct speech for the whole society.

The English sentence selected as an example is: Are you going to eat rice and cassava now? The Javanese words (low forms first) are as follows:

Are	*apa/napa/menapa*
you	*kowé/sampéjan/pandjenengan*
going	*arep/adjeng/baḍé*
to eat	*mangan/neḍa/ḍahar*
rice	*sega/sekul*
and	*lan/kalijan*
cassava	*kaspé*
now	*saiki/saniki/samenika*

1. Although in terms of the total Javanese vocabulary the number of words which show formal changes in terms of status connotations are relatively small in percentage, since they tend to be the most frequently occurring in actual speech, in word counts of common utterances the percentage of status-expression forms is quite high. In general it may be said that there is no set rule by which one can determine which words change in different status situations and which do not, except a vague one that the commoner the word and the more it denotes something fairly closely associated with human beings, the more likely it is that it will have such forms.

Table 1 Dialect of non-Prijaji, urbanized, somewhat educated persons

Level	are	you	going	to eat	rice	and	cassava	now	Complete sentence
3a		pandjenengan		ḍahar		kalijan		samenika	Menapa pandjenengan baḍé ḍahar sekul kalijan kaspé samenika?
3	—— menapa		baḍé		sekul				Menapa sampéjan baḍé neḍa sekul kalijan kaspé samenika?
2	—— napa	sampéjan	adjeng	neḍa		lan	kaspé	saniki	Napa sampéjan adjeng neḍa sekul lan kaspé saniki?
1a					sega				Apa sampéjan arep neḍa sega lan kaspé saiki?
1	—— apa	kowé	arep	mangan				saiki	Apa kowé arep mangan sega lan kaspé saiki?

Table 2 Dialect of peasants and uneducated townspeople

Level	are	you	going	to eat	rice	and	cassava	now	Complete sentence
2	napa	—— sampéjan	adjeng	neḍa	sekul	lan	kaspé	saniki	Napa sampéjan adjeng neḍa sekul lan kaspé saniki?
1a				neḍa	sega			saiki	Apa sampéjan arep neḍa sega lan kaspé saiki?
1	—— apa	kowé	arep	mangan	sega				Apa kowé arep mangan sega lan kaspé saiki?

Table 3 Dialect of the Prijajis

Level	are	you	going	to eat	rice	and	cassava	now	Complete sentence
3a		pandjenengan	badé	dahar	sekul	kalijan	kaspé	samenika	Menapa pandjenengan badé dahar sekul kalijan kaspé samenika?
	menapa								
3		sampéjan	badé	neda	sekul	kalijan	kaspé	samenika	Menapa sampéjan badé neda sekul kalijan kaspé samenika?
1b		pandjenengan	arep	dahar	sega	lan	kaspé	saiki	Apa pandjenengan arep dahar sega lan kaspé saiki?
	apa								
1a		sampéjan	arep	neda	sega	lan	kaspé	saiki	Apa sampéjan arep neda sega lan kaspé saiki?
1		kowé	arep	mangan	sega	lan	kaspé	saiki	Apa kowé arep mangan sega lan kaspé saiki?

The numbers at the sides of the charts indicate the levels, and the sentences, on the right, derived by reading across the chart at each level, are those available to a speaker in the particular dialect concerned. This range of sentences does not represent a mere theoretical set of possibilities. All of these variations are used every day. Moreover the Javanese have names for each of the levels. Level 3a is *krama inggil*; level 3 is *krama biasa*, or just *krama*; level 2 is *krama madya*, or just *madya*. (These three highest levels are often referred to merely as *basa* or language, although by high *prijajis* only the first two would be so considered.) Level 1a is either *ngoko madya*, or just *madya*; and level 1 is *ngoko biasa*, or just *ngoko*. Level 1b, a *prijaji* specialty, is called *ngoko sae* ('fine *ngoko*') or *ngoko alus*.

Krama, *madya*, and *ngoko* – or high, middle, and low – are the three main levels expressing status and/or familiarity available to speakers in the language. They represent sets of linked conjugates (*menapa ... badé ... samenika*; *napa ... adjeng ... saniki*; *apa ... arep ... saiki*; etc.), the occurrence of one of which for any given meaning (e.g., *menapa/napa/apa*) will predict the occurrence of the other if the meaning concerned occurs (i.e., *badé/adjeng/arep*; or *samenika/saniki/saiki*, etc.). In some cases the *madya* conjugate is the same as the *ngoko* (e.g. *lan*); sometimes it is the same as the *krama* (e.g. *sampéjan, neda, sekul*); and of course, sometimes the conjugate is the same in all three cases (e.g. *kaspé*).

In addition to these sets of linked conjugates, there is a group of special words, mostly referring to people, their parts, possessions and actions, which occur independently of the first kinds of conjugates and which act to raise the level of speech indicated by the first, inevitable selection, one 'notch' higher – or, better, one-half notch. *Dahar* and *pandjenengan* are such words in the above sentences, raising level 3, *krama biasa* (literally: 'usual' or 'common' *krama*) to level 3a, *krama inggil* ('high' *krama*). In the *ngoko* level, the use of *krama* words (e.g., *sampéjan*, or *neḍa* in the above) also has an honorific effect, lifting *ngoko biasa* (level 1), to *ngoko madya* (level 1a). As these *krama* words employed in *ngoko* sentences occur with the same meanings as the special honorifics, they might be called 'low honorifics', in contrast to the special 'high honorifics', such as *ḍahar*, *pandjenengan*. Finally, the use of high honorifics in a *ngoko* context yields level 1b, *ngoko sae*. As a result, the intra-dialect system of status symbolization consists, at the most, of three 'stylemes' (high, middle and low) and two types of honorifics (high and low). The honorifics occur, at least in the dialects described here, only with the high and low stylemes, never with the middle one.[2]

2. In utterances of more than minimal length the chance that at least one *krama/madya/ngoko* style marker will occur is nearly unity. I owe the suggestion to treat the 'style' problem and the 'high word' problem separately to Mr Rufus Hendon,

On the basis, then, of how many stylemes and how many types of honorific are customarily employed and what combinations occur, the three 'class dialects' diagrammed in the charts are distinguished. In the dialect of the non-*prijaji*, urbanized, and at least somewhat educated group, Table 1, all three stylemes are customarily used (high, middle, low) and both types of honorific (high and low). Since the high honorifics occur only with the high style and the low ones only with the low style,[3] a speaker of this dialect has five possibilities, represented by the five sentences: 3a, *krama inggil* (i.e., high styleme and high honorifics); 3, *krama biasa* (high styleme without honorifics); 2, *krama madya* (middle styleme without honorifics); 1a, *ngoko madya* (middle styleme with low honorifics); 1, *ngoko biasa* (low styleme, no honorifics).

In the peasant and uneducated townsman dialect or idiom, Table 2, two stylemes (middle and low) and one type of honorific (low) customarily occur, the honorifics occurring only with the low styleme, to raise *ngoko biasa* to *ngoko madya*.[4] Thus the possibilities for the expression of 'status meaning' for a speaker of this dialect are only three: 2, *krama madya* (middle styleme without honorifics); 1a, *ngoko madya* (low styleme plus low honorifics); 1, *ngoko biasa* (low styleme, no honorifics).

Finally, in the *prijaji* dialect, the middle styleme – considered to be vulgar – drops out. Thus, there are two stylemes (high and low) and both high and low honorifics, the high occurring with both high and low stylemes, the low, again, only with the high. This gives five possibilities: 3a, *krama inggil* (high styleme plus high honorifics); 3, *krama biasa* (high styleme without honorifics); 1b, *ngoko sae* (low styleme, high honorifics); 1a, *ngoko madya* (low styleme plus low honorifics); and 1, *ngoko biasa* (low styleme, no honorifics).

It will be noted that sentences 3 and 3a are available to both *prijaji* and educated townsmen; sentence 2 to both educated and uneducated townsmen and to peasants; and 1 and 1a to all three groups (although, as mentioned, 1a tends to be omitted by the more *alus* among the *prijaji*); 1b is characteristically employed only by *prijajis*.

---

who has also suggested that the three linked conjugate sets be dissolved into a new unit, called a 'styleme,' which then occurs once in (nearly) every sentence, and that the high words, which occur sporadically, be called 'honorifics'. The formal parts of the above discussion are heavily dependent upon his analysis.

3. As the two types of honorific are in complementary distribution, high ones occurring only with high stylemes, low ones with low, the difference between them is redundant and could be eliminated in a more elegant analysis.

4. As low honorifics are but high styleme 'markers' occurring in low styleme contexts, a combination of high styleme and low honorifics is, of course, impossible for the honorifics could not be distinguished from the styleme markers.

Given this brief and over-condensed formal analysis of the level problem, the sense in which Javanese linguistic behavior is but a part of their wider system of etiquette and, in fact, a simplified and summarizing model of it is more easily set forth. First, as already noted, the levels themselves reflect the *kasar* to *alus* continuum. *Ngoko*, level 1, is the basic language. People think in this, fall into it whenever the urge to express themselves overcomes the desire to maintain propriety, and generally regard it, like the peasant himself, as the rough, down-to-earth, and necessary foundation on top of which all the *prijaji* fancy work is erected. It is for this reason that all Javanese terms in this report have been given in their *ngoko* forms.

As one moves up the level ladder from *ngoko* toward *krama*, level 3, and *krama inggil*, level 3a, the manner of speaking shifts too: the higher the level one is using, the more slowly and softly one speaks – and the more evenly, in terms both of rhythm and pitch. As, on the whole, the 'higher' conjugates tend to be longer than the lower ones (*kowé/sampéjan/pandjenengan* – and, for the *very* elevated, *pandjenengan dalem* – for 'you'; *kéné/-ingriki* for 'here'), the high language levels, when spoken correctly, have a kind of stately pomp which can make the simplest conversation seem like a great ceremony. Like the forms of etiquette generally, the patterns of linguistic etiquette modulate, regularize, and smooth the processes of social interaction into an *alus*, unvarying flow of quiet, emotionally tranquilizing propriety.

It has already been pointed out how etiquette patterns, including language, tend to be regarded by the Javanese as a kind of emotional capital which may be invested in putting others at ease. Politeness is something one directs toward others; one surrounds the other with a wall of behavioral (*lair*) formality which protects the stability of his inner life (*batin*). Etiquette is a wall built around one's inner feelings, but it is, paradoxically, always a wall someone else builds, at least in part. He may choose to build such a wall for one of two reasons. He and the other person are at least approximate status equals and not intimate friends; and so he responds to the other's politeness to him with an equal politeness. Or the other is clearly his superior, in which case he will, in deference to the other's greater spiritual refinement, build him a wall without any demand or expectation that you reciprocate. This is, of course, but a restatement of the *aṇḍap-asor* pattern discussed more generally above. But in terms of language it is possible to state the exact nature of this pattern, the core of Javanese etiquette, in a rather more precise, abstract and formal manner.

If we take the six levels (or three levels and three half-levels) of speech present in one dialect or another in Modjokuto, we can diagram them in terms of the 'wall' metaphor as follows:

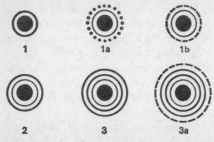

Figure 1

The solid center is intended to represent the *batin*, the inner life. The solid lines represent the stylemes – the low styleme taken as one 'layer', the middle as two, the high as three. Low honorifics are represented by a dotted line, high by a dashed. The circles – solid, dotted, or dashed – around the solid center are thus intended to diagram the *lair*, the behavioral world of etiquette. The higher the level of language spoken *to* an individual, then, the thicker the wall of etiquette protecting his emotional life.

In such terms one can diagram nearly any relationship between two individuals of whatever rank or familiarity.[5] Thus, two close friends of equal rank (that two close friends will be of roughly equal rank is nearly a tautology for most Modjokuto Javanese) will both speak *ngoko* to one another:

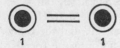

Figure 2

A high official, say the District Officer, and an ordinary educated urbanite will follow a sharply asymmetrical pattern:

5. One complication is that it is not entirely true that the status and/or familiarity relationship between speaker and hearer is the only determinant of status forms, because sometimes the status of a third person referred to, especially if he be quite high, may determine the form used: thus, in speaking to a lower-status person one will use the high, *krama*, forms of 'house' when speaking of the one the District Officer lives in.

Figure 3

– i.e. the District Officer will speak *ngoko biasa*, the ordinary man, *krama inggil*.

Two ordinary townsmen who are not intimate friends tend to speak *krama madya* reciprocally:

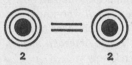

Figure 4

Two *prijajis* who are not intimate friends tend to speak *krama biasa* (if particularly elevated, *krama inggil*) reciprocally:

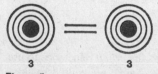

Figure 5

A peasant speaking to a higher status person will use *krama madya*, for the most part, for he doesn't use *krama biasa* or *krama inggil*:

Figure 6

One might get a similar pattern if a 'lower-class' townsman were con- versing with a 'middle-class' townsman, say a carpenter with a well-off storekeeper.

A peasant speaking to a fellow peasant with whom he is not intimate might use *krama madya*, but more commonly he will use *ngoko madya*, reciprocally:

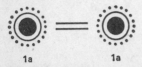

1a   1a

Figure 7

Middle- or lower-ranking townsmen who are casual acquaintances might also use reciprocal *ngoko madya* or *krama madya*, depending mostly on the occasion, the content of what was being communicated, and so on.

Ngoko sae, the *prijaji* speciality, is used between *prijaji* who know one another fairly well and are of equal status but regard each other to be so elevated as to make the reciprocal use of *ngoko biasa*, or *ngoko madya*, which might sometimes be used in this context, unseemly:

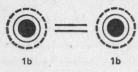

1b   1b

Figure 8

The inclusion of this level in the dialect shows the *prijaji* reluctance to use very low language to anyone of much status. *Ngoko sae* is used to close friends and relatives whom one knows well enough to use familiar speech but to whom one wishes nevertheless to show proper respect. Thus sen- tences on this level resolve the conflict between familiarity and respect implicit in the Javanese etiquette pattern with a greater delicacy and subtlety than is possible in either the 'urbanite' or 'peasant' dialects.

A thorough semantic study of the contexts within which the different levels are employed would in itself be a complex and extended investiga- tion, for the number of variables specifically determining the selection of a particular level are very numerous. They include not only qualitative characteristics of the speakers – age, sex, kinship relation,[6] occupation,

6. For a discussion of the selection of language levels within the kinship and family context, see H. Geertz, (1961).

wealth, education, religious commitment, family background – but also more general factors: for instance, the social setting (one would be likely to use a higher level to the same individual at a wedding than in the street); the content of the conversation (in general, one uses lower levels when speaking of commercial matters, higher ones if speaking of religious or aesthetic matters); the history of social interaction between the speakers (one will tend to speak rather high, if one speaks at all, with someone with whom one has quarreled); the presence of a third person (one tends to speak higher to the same individual if others are listening). All these play a role, to say nothing of individual idiosyncratic attitudes. Some people, particularly, it seems, wealthier traders and self-confident village chiefs, who tend to think the whole business rather uncomfortable and somewhat silly, speak *ngoko* to almost everyone except the very high in status. Others will shift levels on any pretext. A complete listing of the determinants of level selection would, therefore, involve a thorough analysis of the whole framework of Javanese culture.

In terms of the more general relationship between the Javanese language and Javanese culture, it is of interest to note how the three charts when taken together present a picture of how the three groups – 'urbanites' 'peasants' and *prijajis* – perceive the Modjokuto-wide status system, the varying form of their etiquette systems, and how they are related to each other – how, in essence, the ideal model set by the *prijajis* refracts through the rest of the social structure. The *prijaji* chart, Table 3, with its excluded middle, shows the *prijaji* tendency to put people into two categories: those to whom one speaks respectfully, equals and superiors (i.e., other *prijajis*); and those to whom one speaks familiarly, inferiors (i.e., non-*prijajis*) and very close friends and relatives. As noted, level 1b, *ngoko sae* forms a nice compromise between respect and familiarity, and among the more refined *prijajis* in the larger towns, the omission of *ngoko madya*, 1a, in their dialect would even further strengthen the dichotomous nature of their model of the status system.

The peasant chart, Table 2, shows both the peasants' lessened sense of internal differentiation of status within their own group and their view of the whole structure from the bottom, the upper reaches of the system being mostly beyond their ken. The chart, in fact, provides a concrete case in point of the relationship between gentry and peasant culture patterns outlined earlier. Gentry patterns are reflected dimly and in a somewhat distorted fashion in the peasant context, but they are reflected there. *Prijaji* speakers of (what they regard as) 'correct' Javanese are continually making fun – to one another, or to the ethnographer – of 'ignorant' villagers who use *tjinten* as the high form of *tjina* (Chinese), when 'really' there is no higher form. Similarly for the village use of *konten* for *kori* (door) and, worst of all, their creation of high forms for place names which never should alter: *Kedinten* for *Kediri*; *Surobringo* for *Surabaja*.[7] For the *abangan* peasant at any rate, *prijaji* speech, like *prijaji* etiquette, religion, art and style of life, is the ideal form, even though they may regard it as too difficult and restrictive for their own use. For the *santri* the religion and art drop out as patterns worthy of emulation, but the speech, etiquette, and style of life remain as models.

Table 1 shows the results of the jostling together of people from all walks of life in the urban context. Since the average middle-rank urbanite mixes with everyone from *prijaji* to peasant, he employs whatever language level seems reasonable in the situation. To speak respectfully to a peasant, he will use *krama madya*, level 2; to a high *prijaji*, *krama inggil*, 3a; and to people of his own rank or slightly higher he will use *krama biasa*, 3. But he will have little use for the kind of subtleties represented by level 1 b, *ngoko sae*. Thus, in place of the dichotomous (gentry versus the field) view of the status structure of the *prijaji* and the relatively speaking more equalitarian view of the peasant, the urbanite sees a more even gradation of status over quite a wide range.

Lastly, a word should be said about the increasing popularity of Indonesian, the national language based on Malay, among certain groups, particularly the urban youth and the political elite of the town. Indonesian appeals to those whose sense of political nationality as Indonesians rather than as Javanese is most developed, to those who are interested in the cultural products of the new Indonesia's mass media (newspapers, magazines, movies, radio), and those who wish to take leadership positions in government and business. But the use of Indonesian, now taught in all the schools, is spreading very rapidly beyond these somewhat special groups to nearly all townspeople and to a greater and greater number of peasants. As most available reading matter is now in Indonesian rather than Javanese, literacy more or less implies Indonesian, although a reading knowledge does not, of course, imply its use in everyday life. In any case, although the use of Indonesian for everyday conversation is still mostly confined to the more sophisticated urbanites, and its use suggests something of an air of 'public speaking' for most Javanese, it is rapidly becoming more and more an integral part of their daily cultural life and will

7. These 'mistakes' are based on false analogies to types of formal alteration which are common in moving from high to low Javanese. Though there are no specific rules for such changes, a few sorts of changes occur repeatedly (lower terms given first): a shift of final vowel from *a* to *i*: *djawa/djawi*, 'Javanese'; a shift form *i* to *os*: *ganti/gantos*, 'change'; *3* a kind of 'pig-latin' form in the higher term involving, among other processes, various forms of medial or final nasalization: *kena/kenging* 'hit' 'may'; *karep/kadjeng*, 'wish', 'want'; *kari/kantun*, 'left behind'; a complete change of form: *omah/grija*, 'house'.

become even more so as the present generation of school children grows to adulthood. That it will, in the foreseeable future, entirely displace Javanese is, of course, entirely unlikely. Rather, it seems destined, at least in the short run, to become part of the general Javanese linguistic system, to become one more type of sentence among those available, to be selected for use in certain special contexts and for certain special purposes.

Before the meeting began, when they (the members of a mystical religious sect) were discussing language, Sudjoko said that one simply couldn't use Indonesian to discuss mystical philosophy. When I asked him why, he said: 'Well, all the terms are in Javanese in the first place; and in the second place Javanese fits the kind of thought better. It would be very hard to express such thoughts in Indonesian; it just wouldn't feel right.' Contrariwise, he said that, giving a political speech in Javanese is one of the hardest things in the world to do; it just doesn't seem to have the expressions. Someone then noted that even when one goes to a political meeting in the village and they use Javanese, many of the words are Indonesian words which, although the people in the audience perhaps cannot use or at least cannot make into whole Indonesian sentences, they nevertheless understand quite well.

Reference

GEERTZ, H. (1961), *The Javanese Family*, Free Press.

12 W. Labov

The Study of Language in its Social Context

Excerpts from W. Labov, 'The study of language in its social context', *Studium Generale*, vol. 23, 1970, pp. 30–87.

Methodology

In any academic course that deals with research in the speech community, there is always a great deal of interest in the first steps to be taken: 'What do you say to people?' This is not a trivial question. The elementary steps of locating and contacting informants, and getting them to talk freely in a recorded interview, are formidable problems for students. It is an error for anyone to pass over these questions, for in the practices and techniques that have been worked out are embodied many important principles of linguistic and social behavior. Close examination of these methodological assumptions and findings will tell us a great deal about the nature of discourse and the functions of language.

The fundamental sociolinguistic question is posed by the need to understand why anyone says anything. There are methodological questions of sampling and recording which merely set the stage for the basic problems. It was noted above that good data requires good recording, especially for the grammatical analysis of natural speech. After the crucial variables have been defined and isolated, a great deal can be done with hand-written notes. But our initial approach to the speech community is governed by the need to obtain large volumes of well-recorded natural speech.

We can isolate five methodological axioms supported by the findings of the field research projects cited which lead to a methodological paradox; the solution to this paradox is the central methodological problem.

Style shifting. As far as we can see, there are no single-style speakers. Some informants show a much wider range of style shifting than others, but every speaker we have encountered shows a shift of some linguistic variables as the social context and topic change. Some of these shifts can be detected qualitatively in the minor self-corrections of the speaker, which are almost always in a uniform direction.

Attention. There are a great many styles and stylistic dimensions that can be isolated by an analyst. But we find that *styles can be ranged along a single dimension, measured by the amount of attention paid to speech.* The most important way in which this attention is exerted is in audio-monitoring one's own speech, though other forms of monitoring also take place.[1] This axiom (really an hypothesis) receives strong support from the fact that speakers show the same level for many important linguistic variables in casual speech, when they are least involved, and excited speech, when they are deeply involved emotionally. The common factor for both styles is that the minimum attention is available for monitoring one's own speech.

The vernacular. Not every style or point on the stylistic continuum is of equal interest to linguists. Some styles show irregular phonological and grammatical patterns, with a great deal of 'hypercorrection'. In other styles, we find more systematic speech, where the fundamental relations which determine the course of linguistic evolution can be seen most clearly. This is the 'vernacular' – the style in which the minimum attention is given to the monitoring of speech. Observation of the vernacular gives us the most systematic data for our analysis of linguistic structure.

Formality. Any systematic observation of a speaker defines a formal context in which more than the minimum attention is paid to speech. In the main body of an interview, where information is requested and supplied, we would not expect to find the vernacular used. No matter how casual or friendly the speaker may appear to us, we can always assume that he has a more casual speech, another style in which he jokes with his friends and argues with his wife.

Good data. No matter what other methods may be used to obtain samples of speech (group sessions, anonymous observation), the only way to obtain sufficient good data on the speech of any one person is through an individual, tape-recorded interview: that is through the most obvious kind of systematic observation.[2]

Observer's paradox. We are then left with the *observer's paradox*: the aim of linguistic research in the community must be to find out how people talk when they are not being systematically observed; yet we can only obtain this data by systematic observation. The problem is of course not

1. Experiments with white noise which eliminate audio-monitoring show much the same kind of style shift that we observe when attention to speech is distracted by other means.
2. There are some situations where candid recording is possible and permissible, but the quality of the sound is so poor that such recordings are of confirmatory value at best.

insoluble: we must either find ways of supplementing the formal interviews with other data, or change the structure of the interview situation
by one means or another. Of the various research projects mentioned
above, not all have been successful in overcoming this paradox. Many
investigators have completed their work with only a limited range of
stylistic data, concentrated in the more formal ends of the spectrum.
Systematic study of the vernacular has been accomplished primarily in
Gumperz's work, in our own work in New York City and in urban ghetto
areas, and in the Fishman–Gumperz–Ma project in Jersey City.

One way of overcoming the paradox is to break through the constraints
of the interview situation by various devices which divert attention away
from speech, and allow the vernacular to emerge. This can be done in
various intervals and breaks which are so defined that the subject unconsciously assumes that he is not at that moment being interviewed (Labov,
1966). We can also involve the subject in questions and topics which
recreate strong emotions he has felt in the past, or involve him in other
contexts. One of the most successful questions of this type is one dealing
with the 'danger of death': 'Have you ever been in a situation where you
were in serious danger of being killed?' Narratives given in answer to this
question almost always show a shift of style away from careful speech
towards the vernacular.[3]

One cannot expect that such devices will always be successful in obtaining a radical shift of style. A more systematic approach uses the normal
interaction of the peer-group to control speech instead of the one-to-one
confrontation of subject and interviewer. In Gumperz' work (1964), the
fundamental data was obtained through recorded sessions with natural
groups. In our work in South Central Harlem, (Labov *et al.* 1968) we
studied adolescent peer groups through long-term participant observation.
Individual interviews were carried out with all members of the group,
yielding the individual data we needed on each individual. A series of
group sessions were held in which the speech of each member (picked up
from a lavaliere microphone) was recorded on a separate track. There was
no obvious constraint in these group sessions; the adolescents behaved
much as usual, and most of the interaction – physical and verbal – took
place between the members. As a result, the effect of systematic observation was reduced to a minimum.

3. One of the most interesting aspects of this question is that it involves a yes-no
answer, which we normally avoid. The mechanism seems to be that the informant
is willing to commit himself to the fact of having been in such a situation, though he
may be unwilling to volunteer an account. But having so committed himself, he finds
it very difficult to avoid giving a full account when the interviewer asks, after some
delay, 'What happened?' Otherwise, he would appear to have made a false claim.

Rapid and anonymous interviews

In the methods just described, the identity and demographic position of each subject is well known. One can also carry out systematic observation anonymously, in conversations which are not defined as interviews. In certain strategic locations, a great many subjects can be studied in a short period of time, and if their social identity is well defined by the objective situation, the findings can be very rich. In the study of the New York City community, I confirmed the results of a sociolinguistic survey by rapid and anonymous interviews with employees of three large, well-stratified department stores (Labov, 1966, pp. 63–87). The data was easily transcribed in writing, since only one variable was studied: post-vocalic (r) in the expression 'fourth floor'. The sources of error in this study were exactly complementary to those of survey interviews: the data on the demographic characteristics of the population was very rough, but the bias of the interview situation was absent. Subjects did not consider that they had been interviewed or observed, or that any conversation out of the ordinary had occurred. Other such studies have been carried out since in this model, asking for various kinds of information from a stratified population.

Unsystematic observations

The crucial question to be asked in any of these studies is whether one has indeed obtained data on the fundamental, systematic vernacular form of the language. Unsystematic and candid observation of speech at various strategic points can tell us a great deal about our success in this regard. One can record a number of constant and variable features from large numbers of people in public places such as trains, buses, lunch counters, ticket lines, zoos – wherever enough members of the speech community are gathered together so that their speech is naturally and easily heard by others. There are many biases built into such observations – loud and less educated talkers, for example, are strongly selected. But as a corrective to the bias of the interview situation, such data can be very valuable.

Mass media

It is also possible to obtain some systematic data from radio and television broadcasts, although here the selection and the stylistic constraints are usually very strong. In recent years, we have had a great many direct interviews at the scene of disasters, where the speakers are too strongly under the immediate influence of the event to monitor their own speech. Conversation programs and speeches at public events can give us a good cross-section of a population, but here the style is even more formal than that we would obtain in a face-to-face interview.

The formal end of the stylistic range

It is relatively easy to extend the range of styles used by the speaker towards the formal end of the spectrum, where more attention is given to speech. There are many questions which naturally evoke more careful speech (such as questions about speech itself). In most of the urban studies carried out so far, reading texts were used to study phonological variations. In general, linguistic variables show a marked shift from the most formal elicitation to the least formal reading. One can obtain a wide stylistic range within types of reading texts. A well written text that reads well, focusing on vernacular or adolescent themes, will yield much less formal speech than a list of isolated words. Minimal pairs can be embedded in such a test, so that the speaker is not made aware of the contrast; his pronunciation can be compared to his reading of an isolated minimal pair where his attention is directed specifically to the variable being studied, and its use in differentiating words. One can observe the minimal pair *god–guard* in a passage such as '. . . I told him to ask a subway guard. My god! I thought, that's one sure way to get lost in New York City.' Secondly, *god* and *guard* may be included in a long list of other words. Finally, the speaker may be asked to pronounce the two words and say whether they sound the same or different to him. We thus had five stylistic levels for the study of post-vocalic (*r*):

1. Casual speech
2. Careful speech
3. Reading
4. Word lists
5. Minimal pairs

Levine and Crockett (1966) and Anshen (1969) used another method to extend the stylistic range of readings. Sentences were constructed in which the variables were embedded, and at other points in the same sentences blanks were inserted for the subject to fill in lexical items as he read, diverting his attention from the variables. The pronunciation of the phonological variables in this context showed less (r) than in the reading of isolated words.

A number of formal tests do not require any reading on the part of the subjects. *Perception tests* of the ABX form provide useful information: in the case of total merger of a phonological distinction, speakers cannot hear whether X is closer to A or B; but where variable rules are operating, and the merger is not complete, they will show partial success. A surprising amount of grammatical information can be obtained by repetition tests with children two to five years old, but we found to our surprise that with speakers of non-standard dialects the underlying grammatical rules of much older subjects, ten to seventeen years old, controlled the form of their repetitions. Speakers of non-standard Negro English had no difficulty in repeating accurately long sentences within their own grammatical system, but many sentences in standard English were given back instantly in vernacular form (Labov *et al.*, 1968, 39).[4]

A number of formal tests have been developed to isolate social attitudes towards language, and the social information carried by dialect forms. One can play taped sections of 'typical' speakers, and ask subjects to identify their ethnic background, race, social class (Labov *et al.*, 1968, 4.4; Brown, 1969). This tells us whether or not the listeners can obtain this social information from speech, but not where the information is located – in the speaker's grammar, phonology, intonation, or voice qualifiers. *Subjective reaction tests* allow us to separate the linguistic variables from personal factors. The 'matched guise' technique used by Lambert and his students (Lambert, 1968) presents for the subject a series of tape-recorded sections in which voices of the same speakers are heard using different languages or dialects. The subjects are asked to make judgments of the speakers' personalities. As long as they cannot know how they have rated the same speakers before, they unconsciously translate their social attitudes towards language into differential judgements of the speaker's honesty, reliability, intelligence, etc. In our own subjective reaction tests (Labov, 1966, pp. 405–450, Labov *et al.*, 1968; 4.6) the same speakers are heard reading sentences which differ principally by their treatment of the linguistic variable being studied. The subjects' evaluation of the social significance of this variable is registered by their differential responses to the matched sentences, on such scales as 'What is the highest job the speaker could hold, talking as he does?' or 'If the speaker was in a street fight, how likely would he be to come out on top?'

Speakers' attitudes towards well-established linguistic variables will also be shown in *self-evaluation tests*. When asked which of several forms are characteristic of their own speech, their answers reflect which form they believe has prestige or is 'correct', rather than the form they actually use. Here again, this kind of test data cannot be interpreted without data on the subjects' actual speech patterns.

We can investigate speakers' awareness of stigmatized well-marked social variants by *classroom correction tests*, asking them to correct sentences which depart from school or classroom models (Labov *et al.*, 1968; 4.4). But it is almost impossible to obtain interpretable results on the reverse type of *vernacular correction tests*, in which the subject is

4. These observations have since been confirmed by larger-scale tests carried out with school populations, where the subjects' relation to the vernacular was not well known.

asked to correct standard prestige forms to the non-standard vernacular. The influence of the formal test situation is such that the subject cannot perceive accurately the non-standard rules. There is some evidence that the audio-monitoring norm which governed production of the non-standard form in childhood is replaced by the prestige norm, so that it is not possible in general for most speakers to direct their attention accurately to non-standard rules. This result reflects an important axiom of vernacular shifting: whenever a subordinate dialect is in contact with a superordinate dialect, answers given in any formal test situation will shift from the subordinate towards the superordinate in an irregular and unsystematic manner. The terms 'superordinate' and 'subordinate' here refer to any hierarchical social dimension equivalent to 'prestige' and 'stigmatized'. Some linguists hope that by 'educating' the informant in the goals of the analysis, it will be possible to diminish this effect, and gradually obtain answers characteristic of the pure vernacular. But this is an illusion. Instead, the subject may use his knowledge of the prestige dialect to avoid giving any vernacular form which is identical or similar to the standard, and so produce stereotyped forms which are simply a collection of the 'most different' or 'worst' sentence types. Speakers who have had extensive contact with the superordinate form no longer have clear intuitions about their vernacular available for inspection.[5]

There is further reason to regard as suspect, data on a non-standard vernacular gathered from an 'educated' informant. Usually the investigator speaks the standard superordinate dialect which is dominant in this face-to-face interviewing situation. The informant's capacity to learn languages is operating at all times, and there is evidence that his grammatical rules will be heavily influenced by the standard during this period of elicitation.[6]

Once in a great while we encounter an informant who seems almost immune to 'correction' of this sort – who seems to have direct access to his intuitions, despite his knowledge of the standard dialect. An important task for psycholinguists is to identify other traits which accompany or determine this behavior, so that we will be able to search a given population for 'ideal' informants. But it will always be necessary to calibrate the informant's responses against other data of the vernacular to see if he does indeed have access to his original rules. To evaluate this data, we

5. This is obviously true in the case of children. One cannot ask young children whether a non-standard sentence of theirs is well-formed, nor ask adults to reconstruct their childhood grammars. It is true in general that learning one series of rules closely related to the older series makes it impossible to reconstruct the earlier situation.

6. Our own field worker in South Central Harlem, John Lewis, showed a strong shift of the non-standard variables we were investigating from the time that he was first interviewed (1965) to the time that he finished interviewing others (1967).

must already know the rules of the vernacular from the direct observation of casual speech. But the procedure is not entirely circular; for if we have confidence in the introspections of 'immune' informants, we may obtain crucial data on forms which are too rare to find in any body of casual speech. Whether or not we are safe in extrapolating from observed stability on common forms to unobserved stability on rare forms is an open question.

These considerations do not necessarily apply to linguists studying languages through an intermediate language which is not marked socially with regard to their object language.[7] It is normal for a linguist who approaches a language for the first time to work with bilingual informants, who may not even be good speakers of the object language. Such preliminary steps in formal elicitation are of course necessary prerequisites to the accurate study of language in its social context. Good linguists can go further than this, and draw their best data from recordings of native speakers talking to each other – parallel to the group sessions mentioned above. The study of language in its social context can only be done when the language is 'known' in the sense that the investigator can understand rapid conversation. When an anthropological linguist enters into this more advanced study, then the axiom of vernacular shifting will apply, for there will inevitably be stylistic levels which he will want to distinguish.

Although one can achieve a certain amount of insight working with bilingual informants, it is doubtful if as much can be said for 'bi-dialectal' informants, if indeed such speakers exist. We have not encountered any non-standard speakers who gained good control of a standard language, and still retained control of the non-standard vernacular. Dialect differences depend upon low-level rules which appear as minor adjustments and extensions of contextual conditions, etc. It appears that such conditions inevitably interact, and although the speaker may indeed appear to be speaking the vernacular, close examination of his speech shows that his grammar has been heavily influenced by the standard. He may succeed in convincing his listeners that he is speaking the vernacular, but this impression seems to depend upon a number of unsystematic and heavily marked signals.

There are speakers in every community who are more aware than others of the prestige standard of speech, and whose behavior is more influenced by exterior standards of excellence. They will show greater style shifting than those who do not recognize such a standard. This trait can be

7. In his first approach to Lahu, a Lolo-Burmese language of Thailand and Burma, J. Matisoff used an English-Lahu bilingual speaker. It is his opinion that if he had used a more closely related language such as Thai, the distortion of the data would have been much greater.

measured by *linguistic insecurity tests*. For a selected list of socially marked variants, the subject is asked which of two forms is correct; and then which he actually uses himself. The index of linguistic insecurity is simply the number of items for which these two answers are different: that is, the extent to which the speaker recognizes an exterior standard of correctness different from his own speech (Labov, 1966, pp. 474–480). [. . .]

Sociolinguistic structure

We may define a *sociolinguistic variable* as one which is correlated with some non-linguistic variable of the social context: of the speaker, the addressee, the audience, the setting, etc. Some linguistic features (which we will call ·dicators) show a regular distribution over socio-economic, ethnic, or aɡe groups, but are used by each individual in more or less the same way in any context. If the social contexts concerned can be ordered in some kind of hierarchy (like socio-economic or age groups), these indicators can be said to be *stratified*. More highly developed socio-linguistic variables (which we will call *markers*) not only show social distribution, but also stylistic differentiation. As noted earlier, stylistic context can be ordered along a single dimension according to the amount of attention paid to speech, so that we have *stylistic* as well as *social strati-fication*. Early studies such as those of Fischer (1958) or Kučera (1961) observed linguistic variables only one dimension at a time, but more recent studies (Labov, 1966; Wolfram, 1969; Anshen, 1969) look at the interrelation of both dimensions.

A stable sociolinguistic marker: (*th*)

One of the most general and simple sociolinguistic markers in English is (th): the phonetic form of the voiceless interdental fricative /Θ/ in *thing*, *thick*, etc. The prestige form is universally the fricative, while affricates and stops are stigmatized. The influence of other languages without this inderdental fricative may reinforce the development of the stop form in various large cities of the United States, in Anglo-Irish and in NNE; but we also find this sociolinguistic variable in a great many other rural and urban areas in England and the United States. It has apparently had roughly the same status for at least two centuries, and probably more.

There are a number of technical questions in the definition of this variable: the simplest approach is to consider only initial position. In the numerical index to be used here, a stop [t] is counted as 2 points, the affricate [tΘ] as 1, and the prestige variant [Θ] as 0. Invariant use of the stop form would yield an index score of (th) −200; of the prestige form, (th) −00. Figure 2 shows both stylistic and social stratification of (*th*) in New York City displayed on one diagram (Labov, 1966, p. 260).

The vertical axis is the (th) index, and the horizontal axis shows contextual style, ranging from the most informal on the left to the most formal on the right as described in the first section. On the figure, the average (th) values for five different socio-economic groups are plotted, and scores for each group connected with straight lines. Figure 1 thus shows regular stratification of the (th) variable for each contextual style. This is merely one of many such sociolinguistic structures which might be displayed here; there are a number of common properties which Figure 1 exemplifies:

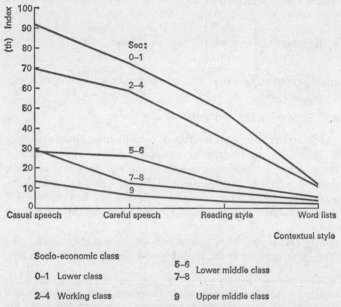

Figure 1 Stylistic and social stratification of *th* in *thing*, *thrice* etc. in New York City

1. In every context, members of the speech community are differentiated by their use of (*th*).

2. Yet every group is behaving in the same way, as indicated by the parallel slope of style shifting for ()*th*.

3. Since Figure 1 is not visible as a whole to members, facts (1) and (2) are not part of general knowledge. The portion of Figure 1 visible to any given individual is usually one vertical and one horizontal section: the range of style shifting used by his own group, and the stratified behavior of other groups in the few contexts where he interacts with them. He is not aware that others shift in the same way he does.

W. Labov 189

4. The same sociolinguistic variable is used to signal social and stylistic stratification. It may therefore be difficult to interpret any signal by itself – to distinguish, for example, a casual salesman from a careful pipefitter.[8]

5. Although it is impossible to predict for any one utterance which variant a speaker will use, the striking regularity of Figure 1 emerges from samples with as few as five individuals in one sub-group, and no more than five or ten utterances in a given style for each individual.

The pattern of Figure 1 shows us the exterior, sociolinguistic controls on the variable rule represented as **1**:

$$\begin{bmatrix} + \text{ cons} \\ - \text{ voc} \end{bmatrix} \rightarrow ([- \text{ cont}]) \ / \ \begin{bmatrix} - \text{ strid} \\ - \text{ back} \\ + \text{ cor} \end{bmatrix}^9 \qquad \qquad 1$$

The variable input to this rule may be shown as a function of socio-economic class and style:

$$k_0 = f(\text{SEC}, \text{Style}) = a(\text{SEC} + b(\text{Style}) + c \qquad \qquad 2$$

These general traits hold for a number of sociolinguistic markers which have been studied in the research groups cited. The complete view of social stylistic stratification is not available in most of these studies: some provide data on relatively small sections of Figure 1 and its equivalents, while others cover a wider range. But all of this data can be interpreted in terms of the configuration shown in Figure 1, and fitted into this framework consistently.

The variable (*th*) is one of a pair which are remarkably similar and parallel. The other member is the voiced interdental fricative (*dh*) in *this*,

8. This is one of the most striking findings of sociolinguistic research, since essays about social usage, written from 'common-sense' knowledge, have tried to distinguish 'functional varieties' and 'cultural levels' as completely independent dimensions. But their interdependence is shown in this and every other careful empirical study to date. Though it may seem inconvenient to have one variable operate on both dimensions, it seems to be an inevitable result of the sociolinguistic processes involving attention to speech and perception of norms, as outlined below.

9. The notation used here differs from that of Chomsky and Halle (1968) only in the use of parentheses around the right hand member to indicate a variable rule. This parenthesis convention provides the automatic interpretation that $\varphi = 1 - k_0$, developed further in (2). The rule may be read as 'Consonants variably lose their continuant or fricative character if they are non-strident and articulated with the forward part of the tongue'. In this form, the rule applies to the voiced counterpart (*dh*) which shows the same structure, and to all environments. Variable constraints may appear to indicate the difference between (*th*) and (*dh*) (as —a tense in the environment shown here) or as variables attached to the preceding or following segments. Our discussion here concerns the variable input k_0, and such details are left unspecified.

then, etc., which has been charted in the general study of New York City (Labov, 1966) and in the Negro community (Labov *et al.*, 1968; Anshen, 1969).[10] A very similar stable sociolinguistic pattern appears for unstressed (*ing*) in *working, nothing*, etc. Almost universally, the (*in*) variant is considered non-standard, and the sociolinguistic structure duplicates Figure 1 (Labov, 1966, p. 398). Confirming data appears in Fischer, 1958, and Anshen, 1969. Such stigmatized variables as negative concord and pronominal apposition have been studied by Shuy, Wolfram and Riley, 1967, for Detroit. Ma and Herasimchuk (see Fishman, 1968), examined style shifting of a number of Puerto Rican variables: final (S) as noted above; (R), the neutralization of *r* and *l*; (RR), alternation of (*r:*) and [ɣ]; and (D), the deletion of intervocalic (*d*).

Figure 1 also has some features that are not shared by all sociolinguistic variables. One can observe a sharp break between the working-class groups and the middle-class groups – a pattern which I have termed 'sharp' stratification (see also Wolfram, 1969, p. 147). There is very little overlap between the working-class treatment of (*th*) and the middle-class values, while that is not the case for many other variables (see Figure 2 below). In a stable sociolinguistic marker, this may reflect discontinuities in the over-all pattern of socio-economic stratification in the society.

Men versus women

There is another aspect to the social stratification of (*th*) which is not shown on Figure 1. In careful speech women use fewer stigmatized forms than men (Labov, 1966, p. 288), and are more sensitive than men to the prestige pattern. They show this in a sharper slope of style shifting, especially at the more formal end of the spectrum. This observation is confirmed innumerable times, in Fischer (1958), throughout Shuy and Fasold's work in Detroit, in Levine and Crockett, and in Anshen's study of Hillsboro. The pattern is particularly marked in lower-middle-class women, who show the most extreme form of this behavior. There is some question as to whether lower-class women are also more sensitive to social speech: the evidence is not clear here.

The hypercorrect pattern of the lower middle class

One of the most solidly established phenomena of sociolinguistic behavior is that the second-highest status group shows the most extreme style shifting, going beyond that of the highest status group in this respect.

10. The (dh) variable (in initial position) is more regular in the Negro community than (th). Final (th) is realized as (*f*) more often than as (*t*), though initially it is not realized as [f] in the Cockney dialect. It should be noted that (th) and (dh) are examples of inherent variation: in particular, we note the absence of hypercorrection, even though the phonetic forms overlap with /t/ and /d/ in some cases. See Wolfram, 1969, pp. 100 ff. for a detailed analysis of the (*th*) variants.

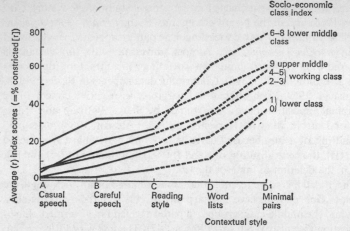

Figure 2 Class stratification of (r) in *guard, car, beer, beard*, etc. for native New York City adults

To see this most clearly, it is necessary to examine the sociolinguistic structure of a change in progress. Figure 2 shows the pattern for final and pre-consonantal (r) in New York City (Labov, 1966, p. 240). This community has a basically r-less vernacular, but shortly after the end of World War II, r-pronunciation became the prestige norm (as to a lesser extent in other r-less areas of the United States). The vertical axis is the (r) index – the percentage of constricted (r) in words like *ear, where, car, board*, etc.[11] Higher scores reflect greater use of prestige form (r). Note the sharp

Table 1 R scores by sentence and word-list and by education and sex in Hillsboro, North Carolina

	Sentence list	Word list	Net increase
Education			
Any college	52·7	58·9	6·2
High school graduate	54·6	65·6	11·0
Some high school	50·0	57·0	7·0
Grade school or none	52·6	57·3	4·7
Sex			
Male	52·3	57·4	5·1
Female	52·9	61·1	8·2

Source: Levine and Crockett, 1966, p. 223.

11. This variable does not include (r) following the mid-central vowel of *her, heard*, etc., which follows a different pattern with either a palatal up-glide or more constriction.

cross-over of the lower middle class group in the two most formal styles. This pattern recurs in several other variables from New York City. One of the most striking instances of quantitative convergence is supplied by Levine and Crockett's study, as shown in Table 1.

Here data from a completely independent study with a more limited stylistic range shows the same cross-over phenomenon. The second highest status group – in this case, high school graduates, show a much greater shift towards the prestige norm in their more formal style. The significance of this pattern for the mechanism of linguistic change has been dealt with specifically in Labov. Here it will be helpful to see what formal simplification can be achieved for this complex pattern, abstractly:

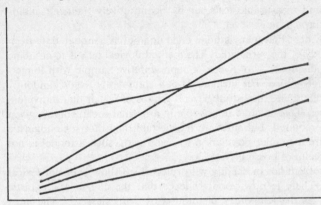

The slope of style shifting is very complex. The highest and lowest group have the shallowest slope. The interior groups follow behind the lead of the second highest group, which is the steepest. How can this be formalized? The rule for the vocalization of (r) in the white community has the general form:

$$[+\text{cen}] \rightarrow ([-\text{cons}]) / [-\text{cons}] \underline{\quad\quad} \sim V.^{12} \qquad\qquad 3$$

The problem here is to write a formula for the basic constraint on the input variable k_0 comparable to the simple and straightforward 2. The solution lies in an understanding of the significance of style shifting: it is governed by the recognition of an exterior standard of correctness. The strength of such behavior can be measured by an index of Linguistic Insecurity which gives us precisely the curvilinear pattern we need to

12. This rule is the formal equivalent of 'A central consonant (r) variably loses its consonantal character after a vowel or glide if a vowel does not follow directly.' If a word boundary follows directly, and then a vowel, this rule is constrained so that (r) appears more often in *four o'clock*.

describe the slope of style shifting in Figure 2, with the lower middle class at a maximum (Labov, 1966, p. 477). We can then write for 3

$$k_0 = f(\text{Class, Style}) = a(\text{SEC}) + b(\text{ILI})(\text{Style}) + c \qquad 4$$

Problems of sociolinguistic structure

Perhaps the most immediate problem to be solved in the attack on sociolinguistic structure is the quantification of the dimension of style. If quantitative studies of attention can be related to style shifting, we will then be able to give more precise form to rules such as 2 or 4 and specify the constants 1, 2, 3. Such quantification may possibly be obtained by studies of pupil dilation, or of systematic divisions of attention through mechanical and measurable tests, or by quantitatively reducing audio-monitoring through noise level.

It is also evident that many studies cited do not have enough data from the direct study of the vernacular. The methodological task is to combine surveys of individuals who give us a representative sample with longer-term studies of groups. The ideal study of a community would randomly locate individuals, and then study several groups of which that individual was a member. That is quite impossible in a normal social survey, given the numbers required, but since we have established that sociolinguistic studies require a smaller population to begin with, such a model is not beyond the realm of possibility.

A third problem lies in dealing with rules which show irregular lexical distribution. There is now good evidence that the course of linguistic change involves the temporary dissolution of word classes.[13] The most difficult problem here is that there are distributions across word classes which we would want to describe, but which are not likely to be a part of the knowledge of the native speaker. For example, only a certain proportion of English verbs with Latinate prefixes show a shift of stress when they appear as nouns like *convíct* [V]: *cónvict* [N]; others retain end stress, like *consént* [V]: *consént* [N]. It can be shown that the proportion of words in any given sub-class is related to the length of the prefix, but this regularity is of no use to the native speaker since most words have a fixed accent. As another example, the tensing rule for short *a* in New York City does not normally operate in $-\text{CV}$ environments, though there are a number

13. Although Figures 1 and 2 show classes moving words as a whole, we have encountered some rules which show a great deal of irregular lexical variation. The tensing of short/a/ in *bad*, *ask*, etc., now being investigated in New York City by Paul Cohen, shows such irregularity, while the raising rule which follows the tensing rule does not (Labov, 1966, pp. 51–2). It is the existence of a variable rule which allows the word class to be reconstituted when the change is completed, since it is defined as the class of lexical items which can vary between X and Y, as opposed to the classes which are always X or always Y. For some structural causes of such lexical variation, see Wang, 1969.

of exceptions. The linguist is interested to discover that most of these exceptions have a sibilant as the medial consonant C. But in such cases, the native speaker again only needs to know in what class a given word falls. The proportion of the original word class which has been affected by the incoming rule is of no immediate interest to him if he has no choice in the pronunciation of any given item. It may be that we will enter rules into our grammar which are *not* a part of the 'knowledge' of native speakers. This particular metaphor may have lost its value at this point in our investigations.

A fourth major challenge is to enter more deeply into the study of higher-level syntactic variables, such as extraposition, nominalization, placement of complementizers, negative raising, wh-attachment, or relativization. The two chief stumbling blocks to investigating these features in their social context is the low frequency of occurrence of the critical sub-cases, and the lack of certainty in our abstract analyses. But some beginning has been made in our recent work in urban ghetto areas, and the challenges to work with more abstract matters cannot be ignored. The study of language in its social context cannot remain at the level of such phonological variables as (th), if it is to have significance.

The fifth problem is to enlarge the scope of these studies beyond individual speech communities, and relate them to larger grammars of the English speech community as a whole. The work of Bailey is most challenging here: particularly his penetrating studies of phonological rules in Southern dialects (1969a), and his broader attempts to incorporate all English phonology into a single, pan-dialectal set of rules (1969b). Though these studies of Bailey are not based upon the study of language in context, one must eventually hope to provide reliable data to support work of this generality and this level of abstraction.

The relation of norms to behavior

So far, in our consideration of sociolinguistic structure, we have taken into account only what people say, and only incidentally what they think they *should* say. These are the 'secondary responses' to language that Bloomfield suggested that we might well observe (1944) as one part of popular lore. There is a very small vocabulary available to most people for talking about language: the same few terms recur over and over as we hear that the other people's pronunciation has a 'nasal twang', is 'sing-song', is 'harsh' or 'guttural', 'lazy' or 'sloppy'. Grammar is said to be 'mixed-up' or 'illogical'.

A small number of sociolinguistic markers rise to overt social consciousness, and become *stereotypes*. There may or may not be a fixed relation between such stereotypes and actual usage. The variables (ing) and (dh) are such stereotypes in the United States: someone may be said to 'drop his g's' or to be one of those 'dese, dem and dose guys'. Most communities have local stereotypes, such as 'Brooklynese' in New York City which focuses on 'thoity-thoid' for *thirty-third*; in Boston, the fronted broad *a* in 'cah' and 'pahk' receives a great deal of attention. Speakers of the isolated Cape Hatteras (North Carolina) dialect are known as 'hoi toiders' because of the backing and rounding of the nucleus in *high, tide*, etc.

Such social stereotypes yield a sketchy and unsystematic view of linguistic structure to say the least. In general, we can assert that over *social correction* of speech is extremely irregular, focusing on the most frequent lexical items, while the actual course of linguistic evolution, which has produced the marked form of these variables, is highly systematic. This is the basic reason why the vernacular, in which minimum attention is paid to speech, gives us the most systematic view of linguistic structure. For example, the evolution of the New York City vernacular has led to the raising of the vowel in *off, lost, shore, more*, etc. until it has merged with the vowel of *sure* and *moor*. This high vowel has been stigmatized, and is now being corrected irregularly by middle-class speakers. But the same vowel, raised simultaneously in the nucleus of *boy, toy*, etc., is never corrected.[14]

But subjective reactions to speech are not confined to the few stereotypes that have risen to social consciousness. Unconscious social judgments about language can be measured by techniques such as Lambert's 'matched guise' test, and others described above. One basic principle emerges: that *social attitudes towards language are extremely uniform throughout a speech community*.[15] Lambert's studies show, for example, that the negative attitude towards Canadian French is not only quite uniform in the English-speaking community, but almost as unanimously held among French speakers in Quebec (1967). In our study of unconscious subjective reactions to markers such as (r), we find the most extraordinary unanimity in speaker's reactions, despite the great variation in the use of [r] just described. There is a general axiom of sociolinguistic structure

14. We also find that the vowels of *my* and *mouth* are affected by the rotation of the long and ingliding vowels of *bad, bar, lost*. As *bar* moves to the back, *my* moves with it, and *mouth* moves in the opposite direction towards the front. But of all the systematically interrelated changes, only the raising of *bad* and *lost* shows style shifting and correction. Even for these cases, the correction is lexically irregular.

15. In fact, it seems plausible to define a speech community as a group of speakers who share a set of social attitudes towards language. In New York City, those raised out of town in their formative years show none of the regular pattern of subjective reactions characteristic of natives where a New York City variable such as the vowel of *lost* is concerned (Labov, 1966, p. 651).

which can be stated as: *the correlate of regular stratification of a socio-linguistic variable in behavior is uniform agreement in subjective reactions towards that variable*. This may be illustrated by Figure 3, which compares behavior and subjective reactions for (r) in New York City. Figure 3a shows the development of stratification of (r) in the vernacular for young adults. For those over 40, there is no particular connection between social class and the use of (r), but for those under 40, there is a striking difference between upper-middle-class and other groups. Figure 3b shows the normative correlate. For those over 40, responses to the subjective reaction test for (r) are close to the random level. But for those between 18 and 39, there is complete unanimity: 42 out of 42 subjects showed responses that unconsciously registered the prestige status of r-pronunciation.

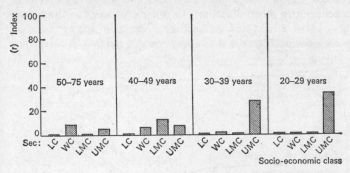

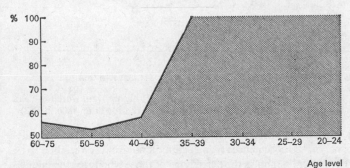

Figure 3 (a) Social stratification of (r) in *ear, board, car* etc. for four age levels in casual speech: New York City (Labov, 1966, p. 344)
(b) per cent showing (r)–positive response on subjective reaction test by age level (two-choice test): New York City (Labov, 1966, p. 435)

As we re-examine the structures shown in Figures 1 and 2, it is apparent that the uniform slope of style shifting also reflects the uniform attitudes held in the community. But for a stable sociolinguistic marker like (th), we can raise the question, what maintains this structure for such a long period of time? Why don't all people speak in the way that they obviously believe they should? The usual response is to cite laziness, lack of concern, or isolation from the prestige norm. But there is no foundation for the notion that stigmatized vernacular forms are easier to pronounce;[16] and there is strong evidence of concern with speech in large cities. Careful consideration of this difficult problem has led us to posit the existence of an opposing set of covert norms, which attribute positive values to the vernacular. In most formal situations in urban areas, such as an interview or a psycholinguistic test, these norms are extremely difficult to elicit. Middle-class values are so dominant in these contexts that most subjects cannot perceive any opposing values, no matter how strongly they may influence behavior in other situations. In our recent work in the Negro community, we have been able to uncover evidence of the existence of such opposing norms. Figure 4 shows responses to the first two items on

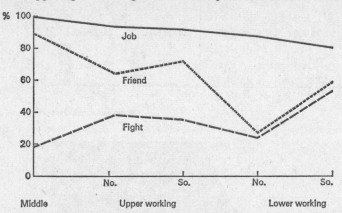

Figure 4 Per cent rating middle-class speaker (S2) higher than working-class speaker (S1) on three scales for five social groups (Labov et al. 1968, p. 242)

our subjective reaction test, opposing a working-class speaker to a middle-class speaker on 'zero' sentences (which contain none of the variables to be tested). The upper line shows the percentage of those who rated the middle-

16. Some of the extreme developments of vernacular vowel shifts in New York City, Detroit or Chicago are tense vowels which seem to involve a great deal of muscular effort compared to the standard. Spectrographic analysis indicates that such vowels as short /a/ rising to the height of *here* are extremely fronted. An interesting correlate of such extreme movements is the pattern of subjective reaction tests which shows that those who use the highest percentage of stigmatized forms are quickest to stigmatize them in the speech of others.

class speaker higher on the scale of 'job-suitability'. It begins very high with middle-class subjects, and falls off slightly as we move to lower socio-economic groups. The lower line is the converse: this registers reactions to the 'fight' or 'toughness' scale: 'If the speaker was in a street fight, how likely would he be to come out on top?' There is a simple inverse relationship here: a stereotype that is probably reinforced by school teachers but also shows some recognition of social reality. But the third set of reactions to the 'friendship scale' shows that there is more involved. This scale is in response to the question 'If you knew the speaker for a long time, how likely would he be to become a good friend of yours?' For the three upper social groups, this follows the job scale closely; but for the lower working class, it switches abruptly, and follows the fight scale. The same phenomenon can be observed for a whole range of variables tested (Labov et al. 1968, 3.6).

We have therefore some empirical support in positing the opposition between two sets of values as the normative correlate of stable sociolinguistic markers such as *(th)* and *(ing)*. In this type of study, we agree with Homans (1955) that the proper object of study should not be behavior alone, or norms alone, but rather the extent to which (and the rules by which) people deviate from the explicit norms which they hold. It is at this level of abstraction that we can best develop linguistic and sociolinguistic theory.

The role of social factors in linguistic evolution

Although this discussion is not primarily concerned with the problems of language change, I have already introduced some data which bears on this question. In speaking of the role of social factors influencing linguistic evolution, it is important not to overestimate the amount of contact or overlap between social values and the structure of language. Linguistic and social structure are by no means co-extensive. The great majority of linguistic rules are quite remote from any social value; they are part of the elaborate machinery which the speaker needs to translate his complex set of meanings or intentions into linear form. For example, the rules governing the crossover of co-referent pronouns discussed above are well below the level of social affect, and their irregular, idiosyncratic distribution in the population reflects this fact.

Variables closer to surface structure frequently are the focus of social affect. In fact, social values are attributed to linguistic rules only when there is variation. Speakers do not readily accept the fact that two different expressions actually 'mean the same' and there is a strong tendency to attribute different meanings to them.[17] If a certain group of speakers uses

17. When New York City *cruller* (Dutch *kroeller*) was replaced by the standard term *doughnut*, the term *cruller* was variously assigned to other forms of pastry. Similarly

a particular variant, then the social values attributed to that group will be transferred to that linguistic variant. Sturtevant (1947) has proposed a general model of linguistic change showing the opposition of two forms, each favored by a particular social group. When the issue is resolved, and one form becomes universal, the social value attached to it disappears.

We may think of social meaning as parasitic upon language. Given a uniform set of linguistic rules used to express certain meanings, language may be considered as a neutral instrument. But in the course of change, there are inevitably variable rules, and these areas of variability tend to travel through the system in a wave-like motion. The leading edge of a particular linguistic change is usually within a single group, and with successive generations the newer form moves out in wider circles to other groups. In New York City, the leading edge in the raising of short *a* is to be found among Italian working-class women, and the raising of open *o* in *off*, *lost*, etc., is most advanced among Jewish lower-middle-class women (Labov, 1966). Fasold's observations of the raising of short *a* in Detroit again show that lower-middle-class women play a leading role. Linguistic *indicators* which show social distribution but no style shifting represent early stages of this process. *Markers* which show both stylistic and social stratification represent the development of social reaction to the change and the attribution of social value to the variants concerned. *Stereotypes*, which have risen to full social consciousness, may be based on older changes which may in fact have gone to completion; or they may actually represent stable oppositions of linguistic forms supported by two opposing sets of underlying social values.

Many of the individual sociolinguistic variables are members of a complex network of linguistic relations, and as change spreads slowly throughout this system (Labov, 1965), there is a gradual shift of social values. Generally speaking, it seems to take about thirty years for a change in one part of a system (as in a front vowel) to be generalized fully to a parallel member (like a back vowel). But social structures are seldom stable over such a period of time. For example, in Martha's Vineyard we see the gradual raising of the nucleus of the diphthong in *nice, right, side*, etc., among Yankee fisherman (Labov, 1963). This sound change was generalized to the corresponding diphthong in *out, proud*, etc. But in the interval, a large number of second- and third-generation Portuguese-Americans entered into the speech community, and for various reasons we find that they

---

the local *pot cheese* (Dutch *pot kees*) was replaced by *cottage cheese* and was differentiated to indicate a drier form. The oscillation of socially marked pronunciations of *vase* led one informant to say, 'These small ones are my [veziz] but these big ones are my [vaziz].'

favor the raising of the second vowel much more than the first, moving the whole process to higher levels. Thus succeeding generations re-interpret the on-going course of a linguistic change in terms of a changing social structure. It is the oscillation between the internal process of structural generalization, and interaction with the external social system, which provides the impetus for continuous linguistic evolution (Labov, 1965).

As far as the synchronic aspect of language structure is concerned, it would be an error to put much emphasis on social factors. Generative grammar has made great progress in working out the invariant relations within this structure, even though it wholly neglects the social context of language. But it now seems clear that one cannot make any major advance towards understanding the mechanism of linguistic change without serious study of the social factors which motivate linguistic evolution. [. . .]

References

ANSHEN, F. (1969), *Speech Variation Among Negroes in a Small Southern Community*, unpublished NYU dissertation.

BAILEY, C-J. N. (1969a), 'The integration of linguistic theory: internal reconstruction and the comparative method in descriptive linguistics', with an appendix of 107 pan-dialectal ordered rules, paper given before Conference on Historical Linguistics in the Light of Generative Theory, Los Angeles.

BAILEY, C-J. N. (1969b), 'Introduction to southern states phonetics', University of Hawaii Working Papers in Linguistics, vols. 4 and 5.

BLOOMFIELD, L. (1944), 'Secondary and tertiary responses to language', *Language*, vol. 20, pp. 45–55.

BROWN, L. (1969), *The Social Psychology of Variations in French Canadian Speech Styles*, unpublished McGill University dissertation.

CHOMSKY, N., and HALLE, M. (1968), *The Sound Pattern of English*, Harper & Row.

FISCHER, J. L. (1958), 'Social influences on the choice of a linguistic variant', *Word*, vol. 14, pp. 47–56.

FISHMAN, J. A. (ed.) (1968), *Readings in the Sociology of Language*, Mouton.

GUMPERZ, J. J. (1964), 'Linguistic and social interaction in two communities', in J. J. Gumperz and D. Hymes (eds.), 'The ethnography of communication', *AmA*, vol. 66, no. 6, part 2.

HOMANS, G. C. (1955), *The Human Group*, Harcourt, Brace & Ward.

KUČERA, H. (1961), *The Phonology of Czech*, Mouton.

LABOV, W. (1963), 'The social motivation of a sound change', *Word*, vol. 19, pp. 273–309.

LABOV, W. (1965), 'On the mechanism of linguistic change', *Language and Linguistics*, Monograph No. 18, Georgetown University, Washington.

LABOV, W. (1966), *The Social Stratification of English in New York City*, Center for Applied Linguistics, Washington.

LABOV, W., COHEN, P., ROBINS, O. and LEWIS, J. (1968), *A Study of the Non-standard English of Negro and Puerto Rican Speakers in New York City*, Final Report, Cooperative Research Project 3288, vols. 1 and 2, Office of Education, Washington.

LAMBERT, W. E. (1967), 'A social psychology of bilingualism', in J. Macnamara (ed.), *Problems of Bilingualism, The Journal of Social Issues*, vol. 23, no. 2.

LEVINE, L., and CROCKETT, H. J. Jr (1966), 'Speech variation in a Piedmont community: post-vocalic *r*', in S. Lieberson (ed.), *Explorations in Sociolinguistics, sociol. Inq.*, vol. 36, no. 2.

SHUY, R., WOLFRAM, W., and RILEY, W. K. (1967), *A Study of Social Dialects in Detroit*, Final Report, Project 6-1347, Office of Education, Washington.

STURTEVANT, E. (1947), *An Introduction to Linguistic Science*, Yale University Press.

WANG, W. S-Y. (1969), 'Competing changes as a cause of residue', *Language*, vol. 45, pp. 9–25.

WOLFRAM, W. (1969), *Linguistic Correlates of Social Stratification in the Speech of Detroit Negroes*, Hartford Seminary Foundation thesis.

13 J. J. Gumperz

Sociolinguistics and Communication in Small Groups

J. J. Gumperz, 'Sociolinguistics and communication in small groups',
Working Paper no. 33, Language Behavior Research Laboratory, 1970,
University of California, Berkeley.

Language is relevant to the study of small groups in two ways. On the one hand, it serves as a medium for the exchange of ideas and interaction among group members, whose conversations can be recorded and analysed by social scientists observing their behavior. On the other hand, the social scientist wishing to study group processes indirectly (through non-observational methods like interviews, projective tests, etc.) must also rely on language for much of his information. In either case, it is necessary for the success of the research that all concerned, participants and researchers, control the same code.

But unfortunately, communality of code has been more frequently assumed than demonstrated empirically. To the extent that they have explicitly dealt with language, social scientists have treated it largely as a reflection of individual psychology. They have focused on the content of what is communicated, assuming that as long as everyone concerned 'speaks the same language', form presents no problem. Choice of expression, words or speech style is regarded primarily as a matter of individual intent, a reflection of a person's attitude or psychic state. Yet, these very choices also convey important information. Members of any speech community ordinarily have little difficulty in distinguishing informal from formal or familiar from deferential speech. They can tell whether people are engaged in a serious discussion, or just chatting, without knowing exactly what is being talked about. Similarly, one can learn much about a speaker's social background, educational achievements, and sometimes also his regional origin just from the way he speaks. Since it conveys important social information, language usage is not, and cannot be, merely a matter of individual choice. It must be rule-governed. This paper will review some recent research on the relationship of group processes and cultural milieux to choice of linguistic form, for its implications for problem solving in small groups.

Linguistics and sociolinguistics

Linguistics is best known as the formal study of grammatical systems. Social scientists in recent years have been particularly interested in

Chomsky's (1965) notion of linguistic competence – that is, the study of the speaker-hearer's knowledge of his language, defined as his control of the rules by which meanings are encoded into sounds. The linguist's remarkably explicit models of these processes have come to serve as examples of scientific rigor to investigators in related fields of psychology and anthropology.

One of the most significant features of the notion of competence is the fact that it deals with underlying constraints upon behavior rather than with actual performance. It refers to ability to act, rather than to what is done in particular instances. The goal of a linguistic analysis of competence is not to classify forms appearing in a particular body of data, but rather to explain occurring patterns in terms of deeper, more abstract regularities. It has been possible to show, for example, that although the number of sentences in a particular language is infinitely varied, they can in fact be generated from a finite body of rules. Generative grammar, as it is called, thus captures the creativity which is inherent in human language processes and which distinguishes them from non-human sign systems (Lenneberg, 1967).

The processes by which speakers code meanings into sound are largely automatic and hence only partially subject to conscious control. Regardless of individual intent, the form of his speech always depends on the grammatical system of his language, and his interpretation of what he hears. There is no such thing as impartial observation or measurement of verbal behavior: measurement is always affected by distortions. To some extent these distortions can be overcome by analytical techniques, however; and the study of linguistic forms provides tools to deal with a level of subconscious behavior which, when compared with an individual's actual behavior on the one hand, and his expressed opinions about his behavior on the other, can offer entirely novel insights into social processes.

The findings of generative grammar and its general orientation to the study of human action have had a profound effect on psychology and anthropological study of cognition (Chomsky, 1959; Smith and Miller, 1966). Attempts to establish direct relationships between grammatical rules and broader social processes, however, suffer from the fact that until quite recently, formal grammatical analysis dealt only with relatively limited aspects of verbal messages. In their search for methodological rigor, linguists tended to confine themselves to the internal linguistic patterning of linguistic forms within isolated sentences, ruling out consideration of the broader conversational context or the social settings in which such sentences are embedded. The resulting grammars account for what can be said in particular language, but they make no attempt to specify what constitutes appropriate behavior in particular social circumstances.

In an effort to extend some of the general principles of formal grammatical analysis to the study of speech as a form of social interaction, sociolinguists have advanced the concept of communicative competence (Hymes, 1967). Whereas linguistic competence covers the speaker's ability to produce grammatically correct sentences, communicative competence describes his ability to select from the totality of grammatically correct expressions available to him, forms which appropriately reflect the social norms governing behavior in specific encounters. The following examples of communication failures will illustrate the contrast between the two approaches to language.

1. From Allen, Ware, and Garrison (1867), quoted by Stewart (1968): A report by a white teacher of a century ago on an interchange with southern Negro boys:

I asked a group of boys one day the colour of the sky.
Nobody could tell me. Presently the father of one of
them came by, and I told him their ignorance, repeating
my question with the same result as before. He grinned:
'Tom, how sky stan'?' 'Blue', promptly shouted Tom.

The difficulties in communication here are linguistic. We assume that since Negro boys did not understand the teacher's question, it was no more grammatically correct in their dialect than 'How sky stan'?' is in English. The boys speak only Gullah, a plantation Creole of the Caroline Coast current at the time; the teacher speaks only standard English. Their languages have different grammatical systems and therefore speaker and addressee are unable to exchange factual information.

2. From a report of a Congressional hearing in the New York Times, 1968:

Studies of the Detroit riot show that Negroes are more interested in human dignity than in jobs, housing, and education. George Romney said.

He quoted a survey showing that 80 per cent of the Negroes of Detroit complain of the way they are treated by whites. They particularly object to being patronized, as when a white policeman addresses a Negro man as 'boy', he said.

Mr (John L.) McClellan broke his silence. In his section of the country, he said, it was an old custom for whites to call Negroes 'boy', and no offense was intended.

'I sometimes use it, as a custom, a habit,' he said. 'But I mean no disrespect.'

'I try to avoid it, but sometimes I say, "Boy, this, or boy, that."'

Negroes are too sensitive about that, he said. It makes no sense to start a riot over such a matter as being called 'boy', he said.

'People have to rise above these little things,' he added.

It was the Governor's turn to sit silent, Then he stammered, 'Well, it's a hard thing –'

Mr McClellan interrupted, 'Yes,' he said sternly, 'and if it comes to it, we can deal with it in a hard way.'

As in the first example, the two speakers do not seem to be communicating. Yet in this case both have the same grammar. They may differ in pronunciation but this is not relevant. What is important here is that they differ in the social norms governing the appropriate use of the address form 'boy'.

A third example illustrates how such divergence in sociolinguistic norms can be used to the communicative advantage of one party to an exchange, and the disadvantage of another.

3. From an experience of a Negro psychiatrist on a street corner in the southern United States in 1967, quoted by Ervin-Tripp (1969d):

'What's your name, boy?' the policeman asked. . . .
'Dr Poussaint. I'm a physician . . .'
'What's your first name, boy? . . .'
'Alvin.'

'As my heart palpitated. I muttered in profound humiliation. . . . For the moment, my manhood had been ripped from me. . . . No amount of self-love could have salvaged my pride or preserved my integrity. . . .'

Here the two speakers understand each other perfectly: the policeman means to insult, and he achieves this by an inappropriate demand for the victim's first name and by addressing a physician with a term reserved for a servant.

All three examples show rule-governed behavior. But only in the first case would the relevant rules be covered in the linguist's analysis. The alternants involved in the second and third examples – 'Alvin', 'Dr Poussaint', and 'boy' – are all equally grammatical and have the same basic function in the sentence. They are terms of address which may refer to the same individual. Use of one term or another does not change the nature of the message as a form of address; but it does determine how the person addressed is to be treated, and to what social category he is to be assigned. Selection among such grammatically equivalent alternants thus serves social rather than linguistic purposes. The study of sociolinguistic categorization processes provides a method of relating verbal behavior to social processes, adding an important dimension to the linguist's grammatical analysis.

Although our evidence is somewhat scanty, there is some reason to believe that sociolinguistic selection, like the coding of meanings into sounds, constitutes automatic behavior. The following example from recent fieldwork in a small Norwegian community (Gumperz, 1964) shows that the discrepancies between actual speech behavior and the speaker's opinions about his actual behavior may be surprisingly large. Residents of this community speak both a local dialect and standard Norwegian (Bokmål) and read the latter. Their feelings about the appropriate times and places in which to use these two varieties are very strong. The standard language is used primarily in formal situations: teaching, business negotiations and church services. On all other occasions, but above all in casual meetings, only the dialect is considered appropriate. To test the relationship of these attitudes about language usage to actual speech practice, we organized a series of informal gatherings for three local groups of differing social characteristics. In each group, various topics of conversation were introduced and the conversations recorded. In two of the three groups, speech practice was found to conform closely to locally-held stereotypes about language usage. Since the gathering was considered an informal one, even such topics as community affairs and the economic development of the region were discussed in the dialect. The third group, however, differed, in that 'serious' topics like economic development and politics usually elicited a shift from the dialect into standard Norwegian, even though the members of the group were friends and the gathering informal. The majority of this group were university students spending about six months of the year in various university centers far distant from the community. Their residence in the city, however, had not changed their attitudes to the dialect. So strong was their allegiance to local values regarding speech behavior that they claimed, with perfect sincerity, that their entire conversation had been in the dialect. When the recorded conversation was played back to them, they were appalled and vowed not to repeat such slips of the tongue again. Yet the same phenomenon was observed during a subsequent meeting of this group! The cause of this group's difference in speech behavior is complex and does not concern us here. What is important for us is the evidence this example provides for the existence of compelling patterns of speech behavior which may not be realized by the speaker at all.

Research in sociolinguistics has dealt with socially determined selection in a variety of societies and at a variety of levels of analysis. What aspects of language are subject to this kind of variation? The problem is one which has never been completely neglected, and social variations in speech have been observed in many different kinds of societies around the world (Hymes, 1964). Until quite recently, however, such social variations have tended to be described only when they were clearly reflected in the data gathered by linguists as part of their ordinary linguistic field-work procedures. What has tended to be studied are phenomena which, like the choice between *tu* and *vous* in French, are reflected in the grammatical system itself. This has created the impression that social distinctions are revealed only in some languages but not in others.

But this is not the case. Although members of all societies categorize each other through speech, groups differ in the linguistic means by which such categorization is accomplished. What some groups accomplish by alternating between familiar and respectful personal pronouns, such as *tu* and *vous*, others achieve by shifting between Mr Smith and John. Still others may achieve similar ends by simply switching from a local dialect to a standard language.

The major reason that such social variation in speech has not been studied systematically in all societies lies not in the speech behavior of the populations concerned, but rather in the way in which their speech has been recorded. The almost exclusive concern of linguistic elicitation procedures with reference (in the sense in which that term was used above) has led to the recording of the most commonly used equivalent for particular objects or ideas. The very artificiality of settings where linguists interview a single informant, and where speech samples must be produced in isolation from the customary circle of friends and family is hardly likely to bring forth the subtleties in selection of speech forms, shifts in formality and informality, which characterize everyday interaction.

The reproduction of natural conversation is difficult even for a highly-skilled writer. It is certainly more than could be expected from the ordinary person. At best the linguist-informant interview yields samples of a single speech style, usually a relatively formal one. Suitable data for the analysis of communication processes has therefore simply not been available. The systematic study of communicative competence requires special elicitation techniques capable of capturing the speaker's skill in responding appropriately to significantly different social stimuli. Complete records of actual conversations must replace the recording of single sentences. Furthermore, comparison of the same speaker's verbal responses in at least two different settings should be emphasized.

Sociolinguistic elicitation techniques

How can such data be collected, and what information do we need to interpret it? One of the most obvious elicitation methods is the recording of naturalistic speech in unobserved settings. In a pioneering study of this type Soskin and John (1963) secured the assistance of a married college student couple for this task. The subjects were given two weeks' free vacation at a holiday resort. After their arrival they were each equipped with small microphones disguised as part of their clothing. They had the option of turning off the microphones when privacy was desired, but they were asked to keep the microphones during much of their day on, especially to record their meetings with other vacationers at the resort. Their speech was recorded through a transmitter station located a few miles from the locale of their activities. Similar naturalistic techniques of observation have been used in studying the behavior of nursery and kindergarten play groups. In one such study (Sher and Harner, 1968) all children were equipped with microphone pins of which all but one or two were dummies. Recordings were then made by experimenters seated behind a one-way mirror. This type of situation offers the advantage of allowing the investigator to make visual observations of the group while they were talking.

Methods of this type have produced some of our first extensive recordings of natural speech, providing much material potentially useful for sociolinguistic analysis. But the analysis of such conversation presents some serious problems. At the outset, masses of recorded data are necessary if a sufficiently large range of stylistic variation is to be obtained. This presents serious transcription problems, since even a roughly accurate transcription of one hour of recorded natural speech requires ten to twelve hours of transcription time. More faithful transcription involves a much heavier investment of time. Even after the material has been recorded, it is sometimes impossible to evaluate its social significance in the absence of ethnographic knowledge about social norms governing linguistic choice in the situation recorded.

Consider the account of the Congressional hearing cited above. In order to understand what is going on, we must be aware of the difference between Senator McClellan's traditional Southern speech norms and Governor Romney's egalitarian Northern values. The policeman in the Poussaint incident effectively degrades Dr Poussaint because both speakers share a common set of values about the social meaning of the alternants employed. One problem with so-called naturalistic observation is that the experimenter sometimes cannot 'understand' what he hears because of his unfamiliarity with the norms of the group he is observing. It is one of the striking characteristics of our society, and for that matter of any society undergoing rapid change, that values about speech behavior may differ from small group to small group and sometimes from generation to generation. Failure to recognize these sources of variation in value systems makes it difficult for us to understand such phenomena as hippie speech or black power rhetoric. Naturalistic observation and random sampling of speech must therefore be preceded by 'ethnographies of communication' (Hymes, 1964a) – that is, by unstructured observation not tied down to any rigid experimental design.

The Norwegian experiment mentioned in the beginning of this paper was based on such fieldwork. The discussion sessions reported above took less than a week to stage, but this phase of the project was preceded by more than two months of intensive ethnographic study by two anthropologists, including an examination of local demographic records, study of economic life, local class stratification and its relation to friendship patterns, formal interviews about speech, and above all, participant observation. One of the investigators was a native Norwegian with several years of ethnographic experience in a village in Norway. Elaborate preparatory field-work of this kind provided the basis for selection of conversational groups whose speech behavior could be predicted by our knowledge of the local social organization.

Several kinds of group elicitation techniques were employed in Labov's (1968a) study of six adolescent and pre-adolescent peer groups in Harlem. Here is Labov's description of his procedures:

The paradigm for investigating the language of these peer groups may be summarized as follows:

1. The group was located by the field worker – in most cases a participant-observer living in the area.

2. Several individuals, including the leaders of the group, were interviewed in face-to-face situations.

3. Our staff met with the group on several outings and trips to various parts of the Metropolitan area. The field worker maintained daily contact with the group, and made notes on group membership and activities.

4. In several group sessions, multi-track recordings were made of the group in spontaneous interaction; in these sessions, the dominant factors controlling speech are the same as those which operate in every-day conversation.

5. All of the remaining individuals were interviewed in face-to-face interaction, and in addition, a large number of isolated individuals in the neighborhood ('lames') were interviewed.

In a recent study of London school children, Bernstein succeeded in generating stylistic variation by exposing children to different communication tasks as part of a half-hour structured interview session (Robinson, 1968). To initiate proceedings the child brought a painting or model to the interview room and talked about it. The child then constructed a model room with furniture and family figures supplied by the interviewer and answered several questions about these. The other tasks comprised the narration of stories about three sets of pictures, the description of objects and events in three postcard-size reproductions of paintings by Trotin, an open-ended story about what a child did in a free day, an explanation of how to play one of three games, and the description and explanation of the behavior of a toy elephant.

In interviews where the investigator brings a portable tape recorder to interview a small group of individuals (as in a family), it has sometimes been found useful for the investigator to leave the room or to step aside for a time, leaving the tape recorder running while participants talk among themselves. This technique proved productive during a recent interview with black West Indian high-school children in Birmingham, England. We had asked the principal of a local school to get together a group of students to talk to us. The students met us in a small seminar room seated around a table. All of them were native speakers of Jamaican Creole who use a very creolized form of English among themselves and in family settings, although most of them can also employ normal Birmingham English in the classroom. When we entered the room, we questioned them about their background, their schoolwork and their interests. They answered in fairly formal English. During the course of the conversation it appeared that the students frequently performed skits in the classroom dealing with everyday life. When they volunteered to put on a skit for us, we offered to step out of the room to give them an opportunity to plan their performance. We left the tape recorder running during our absence, and when we listened to the tape later, we found remarkable shifts both in style and fluency. Students who seemed to have difficulty in talking when we were present suddenly became very fluent when the style of the language shifted to Creole.

While the elicitation procedures reported here differ greatly, they all depend to a large extent on the investigator's knowledge of the cultural norms and behavior patterns of the group concerned. Given such background knowledge, investigation need not be confined to a few small groups randomly selected. There is no reason why systematic and structured interview methods cannot be designed which can accommodate samples of relatively large size. Bernstein's group, for example, sampled a total of 350 children and their mothers in London. It is crucial, however, that procedures are followed which are meaningful to both interviewer and interviewee. The right question must be asked in exactly the right way. This is especially important in working with small friendship or family groups where communication, as Sapir and Bossard have pointed out, relies heavily on shared knowledge. As Labov, a highly-skilled socio-linguistic investigator, remarks: 'If you want a child to tell you about baseball, questions such as "Tell us the rules of baseball" are unlikely to elicit responses.' To obtain a natural answer, the investigator must display his own knowledge of the game by questions like 'How do you know when to steal third base?' Labov's recently completed study of peer group speech in the New York ghetto is perhaps the best example of this approach Labov, 1968b).

Structural aspects of speech behavior

To suggest that the structure of longer conversational passages bears significant resemblances to the structure of sentences is to say that these passages must be patterned along two dimensions: the sequential or syntagmatic, and the paradigmatic. By paradigmatic structure, we refer to the fact that in any one speech event, speakers always select from a limited repertoire of alternates. Take, for example, the sentence, 'We — out to dinner last night.' In filling the slot here, we select one of a number of possible forms of the verb 'go': 'go, goes, went'. Note that selection is determined by the grammatical environment; only the last of the three forms fits, because of the adverbial phrase 'last night'. Since grammatical rules are automatic, all but beginning learners of English as a second language are unaware of the possibility of selection in this case. When we decide how to address someone who enters our office, similar selection among alternates takes place. But here social factors, rather than grammatical rules, are operative. Thus we may say 'Come in and sit down, John,' 'Come in, Mr Smith,' or 'Won't you come in, Sir?' Our choices in these matters are never quite free. We select a form of address on the basis of what we know about our interlocutor and what the behavioral norms allow. The difference between grammatical and sociolinguistic selection rules is one of degree, not one of kind.

By syntagmatic or sequential structuring, we refer to the fact that longer stretches of speech can be divided into distinct elements which are ordered in relation to each other. Just as sentences consist of clauses and phrases, conversations sub-divide into episodes (Watson and Potter, 1962) or discourse stages, as Frake (1964) has termed them in his highly detailed and suggestive analysis of drinking encounters among the Subanun tribe in the Philippines. These drinking encounters are culturally important as dispute-settling mechanisms. Yet the introduction of information about interpersonal conflicts is strictly constrained by the order of discourse stages. Encounters begin with long, ritualized introductions, in which wording is relatively pre-determined. They end with similarly ritualized codes. Only the skilful speaker knows how to introduce new information in the transitions between these ritualized sequences.

A dramatic example of the importance of order in conversations is provided by Schegloff (1969) in an analysis of opening gambits in telephone conversations. Scheglof shows among other things that the person who answers a ringing telephone is always the first speaker, and that the caller speaks next. Thus the conversation has a defined order, like the order of words in a sentence. So strong are our expectations about the order in which the conversation will proceed, Scheglof has discovered, that it is possible to foil obscene telephone calls by simply picking up the ringing telephone but refusing to say 'Hello'. Scheglof further shows how purposeful distortions in sequential ordering can seriously affect the intelligibility of the message.

A phone rings in Jim's home:
Jim: Hello.
George: Hi, how are you?
    Jim: OK, but listen, I'm in a phone booth and this is my last dime. Barbara's phone is busy and I won't be able to meet her at seven. Could you keep trying to get her for me and tell her?
George: what the hell are you talking about?

The key linguistic concept for the analysis of paradigmatic aspects of language behavior has been the notion of sociolinguistic variables as developed by Labov (1966) and others. Alternate terms of address and formal–informal word pairs such as 'buy–purchase', 'munch–eat–dine', can all be regarded as instances of such variables. A striking discovery based on contextual realistic linguistic fieldwork has been that social variation is by no means confined to lexical features and address terms. It affects all aspects of grammar including phonology and syntax. This is true for both monolingual societies like the United States and for bi-dialectal or multilingual societies.

In a pioneering study of verbal behavior in New York City, Labov (1966) noted that variations in the pronunciation of certain words were so extensive as to cut across the articulatory range of what structural dialectologists using traditional field techniques have analysed as distinct phonemes. The vowel in *bad* for example could be homophonous with the *i* in *beard*; the *e* in *bed* or the '*æ*' in *bat*. Three distinct phonemes thus seem to collapse into a single articulatory range. Since there is no phonetic basis for isolating distinct articulation peaks within this range, Labov argues that any attempt to deal with such shifts by postulating alternation between distinct systems is without empirical foundation. They must be treated as variable within a single system. He goes on to suggest that the discreteness of phonemic systems is an artifact of the linguist's field practice of abstracting rules from the speech of one or at most a few informants and of de-emphasizing variation. Intensive study of speech behavior should, in any one speech community, reveal both phonemes and variables. While phonemes are characterized by pronunciations clustering around definable articulation peaks, variables are defined by a starting point and a scale of values varying in a certain direction. The values along such scales are conditioned by social factors in a manner analogous to that in which phonological environments condition the phonetic realizations of allophones.

Not all grammatical or lexical alternates in a language can automatically be regarded as sociolinguistic variables, however. Since the same language may be spoken in a number of socially distinct societies, it must be demonstrated that selection among alternates carries social significance for some group of speakers. Furthermore, since social meaning is always embedded in reference, it is useful to speak of sociolinguistic variables only when alternates are referentially equivalent, i.e. when they signify the same thing in some socially realistic speech event. Items with the same or similar dictionary meanings may not be substitutable in actual conversation and, per contra, some variables are semantically equivalent only in specific contexts. An example will illustrate the problem. Few would ordinarily claim that the words 'wife' and 'lady' are homonyms in English. Yet they are used as such in the following extracts from an invitation to an army social quoted in a recent issue of the San Francisco Examiner: 'Officers with their ladies, enlisted men with their wives'. Referential equivalence here underlines social differences.

There is evidence to show that selection of sociolinguistic variables is rarely completely free. Variables tend to be selected in co-occurrent clusters. In other words, the speaker's selection of a particular value of a variable is always constrained by previous selections of variables. Thus, if a speaker varies between $(i.)$, $(e.)$, and $(æ)$ in *bad*, and, in addition, has alternates *ain't, is not, going'*, and *goin'* he is most likely to say 'This ain't gonna be (bi.d)' in some situations and 'This is not going to be (bæd)' in others. It would be unusual for him to say 'This is not going to be (bi.d).' It is important to note that sociolinguistic selections or constraints which generate such co-occurrences cut across the normal components of grammar. Their study, therefore, extends the application of linguistic analysis to data not ordinarily considered a part of grammar.

So far, our discussion of linguistic variables has dealt only with features of phonology and grammar. During the last few years, some of the methodological principles employed in the study of grammar have also begun to be applied to the sociological analysis of communication content. Content, however, is not studied for its own sake. The goal here is the empirical investigation of the manner in which content is manipulated as part of communicative strategies. Stereotyped opening gambits such as 'What's new?' suggest that the selection of conversational topics often serves social ends other than the transmission of factual information. Here, the speaker identifies himself as a friend and signals his readiness for further talk. Ervin-Tripp (1969, d) points out similarly that when a wife greets her husband by announcing that her visitors are discussing nursery schools, she may be suggesting that he absent himself, since in our culture husbands are not potential members of nursery school mothers' groups. In both cases, the important information in the conversation is contained in inferences hearers are expected to draw from their knowledge of the social relationships underlying the ostensible topic. Choice of content, therefore, is part of the code; like choice of grammatical form, it is a means to an end, not an end in itself.

To say that selection of topic communicates information about social relationships is to imply that these relationships, or for that matter, social structures in general, cannot simply be regarded as fixed, jural rules having an existence of their own apart from human action. They must themselves be a part of the communicative process, and thus presumably subject to change or reinforcement as the cumulative result of everyday communicative acts. The view that social structures are assigned through interaction is most clearly documented in the writings of Erving Goffman (1963). Through his study of interaction in various special settings, such as games, hospitals, work groups, and the like, he provides dramatic evidence for the fact that a single role or relationship may be realized through different types of behavior in different situations.

Building upon similar theoretical premises, Garfinkel (1967) concentrates somewhat more directly on the cognitive rules by which members of a society assess the significance of actions in everyday life. In essence, Garfinkel's view is that a person's previous experience and his knowledge of the institutions and practices of the world around him act to constrain his interpretations of what he sees and hears, in somewhat the same way that grammatical rules constrain his perception of sound sequences. He uses the term 'background expectation' to characterize the outside knowledge that an individual employs in the interpretation of events.

In a study of the function of such 'background expectations' in everyday communication, Garfinkel (1971) asked a group of students to report a conversation in which they had participated in the following fashion: they were to write on the left-hand side of a piece of paper what was actually said, and on the right side they were to explain in detail what they understood the conversation to mean. Here is a sample of the record obtained in this way:

Verbatim transcript	Detailed explanation
Husband	
Dana succeeded in putting a penny in a parking meter today without being picked up.	This afternoon as I was bringing Dana, our four-year-old son, home from the nursery school, he succeeded in reaching high enough to put a penny in a parking meter when we parked in a meter zone, whereas before he had always had to be picked up to reach that high.
Wife	
Did you take him to the record store?	Since he put a penny in a meter that means that you stopped while he was with you. I know that you stopped at the record store either on the way to get him or on the way back.

The interchange in the verbatim transcript would be inexplicable without an assumption of shared 'background expectations'.

Garfinkel then went on to demonstrate the function of 'background expectations' by asking his students to substitute detailed explanations of the kind shown in the right-hand column in the example above for the usual expressions exmployed in ordinary family discourse. The results were instructive: when they did, they were accused of 'acting like strangers'. One wife asked her husband, 'Don't you love me any more?' Thus, the students' relatives perceived detailed explanatory language as a reflection of family values. Reliance on background expectations thus seems to serve an important purpose in distinguishing small group or family conversations from interaction with non-members.

Where Garfinkel points out the importance of background expectations in communication, Sacks (1967) proceeds to specify how the speaker's implicit use of these expectancies generates conversation exchanges. Among the most important of these are the 'social categories' or social reactions implied by speech content. Sacks' basic data is derived from natural conversations. In analysing the following sentence sequence taken from a verbatim transcript of a child's story: 'The baby cried. The mommy picked it up,' he notes that members of our society will automatically recognize the 'mommy' in sentence two as the mother of the infant in sentence one. Yet, there is nothing in the overt linguistic structure of either sentence which provides for this identification. Pronouns such as 'his' or 'her' which ordinarily express such relationships are lacking.

What perceptual or cognitive mechanisms, Sacks asks, must we postulate in order to explain the hearer's understanding of the mother–child relationship in the absence of linguistic clues? Sacks observes that forms like 'mommy' and 'baby' can be regarded as 'membership categorization devices' which assign actors to certain social categories and invest them with the rights and duties implied therein. It is not possible, however, to determine the social category implied by a term by considering that term in isolation. The isolated term 'baby', for example, could be part of the collection baby–child–adult, or of the collection mommy–daddy–baby. In the example given above, we identify it as part of the latter collection by examining both sentences. The cognitive process is somewhat as follows:

1. We perceive a semantic tie between baby and the activity of crying, which is more reminiscent of family relationships (mommy–daddy–baby) than of age grading (baby–child–adult).

2. This hypothesis is confirmed by the fact that the mommy in sentence two forms part of the collectivity (mommy–daddy–baby) but not of the collectivity (baby–child–adult).

The concept of membership categorization device has some similarity to the symbolic interactionists' concept of role. Both Sacks and Garfinkel, however, seem to avoid this conventional terminology in order to circumvent the association of roles with separately existing jural rules which has been built up by much earlier writing on role. As Cicourel (1968) has pointed out, they see social structure as constraining behavior in somewhat the same way that syntax constrains the encoding of sounds. The goal is to devise empirical methods by which to discover social categories directly through conversational data. Despite the newness of these insights, a recent study of Moerman's (1969) shows that Sacks' concepts can be used, with the aid of an informant, to analyse the cultural basis of everyday behavior in groups whose culture is strange to the observer. These techniques should also be applicable to the analysis of sub-cultural difference in family groups in American society, and seem to me to hold considerable potential value for a range of applications, from group therapy for families to social psychological and anthropological analysis of small groups.

Although Sacks limits his analysis to communication content, sociolinguistic variables of the types discussed above can also be regarded as membership categorization devices. In the following joke told to my colleague Alan Dundes by a black student, the social label 'Negro' is conveyed by the syntactically and phonologically marked utterance 'Who dat?':

Governor W. died and went to heaven. When he
knocked on the door, a voice answered: 'Who dat?'
He said, 'Never mind, I'll go to the other place.'

The notion of categorization devices thus extends to both linguistic form
and linguistic content. Although I know of no serious study of the use of
linguistic form as a categorization device, it would seem that both types
of evidence should be utilized in the study of interpersonal relations in
small groups.

How do different groups develop different linguistic codes?

This question is but one aspect of the broader problem of social differentiation in speech: of how a person's social origin affects his ability to
communicate with others. Bernstein's (1965) theories of restricted and
elaborated codes represent the first systematic attempt to deal with this
question in cross-culturally valid or universal terms. In the United States,
Bernstein's earlier work has frequently been taken to assert that there is a
direct or casual relationship between middle- and working-class status and
elaborated and restricted codes, respectively. His recent writings present
a considerably different picture (Bernstein, 1968). The basic assumption
underlying Bernstein's empirical research is that the network of social
relationships in which the individual interacts, and the communicative
tasks which these relationships entail, ultimately shape his linguistic
potential. Following Bott (1957), he makes a scalar distinction in family role
systems between closed or positional systems, and open or person-oriented
systems. The former polar type emphasizes communal values at the
expense of freedom of individual expression and initiative. Such emphasis
tends to limit the introduction of new information through verbal means,
stressing social propriety in speech and leading to a predominance of
ritualized exchanges. Hence the term 'restricted code' to describe a way
of using language which is largely formulaic, and more suited for reinforcing pre-existing social relationships than for the transmission of new
factual information. Person-oriented role systems, on the other hand,
emphasize individual freedom and adaptability. They tend to generate
'elaborated codes', capable of expressing information about the physical
and social environment and emphasizing the ability to use speech creatively,
for the transmission of such information.

While all speakers show some control of both types of speech code,
there are important social differences in the extent to which elaborated
speech is used. Individuals socialized in open-role systems, while they may
use restricted codes in their own family or small-group settings, are
trained to speak in and respond to elaborated codes in serious discussion,

in school, and in public life. Persons socialized in closed-role systems are less flexible. The socialization process they have undergone has generated certain attitudes to speech as a vehicle for the transmission of new information. These attitudes create conflicts when children are faced with the kind of verbal learning tasks usually required in school. Bernstein suggests that it is the schools' inability to bridge the communication gap with restricted code speakers which accounts for the fact that so many children are slow to learn verbal skills. He rejects the notion of cultural or linguistic deprivation: the problem is one of differing socialization methods, and the difficulty lies in devising a strategy for communicating with children unaccustomed to the types of social relations required in school.

The value of Bernstein's theory for sociolinguistics lies in the fact that it postulates a direct relationship between socialization practices and the individual's ability to express social relationships through speech. The relationships thus postulated are subject to empirical verification both through interview methods and the study of natural conversations of mothers and children. Recently published studies conducted by Bernstein's group (Robinson, 1968) have in fact produced some impressive evidence of the connection between mothers' socialization practices and the way their children perform on communicative tasks of the type mentioned in the discussion of field methods given above. There is no doubt that, at least in Britain, children of various groups differ significantly in their ability to take the role of the other, and that this difference is measurable through the study of the children's language.

Recent sociolinguistic research in the United States, however, raises some doubt about the generalizability of the concepts of restriction and elaboration in their present form. Labov (1968b) using elicitation techniques which relied heavily on natural conversation, found that the very children who in school or in interviews with strangers speak only in short and highly formulaic utterances, usually characterized as 'restricted codes', show themselves to be highly creative and effective communicators when they are interviewed in a setting which they perceive culturally realistic, or when their natural interaction with peers is recorded. Similarly, Kohl's (1968) stimulating account of his classroom experiences in ghetto schools shows that children who are placed low on conventional linguistic achievement tests are capable of highly creative and effective writing under the right conditions.

Labov's and Kohl's observations are confirmed by preliminary results from cross-cultural research on language socialization by a group of anthropologists from the University of California, Berkeley, who lived as participant observers with the groups they studied and were thus able to compare psycholinguistic test results with their own observations and tape-recorded natural conversations (C. Kernan, 1969; K. Kernan, 1969; Blount, 1969; Stross, 1969). Findings, some of which are summarized by Ervin-Tripp (1969a), point to the importance of peer group socialization in verbal development in non-Western cultures and in lower-class Western groups. Whereas parent–child interaction tends to be quite restricted, peer group interaction shows a great deal of verbal communication. Black teenage groups in American ghettos place unusual value on such verbal skills as story telling, word games, verbal dueling, etc. (Labov, 1968, b). If they seem uncommunicative in formal interviews or if they perform badly on tests, this may be in large part due to the unfamiliarity of the setting or to their attitude to the test.

The present state of our knowledge therefore provides little justification for associating absolute differences in verbal skills with class or ethnic background. It would be more useful to assume that different social groups use different verbal devices for the transmission of social meaning. 'Lexical elaboration', to paraphrase Bernstein's term for the code which relies most heavily on the expression of non-referential meaning through words, is only one of these devices but by no means the only one. Similar information can be conveyed through style-shifting, intonation, special 'in 4 group' vocabulary, topical selection and like devices. The sense of 'who dat' in the joke cited above could for instance also have been conveyed by the phrase 'A heavily accented negro voice answered: Who is that?' The social significance would have been the same, but the joke less effective.

Differences in communicative devices have important social consequences. Communication through style shifting, special intonation, special in-group terminologies and topical selection basically relies on metaphor and is heavily dependent on shared background knowledge. Only individuals who are aware of the cultural stereotype which associates the pronunciation 'who dat' with Negro race can understand the joke cited above. On the other hand, the greater the verbal explicitness the less the reliance on shared commonality of background. At the extreme end of the explicitness scale an individual needs to know little more than the rules of grammar and the relevant vocabulary. Wherever education is public and open to all these matters can be learned by everyone regardless of family background. The cultural knowledge necessary for the understanding of metaphors is not that easily accessible. Ability to understand and communicate effectively here depends above all on informal learning through regular interaction. Frequency of interaction alone moreover is not enough. The context in which the communication occurs and the social relationships relevant to it are also important. Whites in our society may regularly interact with blacks, but in most cases such interaction is relatively impersonal. Communication in intimate family contexts of the kind which is characterized by free, unguarded give and take, is still quite rare. It is therefore not to be expected that whites have the cultural basis for judging the quality of interaction in black family groups.

Some applications for small group studies

The fact that family communication relies heavily on shared background expectations, which so far have received relatively little formal study has some serious consequences for the investigator working with family groups. Small group studies depend on the observer's or coder's ability to evaluate communication content. Bales' (1950) well known twelve categories for interaction analysis, for example, require that the observer make relatively fine judgement as to the degree of solidarity or tensions expressed in an utterance or that he distinguish between suggestions or expressions of opinions, etc. It is exactly this type of judgement of speech function which is most radically affected by subcultural variation and is likely to cause difficulties for investigators working with populations of social class and ethnic background different from their own. The difficulties are compounded by the fact that speakers think of themselves as speaking the same language. It is assumed that as long as speakers share a grammar and vocabulary they can always make sense of each other's statement. But the investigator's interpretation of what is meant by a particular utterance may be radically different from that of his subjects.

An example from my own recent field work experience will illustrate the problem. In the course of a discussion session with a group of black teenagers in a ghetto neighborhood in which my assistant and I were the only whites present I felt myself repeatedly the target of remarks such as the following; 'You are racist', 'You wouldn't give a black man a chance'. A series of these and similar remarks made me feel increasingly under attack. I responded 'You know nothing about me. How do you know that I discriminate?' The reply was 'You means the system not *you*. We are not blaming you personally.'

Communication difficulties are not confined to evaluation of behavior in small groups. A family therapist attempting intervention techniques may similarly find that his instructions are misunderstood or that his comments unaccountably cause resentment. The white middle-class school teacher's experience with ghetto children provides many examples for this type of failure. How can such communication gaps be overcome? Should the investigator learn to speak his subjects' language? This would be difficult and not necessarily effective. An outsider using 'in group speech' may give the impression of talking down or intruding on others' private affairs. It is more important to concentrate on methods for diagnosing the relevant differences in language usage. In the examples cited above for instance, the problem lies in the ambiguity between the personal and impersonal meaning of 'you'. In middle-class English usage the impersonal 'you' tends to be marked linguistically either by occurring in constructions such as 'you people', or in stereotyped expressions like 'you never know', or by appearing in the same sentence with an abstract impersonal noun. In lower-class English as well as in lower-class black speech the interpretation of 'you' as personal or impersonal is more frequently ambiguous and its interpretation depends on the non-linguistic context. My reaction was due to my failure to see this possible ambiguity. The speaker took advantage of this failure on my part to show me up.

In the absence of detailed ethnographic data, intensive analysis and exposure to natural conversation of culturally different groups is one of the best ways of acquiring the cultural background necessary to interpret their speech. It would be useful here to adopt a practice which is becoming more and more common in minority schools (Labov, 1968b): to employ as an assistant a local resident – not necessarily someone with a proper degree, but a person who through leadership in local groups has shown himself to be a good communicator. Such an individual would act as an intermediary between the researcher and his subjects, to make sure that instructions are given in the right manner and that explanations are properly understood. He would tutor the investigator in the usage rules and politeness formulas of the group, teach him such matters as how best to open a conversation, when to interrupt, when not to speak his mind, etc. and also provide tapes of natural conversation in relevant settings for analysis.

The natural unit for such conversational analysis is the interactional exchange or sequence of two or more utterances, not an isolated utterance. Two questions are relevant in the analysis. (1) What is meant by the exchange? What does it reflect about the speaker's state of mind and his relationship to the group? Comparison of the assistant's judgement in these matters with those of the investigator should be useful to reveal relevant subcultural differences. (2) By what verbal devices are the relevant effects obtained? Are there any special features of style, pronunciation of special vocabulary, which are significant? It is here that the work of Sacks (1967) and Schegloff (1969) and Moerman (1969) should be useful.

With relatively little additional research an investigator with some training in sociolinguistics could develop indices for the study of interaction patterns in family solving groups, to be used in addition to conventional communication indices such as those now employed by Strauss (1968) and others. The method here would be to follow the sociolinguist's practice in studying the same individuals' reaction under varying social stimuli. A subject's performance on similar problem-solving tasks could be measured first in a family group and then in a peer group setting. Techniques for the study of variable selection devised by Labov (1966) as well as the recent linguistic work by Bernstein's group (Mohan and Turner, 1968; Henderson, 1968) on measures of elaboration and restriction could be adapted here.

Throughout our discussion we have given primary attention to sociolinguistic analysis as a diagnostic or ethnographic tool for the study of small group interaction. Little if any attempt has been made to make direct predictions, e.g., of the effect of particular types of speech behavior on problem-solving ability. In part this is due to the newness of sociolinguistics.

Although we have made considerable advances in basic theory we are faced with a great paucity of reliable descriptive data. More direct application would require more detailed research on family problem solving by skilled sociolinguists. In the absence of such work it would seem that the basic understanding we have achieved can aid the student of problem solving primarily by giving him an insight into basic communication processes and thus improve the validity of his own field work both cross-culturally and within his own society.

References

ALLEN, W. F., WARE, C. P., and GARRISON, L. McK. (1867), *Slave Songs of the United States*, p. xxvii.

BALES, R. F. (1950), *Interaction Process Analysis*, Addison-Wesley.

BERNSTEIN, B. (1965), 'A sociolinguistic approach to social learning', *Social Science Survey*, Penguin.

BERNSTEIN, B. (1971), 'A sociolinguistic approach to socialization', in J. J. Gumperz and D. Hymes (eds.), *Directions in Sociolinguistics*, Holt, Rinehart & Winston.

BLOUNT, B. G. (1969), Dissertation, University of California, Berkeley, in preparation.

BOTT, E. (1957), *Family and Social Network in London*, Tavistock.

CHOMSKY, N. (1959), 'Review of B. F. Skinner's "Verbal Behavior"', *Language*, vol. 35, no. 1, pp. 26–8.

CHOMSKY, N. (1965), *Aspects of the Theory of Syntax*, M.I.T. Press.

CICOUREL, A. (1968), 'The acquisition of social structure: towards a developmental sociology of language and meaning', in H. Garfinkel and H. Sacks (eds.), *Contributions to Ethnomethodology*, Indiana University Press, in press.

ERVIN-TRIPP, S. (1969a), 'Sociolinguistics', in L. Berkowitz (ed.), *Advances in Experimental Social Psychology*, vol. 4, Academic Press.

ERVIN-TRIPP, S. (1969b), 'Sociolinguistics Summer Training', *Items*, 1969.

FRAKE, C. O. (1964), 'How to ask for a drink in Subanun', in J. J. Gumperz and D. Hymes (eds.), *The Ethnography of Communication*, *AmA*, vol. 66, no. 6, part 2, pp. 127–32, see also this volume.

GARFINKEL, H. (1971a), *Studies in Ethnomethodology*, Prentice-Hall.

GARFINKEL, H. (1971b), 'Remarks on ethnomethodology', in J. J. Gumperz and D. Hymes (eds.), *Directions in Sociolinguistics*, Holt, Rinehart & Winston.

GOFFMAN, E. (1963), *Behavior in Public Places*, Free Press.

GUMPERZ, J. J. (1964), 'Linguistic and social interaction in two communities', in J. J. Gumperz and D. Hymes (eds.), *The Ethnography of Communication, AmA*, vol. 66, no. 6, part 2, pp. 137–53.

HENDERSON, D. (1968), 'Social class differences in form-class usage and form-class switching among five-year-old children', in W. Brandis and D. Henderson (eds.), *Social Class, Language and Communication*, Routledge & Kegan Paul.

HYMES, D. (ed.) (1964a), *Language in Culture and Society*, Harper & Row.

HYMES, D. (1964b), 'Toward ethnographies of communication', in J. J. Gumperz and D. Hymes (eds.), *The Ethnography of Communication, AmA*, vol. 66, no. 6, part 2, pp. 1–34.

HYMES, D. (1967), 'Models of the interaction of language and social setting', in J. Macnamara (ed.), *Problems of Bilingualism, J. Soc. Iss.*, vol. 23, no. 2.

KERNAN, C. (1969), Dissertation, University of California, Berkeley, in preparation.

KERNAN, K. (1969), Dissertation, University of California, Berkeley, in preparation.

KOHL, H. (1967), *Thirty-six Children*, New American Library; Penguin, 1971.

LABOV, W. (1966), *The Social Stratification of English in New York City*, Center for Applied Linguistics, Washington.

LABOV, W. (1968a), 'Contraction, deletion and inherent variability of the English copula', *Language*, vol. 45, pp. 715–62.

LABOV, W. (1968b), 'A study of the non-standard English of Negro and Puerto Rican speakers in New York City', Columbia University, mimeograph.

LENNEBERG, E. (1967), *Biological Foundations of Language*, Wiley.

MOERMAN, M. (1969), 'Analysis of Lue conversation', Working Paper no. 12. Language Behavior Research Laboratory, University of California, Berkeley.

MOHAN, B. and TURNER, G. J. (1968), 'Grammatical analysis, its computer programme and application', in B. Bernstein (ed.), *Social Class and the Speech of Five-Year-Old Children*, Routledge & Kegan Paul.

ROBINSON, W. P. (1968), 'Social factors and language development in primary school children' (typescript).

SACKS, H. (1967), 'Typescript of classroom lectures', Division of Social Sciences, University of California, Irvine.

SCHEGLOFF, E. (1969), 'Sequencing in conversational openings', *AmA*, vol. 70, no. 6, pp. 1075–95.

SHER and HARNER (1968), typescript.

SMITH, F., and MILLER, G. A. (1966), *The Genesis of Language*, M.I.T. Press.

SOSKIN, W., and JOHN, V. (1963), 'The study of spontaneous talk', in R. G. Barker (ed.), *The Stream of Behavior*, Appleton-Century-Crofts.

STEWART, W. A. (1968), 'Continuity and change in American negro dialects', typescript.

STRAUS, M. A. (1968), 'Communication, creativity, and problem solving ability of middle and working class families in three societies', *Amer. Soc.*, vol. 73. no. 4.

STROSS, B. (1969), Dissertation, University of California, Berkeley, in preparation.

WATSON, G., and POTTER, R. J. (1962), 'An analytic unit for the study of interaction', *Hum. Rel.*, vol. 15, pp. 245–63.

14 S. M. Ervin-Tripp

Sociolinguistic Rules of Address

Excerpt from S. M. Ervin-Tripp 'Sociolinguistics', in L. Berkowitz (ed.),
Advances in Experimental Social Psychology, vol. 4, 1969, pp. 93–107.

Alternation rules

American rules and address

A scene on a public street in contemporary US:
   'What's your name, boy?' the policeman asked. . . .
   'Dr Poussaint. I'm a physician . . .'
   'What's your first name, boy? . . .'
   'Alvin.'

Poussaint (1967, p. 53).

Anybody familiar with American address rules[1] can tell us the feelings reported by Dr Poussaint: 'As my heart palpitated, I muttered in profound humiliation. . . . For the moment, my manhood had been ripped from me. . . . No amount of self-love could have salvaged my pride or preserved my integrity . . . [I felt] self-hate.' It is possible to specify quite precisely the rule employed by the policeman. Dr Poussaint's overt, though coerced, acquiescence in a public insult through widely recognized rules of address is the source of his extreme emotion.

Brown and Ford (Hymes, 1964a) have done pioneering and ingenious research on forms of address in American English, using as corpora American plays, observed usage in a Boston business firm, and reported usage of business executives. They found primarily first name (FN) reciprocation or title plus last name (TLN) reciprocation. However, asymmetrical exchanges were found where there was age difference or occupational rank difference. Intimacy was related to the use of multiple names.

Expanding their analysis from my own rules of address, I have found the structure expressed in the diagram in Figure 1. The advantage of formal diagraming is that it offers precision greater than that of discursive description (Hymes, 1967). The type of diagram presented here, following

---

1. 'Rules' in this article are not prescriptive but descriptive. They may not be in conscious awareness. Unlike habits, they may include complex structures inferred from the occurrence of interpretable and appropriate novel behavior.

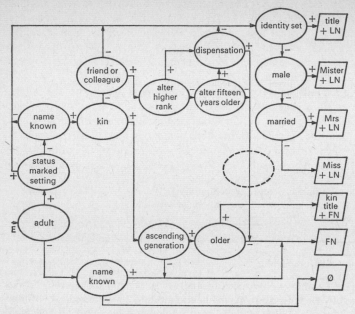

Figure 1 An American address system

Geoghegan (in press), is to be read like a computer flow chart. The entrance point is on the left, and from left to right there is a series of selectors, usually binary. Each path through the diagram leads to a possible outcome, that is, one of the possible alternative forms of address.

Note that the set of paths, or the rule, is like a formal grammar in that it is a way of representing a logical model. The diagram is not intended as a model of a process of the actual decision sequence by which a speaker chooses a form of address or a listener interprets one. The two structures may or may not correspond. In any case, the task of determining the structure implicity in people's knowledge of what forms of address are possible and appropriate is clearly distinct from the task of studying how people, in real situations and in real time, make choices. The criteria and methods of the two kinds of study are quite different. Just as two individuals who share the same grammar might not share the same performance rules, so two individuals might have different decision or interpretation procedures for sociolinguistic alternatives, but still might have an identical logical structure to their behavior.

The person whose knowledge of address is represented in Figure 1 is assumed to be a competent adult member of a western American academic community. The address forms which are the 'outcomes' to be accounted for might fit in frames like 'Look, —, it's time to leave.' The outcomes themselves are formal sets, with alternative realizations. For example, first names may alternate with nicknames, as will be indicated in a later section. One possible outcome is no-naming, indicated in Figure 1 by the linguistic symbol for zero [∅].

The diamonds indicate selectors. They are points where the social categories allow different paths. At first glance, some selectors look like simple external features, but the social determinants vary according to the system, and the specific nature of the categories must be discovered by ethnographic means. For example, 'older' implies knowledge of the range of age defined as contemporary. In some South East Asian systems, even one day makes a person socially older.

The first selector checks whether the addressee is a child or not. In face-to-face address, if the addressee is a child, all of the other distinctions can be ignored. What is the dividing line between adult and child? In my own system, it seems to be school-leaving age, at around age eighteen. An employed sixteen-year-old might be classified as an adult.

Status-marked situations are settings such as the courtroom, the large faculty meeting, or Congress, where status is clearly specified, speech style is rigidly prescribed, and the form of address of each person is derived from his social identity, for example, 'Your honour', 'Mr Chairman'. The test for establishing the list of such settings is whether personal friendships are apparent in the address forms or whether they are neutralized (or masked) by the formal requirements of the setting. There are, of course, other channels by which personal relations might be revealed, but here we are concerned only with address alternations, not with tone of voice, connotations of lexicon, and so on.

Among non-kin, the dominant selector of first-naming is whether alter is classified as having the status of a colleague or social acquaintance. When introducing social acquaintances or new work colleagues, it is necessary to employ first names so that the new acquaintances can first-name each other immediately. Familiarity is not a factor within dyads of the same age and rank, and there are no options. For an American assistant professor to call a new colleague of the same rank and age 'Professor Watkins' or 'Mr Watkins' would be considered strange, at least on the West Coast.

Rank here refers to a hierarchy within a working group, or to ranked statuses like teacher–pupil. In the American system, no distinction in address is made to equals or subordinates since both receive FN. The distinction may be made elsewhere in the linguistic system, for example, in the style of requests used. We have found that subordinates outside the family receive direct commands in the form of imperatives more often than equals, to whom requests are phrased in other ways at least in some settings (see below).

A senior alter has the option of dispensing the speaker from offering T L N by suggesting that he use a first name or by tacitly accepting first name. Brown and Ford (Hymes, 1964a) have discussed the ambiguity that arises because it is not clear whether the superior, for instance, a professor addressing a doctoral candidate or younger instructor, wishes to receive back the FN he gives. This problem is menioned by Emily Post: 'It is also effrontery for a younger person to call an older by her or his first name, without being asked to do so. Only a very underbred, thick-skinned person would attempt it' (Post, 1922, p. 54). In the American system described in Figure 1, age difference is not significant until it is nearly the size of a generation, which suggests its origin in the family. The presence of options, or dispensation, creates a locus for the expression of individual and situational nuances. The form of address can reveal dispensation, and therefore be a matter for display or concealment of third parties. No-naming or Ø is an outcome of uncertainty among these options.[2]

The *identity* set refers to a list of occupational titles or courtesy titles accorded people in certain statuses. Examples are Judge, Doctor, and Professor. A priest, physician, dentist, or judge may be addressed by title alone, but a plain citizen or an academic person may not. In the latter cases, if the name is unknown, there is no address form (or zero, Ø) available and we simply no-name the addressee. The parentheses below refer to optional elements, the bracketed elements to social selectional categories.

Cardinal	Your excellency
U.S. President	Mr President
Priest	Father + LN
Nun	Sister + religious name
Physician	Doctor + LN
Ph.D., Ed.D., etc.	Doctor + LN
Professor	Professor + LN
Adult, etc.	Mister + LN
	Mrs + LN
	Miss + LN

Wherever the parenthetical items cannot be fully realized, as when last name (LN) is unknown, and there is no lone title, the addressee is no-named by a set of rules of the form as follows: Father + Ø → Father,

2. In the system in Figure 1, it is possible to create asymmetrical address by using FN to a familiar addressee who cannot reciprocate because of rank or age difference, and his unwillingness or lack of dispensation, e.g., a domestic servant.

Professor $+ \emptyset \rightarrow \emptyset$, Mister $+ \emptyset \rightarrow \emptyset$, etc. An older male addressee may be called 'sir' if deference is intended, as an optional extra marking.

These are my rules, and seem to apply fairly narrowly within the academic circle I know. Non-academic university personnel can be heard saying 'Professor' or 'Doctor' within LN, as can school teachers. These delicate differences in sociolinguistic rules are sensitive indicators of the communication net.

The zero forms imply that often no address form is available to follow routines like 'yes', 'no', 'pardon me', and 'thank you'. Speakers of languages or dialects where all such routines must contain an address form are likely in English either to use full name or to adopt forms like 'sir' and 'ma'am,' which are either not used or used only to elderly addressees in this system.

One might expect to be able to collapse the rule system by treating kin terms as a form of title, but it appears that the selectors are not identical for kin and non-kin. A rule which specifies that *ascending generation* only receives title implies that a first cousin would not be called 'cousin' but merely FN, whereas an aunt of the same age would receive a kin title, as would a parent's cousin. If a title is normally used in direct address and there are several members of the kin category, a first name may also be given (e.g. Aunt Louise). Frequently there are additional features marked within a given family such as patrilineal v. matrilineal, and near v. distant. Whenever the address forms for an individual person's relatives are studied, this proves to be the case, in my experience.

Presumably, the individual set of rules or the regional dialect of a reader of this article may differ in some details from that reported in Figure 1. Perhaps sociolinguists will begin to use a favorite frame of linguists: 'In my dialect we say . . .' to illustrate such differences in sociolinguistic rules. For example, I have been told that in some American communities there may be a specific status of familiarity beyond first-naming, where a variant of the middle name is optional among intimates. This form then becomes the normal or unmarked address form to the addressee.

What's your name, boy?
Dr Poussaint. I'm a physician.
What's your first name, boy?
Alvin.

The policeman insulted Dr Poussaint three times. First, he employed a social selector for race in addressing him as 'boy', which neutralizes identity set, rank, and even adult status. If addressed to a white, 'boy' presumably would be used only for a child, youth, or menial regarded as a non-person.

Dr Poussaint's reply supplied only TLN and its justification. He made clear that he wanted the officer to suppress the race selector, yielding a rule like that in Figure 1. This is clearly a non-deferential reply, since it does not contain the FN required by the policemen's address rule. The officer next treated TLN as failure to answer his demand, as a non-name, and demanded FN; third, he repeated the term 'boy' which would be appropriate to unknown addressees.

According to Figure 1, under no circumstances should a stranger address a physician by his first name. Indeed, the prestige of physicians even exempts them from first-naming (but not from 'Doc') by used-car salesmen, and physicians' wives can be heard so identifying themselves in public in order to claim more deference than 'Mrs' brings. Thus the policeman's message is quite precise: 'Blacks are wrong to claim adult status or occupational rank. You are children.' Dr Poussaint was stripped of all deference due his age and rank.

Communication has been perfect in this interchange. Both were familiar with an address system which contained a selector for race available to both black and white for insult, condescension, or deference, as needed. Only because they shared these norms could the policeman's act have its unequivocal impact.

Comparative rule studies

The formulation of rules in this fashion can allow us to contrast one sociolinguistic system with another in a systematic way. A shared language does not necessarily mean a shared set of sociolinguistic rules. For instance, rules in educated circles in England vary. In upper-class boarding schools, boys and some girls address each other by LN instead of FN. In some universities and other milieux affected by the public school usage, solidary address between male acquaintances and colleagues is LN rather than FN. To women it may be Mrs or Miss + LN by men (not title + LN) or FN. Women usually do not use LN. Thus sex of both speaker and addressee is important.

In other university circles, the difference from the American rule is less; prior to dispensation by seniors with whom one is acquainted, one may use Mister or Mrs rather than occupational title as an acceptably solidary, but deferential, form. Note that this is the solidary usage to women by some male addressees in the other system. The two English systems contrast with the American one in allowing basically three, rather than two classes of alternatives for non-kin: occupational title + LN, M + LN, and FN/LN. The intermediate class is used for the familiar person who must be deferred to or treated with courtesy.

Two Asian systems of address have been described recently. The pioneering work of Geoghegan (1971) described the naming system of a speaker of Bisayan, a Philippine language. Geoghegan's formal presentation of the system in a talk some years ago was the model for the rules used in the figures in this article. As in most systems, children routinely receive the familiar address form. The Bisayan system, like the American and English, chooses on the basis of relative rank, relative age and friendship. But there are important differences. In the United States, all adult strangers are treated with deference; in the Bisayan system, social inferiors do not receive titled address. In the American system for non-kin, added age, like higher rank, merely increases distance or delays familiar address; in the Bisayan system, inferiors or friends who are older receive a special term of address uniting informality and deference.

The Korean system is even less like the American (Howell, 1967). In Korea, relative rank must first be assessed. If rank is equal, relative age within two years is assessed, and if that is equal, solidarity (e.g. classmates) will differentiate familiar from polite speech. This system differs both in its components and its order from the American and Bisayan rules. Both inferiors and superiors are addressed differently from equals. Many kinds of dyads differ in authority – husband–wife, customer–tradesman, teacher–pupil, employer–employee – and in each case, asymmetrical address is used. Addressees more than two years older or younger than the speaker are differentially addressed, so that close friendship is rigidly age-graded. Solidary relations arise from status, just as they do between equal colleagues in the American system, regardless of personal ties. There are more familiar address forms yet to signal intimacy within solidary dyads. If the English system has three levels, there are even more in the Korean system. Since the criteria were multiple in the Howell study, instead of a single frame, the comparison is not quite exact.

As Howell pointed out, the Korean system illustrates that the dimension of approach that Brown and Gilman (1960) called solidarity may in fact have several forms in one society. In the Korean system intimacy is separable from solidarity. This separation may also exist in the American system but in a different way. One is required to first-name colleagues even though they are disliked. On the other hand, as Brown and Ford (Hymes, 1964a) showed, nicknames may indicate friendship more intimate than the solidarity requiring FN. They found that various criteria of intimacy, such as self-disclosure, were related to the *number* of FN alternates, such as nicknames and sometimes LN, which were used to an addressee, and they suggested that intimacy creates more complex and varied dyadic relations which speakers may signal by address variants. Thus, in the American system two points of major option for speakers exist: the ambiguous address relation between solidary speakers of unequal age or status and intimacy. Systems can be expected to vary in the points where address is prescribed or where options exist; Brown and Ford suggested a universal feature, on the other hand, in saying that in all systems frequent and intimate interaction should be related to address variation.[3] This they suggest is related to a semantic principle of greater differentiation of important domains.

Two-choice systems

The brilliant work of Brown and Gilman (1960) which initiated the recent wave of studies of address systems was based on a study of T and V, the second person verbs and pronouns in European languages. In English, the same alternation existed before 'thou' was lost.

One might expect two-choice systems to be somewhat simpler than a system like Bisayan, which in Geoghegan's description gives nineteen output categories. But the number of outcomes can be few although the number of selectors is many or the kinds of rules relating them complex. Figure 2 gives a description of the nineteenth century rules of the Russian gentry, as I derive them from the excellent analysis by Friedrich (1966), which gives sufficiently full detail to permit resolution of priorities. *Special statuses* refers to the tsar and God, who seem not to fit on any status

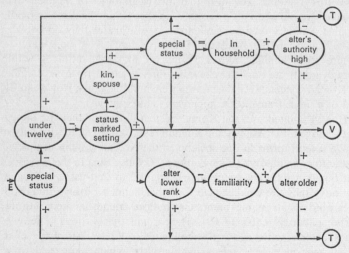

Figure 2 Nineteenth-century Russian address

3. William Geoghegan has privately suggested that in his Philippine studies the extremely high intimacy in families resulted in use of paralinguistic rather than lexical alternatives for 'address variation' of the type Brown and Ford discuss.

continuum. *Status marked settings* mentioned by Friedrich were the court, parliament, public occasions, duels and examinations. *Rank* inferiors might be lower in social class, army rank, or ethnic group, or be servants. *Familiarity* applied to classmates, fellow students, fellow revolutionaries, lovers and intimate friends. There does not seem to be the prescription in the Korean and American solidary relation. A feature of the system which Friedrich's literary examples illustrate vividly is its sensitivity to situational features. Thus T means 'the right to use *Ty*', but not the obligation to do so. Within the kin group, household is of considerable importance because of the large households separated by distance in traditional Russia.

A slightly later Eastern European system described by Slobin (1963) is given in Figure 3. The Yiddish system is somewhat more like the Ameri-

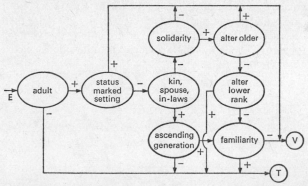

Figure 3 Yiddish address system

can than like the Russian system in that deference is always given adult strangers regardless of rank. However, an older person receives deference, despite familiarity, unless he is a member of the kin group. In the American system, familiarity can neutralize age.

How have these systems changed? We have some evidence from the Soviet Union. The Russian revolutionaries, unlike the French, decreed V, implying that they wanted respect more than solidarity. The current system is identical to the old with one exception: Within the family, asymmetry has given way to reciprocal T, as it has in most of western Europe, at least in urbanized groups. For non-kin in ranked systems like factories, superiors receive *Vy* and give *Ty*:

When a new employee is addressed as *Ty*, she says: 'Why do I call you *"vy"* while you call me *"ty"*?'

Kormilitzyn gleefully shoots back a ready answer: 'If I were to call everyone "*vy*" I'd never get my plan fulfilled. You don't fulfill plans by using *vy*' (Kantorovich, 1966, p. 30).

Evidently the upper-class habit of using '*vy*' until familiarity was established (a system reflecting the fact that the T/V contrast itself came in from above as a borrowing from French) has seeped downward. 'A half-century ago even upon first meeting two workers of the same generation would immediately use '*ty*'. Today things are different. Middle-aged workers maintain '*vy*' for a long time, or else adopt the intermediate form, which is very widespread among people within a given profession: '*ty*' combined with first name and patronymic' (Kantorovich, 1966, p. 81).

Kantorovich, true to the 1917 decree, complains about three features of the current system: *ty* to inferiors regardless of age, *ty* to older kin, and first names alone among young acquaintants. Thus he favors the more deferential alternative in each case. Social change in Russia has been relatively slow in sociolinguistic rules, has affected family life more than public life, and has spread the practices of the gentry among the workers.

The Puerto Rican two-choice system in Figure 4 is quite simple since it

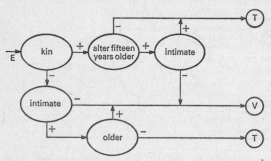

Figure 4 Puerto Rican address system (children)

is a system of children. The data were generously supplied by Wallace Lambert and his collaborators from a large-scale study of comparative address systems in several cultures. Elementary and high-school students filled in questionnaires about the forms of address given and received. In this chart, interlocale and intersubject differences have been suppressed. The striking feature of this system is that it requires only three discriminations. It is likely, of course, that adult informants would elaborate further details. Intimacy, in this system, refers to close ties of friendship, which can occur with others of widely varying age, e.g., with godparents, and is quite distinct from solidarity, which arises from status alone. Adolescent girls, for example, do not give 'tu' to a classmate unless she is a friend.

Lambert and his collaborators have collected slightly less detailed data from samples of schoolchildren in Montreal, from a small town in Quebec, from Mayenne, France, and from St Pierre et Michelon, an island colony with close ties to France, much closer than to nearby Canada (1967b).

The system of kin address varies considerably. In both Mayenne and St Pierre, all kin and godparents receive *tu*. In Quebec, the urban middle class is moving in this direction, but the lower class and the rural regions from which it derives retain an address system like Puerto Rico's in which distance (including age) within the family is important. In some families, even older siblings receive *vous*. If changes in kin address arise during social change, one would expect between-family differences to be greater than in non-kin address, since sanctions are intrafamily. Generally, 'intimate' means parents, then aunts, uncles, and godparents, then grandparents. Some interfamily differences might be accounted for by finding which family members live in the household, which nearby, and which far away.

Lambert and Tucker (in press) have referred to a study of the social connotations of this changing system for urban school children in Montreal. Children were asked to judge taped family interaction varying in *tu* or *vous* to parents, and in the outcome of the interaction – giving or not giving the child a requested bicycle. In addition to the class differences (*tu* users richer, more educated families), the judges drew from the pronoun usage a set of expectations about family values, resulting in favorable judgements when the interaction outcome was congruent. For instance, *tu*-using families sound modern and tolerant, the mothers more active, the fathers more tolerant than *vous*-using families, if they prove child-centered. However, it is *vous*-using families that sound religious, with a good family spirit, an active mother and tolerant father when the decision goes against the child.

Sex of addressee appears to be a feature of adult systems, or may influence the probabilities of intimacy where there is a selector. In Quebec, adults generally give *tu* to children and young men, regardless of familiarity. In St Pierre, except to upper-class girls, who are less likely to receive *tu* under any conditions, acquaintance legitimizes *tu* and is necessary even in addressing children. In Mayenne, middle-class little boys said they received *tu* from everyone (and reported often reciprocating to strangers), but otherwise familiarity seems to be required, as in Puerto Rico, in the Mayenne system. Boys generally receive T from employers, and in the country and the urban lower class they receive T from service personnel. It should be noted that the analysis from the children's standpoint of what they think they receive is an interesting reflection of the fact that people know what they should say themselves, and they also expect some standard form from others. In analysing the adult rule systems, however, the children's data are not the best; the adults of rural or lower class background may have different rules (e.g., service personnel, perhaps) than others.

The compressed presentation here of Lambert's work has indicated several directions for research on social criteria of address selection. Lambert has shown that these rules are sensitive indicators of differences between social groups and of social change. One must look beyond the address system for independent social features correlated with address systems of a defined type. In order to do such studies, a clear-cut formal system for typing properties of address systems (like language typologies) is necessary.

Lambert (1967a) has discussed the development of address rules with age. There are several interesting problems in the learning of these systems, one being the visibility of the various social selectors. One can assume that rank graduations in an adult system might be learned late (at least in terms of generalizability to new addressees), as would generation differentiations not highly related to age. A second problem emphasized by Lambert is the system of alternation itself. Children in most language communities learn fairly early to employ the asymmetry of first and second person (for a case study see McNeill, 1963). Thus if they always received T and gave V, there might be less difficulty; however, they see others exchanging reciprocal V and T as well as asymmetrical address, and they give T to some alters. These problems could be studied in natural language communities where the language structure provides different category systems and social selectors (Slobin, 1967).

Shifting

When there is agreement about the normal address form to alters of specified statuses, then any deviation is a message. In the case of Dr Poussaint, both parties knew that the system required title to a physician; the policeman's use of 'boy' and 'Alvin' denied both rank and age. In the Russian system, the existence of numerous criteria of address permits the expression of delicate nuances of relationship. Friedrich gives convincing cases of momentary shifts at times of personal crises. He points out that in a public setting, friends would mask their intimacy with V; in talking of personal topics they could invoke their friendship with 'ty', remove it for impersonal topics with 'vy'.

Kantorovich (1966, p. 43) gives similar examples in current practice: 'I say "*ty*" to my subordinates, but I certainly don't do this in order to belittle them. I know that they'll answer me with "*vy*", but this isn't grovelling – it's a mark of respect . . . Somebody I call "*ty*" is somehow closer to me than someone I have to call *vy* ... If I get mad at one of my workers, and he needs a bawling out, I frequently switch to *vy* ...' Kantorovich also mentions that two businessmen who normally exchanged '*ty*' switched to '*vy*' and the first name + patronymic when help or advice was needed.

In systems with age or rank asymmetries of address, the use of the more deferential form to an equal or subordinate can either mean that they are receiving respect, or being put off at a distance. To account fully for the interpretation of such actions by the receivers, we need to know the other signals, such as tone of voice, other address features, and the available ambiguities of the relationship. In the case of courtship, for example, the important dimension is closeness or distance, and address change would be so interpreted.

Socialization

Adults entering a new system because of geographical or occupational mobility may have to learn new sociolinguistic rules. A contrastive analysis of formal rules, in combination with a theory of social learning, would allow specification of what will happen.

First, we can predict what the speaker will do. We can expect, on the basis of research on bilinguals (Ervin-Tripp, in press; Haugen, 1956), that the linguistic alternatives will at first be assimilated to familiar forms, to 'diamorphs'. Thus a Frenchman in the United States might start out by assuming that Monsieur = Mister, Madame = Mrs, and so on.

However, the rules for occurrence of these forms are different in France. In the polite discourse of many speakers, routines like *merci,* 'au revoir', 'bonjour', 'pardon' do not occur without an address form in France, although they may in the United States. One always says 'Au revoir, Madame' or some alternative address form. *Madame* differs from 'Mrs' in at least two ways. Unknown female addressees of a certain age are normally called *Madame* regardless of marital status. Further, Mrs + $\emptyset$ = $\emptyset$; Madame + $\emptyset$ = Madame. As a matter of fact, the rule requiring address with routines implies that when LN is not known, there cannot be a 'zero alternate' – some form of address must be used anyway, like the English 'sir'. As a result of these differences in rules, we can expect to hear elderly spinsters addressed as 'Pardon me, Mrs'.

How do listeners account for errors? I suggested earlier that shifting at certain points in sociolinguistic rules is regularly available as an option. Normally, it is interpreted as changing the listener's perceived identity or his relation to the speaker. The result may be complimentary, as 'sir' to an unknown working-class male, or insulting, as 'Mommy' to an adolescent male. If the learner of a sociolinguistic system makes an error that falls within this range of interpretable shifts, he may constantly convey predictably faulty social meanings. Suppose the speaker, but not the listener, has a system in which familiarity, not merely solidarity, is required for use of a first name. He will use TLN in the United States to his new colleagues and be regarded as aloof or excessively formal. He will feel that first-name usage from his colleagues is brash and intrusive. In the same way, encounters across social groups may lead to misunderstandings within the United States. Suppose a used-car salesman regards his relation to his customers as solidary, or a physician so regards his relation to old patients. The American using the rule in Figure 1 might regard such speakers as intrusive, having made a false claim to a solidary status. In this way, one can pinpoint abrasive features of interaction across groups.

Another possible outcome is that the alternative selected is completely outside the system. This would be the case with 'Excuse me, Mrs' which cannot be used under any circumstances by rule one. This behavior is then interpreted with the help of any additional cues available, such as the face, dress, or accent of a foreigner. In such cases, if sociolinguistic rules are imperfectly learned, there may be social utility in retaining an accent wherever the attitude toward the group of foreigners is sufficiently benign; it is better to be designated a foreigner than to risk insulting or offending addressees.

Integrated sociolinguistic rules

The rules given above are fractional. They are selective regarding the linguistic alternations accounted for. They define only specific linguistic entries as the universe of outcomes to be predicted. If one starts from social variables, a different set of rules might emerge. This is the outlook of William Geoghegan (1971) and Ward Goodenough (1965), as well as Dell Hymes (1964b), who suggested taking 'a specific or universal function, such as the distinguishing of the status or role of man and woman, derogation, respect, or the like, and . . . investigating the diverse means so organized within the language habits of the community . . . [rather than] looking for function as a correlative of structure already established' (p. 44).

Using such an approach, Goodenough examined behavior toward a range of statuses, and found that it was possible to rank both the statuses and the forms of behavior into Guttman scales and equivalent classes, grouped at the same scale point (1965). In this way, various kinds of verbal and nonverbal behavior can be shown to be outcomes of the same social selectors.

Deference, the feature studied by Goodenough, may be indicated by pronoun alternations, names or titles, tone of voice, grammatical forms, vocabulary, and so on (Capell, 1966, pp. 104ff; Martin, 1964). Deferential behavior in some systems may be realized only in special situations such as in introductions or in making requests. If one compares an isolated segment of two sociolinguistic systems, one cannot legitimately conclude that a given social variable is more important in one system than in the other. It may simply be realized through a different form of behavior.

It is not clear how the different realizations of social selectors might be important. Address, pronominal selection, or consistent verb suffixing (as in Japanese) can be consciously controlled more readily, perhaps, than intonation contours or syntactic complexity. Frenchmen report 'trying to use *tu*' with friends. Such forms can be taught by rule specification to children or newcomers. Forms which allow specific exceptions, or which have options so that too great or too little frequency might be conspicuous, cannot be taught so easily. Such rules can be acquired by newcomers only by long and intense exposure rather than by formal teaching.

Some alternations are common and required, others can be avoided. Howell reported that in Knoxville, Tennessee, Negroes uncertain of whether or not to reciprocate FN simply avoided address forms to colleagues (Howell, 1967, pp. 81–3), an approach that Brown and Ford also observed in the academic rank system. In a pronominal rank system like French or Russian such avoidance is impossible. Among bilinguals, language switching may be employed to avoid rank signaling (Howell, 1967; Tanner, 1967). The avoidable selector can be considered a special case of the presence of options in the system. Tyler (1965) has noticed that morphological deference features (like the Japanese) are more common in societies of particular kinship types, such as lineage organization.

This description was primarily drawn from the standpoint of predicting a speaker's choice of alternatives in some frame. It is also possible to examine these rules from the standpoint of comprehension or interpretation, as have Blom and Gumperz (1968) in their discussion of *social meaning*. Just as one can comprehend a language without speaking it, as actors we can interpret the social meaning of the acts of others without necessarily using rules identical to our own. The relation between production and comprehension rules remains to be studied.

References

BLOM, J.-P., and GUMPERZ, J. J. (1968), 'Some social determinants of verbal behaviour', in J. J. Gumperz and D. Hymes (eds.), *Directions in Sociolinguistics*, Holt, Rinehart & Winston, pub. 1971.

BROWN, R. W., and GILMAN, A. (1960), 'The pronouns of power and solidarity', in T. Sebeok (ed.), *Style in Language*, MIT Press.

CAPELL, A. (1966), *Studies in Sociolinguistics*, Mouton.

ERVIN-TRIPP, S. M. (in press), 'Becoming a bilingual', in *Proceedings of the 1967 UNESCO Conference on the Description and Measurement of Bilingualism*.

FRIEDRICH, P. (1966), 'Structural implications of Russian pronominal usage', in W. Bright (ed.), *Sociolinguistics*, Mouton.

GEOGHEGAN, W. (1971), 'Information processing systems in culture', in P. Kay (ed.), *Explorations in Mathematical Anthropology*, MIT Press.

GOODENOUGH, W. H. (1965), 'Rethinking "status" and "role": toward a general model of the cultural organization of social relationships', in M. Banton (ed.), *The Relevance of Models for Social Anthropology*, Tavistock.

HAUGEN, E. (1956), *Bilingualism in the Americas: A Bibliography and Research Guide*, American Dialect Society, no. 26.

HOWELL, R. W. (1967), *Linguistic Choice as an Index to Social Change*, Ph.D dissertation, University of California, Berkeley.

HYMES, D. (ed.) (1964a), *Language in Culture and Society*, Harper & Row.

HYMES, D. (1964b), 'Toward ethnographies of communication', in J. J. Gumperz and D. Hymes (eds.), *The Ethnography of Communication, AmA*, vol. 66, no. 6, part 2, pp. 1–34.

HYMES, D. (1967), 'Models of the interaction of language and social setting', *J. of Soc. Iss.*, vol. 23, no. 2, pp. 8–28.

KANTOROVICH, V. (1966), *Ty: vy: Zametki Pisatelya, (Ty + vy: a Writer's Notes)* Izd-vo pol. lit., Moscow.

LAMBERT, W. E. (1967a), 'A social psychology of bilingualism', in J. Macnamara (ed.), *Problems of Bilingualism, J. Soc. Iss.*, vol. 23, no. 2, pp. 91–109.

LAMBERT, W. E. (1967b), 'The use of "tu" and "vous" as forms of address in French Canada: a pilot study', *J. Verb. Learning Verb. Behav.*, vol. 6, no. 4, pp. 614–17.

LAMBERT, W. E., and TUCKER, G. R. (in press) *A social-psychological study of interpersonal modes of address: I. A. French-Canadian illustration*.

McNEILL, D. (1963), 'The psychology of "you" and "I": a case history of a small language system', American Psychological Association meeting.

MARTIN, S. (1964), 'Speech levels in Japan and Korea', in D. Hymes (ed.), *Language in Culture and Society*, Harper and Row.

POST, E. (1922), *Etiquette*, Funk and Wagnalls.

POUSSAINT, A. F. (1967), 'A Negro psychiatrist explains the Negro psyche', *New York Times Magazine*, August 20, p. 52.

SLOBIN, D. I. (1963), 'Some aspects of the use of pronouns of address in Yiddish', *Word*, vol. 19, pp. 193–202.

SLOBIN, D. I. (ed.) (1967), *A Field Manual for Cross-Cultural Study of the Acquisition of Communicative Competence*, University of California, Berkeley, mimeograph.

TANNER, N. (1967), 'Speech and society among the Indonesian élite: a case study of a multilingual community', *anthrop. Linguistics*, vol. 9, part 3, pp. 15–40.

TYLER, S. (1965), 'Koya language morphology and patterns of kinship behaviour', *AmA*. vol. 67, pp. 1428–40.

15 A. McIntosh

Language and Style

A. McIntosh, 'Language and Style', *Durham University Journal*,
vol. 55, no. 3, NS vol. 24, no. 3, 1963, pp. 116–23.

In choosing the title of this lecture, I was seeking to find a form of words
which would permit me to try to bring out some fairly widespread mis-
conceptions about the nature of grammar and to discuss the sort of
relationship it has to our more normal spontaneous linguistic activities.
By these I mean our activities whether we are still learners of a language or
whether we are reasonably mature practitioners, and whether we ourselves
are performing or whether we are engaged in trying to take in what others
are expressing. Such activities as these will normally embrace both what
on the one hand we say or hear, and what on the other we write or read.
And to return for a moment to the first point (i.e. whether or not we are
still learners of the language) it will be a central part of my contention
that we are always, all of us, in some sense still learners of the language,
that there is or at least should be no end to this process.

I shall not attempt here an enumeration and discussion of the various
definitions of grammar that one could dig out; I am more concerned to
consider what, in actual practice, people believe grammatical study to
involve and what purposes if any they feel it serves. And since I am to
consider it in relation to style, I shall concentrate on one or two aspects of
the grammar of our own language in relation to a range of fairly normal
linguistic activities on the part of native users of it.

There are some who believe, or often talk as if they believed, that a due
observance of the so-called rules of grammar is sufficient to ensure that
our linguistic activity will be impeccable. I wish to consider this belief
from several points of view, but first of all I should like to clear one simple
but widespread misconception out of the way. It has to do with this:
that even if we put a very broad interpretation on the word 'grammar',
there are still certain aspects of our linguistic activity which are not so to
speak governed by it. For is it not possible for me to utter all kinds of
sentences, the *grammatical* correctness of which nobody would dispute,
but which, nevertheless, may be dismal flops or colossally off the mark?
The study of howlers is instructive in this respect. The essence of the
appeal of a howler is that, despite some sort of linguistic slip-up, it has a

crazy unintended effect or mad validity, rather like a cricket stroke aimed to mid-on which goes for four over the heads of the slips. And the error may not be *grammatical* at all. What for instance is wrong grammatically with Gerard Hoffnung's Tyrolean hotelier who wrote listing among the amenities of his hotel 'a French widow in every bedroom, affording delightful prospects'? Or with my own son's once remarking that Mrs So-and-so was going to have a baby, and on being asked how he knew, replying 'Oh, because she's started to wear nativity clothes'?

These infelicities or felicities have to do with *lexis* or vocabulary, showing us that an observance of the conventions of *grammar* is only half the battle; the proper use of language also involves due observance of the equally important conventions of lexis. In other words, no amount of grammatical knowledge will in itself save us from errors or mis-hits of this kind, and the achievement of correct or 'good' grammar is just a part of the whole business of adequate linguistic performance. We should note that there are other howlers which illustrate grammatical infelicities rather than lexical ones; that is to say, where confusion is caused because a syntactic pattern or relationship is interpreted as a different one from that which was intended. In this category belong such things as 'Second-hand piano for sale belonging to retired schoolteacher with carved legs'. This time it is the *vocabulary* there is nothing wrong with. Another example of a similar kind (one much more likely to be misinterpreted when read than when heard) is quoted by Denys Parsons in his collection of such things in the book called *True to Type*: 'If you shoot yourself and have not used —'s ammunition, you have missed one of the pleasures of life'.

The second point that I wish to consider in relation to the insufficiency of traditional grammatical approaches is of a rather different kind. It has to do with the fact that they tend to consist of little more than a series of warnings or red lights. It is *wrong*, we are often told, to end a sentence with a preposition. It is *wrong* (as I was taught at school) to begin a sentence with *and*, though I have already disregarded this so-called 'rule' in the present paper. It is *wrong* to say (or write) *I seen him yesterday* or *If he didn't do it, he should of.* What I want to suggest in this connection is that (whether we agree with all these prohibitions or not) a series of red lights is not enough, either in matters like these, or in such others as the proper selection of words or the way they should be spelt.

For, from this purely red-light point of view, it would be wrong (in the same sense of that word) to play rugby with a soccer ball, or to putt at golf (as I'm often tempted to do) with a billiard cue. But if we can regard games as having so to speak a structure and a grammar, such prohibitions as I have mentioned would not begin to get to grips with the finer points of their structure; for this something more positive is needed. This is clear enough if one considers the case of users of a language, and this applies to most of us, who after a certain age do not perpetrate linguistic errors in the crude sense, or at least not to an extent which need cause any anxiety. For surely this merely red-light kind of grammar has no great relevance to us. Yet can we, I would ask, claim that we take in and give out with maximal efficiency, or do we not quite often, in all sorts of different situations, fall somewhat short of perfection in the handling of language? And if so, is there not a need for this more positive kind of grammar to help us with some of these more serious problems?

I suggest that we should put matters of rank error or sheer wrongness into a quite secondary and preliminary branch of grammar, and go on from there to a higher branch which pays more attention to what I might call grades of rightness. For with language, as with most other human activity, the mere avoidance of rank error should surely not be the extent of our goal. And here we come to what in a very broad sense we might call 'style'. For I like to think of style as a word we may apply not only to the way Milton writes epic verse or Gibbon writes historical prose, but also (though I should not want to use the word 'style' to cover *all* such diversities) to the various ways in which people may talk or write in quite ordinary circumstances, such as when ordering a goose for Christmas, or talking to a small child, or communicating with a prospective mother-in-law, or complaining about the price of bus fares. All these activities, Milton's, Gibbon's, your own, call for different kinds of linguistic behaviour. We are all perfectly aware of this to some degree; people may vary in their linguistic flexibility, in their ability to adjust to different situations, but there can be none who make (or should I say *none who makes*?) no adjustments at all. I do not forget that a good deal of the variation will often best be described under the category of lexis rather than that of grammar, that is to say that there will often be times when the main change, between one situation and another, will be in the vocabulary rather than in the grammatical patterns. In other words, I do not forget and have indeed been insisting that grammar, even in a fairly wide interpretation of that term, is only part of the whole business. But it is an important part, and it merits attention.

Let us, then, consider its place in the understanding and manipulating of such differing stylistic modes as I have given instances of. Let us suppose that we are considering a problem of how someone might best 'put something', and how a knowledge of alternative grammatical resources might help us in such a case. Our main problem now, it should be clear, has little or nothing to do with rank error, for there may well be no danger of this at all. It is, rather, to assess the degree of *adequacy* of this or that grammatical pattern in immediate relation to the need to express something which has arisen in a particular situation. So if someone says, or considers saying, *I have direct personal ocular evidence of John's having been in this place some twenty to twenty-four hours ago*, our problem now is not of worrying about whether this is a grammatical sentence. We can perhaps pass it on that score. But our real problem is 'how fitting is it, grammatically, in the circumstances?' And you will readily see that we may often be constrained to admit that though – by some abstract general standard – there is nothing fatally wrong with the grammar of a particular sentence, yet – for the particular purpose intended – it may well leave something to be desired. And as far as *this* sentence is concerned, there are numerous situations in which we might well rate higher, all in all, the linguistic *savoir faire* of a man who chose rather to say *I seen John here yesterday evening*. For though the latter sentence perpetrates, in terms of the conventions of Standard English, a certain rank error, it would have, in some situations at least, a distinct superiority. And my point is that it is the kind of superiority to which red-light grammar, which is always straining at gnats and swallowing camels, is in danger of giving no credit whatever.

The main point I am trying to make here is simply this: that the mere abstract grammatical rightness of a sentence does not necessarily make it even *grammatically* appropriate in a particular setting or context. I might also mention here in passing another point which grammars pay little attention to: that two sentences which, considered each in its own right, are quite impeccable grammatically, may be very uneasy bedfellows when juxtaposed. I well remember the stir caused by my old headmaster when once he inadvertently slipped up on this matter. One day after lunch two of my friends wandered outside the school grounds, which was illegal, and they had the misfortune to meet him as they returned. I do not recall what extralinguistic consequences the episode had, but I remember vividly the two sentences he shot at them in swift succession when he saw them. The first was 'Where've you been?' The second was 'Answer me "yes" or "no"!'

So far I have considered two shortcomings in our normal approaches to grammar which seem to me to be closely related. One is the emphasis on rooting out rank error, the other is the failure to make it sufficiently clear that a grammatically correct sentence is not necessarily grammatically *good* in a particular context. It is unfortunate that these shortcomings are seriously and critically supported by the current patterns and conventions of our examinations, at various levels, in such subjects as English Language, the Use of English and so forth. It is not only that the examiners concentrate so much on testing the capacity to avoid mere rank error; or that they set so much store by the carrying out of certain verbal gymnastics which happen to have the superficial virtue of being easily marked (such as turning direct into indirect speech) but which bear very little relation to the normal *creative* activities of speech or writing. Worse than such things in themselves is that when you get examinations so one-sidedly constructed, then you *force* teachers, however able and enlightened they may be, to toe the line, to concentrate on the inculcation of these particular skills and verbal tricks rather than on other matters of greater importance. This is why I am pleased to see approaches like Margaret Langdon's little book *Let the Children Write*, where emphasis is placed on the *positive* side, on ability to express freely and fully, rather than on incidental error.

Let the Children Write does not offer a formal grammatical approach; it simply gets away from this perpetual straining at gnats. But at more advanced stages something further is needed. The gist of my belief about what *is* needed was summed up admirably for me the other day by an old student of mine, now an English master, who came to talk to my staff about the problems of grammar, style, self-expression, interpretation and the like as they confronted him in relation to his own pupils. What he said was that the grammatical approach should for his kind of need and purpose be *generative* rather than merely *analytical*. By this he meant that it was not meeting his problems simply to analyse or parse chunks of prose or verse in the dreary dead formal way that is still not infrequent. For this is something like taking some finished and perhaps dauntingly complicated model made of Meccano or some similar material and then analysing its structure as a finished entity. The more generative or creative alternative which he suggested was that one should show pupils the various kinds of grammatical patterns that are available to them (and to others) for particular specifiable purposes, and above all to give a great deal of attention to relating the patterns very carefully to these purposes. This would be like introducing a pupil gradually to simple constructional techniques in Meccano and getting him accustomed, step by step, by direct experience and practice, to their uses and functions. Needless to say, this alternative approach can be made both in relation to a student's *own* linguistic activity, and in relation to suitably selected structural aspects of something which has been said or written by someone else.

This way of doing things does not in any sense banish processes of analysis. But it does imply that it is not enough just to take a sentence and proclaim that it consists (let us say) of a subject and a predicate, and that the predicate consists of a transitive verb plus an object. And that the object consists of a noun group 'qualified' by an adjectival clause introduced by *which* and so forth. Indeed, the more one goes into this kind of mechanical detail, the greater is the danger of the whole thing being a kind of mumbo jumbo about as remote from linguistic practice as anything could well be. One need not therefore be surprised if the reaction to this kind of approach is 'So what?' Surely from the very beginning the objective should be to relate all analysis to what in a vague way we may call the purpose of the sentence, the reason for it having, of all things, *this* structure, rather than many other possible ones. And of course to show that vocabulary comes in here too, and that vocabulary and grammar necessarily interact. But above all to display and consider the make-up of a sentence in relation to its purpose and its environment. For it seems to me that linguistic study of this general kind, to be of any use at all, must be married to the broader understanding of how to write well and speak well and how to appreciate to the full good writing and good speaking by others. And the present funeral-baked grammatical meats can at best coldly furnish forth any such marriage-feast. For the mechanicalness and the remoteness of approach of the traditional methods of grammatical analysis are sometimes quite frightening. It is almost as if one were to expound to someone what we might not unreasonably call the 'grammar' of a Ferguson tractor and of an Austin Princess (i.e. their mechanical structure and so forth) without any explicit reference to the differing functions of each, and then being surprised and indignant to find our pupil using the Austin Princess to do his ploughing with.

Of course the strictly analytical and non-generative approach to grammar has its reasons. It enables us, by direct observation, to establish the totality of legitimate grammatical structures. It also *appears* at least to have the merit of objectivity and detachment, of not meddling or judging, though in fact, in various ways, it is judging all the time. It usually takes for granted – and I think that this is a mistake – that the choice (at some given point in an utterance) of a particular grammatical structure or complex of structures is obvious; it says in effect, 'You know as well as I do that the Ferguson is for ploughing and the Austin Princess for conveying business men to expensive lunches: don't tell me I need to go into all that.'

Unfortunately such things are *not* always obvious, especially as we move from cruder to more subtle problems of choice. So what we often get in grammars is comparable to what we should have if a lexicographer offered us a sort of dictionary with an imposing inventory of words suitably arranged according to some no doubt laudably logical scheme, but without such elementary trifles as the actual *meanings* of the words. After all, he might argue, why give the meanings of words in a dictionary when most of us know the majority of them already? It is the *meaning* of grammatical patterns in a similar kind of sense, and the degree of superiority or inferiority of one pattern to another in sheer terms of suitability in a specific situation, that I consider to be very much neglected. The result is that the ordinary student of grammar tends to disassociate almost entirely the two activities of linguistic creation and of grammatical analysis. Grammar reeks of formalin and suggests the scalpel and the anatomy room. This is what I meant when I said that grammar as it tends to be taught is not generative but merely analytical.

One way in which it could be made more generative would be to show how some particular effect (if possible, to begin with some quite *obvious* effect) is often achieved by drawing upon the combined resources of a whole conglomeration of grammatical devices. This is precisely the kind of thing that traditional grammarians are not happy about tackling, since they like their material to be organized in an orderly, and what to them may seem a logical, way. To illustrate my point, I shall take an example from *As You Like It*. It has a relevance to our own day-to-day linguistic behaviour, for we can (if we want to) act upon it, as well as merely observe it being put into use by a great writer.

I was recently concerned, from a rather different point of view, with some of the linguistic devices whereby Shakespeare adumbrates the nature of the relationship between Celia and Rosalind and the way this shifts in the course of the play (see McIntosh, 1963). It will be recalled that when they are first together, not only is Rosalind more taciturn than Celia, but she seems to be more detached and impersonal. Then in the course of Act I, Scene iii, certain stylistic shifts may be observed which serve to convey to us a change in Rosalind. And though I call them stylistic shifts, I would point out that many of these are grammatical in nature, so that the understanding of the whole tone of the language becomes partly a matter of feeling the effect of nuances of a specifically grammatical kind. Up to line 104 of that scene, whenever Rosalind speaks, she tends much less to involve Celia directly than Celia does when speaking to her. By this I mean that Celia brings Rosalind right into the conversation in the manner of people who say 'Darling, how are you?' or 'Please pass me the cigarettes,' whereas Rosalind is the kind of person who doesn't get much beyond saying things like 'My nephew got back from Paris yesterday' or 'It'll probably rain tomorrow.'

If we want to involve another person to some degree beyond what is achieved by merely speaking to them at all, what are the linguistic devices at our disposal? First of all we can use the second person pronoun: 'What a lovely dress you are wearing'; this at once brings our interlocutor in out of the psychological cold. Or one can use the inclusive *we*, i.e. the *we* which means *you and I* or *you and we*: *I suggest we go and have a cup of tea*. Or one can use vocatives like *My dear*; or again question-carrying patterns like *Has John got back yet?* Or yet again one can use the imperative, whether in severe or gentle fashion: *Get out of my way* or *Be a dear and get me a cup of tea.* Or you can brew up a judicious combination of one or more of these devices – even, if you wish, the whole lot: *Get us out of here, you dope, do you hear me?*; this is a very involving sentence indeed. I call all such different pattern-resources 'markers of involvement'; my list, I should add, is not exhaustive.

Now if these markers of involvement are part of grammar, we may say that Rosalind for a short while *changes her grammar* at line 105 of Act I, Scene iii, of *As You Like It*. This does not mean of course that she suddenly becomes more, or suddenly becomes less, grammatically correct; it is simply that for reasons connected with the situation, she now tends to select certain patterns from the total number of possible patterns available to her which she did not select before, or else to make changes in the *frequency* with which she selects them. Style, we might almost say, is a matter of the selection of particular grammatical patterns and sequences of patterns, and of particular items of vocabulary and sequences of items; and of course (by implication) the avoidance of others. Let us see what use Rosalind makes of the possibility of selecting differently as her mood changes. In the first 104 lines of that scene she speaks 124 words, and in what she says there are only five examples of any of the 'involving' devices I have been talking about, i.e. only one every twenty-five words or so.

When we compare Rosalind's linguistic behaviour in this respect with that of Celia we can see very clearly that she is very much more drawn in upon herself than her cousin. For Celia (in the same passage) not only speaks twice as much but she uses one or other of these markers of involvement with far higher relative frequency, namely fifty-six times; i.e. once every six words, as against Rosalind's once every twenty-five words. So Celia is always producing remarks like 'Oh my poor Rosalind! Whither wilt thou go?' whereas Rosalind without any similarly direct involvement of Celia says such things as 'Oh, how full of briers is this working-day world!' Rosalind never quite gets so outgiving and matey as Celia habitually is, but in the succeeding part of this same scene she almost trebles the frequency of her use of such markers, using one or another of them sixteen times in the next 142 words. I am not specially concerned here with the reasons for this psychological shift on Rosalind's part, but it has something to do with the sudden crisis of her banishment from court. For Celia's impulsive and generous proposal that they should *both* flee finally shakes Rosalind out of her self-centred preoccupations, and she then starts with a quite new vigour and warmth to discuss plans for their joint flight. For example (lines 128–30):

But, cousin, what if we assay'd to steal
The clownish fool out of your father's court?
Would he not be a comfort to our travel?

Here we have two uses of the first person plural pronoun (*we, our*), one of the second (*your*), one vocative and two questions: six markers all in three lines.

My main purpose in sketching this example has been to show that a preoccupation with a certain kind of stylistic 'tone' or 'atmosphere' forced me to consider, all in one group, a heterogeneous collection of grammatical resources – questions, imperatives, vocatives, pronouns and so on – which grammarians themselves would not normally bring together in this way, but would tend to treat quite separately in different sections or chapters, with little concern for the precise kind of effects their combined use might produce.

Another matter of perhaps even wider relevance and application, in which even advanced users of the language might profit by help from the illumination which grammar could well provide, has to do with the linking together of clauses, sentences and larger units in such a way that the totality coheres and runs smoothly from beginning to end. Here again I want to stress that the relevant devices are – from the narrow conventional grammatical point of view – very varied and miscellaneous, and would rarely, if ever, be discussed together at any one point in a grammar.

I am thinking here of such things as the following: of what Mrs Barbara Strang in her admirable recent work, *Modern English Structure,* calls (page 175) 'response utterances', that is, ways of helping to link what *I* am about to say with what *you* have just said; and then also of forms which link what I am about to say with what *I* have already said, like the phrase *and then also* which I have just used. Again (and notice that 'again' is another such linking device) I am thinking of certain types of intonation and, in writing, of certain types of punctuation which help to weld things together. Fourthly there is the welding and linking effect of the repetition of words and phrases which, like fibres in a thread, stretch back-over and forwards, knitting everything tightly together; I have noticed recently how full some of the writings of John Wycliff are of such repetitions. Finally there is the whole complicated grammar of what we call anaphoric reference, i.e. the way I can hold a stretch of text together by letting words like *he* and *it* and *them* run through it in what is a kind of repeated shorthand reference to, and taking up of, something that has occurred earlier in the text. One has, of course, to be careful about these, or the meaning can go wildly wrong. Consider for example another sentence quoted by Denys Parsons: 'to keep flies from marking electric light bulbs, smear them with camphorated oil'. We should note that some of these 'referring' words may link up not just with single words or phrases, but with whole sentences or even larger units.

It is a useful practical experience to try to write or rewrite a piece of

English denying oneself the advantage of these linking devices; in this way the value and potentialities of these such grammatical resources become clear in a very vivid way. About the machinery of this whole art of the linking of units of utterance there is much still to be discovered, and I know of no grammar which treats adequately, all under one heading, what is after all a fundamentally important everyday stylistic problem.

If, as in such matters as I have touched upon, we can see the kinds of devices in which we may attain the sort of end that is usually desirable, we can also achieve, for some special purpose, the opposite kind of effect of avoiding these devices. One must acknowledge that the greater writers and orators and the like may well achieve such an aim by some more intuitive process, without analysis. But most of us would be no worse off for having a less hazy knowledge of the devices at our disposal and the facilities they provide. Thus if for a special purpose (for example in setting on record my fragmentary recollection of the events of some chaotic battle) I wish specifically *not* to produce a smooth sequential narrative flow, then I can probably better achieve this special aim if I have a clear knowledge of those devices which *would* produce, or help to produce, just such a flow. In other words, I believe it to be true of most of us that the more we know about what the utilization of certain grammatical devices will accomplish (and the same is true on the lexical side), the better shall we be equipped to achieve more unusual ends by more unusual procedures. If there had been time, I should have liked to illustrate what I mean by discussing some aspects of the poetry of Gerard Manley Hopkins. For Hopkins as a poet, though not very much as a prose-writer, felt it necessary to depart from certain grammatical conventions because he came to believe that they distorted his own intuitions about reality. (See McIntosh, 1959). It is sufficient to say here that the most impressive innovators, whether it be in poetry or in music or in painting or in sculpture, are often those who have learnt what we might call the normal or everyday grammar of their subject, and then and only then deviated consciously from it. This is certainly what happened with Hopkins. If we understand the rather special grammar of such innovational deviations as those of Hopkins, we shall see the more readily what it is which helps them to make their own powerful impact.

In all this, so far as literature is concerned, we must remember what I began by saying: that grammar is only one branch of linguistic study and analysis, and that, in particular, equally meticulous scrutiny of the selection made from vocabulary and the way the words used are brought into juxtaposition, is important. But once we recognize this, and the link between these two aspects of language, I see no difficulty about our being able to make helpful grammatical and lexical statements about particular stylistic modes and effects of many different kinds. Meanwhile, however, too much dead and unimaginative teaching of grammar goes on, largely – as I have already suggested – because of the out-of-date ideas of examiners about what should go into the papers they set. And also, I should add now, because there are not enough good text books. I may say that if it were decreed (and why not?) that for the next ten years a certain number of able teachers in our universities and schools were to write text books as their *main* duty, and were only allowed to teach in their spare time, instead of the other way around, then in ten years we should have a very different situation from what we have now.

We are just beginning, in my opinion, to face many of the problems that should be faced in this kind of work, and are still in grave danger of just muddling along as we have tended to do in the past. But I see signs of hope. For instance, committees have recently been set up to scrutinize English examinations. And publishers seem to be ready now to tackle the problems of getting out better text books. And the growing importance of English as a world language offers new challenges. The tasks to be faced are after all quite exciting; if their importance happens to straddle the practical world of international communication, science and business, and the other world of literature proper, then so much the more reason for our facing them with due seriousness and responsibility.

References

MCINTOSH, A. (1963), '"As You Like It": a grammatical clue to character', *A Review of English Literature*, vol. 4, no. 2, April.

MCINTOSH, A., (1959), 'Linguistics and English Studies', in A. McIntoch and M. A. K. Halliday (eds.), *Patterns of Language*, Longman.

STRANG, B. M. H. (1962), *Modern English Structure*, St Martin's Press; Edward Arnold.

16 B. W. Andrzejewski

Poetry in Somali Society

B. W. Andrzejewski, 'Poetry in Somali Society', *New Society*,
no. 25, 1963, pp. 22–4.

The Somali Republic is one of the few countries in Africa where one
language is spoken over almost the entire territory, and the Somali language even spreads over the borders into vast regions of Ethiopia and
Kenya, and into French Somaliland. Paradoxically, this great national
asset, valuable as it proves itself in spoken communication, is not used for
the purpose of writing. Various scripts using Arabic, Roman or invented
symbols have been put forward by both Somalis and Europeans, but so
far none has achieved the status of a national orthography.

There are many reasons for this, but the most important seems to be a
deeply ingrained predilection for the use of two languages. For almost a
thousand years, until the colonial powers introduced their languages into
Somali society, Arabic was the chosen medium for correspondence, commercial records and for communicating with the outside world. Somali
has always been used only for speech, and no doubt this gives the speakers
a sense of exclusiveness, of cosiness and security in a private world to
which foreigners have little access: in fact, they have the advantage of
speaking 'off the record' all the time.

Since the early ages of Islam the Horn of Africa has been exposed to the
powerful influence of Arabia, Arab traders, settlers and refugees established their culture and religion among the autochthonous inhabitants, and
centres of Islamic and Arabic scholarship flourished in all Somali towns.
Even in the remote nomadic hamlets teachers have taught the Quran for
centuries, and future teachers and judges have learned their Muslim
theology and law in itinerant colleges. When English, French and Italian
came on the Somali scene, in colonial times, they fell quite naturally in
the familiar pattern of a dichotomy between the spoken language used
among the Somalis themselves, and another language used for writing
and contact with foreigners.

These European languages, in spite of their undoubted advantages of
contact with modern civilizations, have not as yet had enough time to make
any appreciable impact on Somali culture. The Arabic language and
literature, on the other hand, have proved so attractive, particularly for

the pious, that a sizeable Somali literature written in Arabic has developed. It consists chiefly of religious poetry, some of which even surpasses, for ardour and zeal, similar compositions by the Arabs. But in spite of its undoubted charm and imaginative power, Somali literature in Arabic belongs to the Arabic classical tradition and does not assert with any vigour or individuality the Somali national character. It is in the poetry in the Somali language – composed, recited and remembered without the aid of writing – that we find the real genius of this remarkable nation.[1]

Anyone who comes into close contact with the Somalis of the nomadic interior is deeply impressed by the strange contrast between the poverty of their material civilization and the refinement of their culture in other respects. In the life of the pastoral nomad, there is a premium on the portability of his belongings: adjustable huts are made of light wooden poles and grass mats; vessels are made of bark or light wood; and the only things which of necessity have to be made of iron or clay are cooking pots. Some of these few possessions are decorated with graceful designs, but generaly speaking a nomadic village gives an impression of austere simplicity.

During the dry season, when the struggle with an inclement environment is fierce, Somali pastoral life seems to be entirely centred round the urgent necessity of finding enough water and enough grass to survive with the herds to the next rainy season. When the first rains come, the whole pattern of life changes. There are no more exhausting journeys to distant wells; grass springs up all around, and the heavy toil of seeking new grazing grounds is abandoned. Everyone becomes healthier, visibly fatter, and better-tempered, and rest and recreation replace the relentless struggle of the dry season.

It is particularly at this time that the Somalis turn to their favourite entertainment: the art of alliterative poetry. The demands of prosody and the cultivated taste of the audiences make the composition of poetry a major intellectual and artistic task: the rules of alliteration, for instance, require the poet to use at least one word beginning with the alliterative sound in each half line of a poem, no small achievement if the poem is a hundred lines long. As well as this, a subtle rhythmic pattern must be followed, and the audience naturally expects forceful imagery and a good style. Talented men compose poetry in impressive quantities: there are no professional bards, but a popular poet achieves the kind of nation-wide prestige which can certainly be envied by the unappreciated poets of modern Europe.

1. A bibliography of texts, translations and works on Somali poetry can be found in Johnson (1969).

The formal restrictions of the poetic form often lead to obscurity in diction and the use of veiled imagery, and there is, among the lesser poets, a good deal of 'dragging in' of inappropriate but alliterating words when inspiration has failed. But the decoding of the meaning is a delight to the Somalis and the subject of endless discussions, which add to the aesthetic pleasure of listening to beautiful words well chanted.

Of the several types of Somali poetry, the work and dance songs, though interesting and entertaining, neither merit nor receive serious intellectual attention. Somewhat higher in the scale come the ephemeral love songs, short apostrophes usually strung together to make a sizeable song. These are as likely to be denounced by Somali elders as are pop songs by their contemporaries here, and for much the same reasons.

When a poem is first composed and recited it is always topical and related to some true life situation of the poet or his clan: it is composed for a particular purpose, at a particular moment of time, and these circumstances are an integral part of the poem. If it achieves popularity in areas where the happenings would not be common knowledge, the reciter takes care to explain them. With the passage of time the memory of the particular event is likely to fade even among the poet's clansmen, and the reciter will then use his judgement as to whether they need a history lesson or not. The topicality of a poem does not detract from its continued popularity, if it is good enough. One might think of it as a news commentary in poetic form: one is interested today in both news and poetry, and tomorrow the news has turned into history and the poetry is still there.

Somali poems may be composed to stir up quarrels, to make peace, to rebuke sluggards or hotheads, to publish grievances, or simply to mark a special occasion, such as one recited by the leader of the Dervish movement, Mahammed 'Abdille Hassan (the so-called 'Mad Mullah'), when he gave his favourite horse to a potential ally. This great nationalist leader was also a great poet, and used his talent as a powerful means of propaganda in his war against Great Britain, Italy and Ethiopia. He sometimes even gave instructions to his spies in the form of poems, some of which have survived and acquired wide publicity. The following extract is from a poem composed to denounce some of his countrymen who had joined the enemy.

Listen to the call of the muezzin – it calls people to prayer;
Consider God, who created people, and the people who reject His
    commands
The prophets, and those who do not follow the saints
Those who took long, heavy spears against the elders of the Order
Those who have become children of the Christians and look on
    Europeans as their relatives

Those who of their own free will performed menial tasks for the infidels
Those who, though not forced to do it, followed them and fawned on
them
Those for whom Menelik is like a father who deals with their affairs
Those for whom Abyssinians have become God, and who babble
prayers to them
Those who have hunted me out of the land of my God like wild game
Those who have driven me into the dusty sands of the desert. . . .

Somalis often say that a good poet can sow peace and also hatred: he can
win friendship by praise and appreciation, deepen an existing feud, or lead
to a new one. In the pastoral interior, poets often act as spokesmen for
their clans in disputes, and one can even find interclan treaties in poetic
form; it is not unusual for a poet to rise to the tank of a clan leader, if he
is not one already.

The amount of local history enshrined in Somali poetry is enormous,
though the historian is to be pitied who tries to find his way through the
labyrinthine clan feuds and alliances, obscured as they are by poetic
imagery and hyperbole. In the almost total lack of documentation of
clan history, however, poetry is the only source of such information apart
from the memories, admittedly prodigious, of the Somalis themselves.

There is little or no overt didactic intention in the kind of poetry we are
discussing, but the young men of the clans who are beginning to feel their
way in the adult world of public affairs must absorb a great deal of useful
knowledge in an easily remembered form; they must also be influenced
by the many philosophical observations scattered throughout all Somali
verse, as well as by the emphasis on the moral values of prudence, courage
and loyalty.

In the nomadic interior the composition and enjoyment of poetry is not
limited to any particular group: it goes on round every camp fire and in
every assembly under a shady tree. What is particularly striking is that it
does not function in isolation in separate villages, settlements or clans, but
spreads with astonishing rapidity over vast areas. In fact its swift movements across the plains of the Horn of Africa have led some Somalis to
believe that poems are carried by a mystic wind, or by djinns, or even by
God Himself. A poem recited in one nomadic settlement may in a few
months or even weeks acquire wide currency over a region the size of
Scotland. People who meet on journeys, at wells or trading posts, pass
poems from mouth to mouth, and as there is little else to fill the mind,
some people acquire large repertoires which even a whole evening of non-
stop recitation cannot exhaust. In the storerooms of their memories one

can find poems freshly composed and freshly learned by heart side by side with poems, perhaps a century old, passed on from reciter to reciter.

No doubt the rigid framework of the rhythm and alliteration assists in the achievement of these feats of memory, but some Somalis even have the reputation of being able to learn a poem of one hundred lines after hearing it chanted once only. Others spend hours 'receiving' it, as they say, from a poet or reciter.

The sheer joy of reciting good poetry is often a sufficient incentive for this effort, but there may also be the anticipation of gaining friends and popularity by repeating the poem to fresh audiences. In a society such as this, the winning of allies is an unceasing preoccupation of every pastoralist: he wants to know where he can turn for help in hard times or in war, and he is perfectly aware of the warmth of friendly feeling created by the well-spoken recitation of a good poem.

Apart from the interest of its themes, and the social use made of it, Somali poetry contributes to the maintenance of a high standard of cultivation in speech. Indeed, as the language is not written, there are no rival influences: no newspapers, no novels to drive a wedge between the spoken and written word. Everybody recognizes that the highest form of verbal communication is poetry, and it sets the cultural tone of society even for those who show no particular zeal for it. A rather serious style of speech is used in all public encounters, and quotations from poems and alliterative proverbs are regarded as signs of elegance and refinement.

The poverty and debasement of speech so often met with among the industrial masses in this country is unknown among the common run of camel herders in the Somali Republic, who can as often as not express themselves succinctly or elaborately as the occasion demands, and with a wit and urbanity in contrast with their meagre material surroundings.

No doubt this will gradually change as the opportunities for education skim off the cream of the pastoral talent; the attractions of an urban and 'higher' life are unlikely to be resisted for very long even by the conservative-minded pastoralists, and it is anybody's guess whether the art of poetry will survive a struggle with formal education of a modern type. Even now, in the towns where the influence of Arabic and European culture is stronger than in the interior, traditional poetry is not so extensively cultivated, though it can often be heard in cafés and at public meetings. Especially since the last war, the themes which in the past were connected with interclan affairs have often been replaced by ones connected with party politics. For a political party it is a great asset to have a good poet devoted to its cause: poems in praise of sultans and clan chiefs are increasingly giving way to panegyrics on party leaders and members of the government, and political crises are enlivened by poetic bombard-ments from all sides. Such polemical pieces seldom descend to the scur-rility and churlishness of eighteenth century English lampoons, but use such weapons as exhortation, praise, reproach and emotional blackmail.

A people as politically aware as the Somalis have naturally always extended their interest to world affairs. The advent of broadcasting in Somali provided the poets with further material and a new stimulus to comment on the state of the world. Short-wave sets installed in shops and remote trading posts became centres of attraction: even before the inven-tion of transistors, the small battery set found its way into the camel saddle-pack. These lines are from a poem on the Suez crisis, and show keen interest, but a strange lack of involvement.

Oh men,[2] the beautiful world is going to be spoiled
The nations assembled in London have brought about this trouble
The West and East have approached each other ready for war . . .
See the pride of Nasser, the Chinese, the yelling Arabs,
Nehru negotiating with all ingenuity,
Whenever the sun sets, the Russians bring equipment;
Power has been launched on the sea.
See Eden, proud and strutting
And Dulles, inciting him to conquest yet unwilling to take part himself;
The French, driven by jealousy and zeal, yearning for the din of an
    explosion.
If the United Nations make no decisions with mighty pens
A great explosion will come from the Suez Canal.
The people who have done this do not know the value of their lives;
If planes drop the equipment entrusted to them,
If cannons, resounding, fire without ceasing,
If the hidden submarines come to face each other
It is certain that smoke will billow and boil there!
Certainly, of the two sides, one will subjugate the other, as with a
    burden saddle;
How horrible is the smoke and perdition which they pursue:
Oh God, the Powerful, save us from the roaring thunderbolts!

All the local stations broadcasting in Somali find in poetry an inexhaustible supply of programme material, of which the listeners never seem to tire. Hour after hour the sonorous verses are chanted: here we have a people who are prepared to argue, even quarrel, over the interpretation of a line or the admissibility of a neologism, who cherish wit and the intelligent use of language as part of a man's equipment for life, who really understand

2. For the original Somali version of this poem see Geydh (1965) p. 23.

the power of words. My last quotation is from a poem addressed to a sultan who was ignoring his clan assembly and trying to assume dictatorial powers. The sultan, no match for a poet, was deposed.

The vicissitudes of the world,[3] oh 'Olaad, are like the clouds of the
    seasons
Autumn weather and spring weather come after each other in turn
Into an encampment abandoned by one family, another family moves
If a man is killed, one of his relatives will marry his widow
Last night you were hungry and alone, but tonight people will feast
    you as a guest
When fortune places a man even on the mere hem of her robe, he
    quickly becomes proud and overbearing
A small milking vessel, when filled to the brim, soon overflows. . . .

A supplementary note
The Somali theatre

When this article was originally published I had to omit, for lack of space, any mention of the use of poetry in Somali drama, which has been a very popular form of entertainment in towns since about 1940.

It is essentially an oral art, since the actors learn their roles by heart from the playwright without the use of any script. Although the concepts of plot and imitation of life on the stage are innovations inspired by foreign films and plays, most of the dialogue is conducted in the traditional metres of alliterative verse, the themes are drawn from topical issues of Somali life, and the humour derives from situations and characters familiar to the audiences.

Somali drama has proved to be an unusually successful case of the syncretism of a foreign influence with the traditional art of poetry, and it has attracted some of the most talented poets in the country. The culminating point in its development was the building of the National Theatre in Mogadishu in 1967.

The poetry used in Somali plays can be illustrated by the following extract which comes from a dialogue between a middle-aged couple, Cateeye and his wife Cutiya, on the engagement of their daughter. It is taken from a play by Ali Sugule called *Kalahaab iyo kalahaad* 'Wide apart and flown asunder' (1966), which has marriage problems as its theme.

CATEEYE: We often suffered thirst and hunger
    Yet we were not unlucky. Life is full of trouble
    And is but a journey one night-stop long. Often meagre fare

3. For the original Somali version of this poem see Gabay-Shinni (1965) p. 19.

We had, but also we ate meat and drank milk in plenty,
And there were nights and there were days one doesn't forget.
You remember them, don't you? If God allows it,
More days that are wonderful are still in store for us.

CUTIYA: Oh Cateeye, those nights and those days one doesn't forget.
That is what our bond and our coming together in the bridal room
were all about.

CATEEYE [*aside*]: Ah, how right she is!

CUTIYA: The rain clouds thundered and the lightning flashed
And fresh grass was engendered from them on the land; when fruit
ripened
And the *higlo* tree and the *hohob* bush put forth their berries, we
picked them
And ate our fill. I have never forgotten all that:
I keep it in my mind, my bosom and my belly.

References

GEYDH, F. C. (1965), 'Oh men the beautiful world', in Achmed, S. J. (ed.),
Gabayo, Maahmaah iyo Sheekooyin Yaryar, The National Printer, Mogadishu.
GABAY-SHINNI (1965), 'The vicissitudes of the world', in Achmed, S. J. (ed.)
Gabayo, Maamaah iyo Sheekooyin Yaryar, The National Printer, Mogadishu.
JOHNSON, J. W. (1969) 'A Bibliography of Somali language and literature',
African Language Rev., vol. 8, pp. 279–97.

17 C. O. Frake

How to Ask for a Drink in Subanun[1]

C. O. Frake, 'How to ask for a drink in Subanun', *American Anthropologist*, vol. 66:6 part 2, 1964, pp. 127–32.

Goodenough (1957) has proposed that a description of a culture – an ethnography – should properly specify what it is that a stranger to a society would have to know in order appropriately to perform any role in any scene staged by the society. If an ethnographer of Subanun culture were to take this notion seriously, one of the most crucial sets of instructions to provide would be that specifying how to ask for a drink. Anyone who cannot perform this operation successfully will be automatically excluded from the stage upon which some of the most dramatic scenes of Subanun life are performed.

To ask appropriately for a drink among the Subanun it is not enough to know how to construct a grammatical utterance in Subanun translatable in English as a request for a drink. Rendering such an utterance might elicit praise for one's fluency in Subanun, but it probably would not get one a drink. To speak appropriately it is not enough to speak grammatically or even sensibly (in fact some speech settings may require the uttering of nonsense as is the case with the semantic-reversal type of speech play common in the Philippines. See Conklin, 1959). Our stranger requires more than a grammar and a lexicon; he needs what Hymes (1962) has called an ethnography of speaking: a specification of what kinds of things to say in what message forms to what kinds of people in what kinds of situations. Of course an ethnography of speaking cannot provide rules specifying exactly what message to select in a given situation. If messages were perfectly predictable from a knowledge of the culture, there would be little point in saying anything. But when a person selects a message, he does so from a set of appropriate alternatives. The task of an ethnographer of speaking is to specify what the appropriate alternatives are in a given

1. The Subanun are pagan swidden agriculturists occupying the mountainous interior of Zamboanga Peninsula on the island of Mindanao in the Philippines. This paper refers to the Eastern Subanun of Zamboanga del Norte Province. Descriptions of Subanun social structure, festive activities, and some aspects of *gasi* manufacture are given in Frake (1960, 1963, 1964a, and 1964b). The ethnographic methodology of this paper is that described in Frake (1964b). Single quotation marks enclose English substitutes for (but not translations of) Subanun expressions.

situation and what the consequences are of selecting one alternative over another.

Drinking defined. Of the various substances which the Subanun consider 'drinkable', we are here concerned only with a subset called *gasi*, a rice-yeast fermented beverage made of a rice, manioc, maize, and/or Job's tears mash. *Gasi*, glossed in this paper as 'beer', contrasts in linguistic labelling, drinking technique, and social context with all other Subanun beverages (*tebaq* 'toddy', *sebug* 'wine', *binu*, 'liquor,' *sabaw* 'juice-broth,' *tubig* 'water').

The context of drinking. Focused social gatherings (Goffman, 1961) among the Subanun fall into two sharply contrasted sets: festive gatherings or 'festivities' and nonfestive or informal gatherings (Frake, 1964b). The diagnostic feature of a festivity is the consumption of a festive meal as a necessary incident in the encounter. A 'meal' among the Subanun necessarily comprises a serving of a cooked starchy-staple food, the 'main dish', and ordinarily also includes a 'side dish' of vegetables, fish or meat. A festive meal or 'feast' is a meal with a meat side dish. A 'festivity' comprises all socially relevant events occurring between the arrival and dispersal of participants in a feast. Apart from a feast, the necessary features of a festivity are (1) an occasioning event, (2) multi-family participation, and (3) beer. The drinking of beer, unlike the consumption of any other beverage, occurs only during a festivity and must occur as part of any festivity. It occupies a crucial position as a focus of formal social gatherings.

Drinking technique. 'Beer', uniquely among Subanun drinks, is drunk with bamboo straws inserted to the bottom of a Chinese jar containing the fermented mash. Just prior to drinking, the jar is filled to the rim with water. Except in certain types of game drinking, one person drinks at a time, after which another person replenishes the water from an agreed-upon 'measure'. As one sucks on the straw, the water disappears down through the mash where it picks up a surprising amount of alcohol and an indescribable taste. After initial rounds of tasting, drinking etiquette requires one to gauge his consumption so that when a full measure of water is added, the water level rises exactly even with the jar rim.

The drinking encounter. Each beer jar provided for a festivity becomes the focus of a gathering of persons who take turns drinking. A *turn* is a single period of continuous drinking by one person. Each change of drinkers marks a new turn. A circuit of turns through the gathering is a *round*. As drinking progresses, rounds change in character with regard to the number and length of constituent turns and to variations in drinking techniques.

Differences in these features among successive sets of rounds mark three distinct stages of the drinking encounter: tasting, competitive drinking, and game drinking (Table 1).

Table 1 **Subanun drinking talk**

Encounter stages	Discourse stages	Focus of speech acts	Function
1. Tasting	1. Invitation – permission	Role expression	Assignment of role distances and authority relations to participants
2. Competitive drinking	2. Jar talk	Role expression and context definition	Allocation of encounter resources (turns at drinking and talking)
	3. Discussion 3.1 Gossip 3.2 Deliberation	Topic	Exchange of information; disputation, arbitration; deciding issues on basis of cogent argument
3. Game drinking	4. Display of verbal art	Stylistic	Establishment of euphoria. Deciding issues on basis of skill in use of special styles of discourse (singing, verse)

Segments of a drinking encounter:
1. A turn (continuous drinking by one person); 2. A round (a set of related turns); 3. Encounter stage (a set of related rounds)

Segments of drinking talk:
1. An utterance (continuous speech by one person); 2. An exchange (a set of related utterances); 3. Discourse stage (a set of related exchanges)

The first round is devoted to *tasting*, each person taking a brief turn with little regard to formal measurement of consumption. Successive turns become longer and the number of turns per round fewer, thus cutting out some of the participants in the encounter. These individuals go to other jars if available or withdraw from drinking during this stage of *competitive drinking*. Measurement is an important aspect of competitive rounds, participants keeping a mental record of each other's consumption. Within a round, successive drinkers must equal the consumption of the drinker who initiated the round. In later rounds, as the brew becomes weaker, the measure tends to be raised. Continued competitive drinking may assume an altered character signaled by accompanying music, dancing, and singing. The scope of the gathering may enlarge and turns become shorter. Special types of drinking games occur: 'chugalug' (*saŋgayuq*) and dual-drinking by opposite-sexed partners under the cover of a blanket. These rounds form a stage of *game drinking*.

Drinking talk. The Subanun expression for drinking talk, *taluq bwat dig beksuk* 'talk from the straw', suggests an image of the drinking straw as a channel not only of the drink but also of drinking talk. The two activities, drinking and talking, are closely interrelated in that how one talks bears on how much one drinks and the converse is, quite obviously, also true. Except for 'religious offerings', which must precede drinking, whatever business is to be transacted during a festivity occurs during drinking encounters. Consequently drinking talk is a major medium of interfamily communication. Especially for an adult male, one's role in the society at large, insofar as it is subject to manipulation, depends to a considerable extent on one's verbal performance during drinking encounters.

Subanun society contains no absolute, society-wide status positions or offices which automatically entitle their holder to deference from and authority over others. The closest approximation to such a formal office is the status of religious specialist or 'medium' who is deferred to in religious matters but who has no special voice in affairs outside his domain (Frake, 1964b). Assumption of decision-making roles in legal, economic, and ecological domains depends not on acquisition of an office but on continuing demonstration of one's ability to make decisions within the context of social encounters. This ability in turn depends on the amount of deference one can evoke from other participants in the encounter. Although relevant, no external status attributes of sex, age, or wealth are sufficient to guarantee such deference; it must be elicited through one's skill in the use of speech. Apart from age, sex, and reputation from performances in previous encounters, the most salient external attributes brought to an encounter by a participant are his relational roles based on kinship, neighborhood, and friendship with specific other participants. Because of consanguineal endogamy and residential mobility, the relationship ties between an ego and any given alter are likely to be multiple and complex, giving wide latitude for manipulation of roles within particular encounters. Moreover, most kinship roles permit a range of interpretation depending upon other features of the relationship such as friendship and residential proximity.

The strategy of drinking talk is to manipulate the assignment of role relations among participants so that, within the limits of one's external status attributes, one can maximize his share of encounter resources (drink and talk), thereby having an opportunity to assume an esteem-attracting and authority-wielding role. Variations in the kinds of messages sent during periods devoted to different aspects of this strategic plan mark four distinct *discourse stages* within the drinking talk of the encounter: invitation-permission, jar talk, discussion, and display of verbal art (Table 1). The constituents of a discourse stage are *exchanges*: sets of utterances with a common topic focus. (Boundaries of exchanges in American speech are often marked by such expressions as 'Not to change the subject, but . . .' or 'By the way, that reminds me . . .'.) The constituents of exchanges are *utterances*: stretches of continuous speech by one person.

1. *Invitation-permission.* The Subanun designate the discourse of the initial tasting round as 'asking permission'. The provider of the jar initiates the tasting round by inviting someone to drink, thereby signaling that this person is the one to whom he and those closest to him in the encounter owe the greatest initial deference on the basis of external status attributes. The invited drinker squats before the jar and asks permission to drink of the other participants. He has two variables to manipulate: the order in which he addresses the other participants and the terms of address he employs. Apart from the latter variable, message form remains relatively constant: *naa*, A, *sep pa u* 'Well, A, I will be drinking'. (A represents a term of address.) Role relations with persons who are not lineal consanguineal or lineal affinal kin (Mo, F, Ch, Sp, SpPr, ChSp, ChSpPr) permit a variety of forms of address each with different implications for social distance with respect to ego (Frake, 1960). The drinker's final opportunity to express role relations comes when he finishes tasting and invites another (ordinarily the person who invited him) to drink.

2. *Jar talk.* As competitive drinking begins, asking permission is reduced in scope and importance, and there is an increase in messages sent during drinking itself. The topic focus of these exchanges is the drink being consumed. The drinker responds to queries about the taste and strength of the beer, explanations are advanced for its virtues and defects, and the performance of drinkers is evaluated. During this stage the topic of messages is predictable. The informative aspect of the messages is the quantity and quality of verbal responses a drinker can elicit. This information signals the amount of drinking and talking time the gathering will allot him. Those who receive little encouragement drop out, and the encounter is reduced generally to less than half a dozen persons, who can thereby intensify their interaction with each other and with the beer straw.

3. *Discussion.* As the size and role-structure of the gathering becomes defined, discourse changes in topic to removed referents, usually beginning with relatively trivial gossip, proceeding to more important subjects of current interest, and, finally, in many cases arriving at litigation. Since there are no juro-political offices in Subanun society, a legal case is not

only a contest between litigants, but also one between persons attempting to assume a role of legal authority by settling the case. Success in effecting legal decisions depends on achieving a commanding role in the encounter and on debating effectively from that position. Since there are no sanctions of force legally applicable to back up a decision, the payment of a fine in compliance with a decision is final testimony to the prowess in verbal combat of the person who made the decision.

4. *Display of verbal art.* If drinking continues long enough, the focus of messages shifts from their topics to play with message forms themselves, following stylized patterns of song and verse composition. Songs and verses are composed on the spot to carry on discussions in an operetta-like setting. Even unsettled litigation may be continued in this manner, the basis for decision being shifted from cogent argument to verbal artistry. The most prestigious kinds of drinking songs require the mastery of an esoteric vocabulary by means of which each line is repeated with a semantically equivalent but formally different line. Game drinking is a frequent accompaniment to these displays of verbal art. Together they help assure that the festivity will end with good feelings among all participants, a goal which is explicitly stated by the Subanun. Participants who have displayed marked hostility toward each other during the course of drinking talk may be singled out for special ritual treatment designed to restore good feelings.

The Subanun drinking encounter thus provides a structured setting within which one's social relationships beyond his everyday associates can be extended, defined, and manipulated through the use of speech. The cultural patterning of drinking talk lays out an ordered scheme of role play through the use of terms of address, through discussion and argument, and through display of verbal art. The most skilled in 'talking from the straw' are the *de facto* leaders of the society. In instructing our stranger to Subanun society how to ask for a drink, we have at the same time instructed him how to get ahead socially.

References

CONKLIN, H. C. (1959), 'Linguistic play in its cultural setting', *Language*, vol. 35, pp. 631–6.

FRAKE, C. O. (1960), 'The Eastern Subanun of Mindanao', in G. P. Murdock (ed.), *Social Structure in Southeast Asia*, Viking Publications in Anthropology, vol. 29, pp. 51–64.

FRAKE, C. O. (1963), 'Litigation in Lipay: a study in Subanun law', *The Proceedings of the Ninth Pacific Science Congress*, 1957, vol. 3, Bangkok.

FRAKE, C. O. (1964a), 'Notes on queries in ethnography', *AmA*, vol. 66, no. 3, part 2, pp. 132–45.

FRAKE, C.O. (1964b), 'A structural description of Subanun "religious behaviour"', in W. G. Goodenough (ed.), *Explorations in Cultural Anthropology: Essays in Honor of George Peter Murdock*, McGraw Hill.

GOFFMAN, E. (1961), *Encounters: Two Studies in the Sociology of Interaction*, Bobbs-Merrill.

GOODENOUGH, W. G. (1957), 'Cultural anthropology and linguistics', in P. L. Garvin (ed.), *Report of the Seventh Annual Round Table Meeting on Linguistics and Language Study*, Georgetown University Monograph Series on Language and Linguistics, vol. 9, pp. 167–73.

HYMES, D. H. (1962), 'The ethnography of speaking', in T. Gladwin and W. C. Sturtevant (eds.), *Anthropology and Human Behavior*, Anthropological Society of Washington.

Part Four
Acquisition and Proficiency

In this final section the articles are concerned with first and second
language acquisition. They all deal with the effect of the social context
in which a language is learned on the linguistic competence which the
individual attains in the language. Hymes' paper is theoretical; he
introduces the concept of 'communicative competence' which is taken
up later by Cazden and related to social class differences. Henderson
is similarly concerned with the effect of a family's social class on the
kind of language the child may acquire. Lambert and Rubin examine
two different influences on the degree of proficiency acquired in a
language. Lambert stresses the psychological effects of social stereotypes on language-learning motivation, while Rubin examines situational
variables which determine the context in which the child acquires a
language and the degree of proficiency he achieves. This section is
concerned then with the effect of social factors on the communicative
competence acquired by the individual.

18 D. H. Hymes

On Communicative Competence

Excerpts from D. H. Hymes, *On Communicative Competence*, Philadelphia: University of Pennsylvannia Press, 1971.[1]

I

This paper is theoretical. One connotation of 'theoretical' is 'programatic'; a related connotation is that one knows too little about the subject to say something practical. Both connotations apply to this attempt to contribute to the study of the 'language problems of disadvantaged children'. Practical work, however, must have an eye on the current state of theory, for it can be guided or misguided, encouraged or discouraged, by what it takes that state to be. Moreover, the language development of children has particular pertinence just now for theory. The fundamental theme of this paper is that the theoretical and the practical problems converge.

It is not that there exists a body of linguistic theory that practical research can turn to and has only to apply. It is rather that work motivated by practical needs may help build the theory that we need. To a great extent programs to change the language situation of children are an attempt to apply a basic science that does not yet exist. Let me review the present stage of linguistic theory to show why this is so.

Consider a recent statement, one that makes explicit and precise an assumption that has underlain much of modern linguistics (Chomsky, 1965, p. 3):

Linguistic theory is concerned primarily with an ideal speaker-listener, in a completely homogeneous speech community, who knows its language perfectly and is unaffected by such grammatically irrelevant conditions as memory limitations, distractions, shifts of attention and interest, and errors (random or characteristic) in applying his knowledge of the language in actual performance.

1. This paper is revised from one presented at the Research Planning Conference on Language Development Among Disadvantaged Children, held under the sponsorship of the Department of Educational Psychology and Guidance, Ferkauf Graduate School, Yeshiva University, June 7-8, 1966. The original paper is included in the report of that conference, issued by the Department of Educational Psychology and Guidance (pp. 1-16). I wish to thank Dr Beryl Bailey and Dr Edmund Gordon of Yeshiva University for inviting me to participate and Dr Courtney Cazden, Dr John Gumperz, Dr Wayne O'Neill and Dr Vera John for their comments at that time.

From the standpoint of the children we seek to understand and help, such a statement may seem almost a declaration of irrelevance. All the difficulties that confront the children and ourselves seem swept from view.

One's response to such an indication of the state of linguistic theory might be to ignore fundamental theory and to pick and choose among its products. Models of language structure, after all, can be useful in ways not envisioned in the statements of their authors. Some linguists (e.g., Labov, Rosenbaum, Gleitman) use transformational generative grammar to study some of the ways in which a speech community is not homogeneous and in which speaker-listeners clearly have differential knowledge of a language. Perhaps, then, one ought simply to disregard how linguists define the scope of 'linguistic' theory. One could point to several available models of language – Trager-Smith-Joos, tagnemic, stratificational, transformational-generative (in its MIT, Pennsylvania, Harvard and other variants), and, in England, 'system-structure' (Halliday and others); remark that there are distinguished scholars using each to analyse English; regret that linguists are unable to agree on the analysis of English; and pick and choose, according to one's problem and local situation, leaving grammarians otherwise to their own devices.

To do so would be a mistake for two reasons: on the one hand, the sort of theoretical perspective quoted above *is* relevant in ways that it is important always to have in mind; on the other hand, there is a body of linguistic data and problems that would be left without theoretical insight, if such a limited conception of linguistic theory were to remain unchallenged.

The special relevance of the theoretical perspective is expressed in its representative anecdote (to use Kenneth Burke's term), the image it puts before our eyes. The image is that of a child, born with the ability to master any language with almost miraculous ease and speed; a child who is not merely molded by conditioning and reinforcement, but who actively proceeds with the unconscious theoretical interpretation of the speech that comes its way, so that in a few years and with a finite experience, it is master of an infinite ability, that of producing and understanding in principle any and all grammatical sentences of language. The image (or theoretical perspective) expresses the essential equality in children just as human beings. It is noble in that it can inspire one with the belief that even the most dispiriting conditions can be transformed; it is an indispensable weapon against views that would explain the communicative differences among groups of children as inherent, perhaps racial.

The limitations of the perspective appear when the image of the unfolding, mastering, fluent child is set beside the real children in our schools. The theory must seem, if not irrelevant, then at best a doctrine of poignancy:

poignant, because of the difference between what one imagines and what one sees; poignant too, because the theory, so powerful in its own realm, cannot on its terms cope with the difference. To cope with the realities of children as communicating beings requires a theory within which socio-cultural factors have an explicit and constitutive role; and neither is the case.

For the perspective associated with transformational generative grammar, the world of linguistic theory has two parts: linguistic *competence* and linguistic *performance*. Linguistic competence is understood as concerned with the tacit knowledge of language structure, that is, knowledge that is commonly not conscious or available for spontaneous report, but neces-sarily implicit in what the (ideal) speaker-listener can say. The primary task of theory is to provide for an explicit account of such knowledge, especially in relation to the innate structure on which it must depend. It is in terms of such knowledge that one can produce and understand an infinite set of sentences, and that language can be spoke of as 'creative', as *energeia*. Linguistic performance is most explicitly understood as con-cerned with the processes often termed encoding and decoding.

Such a theory of competence posits ideal objects in abstraction from sociocultural features that might enter into their description. Acquisition of competence is also seen as essentially independent of sociocultural features, requiring only suitable speech in the environment of the child to develop. The theory of performance is the one sector that might have a specific sociocultural content; but while equated with a theory of language use, it is essentially concerned with psychological by-products of the analysis of grammar, not, say, with social interaction. As to a constitutive role for sociocultural features in the acquisition or conduct of performance, the attitude would seem quite negative. Little or nothing is said, and if something were said, one would expect it to be depreciatory. Some aspects of performance are, it is true, seen as having a constructive role (e.g., the cycling rules that help assign stress properly to sentences), but if the passage quoted at the outset is recalled, however, and if the illustrations of performance phenomena in the chapter from which the passage comes are reviewed, it will be seen that the note struck is persistently one of limitation, if not disability. When the notion of performance is introduced as 'the actual use of language in concrete situations', it is immediately stated that only under the idealization quoted could performance directly reflect competence, and that in actual fact it obviously could not. 'A record of natural speech will show numerous false starts, deviations from rules, changes of plan in mid-course, and so on.' One speaks of primary linguistic data as 'fairly degenerate in quality' (Chomsky, 1965, p. 31), or even of linguistic performance as 'adulteration' of ideal competence (Katz,

1967, p. 144). While 'performance' is something of a residual category for the theory, clearly its most salient connotation is that of imperfect manifestation of underlying system.

I do not think the failure to provide an explicit place for sociocultural features to be accidental. The restriction of competence to the notions of a homogeneous community, perfect knowledge, and independence of sociocultural factors does not seem just a simplifying assumption, the sort that any scientific theory must make. If that were so, then some remark to that effect might be made; the need to include a sociocultural dimension might be mentioned; the nature of such inclusion might even be suggested. Nor does the predominant association of performance with imperfection seem accidental. Certainly, any stretch of speech is an imperfect indication of the knowledge that underlies it. For users that share the knowledge, the arrangement might be thought of as efficient. And if one uses one's intuitions as to speech, as well as to grammar, one can see that what to grammar is imperfect, or unaccounted for, may be the artful accomplishment of a social act (Garfinkel, in press), or the patterned, spontaneous evidence of problem solving and conceptual thought (John, 1967, p. 5). These things might be acknowledged, even if not taken up.

It takes the absence of a place for sociocultural factors, and the linking of performance to imperfection, to disclose an ideological aspect to the theoretical standpoint. It is, if I may say so, rather a Garden of Eden view. Human life seems divided between grammatical competence, an ideal innately-derived sort of power, and performance, an exigency rather like the eating of the apple, thrusting the perfect speaker-hearer out into a fallen world. Of this world, where meanings may be won by the sweat of the brow, and communication achieved in labor (cf. Bonhoffer, 1965, p. 365), little is said. The controlling image is of an abstract, isolated individual, almost an unmotivated cognitive mechanism, not, except incidentally, a person in a social world.

Any theoretical stance of course has an ideological aspect, and that aspect of present linguistic theory is not its invention. A major characteristic of modern linguistics has been that it takes structure as primary end in itself, and tends to depreciate use, while not relinquishing any of its claim to the great significance that is attached to language. (Contrast classical antiquity, where structure was a means to use, and the grammarian subordinate to the rhetor.) The result can sometimes seem a very happy one. On the one hand, by narrowing concern to independently and readily structurable data, one can enjoy the prestige of an advanced science; on the other hand, despite ignoring the social dimensions of use, one retains the prestige of dealing with something fundamental to human life.

In this light, Chomsky is quite correct when he writes that his conception of the concern of linguistic theory seems to have been also the position of the founders of modern general linguistics. Certainly if modern structural linguistics is meant, then a major thrust of it has been to define the subject matter of linguistic theory in terms of what it is not. In de Saussure's linguistics, as generally interpreted, *la langue* was the privileged ground of structure, and *la parole* the residual realm of variation (among other things). Chomsky associates his views of competence and performance with the Saussurian conceptions of langue and parole, but sees his own conceptions as superior, going beyond the conception of language as a systematic inventory of items to renewal of the Humboldtian conception of underlying processes. The Chomsky conception is superior, not only in this respect, but also in the very terminology it introduces to mark the difference. 'Competence' and 'performance' much more readily suggest concrete persons, situations, and actions. Indeed, from the standpoint of the classical tradition in structural linguistics, Chomsky's theoretical standpoint is at once its revitalization and its culmination. It carries to its perfection the desire to deal in practice only with what is internal to language, yet to find in that internality that in theory is of the widest or deepest human significance. No modern linguistic theory has spoken more profoundly of either the internal structure or the intrinsic human significance.

This revitalization flowers while around it emerge the sprouts of a conception that before the end of the century may succeed it. If such a succession occurs, it will be because, just as the transformational theory could absorb its predecessors and handle structural relationships beyond their grasp, so new relationships, relationships with an ineradicable social component, will become salient that will require a broader theory to absorb and handle them. I shall return to this historical conjecture at the end of this paper. Let me now sketch considerations that motivate a broader theory. And let me do this by first putting forward an additional representative anecdote.

II

As against the ideal speaker-listener, here is Bloomfield's account of one young Menomini he knew (1927, p. 395):

White Thunder, a man around forty, speaks less English than Menomini, and that is a strong indictment, for his Menomini is atrocious. His vocabulary is small; his inflections are often barbarous; he constructs sentences of a few threadbare models. He may be said to speak no language tolerably. His case is not uncommon among younger men, even when they speak but little English.

Bloomfield goes on to suggest that the commonness of the case is due, in some indirect way, to the impact of the conquering language. In short, there is here *differential competence* within a *heterogeneous speech community*, both undoubtedly shaped by acculturation. (The alternative to a constitutive role for the novel sociocultural factor is to assume that atrocious Menomini was common also before contact. If taken seriously, the assumption would still implicate sociocultural factors). Social life has affected not merely outward performance, but inner competence itself.

Let me now review some other indications of the need to transcend the notions of perfect competence, homogeneous speech community, and independence of sociocultural features.

In her excellent article reviewing recent studies of subcultural differences in language development in the United States, Cazden (1966, p. 190) writes that one thing is clear:

The findings can be quickly summarized: on all the measures, in all the studies, the upper socio-economic status children, however defined, are more advanced than the lower socio-economic status children.

The differences reviewed by Cazden involve enabling effects for the upper status children just as much as disabling effects for the lower status children. Moreover, given subcultural differences in the patterns and purposes of language use, children of the lower status may actually excel in aspects of communicative competence not observed or measured in the tests summarized. And among the Menomini there were not only young men like White Thunder, but also those like Red Cloud Woman, who

speaks a beautiful and highly idiomatic Menomini . . . (and) speaks Ojibwa and Potawatomi fluently. . . . Linguistically, she would correspond to a highly educated American woman who spoke, say, French and Italian in addition to the very best type of cultivated, idiomatic English (Bloomfield, 1927, p. 394).

There are tribes of the northeast Amazon among whom the normal scope of linguistic competence is a control of at least four languages, a spurt in active command coming during adolescence, with repertoire and perfection of competence continuing to be augmented throughout life. Here, as in much of our world, the ideally fluent speaker-listener is multilingual. (Even an ideally fluent monolingual of course is master of functional varieties within the one language.)

In this connection it should be noted that fluent members of communities often regard their languages, or functional varieties, as not identical in communicative adequacy. It is not only that one variety is obligatory or preferred for some uses, another for others (as is often the case, say, as between public occasions and personal relationships). Such intuitions reflect experience and self-evaluation as to what one can in fact do with a given variety. This sort of differential competence has nothing to do with 'disadvantage' or deficiency relative to other normal members of the community. All of them may find Kurdish, say, the medium in which most things can best be expressed, but Arabic the better medium for religious truth; users of Berber may find Arabic superior to Berber for all purposes except intimate domestic conversation (Ferguson, 1966).

The combination of community diversity and differential competence makes it necessary not to take the presence in a community of a widespread language, say, Spanish or English, at face value. Just as one puts the gloss of a native word in quotation marks, so as not to imply that the meaning of the word is thereby accurately identified, so one should put the name of a language in quotation marks, until its true status in terms of competence has been determined. (Clearly there is need for a theoretically motivated and empirically tested set of terms by which to characterize the different kinds of competence that may be found.) In an extreme case what counts as 'English' in the code repertoire of a community may be but a few phonologically marked forms (the Iwam of New Guinea). The cases in general constitute a continuum, perhaps a scale, from more restricted to less restricted varieties, somewhat crosscut by adaptation of the same inherited 'English' materials to different purposes and needs. A linguist analysing data from a community on the assumption 'once English, always English' might miss and sadly misrepresent the actual competence supposedly expressed by his grammar.

There is no way within the present view of linguistic competence to distinguish between the abilities of one of the pure speakers of Menomini noted by Bloomfield and those of whom White Thunder was typical. Menomini sentences from either would be referred to a common grammar. Perhaps it can be said that the competence is shared with regard to the recognition and comprehension of speech. While that would be an important (and probably true) fact, it has not been the intention of the theory to distinguish between models of competence for reception and models of competence for production. And insofar as the theory intends to deal with the 'creative' aspect of language, that is, with the ability of a user to devise novel sentences appropriate to situations, it would seem to be a retrenchment, if not more, to claim only to account for a shared ability to *understand* novel sentences produced by others. In some fundamental sense, the competence of the two groups of speakers, in terms of ability to make 'creative' use of Menomini, is clearly distinct. Difference in judgement of acceptability is not in question. There is simply a basic sense in which users of Menomini of the more versatile type have a knowledge (syntactic as well as lexical) that users of White Thunder's type do not. [...]

Labov has documented cases of dual competence in reception, but single competence in production, with regard to the ability of lower-class

Negro children to interpret sentences in either standard or substandard phonology, while consistently using only substandard phonology in speaking themselves. An interesting converse kind of case is that in which there is a dual competence for production, a sort of 'competence for incompetence' as it were. Thus among the Burundi of East Africa (Albert, 1964) a peasant may command the verbal abilities stressed and valued in the culture but cannot display it in the presence of a herder or other superior. In such cases appropriate behavior is that in which 'their words are haltingly delivered, or run on uncontrolled, their voices are loud, their gestures wild, their figures of speech ungainly, their emotions freely displayed, their words and sentences clumsy.' Clearly the behavior is general to all codes of communication, but it attaches to the grammatical among them.

Such work as Labov's in New York City, and examples such as the Burundi, in which evidence for linguistic competence co-varies with inter- locutor, point to the necessity of a social approach even if the goal of description is a single homogeneous code. Indeed, much of the difficulty in determining what is acceptable and intuitively correct in grammatical description arises because social and contextual determinants are not controlled. By making explicit the reference of a description to a single use in a single context, and by testing discrepancies and variations against differences of use and context, the very goal of not dealing with diversity can be achieved – in the limited, and only possible, sense in which it can be achieved. The linguist's own intuitions of underlying knowledge prove difficult to catch and to stabilize for use (and of course are not available for languages or varieties he does not himself know). If analysis is not to be reduced to explication of a corpus, or debauch into subjectivity, then the responses and judgements of members of the community whose language is analysed must be utilized – and not merely informally or *ad hoc*, but in some explicit, systematic way. In particular, since every response is made in some context, control of the dependence of judgements and abilities on context must be gained. It may well be that the two dimensions found by Labov to clarify phonological diversity – social hierarchy of varieties of usage, and range (formal to informal) of 'contextual styles', together with marking for special functions (expressivity, clarity, etc.) will serve for syntactic diversity as well. Certainly some understanding of local criteria of fluency, and conditions affecting it, is needed just insofar as the goal is to approximate an account of ideal fluency in the language in question. In sum, if one analyses the language of a community as if it should be homogeneous, its diversity trips one up around the edges. If one starts with analysis of the diversity, one can isolate the homogeneity that is truly there.

Clearly work with children, and with the place of language in education, requires a theory that can deal with a heterogeneous speech community, differential competence, the constitutive role of sociocultural features – that can take into account such phenomena as White Thunder, socio-economic differences, multilingual mastery, relativity of competence in 'Arabic', 'English', etc., expressive values, socially determined perception, contextual styles and shared norms for the evaluation of variables. Those whose work requires such a theory know best how little of its content can now be specified. Two things can be said. First, linguistics needs such a theory too. Concepts that are unquestioningly postulated as basic to linguistics (speaker-listener, speech community, speech act, acceptability, etc.) are, as we see, in fact sociocultural variables, and only when one has moved from their postulation to their analysis can one secure the foundations of linguistic theory itself. Second, the notion of competence may itself provide the key. Such comparative study of the role of language as has been undertaken shows the nature and evaluation of linguistic ability to vary cross-culturally; even what is to count as the same language, or variety, to which competence might be related, depends in part upon social factors (cf. Gumperz, 1964; Hymes, 1968a; Labov, 1966). Given, then, the assumption that the competency of users of language entails abilities and judgements relative to, and interdependent with, sociocultural features, one can see how to extend the notion to allow for this. I shall undertake this, by recasting first the representative anecdote of the child, and then the notions of competence and performance themselves.

III

Recall that one is concerned to explain how a child comes rapidly to be able to produce and understand (in principle) any and all of the grammatical sentences of a language. Consider now a child with just that ability. A child who might produce any sentence whatever – such a child would be likely to be institutionalized: even more so if not only sentences, but also speech or silence was random, unpredictable. For that matter, a person who chooses occasions and sentences suitably, but is master only of fully grammatical sentences, is at best a bit odd. Some occasions call for being appropriately ungrammatical.

We have then to account for the fact that a normal child acquires knowledge of sentences, not only as grammatical, but also as appropriate. He or she acquires competence as to when to speak, when not, and as to what to talk about with whom, when, where, in what manner. In short, a child becomes able to accomplish a repertoire of speech acts, to take part in speech events, and to evaluate their accomplishment by others. This competence, moreover, is integral with attitudes, values, and motivations concerning language, its features and uses, and integral with competence for, and attitudes toward, the interrelation of language with the other code of communicative conduct (cf. Goffman, 1956, p. 477; 1963, p. 335; 1964). The internalization of attitudes towards a language and its uses is particularly important (cf. Labov, 1965, pp. 84–5, on priority of subjective evaluation in social dialect and processes of change), as is internalization of attitudes toward use of language itself (e.g. attentiveness to it) and the relative place that language comes to play in a pattern of mental abilities (cf. Cazden, 1966), and in strategies – what language is considered available, reliable, suitable for, *vis-à-vis* other kinds of code.

The acquisition of such competency is of course fed by social experience, needs, and motives, and issues in action that is itself a renewed source of motives, needs, experience. We break irrevocably with the model that restricts the design of language to one face toward referential meaning, one toward sound, and that defines the organization of language as solely consisting of rules for linking the two. Such a model implies naming to be the sole use of speech, as if languages were never organized to lament, rejoice, beseech, admonish, aphorize, inveigh (Burke, 1966, p. 13), for the many varied forms of persuasion, direction, expression and symbolic play. A model of language must design it with a face toward communicative conduct and social life.

Attention to the social dimension is thus not restricted to occasions on which social factors seem to interfere with or restrict the grammatical. The engagement of language in social life has a positive, productive aspect. There are rules of use without which the rules of grammar would be useless. Just as rules of syntax can control aspects of phonology, and just as semantic rules perhaps control aspects of syntax, so rules of speech acts enter as a controlling factor for linguistic form as a whole. Linguists generally have developed a theory of levels by showing that what is the same on one level of representation has in fact two different statuses, for which a further level must be posited. The seminal example is in Sapir (1925) on phonology, while the major recent examples are in the work of Chomsky and Lamb. A second aspect is that what is different at one level may have in fact the same status at the further level. (Thus the two interpretations of 'He decided on the floor' – the floor as what he decided on/as where he decided – point to a further level at which the sameness of structure is shown.) Just this reasoning requires a level of speech acts. What is grammatically the same sentence may be a statement, a command, or a request; what are grammatically two different sentences may as acts both be requests. One can study the level of speech acts in terms of the conditions under which sentences can be taken as alternative types of act, and in terms of the conditions under which types of act can be realized as alternative types of sentence. And only from the further level of acts can some of the relations among communicative means be seen, e.g. the mutual substitutability of a word and a nod to realize an act of assent, the necessary co-occurence of words and the raising of a hand to realize an oath.

The parallel interpretations of 'he decided on the floor' and 'she gave up on the floor' point to a further at which the sameness in structure is shown.

Rules of use are not a late grafting. Data from the first years of acquisition of English grammar show children to develop rules for the use of different forms in different situations and an awareness of different acts of speech (Ervin-Tripp, personal communication). Allocation of whole languages to different uses is common for children in multilingual households from the beginning of their acquisition. Competency for use is part of the same developmental matrix as competence for grammar.

The acquisition of competence for use, indeed, can be stated in the same terms as acquisition of competence for grammar. Within the developmental matrix in which knowledge of the sentences of a language is acquired, children also acquire knowledge of a set of ways in which sentences are used. From a finite experience of speech acts and their interdependence with sociocultural features, they develop a general theory of the speaking appropriate in their community, which they employ, like other forms of tacit cultural knowledge (competence) in conducting and interpreting social life (cf. Goodenough, 1957; Searle, 1967). They come to be able to recognize, for example, appropriate and inappropriate interrogative behavior (e.g. among the Araucanians of Chile, that to repeat a question is to insult; among the Tzeltal of Chiapas, Mexico, that a direct question is not properly asked (and to be answered 'nothing'); among the Cahinahua of Brazil, that a direct answer to a first question implies that the answerer has no time to talk, a vague answer that the question will be answered directly the second time, and that talk can continue).

The existence of competency for use may seem obvious, but if its study is to be established, and conducted in relation to current linguistics, then the notions of competence and performance must themselves be critically analysed, and a revised formulation provided.

The chief difficulty of present linguistic theory is that it would seem to require one to identify the study of the phenomena of concern to us here with its category of performance. The theory's category of competence, identified with the criterion of grammaticality, provides no place. Only performance is left, and its associated criterion of acceptability. Indeed, language use is equated with performance: 'the theory of language use – the theory of performance' (Chomsky, 1965, p. 9).

The difficulty with this equation, and the reasons for the making of it, can be explained as follows. First, the clarification of the concept of performance offered by Chomsky (1965, pp. 10–15), as we have seen, omits almost everything of sociocultural significance. The focus of attention is upon questions such as which among grammatical sentences are most likely to be produced, easily understood, less clumsy, in some sense more natural; and such questions are studied initially in relation to formal tree-structures, and properties of these such as nesting, self-embedding, multiple-branching, left-branching, and right-branching. The study of such questions is of interest, but the results are results of the psychology of perception, memory, and the like, not of the domain of cultural patterning and social action. Thus, when one considers what the sociocultural analogues of performance in this sense might be, one sees that these analogues would not include major kinds of judgement and ability with which one must deal in studying the use of language (see below under appropriateness).

Second, the notion of performance, as used in discussion, seems confused between different meanings. In one sense, performance is observable behavior, as when one speaks of determining from the data of performance the underlying system of rules (Chomsky, 1965, p. 4), and of mentalistic linguistics as that linguistics that uses performance as data, along with other data, e.g. those of introspection, for determination of competence (p. 193). The recurrent use of 'actual' implies as much, as when the term is first introduced in the book in question, 'actual performance', and first characterized: 'performance (the actual use of language in concrete situations)' (pp. 3–4). In this sense performance is 'actual', competence underlying. In another sense, performance itself also underlies data, as when one constructs a performance model, or infers a performative device (e.g. a perceptual one) that is to explain data and be tested against them (p. 15); or as when, in a related sense, one even envisages the possibility of stylistic 'rules of performance' to account for occurring word orders not accounted for by grammatical theory (p. 127).

When one speaks of performance, then, does one mean the behavioral data of speech? or all that underlies speech beyond the grammatical? or both? If the ambiguity is intentional, it is not fruitful; it smacks more of the residual category and marginal interest.

The difficulty can be put in terms of the two contrasts that usage manifests:

1. (underlying) competence v. (actual) performance;
2. (underlying) grammatical competence v. (underlying) models/rules of performance.

The first contrast is so salient that the status of the second is left obscure.

In point of fact, I find it impossible to understand what stylistic 'rules of performance' could be, except a further kind of underlying competence, but the term is withheld. [. . .]

It remains that the present vision of generative grammar extends only a little way into the realm of the use of language. To grasp the intuitions and data pertinent to underlying competence for use requires a sociocultural standpoint. To develop that standpoint adequately, one must transcend the present formulation of the dichotomy of competence: performance, as we have seen, and the associated formulation of the judgements and abilities of the users of a language as well. To this I now turn.

IV

There are several sectors of communicative competence, of which the grammatical is one. Put otherwise, there is behavior, and, underlying it, there are several systems of rules reflected in the judgements and abilities of those whose messages the behavior manifests. (The question of how the interrelationships among sectors might be conceived is touched upon below.) In the linguistic theory under discussion, judgements are said to be of two kinds: of *grammaticality*, with respect to competence, and of *acceptability*, with respect to performance. Each pair of terms is strictly matched; the critical analysis just given requires analysis of the other. In particular, the analysis just given requires that explicit distinctions be made within the notion of 'acceptability' to match the distinctions of kinds of 'performance', and at the same time, the entire set of terms must be examined and recast with respect to the communicative as a whole.

If an adequate theory of language users and language use is to be developed, it seems that judgements must be recognized to be in fact not of two kinds but of four. And if linguistic theory is to be integrated with theory of communication and culture, this fourfold distinction must be stated in a sufficiently generalized way. I would suggest, then, that for language and for other forms of communication (culture), four questions arise:

1. Whether (and to what degree) something is formally *possible*;
2. Whether (and to what degree) something is *feasible* in virtue of the means of implementation available;
3. Whether (and to what degree) something is *appropriate* (adequate, happy, successful) in relation to a context in which it is used and evaluated;
4. Whether (and to what degree) something is in fact done, actually *performed*, and what its doing entails.

A linguistic illustration: a sentence may be grammatical, awkward, tactful and rare. (One might think of the four as successive subsets; more likely they should be pictured as overlapping circles.)

These questions may be asked from the standpoint of a system *per se*, or from the standpoint of persons. An interest in competence dictates the latter standpoint here. Several observations can be made. There is an important sense in which a normal member of a community has knowledge with respect to all these aspects of the communicative systems available to him. He will interpret or assess the conduct of others and himself in ways that reflect a knowledge of each (possible, feasible, appropriate), done (if so, how often). There is an important sense in which he would be said to have a capability with regard to each. This latter sense, indeed, is one many would understand as included in what would be meant by his competence. Finally, it cannot be assumed that the formal possibilities of a system and individual knowledge are identical; a system may contain possibilities not part of the present knowledge of a user (cf. Wallace, 1961b). Nor can it be assumed that the knowledge acquired by different individuals is identical, despite identity of manifestation and apparent system.

Given these considerations, I think there is not sufficient reason to maintain a terminology at variance with more general usage of 'competence' and 'performance' in the sciences of man, as is the case with the present equations of competence, knowledge, systemic possibility, on the one hand, and of performance, behavior, implementational constraints, appropriateness, on the other. It seems necessary to distinguish these things and to reconsider their relationship, if their investigation is to be insightful and adequate.

I should take *competence* as the most general term for the capabilities of a person. (This choice is in the spirit, if at present against the letter, of the concern in linguistic theory for underlying capability.) Competence is dependent upon both (tacit) *knowledge* and (ability for) *use*. *Knowledge* is distinct, then, both from competence (as its part) and from systemic possibility (to which its relation is an empirical matter.) Notice that Cazden (1967), by utilizing what is in effect systemic possibility as a definition of competence is forced to separate it from what persons can do. The 'competence' underlying a person's behavior is identified as one kind of 'performance' (performance A, actual behavior being performance B). The logic may be inherent in the linguistic theory from which Cazden starts, once one tries to adapt its notion of competence to recognized facts of personal knowledge. The strangely misleading result shows that the original notion cannot be left unchanged.

Knowledge also is to be understood as subtending all four parameters of communication just noted. There is knowledge of each. *Ability for use* also may relate to all four parameters. Certainly it may be the case that individuals differ with regard to ability to use knowledge of each: to interpret, differentiate, etc. The specification of *ability for use* as part of competence allows for the role of noncognitive factors, such as motivation, as partly determining competence. In speaking of competence, it is especially important not to separate cognitive from affective and volitive factors, so far as the impact of theory on educational practice is concerned; but also with regard to research design and explanation (as the work of Labov indicates). Within a comprehensive view of competence, considerations of the sort identified by Goffman (1967, pp. 218–26) must be reckoned with – capacities in interaction such as courage, gameness, gallantry, composure, presence of mind, dignity, stage confidence, capacities which are discussed in some detail by him and, explicitly in at least one case, as kinds of competency (p. 224).

Turning to judgements and intuitions of persons, the most general term for the criterion of such judgements would be acceptable. Quirk (1966) so uses it, and Chomsky himself at one point remarks that 'grammaticalness is only one of the many factors that interact to determine acceptability' (1965, p. 11). (The term is thus freed from its strict pairing with 'performance'.) The sources of acceptability are to be found in the four parameters just noted, and in interrelations among them that are not well understood.

Turning to actual use and actual events, the term *performance* is now free for this meaning, but with several important reminders and provisos. The 'performance models' studied in psycholinguistics are to be taken as models of aspects of ability for use, relative to means of implementation in the brain, although they could now be seen as a distinct, contributory factor in general competence. There seems, indeed, to have been some unconscious shifting between the sense in which one would speak of the performance of a motor, and that in which one would speak of the performance of a person or actor (cf. Goffman, 1959, pp. 17–76, 'Performances') or of a cultural tradition (Singer, 1955; Wolf, 1964, pp. 75–6). Here the performance of a person is not identical with a behavioral record, or with the imperfect or partial realization of individual competence. It takes into account the interaction between competence (knowledge, ability for use), the competence of others, and the cybernetic and emergent properties of events themselves. A performance, as an event, may have properties (patterns and dynamics) not reducible to terms of individual or standardized competence. Sometimes, indeed, these properties are the point (a concert, play, party).

The concept of 'performance' will take on great importance, insofar as the study of communicative competence is seen as an aspect of what from another angle may be called the ethnography of symbolic forms – the study of the variety of genres, narration, dance, drama, song, instrumental music, visual art, that interrelate with speech in the communicative life of a society, and in terms of which the relative importance and meaning of speech and language must be assessed. The recent shift in folklore studies and much of anthropology to the study of these genres in terms of performances with underlying rules (e.g. Abrahams, 1967) can be seen as a reconstruction on an ethnographic basis of the vision expressed in Cassirer's philosophy of symbolic forms. (This reconstruction has a direct application to the communicative competence of children in American cities, where identification and understanding of differences in kinds of forms, abilities, and their evaluation is essential.)

The concept of 'performance' will be important also in the light of sociological work such as that of Goffman (cited above), as its concern with general interactional competence helps make precise the particular role of linguistic competence.

In both respects the interrelation of knowledge of distinct codes (verbal: non-verbal) is crucial. In some cases these interrelations will bespeak an additional level of competence (cf., e.g., Sebeok, 1959, pp. 141–2): 'Performance constitutes a concurrently ordered selection from two sets of acoustic signals – in brief, codes – language and music. . . . These are integrated by special rules. . . .'). In others, perhaps not, as when the separate cries of vendors and the call to prayer of a muezzin are perceived to fit by an observer of an Arabic city, but with indication of intent or plan.

The nature of research into symbolic forms and interactional competence is already influenced in important part by linguistic study of competence (for some discussion see Hymes, 1968b). Within the view of communicative competence taken here, the influence can be expected to be reciprocal.

Having stated these general recommendations, let me now review relations between the linguistic and other communicative systems, especially in terms of cultural anthropology. I shall consider both terminology and content, using the four questions as a framework.

1. Whether (and to what degree) something is formally possible

This formulation seems to express an essential concern of present linguistic theory for the openness, potentiality, of language, and to generalize it for cultural systems. When systemic possibility is a matter of language, the corresponding term is of course *grammaticality*. Indeed, language is so much the paradigmatic example that one uses 'grammar' and 'grammaticality' by extension for other systems of formal possibility (recurrent references to a cultural grammar, Kenneth Burke's *A Grammar of Motives*, etc.). For particular systems, such extension may well be the easiest course; it is much easier to say that something is 'grammatical' with respect to the underlying structure of a body of myth, than to say in a new sense that it is 'mythical'. As a general term, one does readily enough speak of 'cultural' in a way analogous to grammatical (Sapir once wrote of 'culturalized behavior', and it is clear that not all behavior is cultural). We may say, then, that something possible within a formal system is grammatical, cultural, or, on occasion, communicative (cf. Hymes, 1967b). Perhaps one can also say uncultural or uncommunicative, as well as ungrammatical, for the opposite.

2. Whether (and to what degree) something is feasible

The predominant concern here, it will be recalled, has been for psycho-linguistic factors such as memory limitation, perceptual device, effects of properties such as nesting, embedding, branching, and the like. Such considerations are not limited to linguistics. A parallel in cultural anthropology is Wallace's hypothesis (1961a, p. 462) that the brain is such that culturally institutionalized folk taxonomies will not contain more than twenty-six entities and consequently will not require more than six orthogonally related binary dimensions for the definitions of all terms. With regard to the cultural, one would take into account other features of the body and features of the material environment as well. With regard to the communicative, the general importance of the notion of means of implementation available is clear.

As we have seen, question 2 defines one portion of what is lumped together in linguistic theory under the heading of performance, and, correspondingly, acceptability. Clearly a more specific term is needed for what is in question here. No general term has been proposed for this property with regard to cultural behavior as a whole, so far as I know, and *feasible* seems suitable and best for both. Notice, moreover, that the implementational constraints affecting grammar may be largely those that affect the culture as a whole. Certainly with regard to the brain there would seem to be substantial identity.

3. Whether (and to what degree) something is appropriate

As we have seen, appropriateness is hardly brought into view in the linguistic theory under discussion, and is lumped under the heading of performance, and, correspondingly, acceptability. With regard to cultural anthropology, the term *appropriate* has been used (Conklin, Frake, etc.), and has been extended to language (Hymes, 1964, pp. 39–41). 'Appropriateness' seems to suggest readily the required sense of relation to contextual features. (Since any judgement is made in some defining context, it may always involve a factor of appropriateness, so that this dimension must be controlled even in study of purely grammatical competence (cf. Labov, 1966). From a communicative standpoint, judgements of appropriateness may not be assignable to different spheres, as between the linguistic and the cultural; certainly, the spheres of the two will intersect. (One might think of appropriateness with regard to grammar as the context-sensitive rules of sub-categorization and selection to which the base component is subject; there would still be intersection with the cultural.)

Judgement of appropriateness employs a tacit knowledge. Chomsky himself discusses the need to specify situations in mentalistic terms, and refers to proper notions of 'what might be expected from anthropological research' (1965, p. 195, n. 5). Here there would seem to be recognition that an adequate approach to the relation between sentences and situations must be 'mentalistic', entailing a tacit knowledge, and, hence, competence (in the usage of both Chomsky and this paper). But the restriction of competence (knowledge) to the grammatical prevails, so far as explicit development of theory is concerned. By implication, only 'performance' is left. There is no mention of what might contribute to judgement of sentences in relation to situations, nor how such judgements might be analysed. The lack of explicitness here, and the implicit contradiction of a 'mentalistic' account of what must in terms of the theory be a part of 'performance' show again the need to place linguistic theory within a more general sociocultural theory.

4. Whether (and to what degree) something is done

The study of communicative competence cannot restrict itself to occurrences, but it cannot ignore them. Structure cannot be reduced to probabilities of occurrence, but structural change is not independent of them. The capabilities of language users do include some (perhaps unconscious) knowledge of probabilities and shifts in them as indicators of style, response, etc. Something may be possible, feasible, and appropriate and not occur. No general term is perhaps needed here, but the point is needed, especially for work that seeks to change what is done. This category is necessary also to allow for what Harold Garfinkel (in discussion in Bright, 1966, p. 323) explicates as application of the medieval principle, *factum valet*: 'an action otherwise prohibited by rule is to be treated as correct if it happens nevertheless'.

In sum, the goal of a broad theory of competence can be said to be to show the ways in which the systemically possible, the feasible, and the appropriate are linked to produce and interpret actually occurring cultural behavior. [. . .]

V

We spoke first of a child's competence as 'in principle'. Of course no child has perfect knowledge or mastery of the communicative means of his community. In particular, differential competence has itself a developmental history in one's life. The matrix formed in childhood continues to develop and change throughout life with respect both to sentence structures and their uses (cf. Labov, 1965, pp. 77, 91–2; Chomsky, 1965, p. 202) and recall the northeast Amazon situation mentioned earlier. Tanner (1967, p. 21) reports for a group of Indonesians: 'Although the childhood speech patterns . . . foreshadowed those of the adult, they did not determine them. . . . For these informants it is the principle of code specialization that is the important characteristic of childhood linguistic experience, not the pattern of code specialization itself. (All are multilingual from childhood.) Not one person interviewed reported a static linguistic history in this respect.' See now also Carroll, 1968).

Perhaps one should contrast a 'long' and a 'short' range view of competency, the short range view being interested primarily in understanding innate capacities as unfolded during the first years of life, and the long range view in understanding the continuing socialization and change of competence through life. In any case, here is one major respect in which a theory of competence must go beyond the notion of ideal fluency in a homogeneous community, if it is to be applicable to work with disadvantaged children and with children whose primary language or language variety is different from that of their school; with intent to change or add, one is presupposing the possibility that competence that has unfolded in the natural way can be altered, perhaps drastically so, by new social factors. One is assuming from the outset a confrontation of different systems of competency within the school and community, and focusing on the way in which one affects or can be made to affect the other. One encounters phenomena that pertain not only to the separate structures of languages, but also to what has come to be called *interference* (Weinreich, 1953) between them: problems of the interpretation of manifestations of one system in terms of another.

Since the interference involves features of language and features of use together, one might adopt the phrase suggested by Hayes, and speak of *sociolinguistic interference*. (More generally, one would speak of *communicative interference* to allow for the role of modes of communication other than language; in this section, however, I shall focus on phenomena of language and language *per se*.)

When a child from one developmental matrix enters a situation in which the communicative expectations are defined in terms of another, misperception and misanalysis may occur at every level. As is well known, words may be misunderstood because of differences in phonological systems; sentences may be misunderstood because of differences in grammatical systems; intents, too, and innate abilities, may be misevaluated because of differences of systems for the use of language and for the import of its use (as against other modalities).

With regard to education, I put the matter some years ago in these words (Hymes, 1961, pp. 65–6):

... new speech habits and verbal training must be introduced, necessarily by particular sources to particular receivers, using a particular code with messages of particular forms via particular channels, about particular topics and in particular settings – and all this from and to people for whom there already exist definite patternings of linguistic routines, of personality expression via speech, of uses of speech in social situations, of attitudes and conceptions toward speech. It seems reasonable that success in such an educational venture will be enhanced by an understanding of this existing structure, because the innovators' efforts will be perceived and judged in terms of it, and innovations which mesh with it will have greater success than those which cross its grain.

The notion of sociolinguistic interference is of the greatest importance for the relationship between theory and practice. First of all, notice that a theory of sociolinguistic interference must begin with heterogeneous situations, whose dimensions are social as well as linguistic. (While a narrow theory seems to cut itself off from such situations, it must of course be utilized in dealing with them. See, for example, Labov and Cohen (1967) on relations between standard and non-standard phonological and syntactic rules in Harlem, and between receptive and productive competence of users of the non-standard vernacular.)

Second, notice that the notion of sociolinguistic interference presupposes the notion of sociolinguistic systems between which interference occurs, and thus helps one see how to draw on a variety of researches that might be overlooked or set aside. (I have in mind for example obstacles to use of research on 'second-language learning' in programs for Negro students because of the offensiveness of the term.) The notions of sociolinguistic interference and system require a conception of an *integrated theory of sociolinguistic description*. Such work as has been done to contribute to such a theory has found it necessary to start, not from the notion of a language, but from the notion of a *variety* or *code*. In particular, such a descriptive theory is forced to recognize that the historically derived status of linguistic resources as related or unrelated languages and dialects, is entirely secondary to their status in actual social relationships. Firstly, recall the need to put language names in quotes (section II). Secondly, the degree of linguistic similarity and distance cannot predict mutual intelligibility, let alone use. Thirdly, from the functional standpoint of a sociolinguistic description, means of quite different scope can be employed in equivalent roles. A striking example is that the marking of intimacy and respect served by shift of second person pronoun in French (*tu* : *vous*) may be served by shift of entire language in Paraguay (Guarani : Spanish). Conversely, what seem equivalent means from the standpoint of languages may have quite different roles, e.g., the elaborated and restricted codes of English studied by Bernstein (1965). In short, we have to break with the tradition of thought which simply equates one language, one culture,and takes a set of functions for granted. In order to deal with the problems faced by disadvantaged children, and with education in much of the world, we have to begin with the conception of the speech habits, or competencies, of a community or population, and regard the place among them of the resources of historically-derived languages as an empirical question. As functioning codes, one may find one language, three languages; dialects widely divergent or divergent by a hair; styles almost mutually incomprehensible, or barely detectable as different by the outsider; the objective linguistic differences are secondary, and do not tell the story. What must be known is the attitude toward the differences, the functional role assigned to them, the use made of them. Only on the basis of such a functionally motivated description can comparable cases be established and valid theory developed.

Now with regard to sociolinguistic interference among school children, much relevant information and theoretical insight can come from the sorts of cases variously labelled 'bilingualism', 'linguistic acculturation', 'dialectology', 'creolization', whatever. The value of an integrated theory of sociolinguistic description to the practical work would be that

1. it would attempt to place studies, diversely labelled, within a common analytical framework; and

2. by placing such information within a common framework, where one can talk about relations among codes, and types of code-switching, and types of interference as between codes, one can make use of the theory while perhaps avoiding connotations that attach to such labels as 'second-language learning'. (I say perhaps because of course it is very difficult to avoid unpleasant connotations for any terms used to designate situations that are themselves intrinsically sensitive and objectionable.)

William Stewart's (1965, p. 11, n. 2) suggestion that some code relation-ships in the United States might be better understood if seen as part of a continuum of cases ranging to the Caribbean and Africa, for example, seems to me from a theoretical standpoint very promising. It is not that most code relationships in the United States are to be taken as involving different languages, but that they do involve relationships among different codes, and that the fuller series illuminates the part. Stewart has seen through the different labels of dialect, creole, pidgin, language, bilingualism, to a common sociolinguistic dimension. Getting through different labels to the underlying sociolinguistic dimensions is a task in which theory and practice meet.

Let me now single out three interrelated concepts, important to a theory of sociolinguistic description, which have the same property of enabling us to cut across diverse cases and modes of reporting, and to get to basic relationships. One such concept is that of *verbal repertoire*, which Gumperz (1964) has done much to develop. The heterogeneity of speech communities, and the priority of social relationships, is assumed, and the question to be investigated is that of the set of varieties, codes, or subcodes, commanded by an individual, together with the types of switching that occur among them. (More generally, one would assess communicative repertoire.)

A second concept is that of *linguistic routines*, sequential organizations beyond the sentence, either as activities of one person, or as the interaction of two or more. Literary genres provide obvious examples; the organization of other kinds of texts, and of conversation, is getting fresh attention by sociologists, such as Sacks, and sociologically oriented linguists, such as Labov. One special importance of linguistic routines is that they may have the property that the late English philosopher Austin dubbed *performative* (Searle, 1967). That is, the saying does not simply stand for, refer to, some other thing; it is itself the thing in question. To say 'I solemnly vow' is to solemnly vow; it does not name something else that is the act of vowing solemnly. Indeed, in the circumstances no other way to vow solemnly is provided other than to do so by saying that one does so. From this standpoint, then, disability and ability with regard to language involve questions that are not about the relation between language and something else that language might stand for or influence; sometimes such questions are about things that are done linguistically or not at all. (More generally, one would analyse linguistic routines, comprising gesture, paralinguistics, etc. as well.)

A third concept is that of *domains of language behavior*, which Fishman has dealt with insightfully in his impressive work on *Language Loyalty in the United States* (1966, pp. 424–39). Again, the complexity and patterning of use is assumed, and the focus is upon 'the most parsimonious and fruitful designation of the occasions on which one language (variant, dialect, style, etc.) is habitually employed rather than (or in addition to) another' (p. 428). (More generally, one would define domains of communicative behavior.)

Too often, to be sure, the significance of a sociolinguistic feature, such as a code, routine, or term or level of address, is sought by purely distributional means. The feature is traced through the set of contexts in which it can be used without regard to an intervening semantic structure. Such an approach neglects the fact that sociolinguistic features, like linguistic features, are 'signs' in the classical Saussurean sense, comprising both a form and a meaning (*signifiant* and *signifié*). The difference is that one thinks of a typical linguistic sign as comprising a phonological form and a referential meaning (*chien* and the corresponding animal), whereas a sociolinguistic sign may comprise with respect to form an entire language, or some organized part of one, while meaning may have to do with an attitude, norm of interaction, or the like. (Recall the Paraguayan case of Spanish/distance : Guarani/closeness (among other dimensions)). Thus the relation between feature and context is mediated by a semantic paradigm. There is an analogue here to the representation of a lexical element in a language in terms of form (phonological features), meaning (semantic features), and context (features of syntactic selection), or, indeed, to the tripartite semiotic formula of Morris, syntactics, semantics, pragmatics, if these three can be interpreted here as analogous of form, meaning and context.

If the distributional approach neglects semantic structure, there is a common semantic approach that neglects context. It analyses the structure of a set of elements (say, codes, or terms of personal reference) by assuming one normal context. This approach (typical of much componential analysis) is equally unable to account for the range of functions a fluent user of language is able to accomplish (cf. Tyler, 1966). It is true that the value of a feature is defined first of all in relation to a set of normal contexts (settings, participants, personal relationships, topics, or whatever). But given this 'unmarked' (presupposed) usage, an actor is able to insult, flatter, color discourse as comic or elevated, etc., by 'marked' use of the feature (code, routine, level of address, whatever) in other contexts. Given their tacit knowledge of the normal values, hearers can interpret the nature and degree of markedness of the use.

Thus the differences that one may encounter within a community may have to do with:

1. Presence or absence of a feature (code, routine, etc.).
2. The semantic value assigned a feature (e.g., English as having the value of distance and hostility among some American Indians).
3. The distribution of the feature among contexts, and
4. The interrelations of these with each other in unmarked and marked usages.

This discussion does not exhaust the concepts and modes of analysis relevant to the sort of theory that is needed. A number of scholars are developing relevant conceptual approaches, notably Bernstein, Fishman, Gumperz, Labov (my own present formulation is indicated in Hymes, 1967a). The three concepts singled out do point up major dimensions: the capacities of persons, the organization of verbal means for socially defined purposes, and the sensitivity of rules to situations. And it is possible to use the three concepts to suggest one practical framework for use in sociolinguistic description. [. . .]

Reference

ABRAHAMS, R. D. (1967), 'Patterns of performance in the British West Indies', mimeographed working paper.

ALBERT, E. M. (1964), 'Rhetoric, logic and poetics in Burundi: culture patterning of speech behaviour', in J. J. Gumperz and D. Hymes (eds.), *The Ethnography of Communication, AmA*, vol. 66, no. 6, part 2.

BERNSTEIN, B. (1965), 'A sociolinguistic approach to social learning', in J. Gould (ed.), *Social Science Survey*, Penguin.

BLOOMFIELD, L. (1927), 'Literate and illiterate speech', *Amer. Speech*, vol. 2, pp. 432-9.

BONHOFFER, D. (1965), 'What is meant by "telling the truth"?', *Ethics*, pp. 363-72.

BRIGHT, W. (1966), *Sociolinguistics*, Mouton.

BURKE, K. (1966), *Towards a Better Life. Being a Series of Epistles, or Declamations*, University of California Press (first published 1932).

CARROLL, J. B. (1968), 'Development of native language skills beyond the early years', in Reed and J. B. Carroll (eds.), *Language Learning*, National Council of Teachers of English.

CAZDEN, C. B. (1966), 'Subcultural differences in child language: an interdisciplinary review', *Merrill-Palmer Q.*, vol. 12, pp. 185-218.

CAZDEN, C. B. (1967), 'On individual differences in language competence and performance', *J. Spec. Educ.*, vol. 1, pp. 135-50.

CHOMSKY, N. (1965), *Aspects of the Theory of Syntax*, MIT Press.

FERGUSON, C. A. (1966), 'On sociolinguistically oriented surveys', *Linguistic Reporter*, vol. 8, no. 4, pp. 1-3.

FISHMAN, J. A. (1966), *Language Loyalty in the United States*, Mouton.

GARFINKEL, H. (in press), 'Remarks on ethnomethodology', in J. J. Gumperz and D. Hymes (eds.), *Directions in Sociolinguistics*, Holt, Rinehart & Winston.

GOFFMAN, E. (1956), 'The nature of deference and demeanor', *AmA*, vol. 58, pp. 473-502.

GOFFMAN, E. (1959), *The Presentation of Self in Everyday Life*, Doubleday; Allen Lane The Penguin Press.

GOFFMAN, E. (1963), *Behavior in Public Places*, Free Press.

GOFFMAN, E. (1964), 'The neglected situation', in J. J. Gumperz and D. Hymes (eds.), *The Ethnography of Communication, AmA*, vol. 66, no. 6, part 2.

GOFFMAN, E. (1967), *Interaction Ritual*, Doubleday.

GOODENOUGH, W. H. (1957), 'Cultural anthropology and linguistics', in P. Garvin (ed.), *Report of the Seventh Annual Round Table Meeting on Languages and Linguistics*, Georgetown University Press.

GUMPERZ, J. J. (1964), 'Linguistic and social interaction in two communities', in J. J. Gumperz and D. Hymes (eds.), *The Ethnography of Communication*, *AmA*, vol. 66, no. 6, part 2.

HYMES, D. (1961), 'Functions of speech: an evolutionary approach', in F. Gruber (ed.), *Anthropology and Education*, University of Pennsylvania.

HYMES, D. (1964), 'Directions in (ethno-) linguistic theory', in A. K. Romney and R. G. D'Andrade (eds.), *Transcultural Studies of Cognition*, American Anthropological Association.

HYMES, D. (1967a), 'Models of the interaction of language and social setting', *J. Soc. Iss.*, vol. 23, pp. 8–28.

HYMES, D. (1967b), 'The anthropology of communication', in F. Dance (ed.), *Human Communication Theory: Original Essays*, Holt, Rinehart & Winston.

HYMES, D. (1968a), 'Linguistic problems in defining the concept of the tribe', in J. Helm (ed.), *Proceedings of the 1967 Spring Meeting of the American Ethnological Society*, University of Washington Press.

HYMES, D. (1968b), 'Linguistics – the field', *International Encyclopedia of the Social Sciences*, Macmillan Co.

HYMES, D. (in press), Review of Kenneth Burke, *Language as Symbolic Action*, *Language*.

JOHN, V. (1967), 'Communicative competence of low-income children: Assumptions and programs', *Report of Language Development Study Group*, Ford Foundation.

KATZ, J. J. (1967), 'Recent issues in semantic theory', *Foundations of Language*, vol. 3, pp. 124–94.

LABOV, W. (1965), 'Stages in the acquisition of standard English', in R. Shuy (ed.), *Social Dialects and Language Learning*, National Council of Teachers of English.

LABOV, W. (1966), *The Social Stratification of English in New York City*, Center for Applied Linguistics.

LABOV, W., and COHEN, P. (1967), 'Systematic relations of standard and non-standard rules in the grammar of Negro speakers', paper for Seventh Project Literacy Conference, Cambridge, Mass.

QUIRK, R. (1966), 'Acceptability in language', *Proceedings of the University of Newcastle-upon-Tyne Philosophical Society*, vol. 1, no. 7, pp. 79–92.

SAPIR, E. (1925), 'Sound patterns in language', *Language*, vol. 1, pp. 37–51.

SEARLE, J. (1967), 'Human communication theory and the philosophy of language: some remarks', in F. Dance (ed.), *Human Communication Theory*, Holt, Rinehart & Winston.

SEBEOK, T. (1959), 'Folksong viewed as code and message', *Anthropos*, vol. 54, pp. 141–53.

SINGER, M. (1955), 'The cultural pattern of Indian civilization: a preliminary report of a methodological field study', *Far East. Q.*, vol. 15, pp. 223–36.

STEWART, W. (1965), 'Urban Negro speech: sociolinguistic factors affecting English teaching', in R. Shuy (ed.), *Social Dialects and Language Learning*, National Council of Teachers of English.

TANNER, N. (1967), 'Speech and society among the Indonesian élite: a case study of a multilingual community', *Anthrop. Linguistics*, vol. 9, no. 3, pp. 15–40. (See also this volume.)

TYLER, S. (1966), 'Context and variation in Koya kinship terminology', *AmA*, vol. 68, pp. 693–707.

WALLACE, A. F. C. (1961a), 'On being just complicated enough', *Proceedings of the National Academy of Sciences*, vol. 47, pp. 438–64.

WALLACE, A. F. C. (1961b), *Culture and Personality*, Random House.

WEINREICH, U. (1953), *Languages in Contact*, Linguistic Circle of New York.

WOLF, E. (1964), *Anthropology*, Prentice-Hall.

19 C. B. Cazden

The Situation: a Neglected Source of Social Class
Differences in Language Use

Excerpts from C. B. Cazden, 'The situation: a neglected source of social class
differences in language use', *Journal of Social Issues*, vol. 26, no. 2, 1970, pp. 35–60.

Study of the acquisition of language has been based on the assumption
that what had to be described and explained was the acquisition of a
repertoire of responses (in the terminology of behaviorism) or the acquisition of a finite set of rules for constructing utterances (in the terminology
of developmental psycholinguistics). On this assumption, the school
language problems of lower-class (LC) children can have two explanations:
either they have acquired less language than middle-class (MC) children
or they have acquired a different language. The 'less language' explanation
has been given various names – cultural deprivation, deficit hypothesis,
vacuum ideology – all with the same connotation of a nonverbal child
somehow emptier of language than his more socially fortunate age-mates.
The 'different language' explanation is forcefully argued by Stewart and
Baratz (Baratz, 1969a; Baratz, 1969b; Aarons, Gordon, and Stewart,
1970). It states that all children acquire language but that many children,
especially LC black children, acquire a dialect of English so different in
structural (grammatical) features that communication in school, both oral
and written, is seriously impaired by that fact alone. [. . .]

The inadequacy of both the 'less language' and the 'different language'
characterizations is twofold. First, both refer only to patterns of structural
form and ignore patterns of use in actual speech events. Second, they
assume that the child learns only one way to speak which is reflected in
the same fashion and to the same extent at all times. On both theoretical
and practical grounds, we can no longer accept such limitations. We must
attend not only to the abilities of individuals and how they develop, but
to qualities of the situation, or temporary environment, in which those
abilities are activated. Such attention to the interaction of abilities and
environments is increasing in psychology, linguistics and education.

The power of environments

Barker has coined the name 'ecological psychology' and argues for its
importance:

When environments are relatively uniform and stable, *people* are an obvious source of behavior variance, and the dominant scientific problem and the persistent queries from the applied fields are: What are people like? What is the nature and what are the sources of individual differences? . . . But today *environments* are more varied and unstable than heretofore and their contribution to the variance of behavior is enhanced. Both science and society ask with greater urgency than previously: What are environments like? . . . How do environments select and shape the people who inhabit them? . . . These are questions for ecological psychology (1968, p. 3).

When Kagan (1967) issued a call for 'relativism' in psychology which would include the context or situation in descriptions of behavior, Psathas answered:

When Kagan uses the term 'relativistic', he says that it 'refers to a definition in which context and state of the individual are part of the defining statement.' The 'neglected situation' as Goffman (1964) has called it and the state of the individual, particularly his internal symbol manipulating state, need to be considered. They would involve Kagan in sociology and anthropology much more than he recognizes. The 'context' that he refers to is one that has *socially* defined stimulus value. The social definitions for a situation are pregiven, i.e. exist before the psychologist or experimenter enters on the scene. He must, therefore, understand what these are and how they are perceived by the subject before he can claim to understand why the subject behaves the way he does. The 'state of the individual' includes not only his biological and physiological state but his interpretive structuring of the world as he experiences it, based on his previous socialization experiences as a member of the culture (1968, p. 136).

While Barker seeks an objective description of the environment – analogous to the characteristics of light or sound in the study of perception, Psathas calls for study of the environment as socially defined and perceived by individuals.

Communicative competence

Applied to language this means that we have to describe more than the child's grammatical competence; we have to describe what Hymes (1972) calls 'communicative competence', which is how the child perceives and categorizes the social situations of his world and differentiates his ways of speaking accordingly. The important point here is not a contrast between competence or knowledge on the one hand, and performance or behavior on the other hand, though many people – including myself in an earlier paper (Cazden, 1967) – have formulated the question in this way. A child's manifest verbal behavior, or performance, has both grammatical and pragmatic aspects. And it is a reflection of implicit knowledge or competence, both of grammar and of use.

The acquisition of competence for use, indeed, can be stated in the same terms as acquisition of competence for grammar. Within the developmental matrix in which knowledge of the sentences of a language is acquired, children also acquire knowledge of a set of ways in which sentences are used. From a finite experience of speech acts and their interdependence with socio-cultural features they develop a general theory of the speaking appropriate in their community, which they employ, like other forms of tacit cultural knowledge (competence) in conducting and interpreting social life (Hymes, 1972).

Social class differences in the explicit expression of meaning

We are a long way from understanding the range of communicative competences that different children have or how they develop. In fact, research on this enlarged question about the child's acquisition of language has only begun. Bernstein (in press) has been a pioneer here. Unfortunately, although Bernstein himself has repeatedly said that he is describing patterns of use in actual speech performance, his work is frequently cited in support of 'less language' assertions about grammatical competence. The unpublished research of Tough at the University of Leeds replicates some of Bernstein's findings with preschool-age children who are matched on Standford-Binet IQ but differ in social class background (see Cazden, in press). Both Bernstein and Tough find social class differences in the degree to which meaning is expressed explicitly, or independent of context. Explicitness is probably also related to what Labov calls 'attention paid to the monitoring of [one's own] speech' (1969, p. 32).

The speech situation as an independent variable

Our eventual goal is to understand how a person's previous experience (of which his social class is simply a rough and composite index) interacts with factors in the momentary situation to affect his behavior. At any one moment, a child decides to speak or be silent, to adopt communicative intent *a* or communicative intent *b*, to express idea *x* or idea *y*, in form 1 or in form 2. The options the child selects will be a function of characteristics of the situation as he perceives it on the basis of his past experience. We observe that a particular child in a particular situation either makes or fails to make a particular utterance. Traditionally, we have related that utterance only to characteristics of the child, such as his social class, while ignoring characteristics of the situation. As Robinson points out, the tendency in child language research has been to ignore situational or contextual variables, or to combine speech data from several contexts. Instead, Robinson suggests, 'it may be wiser methodologically to accumulate the (social class) differences within contexts and to see what higher order generalizations can be made about them' (1968, p. 6).

The next section is a survey of research on child language which includes aspects of the speech situation as independent variables, regardless of the social class of the subjects. The purpose is to illustrate the idea of situational relativity and to suggest significant variables which should be explored more systematically. While the research to be reported is all about monolingual children, the notion of a diversified speech repertoire applies even more obviously to bilinguals (Herman, 1961; McNamara, 1967, especially the chapter by Hymes).

The final section of the paper raises questions about other necessary ingredients of a theory of oral language education.

The effects of situations

Relevant studies are listed in Table 1. Columns represent a very gross categorization of situational differences (the independent variables in the research): topic, task, listener(s), interaction, and situations with mixed language (the dependent variables): fluency and/or spontaneity length and/or complexity, some characteristic of speech content such as abstractness, and degree of approximation to Standard English. Unless otherwise specified, all differences to be discussed below are differences in the way the same child, or group of children, speaks in different situations; occasionally, differences between similar groups of children are reported. All but two (Moffett, 1968; Robinson, 1965) deal with oral language.

Topic

Pictures. Four studies used different kinds of pictures. Strandberg (1969) found that four- and five-year-old children above average in intelligence (with different children in each stimulus group) talked more about either a toy or a twenty-second silent film of that toy than they did about a still color photograph of it. There was no difference, however, in either average length or complexity of the responses. Strandberg and Griffith (1968) gave four- and five-year-old children in a university laboratory school Kodak Instamatic cameras loaded with color film and then elicited conversation about the remarkably successful pictures the children took. The children talked more spontaneously (i.e. required fewer adult probes) and talked in longer and more complex utterances about the pictures they took at home of personally significant objects (like a favorite climbing tree or a closeup of Mother's mouth) than they did about pictures taken under adult direction during the period of orientation to the camera. Since the pictures taken at home were also frequently of only one object, the authors conclude that the difference lies in the degree of personal involvement. Although topic is compounded with order since all children told stories about the preselected objects first, it seems unlikely that this

Table 1 Effects of the situation on child language (classification of relevant studies)

Language characteristics	Characteristics of the situation				
	Topic	Task	Listener(s)	Interaction	Mixed
Fluency/ Spontaneity	Strandberg Strandberg & Griffith Williams & Naremore (a, b) Berlyne & Frommer	Heider et al. Brent & Katz	Labov et al.	Cooperman (personal communication)	Cowan et al. Cazden (1965) Labov et al. Pasamanick & Knobloch Resnick, Weld, & Lally (1969) Kagan (1969) Jensen
Length/ Complexity	Strandberg & Griffith Cowan et al. Moffett Williams & Naremore (a, b) Labov et al. Mackay & Thompson	Brent & Katz Cazden (1967) Lawton Robinson (1965) Williams & Naremore (a, b)	Cazden (1967) Smith	Plumer	Cowan et al.
Content or Style	Labov et al.	Lawton			
Approximation of Standard English	Labov et al.	Labov et al.			

Note: dates are cited here only where the Reference list contains more than one item by the same author(s).

accounts for all the difference. Following are examples of one five-year-old's stories, first about an assigned picture and then about one of his choices:

That's a horse. You can ride it. I don't know any more about it. It's brown, black and red, I don't know my story about the horse.
There's a picture of my tree that I climb in. There's – there's where it grows at and there's where I climb up – and sit up there – down there and that's where I look out at. First I get on this one and then I get on that other one. And then I put my foot under that big branch that are strong. And then I pull my face up and then I get ahold of a branch up at that place – and then I look around (Strandberg & Griffith, personal communication, 1969).

Cowan et al. (1967) presented elementary school children of mixed socioeconomic status with ten colored pictures from magazine covers. The effect of the particular picture on the mean length of response (MLR) was strong across all age, sex, socioeconomic class, and experimenter categories. One picture of a group standing around a new car elicited significantly shorter MLRs and one picture of a birthday party elicited significantly longer MLRs, while the other eight pictures were undifferentiated between the two extremes. Although the authors cannot specify the source of the stimulus effect, they conclude that 'the implicit assumption that magnitude of MLR is a property of the subject independent of his setting should be permanently discarded' (Cowan, Weber, Hoddinott, and Klein, 1967, p. 202).

Finally, Berlyne and Frommer (1966) studied the properties of different pictures and stories in eliciting one particular form of speech – questions. They presented children from kindergarten and grades three, five, and six at a university laboratory school with stories, pictures, and stories accompanied by pictures, and then invited the children to ask questions about them. Novel, surprising, and incongruous items elicited more questions than others, but provision of answers (an interaction characteristic) had little effect.

TV Narratives. Two studies compared narratives about TV programs with other topics. Williams and Naremore (1969, a and b) analysed forty interviews with Negro and white fourth- through sixth-graders who were selected from the extremes of the socioeconomic distribution of a larger group of 200 interviewees in a Detroit dialect study (Shuy, Wolfram and Riley, 1967). All informants had responded to three topics: games ('What kinds of games do you play around here?'); television ('What are your favorite TV programs?'); and aspirations ('What do you want to be when you finish school?'). Social class differences in number of words spoken – on an elaboration index (the proportion of utterances which went beyond a simple yes–no answer or a label to a description or explanation), on a ranking of the degree of connectedness of the utterances in a response, and on verbal indices of specific grammatical features – appeared only for the topic of TV.

Although it is at best a subjective interpretation, the concentration of status differences in three of the clause indices on the TV topic seem to be a reflection of the tendency of the HS (high status) children to engage in story-telling or narrative while the LS (low status) children tended to itemize instances of what they had seen or preferred. The language used by the child in an interview is as much a reflection of his engagement within the constraints of a communication situation as it is a reflection of his linguistic capabilities (Williams & Naremore, 1969b).

Labov has collected narratives of TV programs and personal experience from pre-adolescent boys attending vacation day camps (VDC) in Central Harlem. Following are two such narratives by two different eleven-year-old boys – the first about 'The Man From Uncle' and the second about a personal fight.

1. This kid – Napoleon got shot
2. and he had to go on a mission
3. And so this kid, he went with Solo.
4. So they went
5. And this guy – they went through this window.
6. and they caught him.
7. And then he beat up them other people
8. And they went
9. and then he said
   that this old lady was his mother
10. and then he – and at the end he say that he
    was the guy's friend.
    (Carl, 11, VDC, No. 386)
1. When I was in fourth grade –
   no it was in third grade –
2. This boy he stole my glove.
3. He took my glove
4. and said that his father found it downtown on
   the ground
   (And you fight him?)
5. I told him that it was impossible for him
   to find downtown cause all those people were walking by and
   just his father was the only one that found it?
6. So he got all (mad).
7. So then I fought him.

8. I knocked him all out in the street.
9. So he say he give.
10. and I kept on hitting him.
11. Then he started crying
12. and ran home to his father
13. And the father told him
14. that he didn't find no glove.
    (Norris, W., 11, VDC, No. 378)
    (Labov *et al.*, 1968, vol. 2, pp. 298–99.)

Labov finds that the main difference between the two sets of narratives is the absence of evaluation in the TV narratives: 'the means used by the narrator to indicate the point of the narrative, its *raison d'être*, why it was told, and what the narrator is getting at' (Labov *et al.*, 1968, vol. 2, p. 297). Absence of evaluation from accounts of vicarious experience reduces structural complexity. 'The syntax of the narrative clause itself is one of the simplest structures that may be found even in colloquial language' (Labov *et al.*, 1968 vol. 2, p. 308). But explanations, one of the devices for evaluation, may be exceedingly complex. Following is the diagram (Figure 1) for one section of the personal experience narrative; the symbol S indicates that one sentence has been embedded in another (Labov *et al.*, 1968, vol. 2, p. 332):

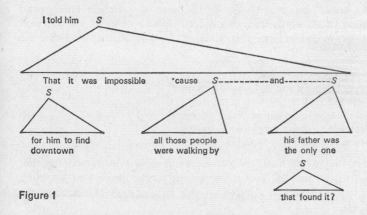

Figure 1

It does not seem far-fetched to suggest a common element in these findings: the greater the degree of affect or personal involvement in the topic of conversation, the greater the likelihood of structural complexity.

Some final examples of the effect of topic on linguistic structure are, first, Moffett:

While watching some third-graders write down their observations of candle-flame – deliberately this time, not merely in note form – I noticed that sentences beginning with if-and-when clauses were appearing frequently on their papers. Since such a construction is not common in thirdgrade writing, I became curious and then realized that these introductory subordinate clauses resulted directly from the children's *manipulation of what* they were observing. Thus: 'If I place a glass over the candle, the flame turns blue.' Here we have a fine example of a physical operation being reflected in a cognitive operation and hence in a linguistic structure. . . . The cognitive task entailed in the candle tests *created a need* for subordinate clauses, because the pupils were not asked merely to describe a static object but to describe changes in the object brought about by changing conditions (*if* and *when*), (1968, p. 180).

My last example comes from my observations of the written compositions by five-year-old children in two English infant schools, both in neighborhoods of mixed socioeconomic status (Cazden, in press). In the first school, all the children were given their first writing books (blank with unlined pages for pictures and related stories), asked to draw a picture and then dictate a story for the teacher to write. All the resulting stories were simple sentences and all but one was of the form *This is a* —. The exception was the sentence *This boy is dead.* In the second school, children were using experimental beginning reading materials developed by Mackay and Thomson (1968). Each child had a word folder with a preselected store of basic words plus some blanks for his personal collection. He also had a stand on which words from the folder could be set up as a text. These children composed sentences very different from each other, including the following:

My Mum takes me to school.
Is my sister at school and is my baby at home?
My cousin is skinny.
I like Siam she gave me one of David's doggies.
On Tuesday the movie camera man is coming.
I ask Helen to come to my birthday.

Whereas the presence of the pictures somehow constrained the first children to the simplest and most routine labels, absence of a picture seemed to free the second children to work with far more of their linguistic knowledge.

Task

In some studies, differences are found which seem to relate more to what the subject is asked to do with the topic than to the topic itself. For instance, Brent and Katz (1967) asked white Headstart children to tell stories about pictures from the WISC picture arrangement task, then removed the pictures and asked the children to tell the stories again. They found that the stories told without the pictures were superior. The children produced longer stories without prompting, and ideas were related more logically and explicitly. Brent and Katz suggest that 'the actual presence of the pictures, which constitute a *spatially distributed* series of *perceptually discrete events*, may in fact interfere with our younger subjects' ability to form a *temporally distributed* and *logically continuous* story, a task which required a conceptual and linguistic "bridging-the-gap" between discrete frames' (1967, pp. 4–5). We cannot tell from this study whether first telling the stories with the pictures present contributes to the more successful attempt when they are removed.

Lawton (1968), a student and then colleague of Bernstein's in London, gave a series of language tasks to boys aged twelve–fifteen years. In an interview he elicited both descriptive and more abstract speech, e.g. describe your school and then answer 'what do you think is the real purpose of education?' All the boys used more subordinate clauses and complex constructions on the abstraction task than on the description task.

The structure of directions. Four studies report differences which result from different degrees of structure or constraint in the directions. With the same boys, Lawton also conducted a discussion of capital punishment, replicating an earlier study by Bernstein (1962), and gave assignments to write on four topics such as 'My life in ten years' time'. In the more open unstructured discussions, middle-class boys used more abstract arguments and hypothetical examples, while the working-class boys used more concrete examples and clichés or anecdotes. But in the abstract sections of the interviews, social class differences were much smaller.

The inference I would draw is that in an 'open' situation the working-class boys tend to move towards concrete, narrative/descriptive language, but in a 'structured' situation where they have little or no choice about making an abstract response, they will respond to the demand made upon them. They may have found the task extremely difficult, but it was not impossible for them (Lawton, 1968, p. 138).

Comparable results were obtained by Williams and Naremore (1969b) and Heider *et al.* (1968). One way in which Williams and Naremore scored the interviews on games, aspirations, and TV was by the type of questions asked by the interviewer and the corresponding type of child response. There were three types of probe constraints:

1. Simple (Do you play baseball?)
2. Naming (What television programs do you watch?)

3. Elaboration (How do you play kick-the-can?).
Response-style was categorized as follows:
1. Simple (Yeah).
2. Naming (Baseball).
3. Qualified naming (I usually watch the Avengers and lots of cartoons).
4. Elaboration (Last night the Penguin had Batman trapped on top of this tower . . .).

Results show that in response to the first two probes, 'The lower status children had more of a tendency to supply the minimally acceptable response, whereas their higher status counterparts had a greater tendency to elaborate their remarks' (Williams and Naremore, 1969a). Following the probe for elaboration, however, these differences disappeared. 'The mark of a lower-status child was that he had some tendency to provide the type of response which would minimally fulfill the field worker's probe, [but] not go on to assume a more active role in the speech situations including elaboration of more of his own experience' (Williams and Naremore, 1969a).

Heider et al. (1968) report an experiment in which lower- and middle-class white ten-year-old boys were asked to describe a picture of one animal out of a large array. Criterial or essential attributes were the name of the animal and three others: number of spots, standing or lying down, and position of the head. The density of criterial attributes named by the children was almost identical for the two groups: MC children mentioned 67 attributes of which 18 were criterial, while LC children mentioned 69 attributes of which 16 were criterial. But there was a significant social class difference in the number of requests the listener had to make for more information before the picture was adequately specified: LC mean $= 6 \cdot 11$ requests; MC mean $= 3 \cdot 56$ requests. Thus the lower-class children's performance was far superior to what it would have been if the amount of probing or feedback had been standardized for the two groups as it usually is in both experimental situations and classrooms.

Robinson (1965), another colleague of Bernstein, gave two writing assignments to 120 middle-class and working-class twelve- and thirteen-year-old boys and girls in a comprehensive school. One assignment, to tell a good friend news of the past fortnight, presumably elicited informal or restricted codes from all subjects. The other assignment, advising a governor of the school how some money he had donated might be spent, presumably elicited a formal or elaborated code from anyone who could use one. Contrary to expectations, there were no significant differences between the middle-class and working-class formal letters, and differences only in lexical diversity (number of different nouns, adjectives, etc.) between the informal letters where the topic was less constrained.

While the results of Lawton, Williams and Naremore, Heider *et al.*, and Robinson have indicated that working-class children display greater abstraction, elaboration, or informational analysis when it is demanded by an adult, analyses by Anita R. Olds and myself (Cazden, 1967) of the speech of two first-grade children in eight situations showed different results when the dependent variable is simply mean length of utterance in morphemes (utterance defined as an independent clause and any syntactically related dependent clauses). Martin, a middle-class white boy, spoke longer utterances on the average in the three structured task situations: retelling *Whistle for Willie* – 7·09; describing an object hidden in a cloth bag – 6·52; and describing five pictures about school – 6·44. By contrast Rita, a lower-class Negro girl, spoke longer utterances on the average in three more informal interviews: 7·94, 7·53, and 6·20. While this study of two children must be considered only a pilot venture, it does provide an example of interaction between a child's background and the situations which elicit the longest utterances. Presumably, there are more such interactions to be discovered if we knew where and how to look for them.

Formality of the situation. Speech situations can also be differentiated on an informal-formal continuum, according to the amount of attention paid to language itself. Labov *et al.* (1968, vol. 1) has collected speech samples at several points along such a continuum from the least self-conscious and most excited speech in peer group sessions, through accounts of fights in individual interviews and other interview speech, to reading a connected sentence, and finally to reading a list of unconnected words. All speakers speak more standard English in their most formal and careful speech.

Listener(s)

One important characteristic of the listener is age in relation to the speaker. In an early study, Smith (1935) found that children 18 to 70 months old spoke longer sentences at home with adults than at play with other children, presumably because at home they gave fewer answers to questions and fewer imperatives, and had greater opportunity for more connected discourse with less active play and less frequent interruptions. We also found (Cazden, 1967) that both Rita and Martin spoke their shortest sentences, on the average, in two experimental situations with their peers: an arithmetic game where Rita averaged 4·50 and Martin 4·78, and a telephone conversation where Rita scored 5·60 and Martin 3·58.

Two students at Harvard found that children modified their speech when speaking to younger children. Yurchak (1969) analysed the language of her three-year-old daughter, Kathleen, as she talked to herself, her mother, and her eighteen-month-old baby sister. Kathleen's longest utterances were spoken to her mother, her shortest utterances to her sister, while speech to herself was somewhere in between. Bernat (1969) taped the speech of three girls, 9 and 11 and 13 years old, when talking to younger boys ages 18, 30, and 29 months. The extent to which the girls adapted their speech to their young listener depended not on his age, but on evidence of his capacity to talk and understand. Their average sentence length with the first child was 4·06 morphemes, with the second 5·23 morphemes; but with the third – a very verbal child with excellent comprehension – they talked in normal, mature sentences. On replaying the tape, Bernat, found to her surprise, that she herself did too.

Younger listeners aren't the only restraining influence. Power relations between older and younger children can also influence speech:

Stevie: He gon' getchyou with 'Is li's . . . he got li-' he got leg like di – like –
Stevie is ordinarily very fast and fluent with words, but he finds it very difficult to say what he means to these sixteen-year-olds – another example of how power relations can determine verbal ability available at the moment (Labov et al., 1968, vol. 2, p. 117).

Interaction of speakers

Here we have only one report from a pilot study and one hypothesis now being tested. But both are worth consideration by others. Oliver Cooperman, a student at Harvard Medical School on leave to work with Barbara Tizard at the University of London on the effects of various conditions of residential care on pre-school age children, conducted a pilot study of various aspects of conversation. He found that 'conversation is more likely to occur and include a greater number of exchanges back and forth when initiated by the child' and 'a child almost never responds verbally to an adult command "Stop doing X" except rarely, to say "no"; on the other hand, commands to initiate action, to "do X", frequently provoked verbal reply' (personal communication, 1969).

A student at Harvard, Davenport Plumer, is conducting his doctoral research on dialogue strategies among twelve families with children seven or eight years old, six with sons of high verbal ability (as measured on the Stanford-Binet and a combination of WISC-ITPA), and six with sons of average verbal ability. Recording equipment is given to each family in turn, and dialogue is recorded from a wireless microphone worn by the focal child. Each family records a total of seven hours during one week, including twenty-minute sessions at breakfast, supper and bedtime. One measure used will be the length of a dialogue–the number of verbal exchanges between the initiation and termination of a topic; one analysis undertaken will be the relation of length of dialogue to complexity of the child's utterances.

A major assumption underlying this study is that the longer the dialogue the more likely the child is to hear and use a wide range of the resources and strategies of his language. The ability to elaborate and qualify – or to follow elaboration and qualification – is most likely to be learned in an extended dialogue after an initial exchange has set up the need for clarification and elaboration (Plumer, 1969, pp. 7–8).

If either Cooperman's or Plumer's hypothesis is borne out in further research, it would have important implications for planning classrooms for maximally productive conversation. For instance, initiation of conversation probably takes place more often in a classroom where children carry major responsibility for planning their activities. But this may only be productive for language usage if involvement, and thereby conversation on a topic, is sustained over some period of time.

Mixed aspects of situations

Classrooms. Two kinds of situations which seem to contain a mixture of relevant aspects are the various activities in any classroom and the testing situations. Cowc (1967) has recorded the conversations of kindergarten children in nine activities. In both amount and maturity of speech, housekeeping play and group discussion held the greatest potential for language, while play with blocks, dance, and woodworking held least. She suggests that factors influencing speech are adult participation, something concrete to talk about, physical arrangements, and noise. I made similar observations when selecting play materials for the tutorial language program (Cazden, 1965).

Tests. Testing situations contain the effects of interpersonal formality and power relationship mixed with the cognitive demands of particular tasks. Pasamanick and Knobloch (1955) and Resnick, Weld, and Lally (1969) report evidence that the verbal expressiveness of working-class Negro two-year-olds is artificially depressed in testing situations. Even Jensen, arguing that social-class differences in intelligence are largely inherited, reports from his own clinical experience that he regularly raised IQ scores on the Stanford-Binet (largely a test of verbal performance) eight to ten points by having children from an impoverished background come in for two to four play sessions in his office so that the child could get acquainted and feel more at ease (Jensen, 1969).

Kagan, in answer to Jensen, reports the experience of Francis Palmer in New York City:

Dr Palmer administered mental tests to middle- and lower-class black children from Harlem. However, each examiner was instructed not to begin testing with any child until she felt that the child was completely relaxed, and understood what was required of him. Many children had five, six, and even seven hours of rapport sessions with the examiner before any questions were administered. Few psychological studies have ever devoted this much care to establishing rapport with the child. Dr Palmer found few significant differences in mental ability between the lower- and middle-class populations. This is one of the first times such a finding has been reported and it seems due, in part, to the great care taken to insure that the child comprehended the nature of the test questions and felt at ease with the examiner (1969, p. 276).

Labov provides a dramatic example of the effect of the test situation on an older child. Attacking the conditions under which much of the data on 'verbal deprivation' is collected, he quotes an entire interview with a pre-adolescent boy in a New York City school and contrasts it with his own methods and findings:

The child is alone in a school room with the investigator, a young, friendly white man, who is instructed to place a toy on the table and say 'Tell me everything you can about this.' The interviewer's remarks are in parentheses.
(Tell me everything you can about *this*.) [Plunk]
   [*12 seconds of silence*]
(What would you say it looks like?)
   [*8 seconds of silence*]
A space ship.
(Hmmmm.)
   [*13 seconds of silence*]
Like a je-et.
   [*12 seconds of silence*]
Like a plane.
   [*20 seconds of silence*]
(What color is it?)
Orange. [*seconds*] An' whi-ite. [*seconds*] An' green.
   [*6 seconds of silence*]
(And what could you use it for?)
   [*8 seconds of silence*]
A jet.
   [*6 seconds of silence*]
(If you had two of them, what would you do with them?)
   [*6 seconds of silence*]
Give one to some-body.
(Hmmmm. Who do you think would like to have it?)
   [*10 seconds of silence*]
Clarence.
(Mm. Where do you think we could get another one of these?)
At the store.
(O-Ka-ay!)
The social situation which produces such defensive behavior is that of an adult asking a lone child questions to which he obviously knows the answers, where

anything the child says may well be held against him. It is, in fact, a paradigm of the school situation which prevails as reading is being taught (but not learned). We can obtain such results in our own research, and have done so in our work with younger brothers of the 'Thunderbirds' in 1390 Fifth Avenue. But when we change the social situation by altering the height and power relations, introducing a close friend of the subject, and talking about things we know he is interested in, we obtain a level of excited and rapid speech (Labov *et al.*, 1968, vol. 2, pp. 340–41).

The situation as a source of social class differences

Because all the above examples illustrate how the same children respond in different situations, it may not be clear how the situation can be considered a neglected source of social class differences. Two ways are possible. Differential responses according to aspects of the situation may be intensified for lower-class speakers (an ordinal interaction). So for example, all children may be constrained in a testing situation and lower-class children especially so. Labov found this kind of interaction between style shifting and social stratification in his study of phonological and grammatical features:

The same variables which are used in style shifting also distinguish cultural or social levels of English. This is so for stable phonological variables such as *-th* and *-ing*, for such incoming prestige forms as *-r*; for the grammatical variables such as pronominal opposition, double negative, or even the use of *ain't* (1969, p. 17).

For instance, all speakers shift from *workin'* to *working* as they shift from casual speech to reading style. But the shift is much greater for lower-class speakers.

Alternatively, there may be interactions between language and situation in which the relationships are reversed (a disordinal interaction) rather than varying in intensity for the different social class groups. Middle-class children may be more fluent in one set of situations, while lower-class children talk more fluently in another. Such a finding was suggested for our research subjects, Martin and Rita, above. Only further research can sort these possibilities out.

Towards a theory of oral language education

Even if we had the kind of understanding of communicative competence among diverse groups of children which Hymes calls for, we would still be far from a theory of oral language education. That requires, in addition, decisions about which goals are important, what communicative competence we seek. Sociolinguistic interference from contrasting communicative demands outside and in school are almost certainly more important than grammatical interference (Hymes, 1972; Labov, Cohen, Robins and Lewis, 1968). To reduce this interference, we have to know both what capabilities the child brings and what we want him to be able to do.

Language use rather than language form is important

Discussions of the goals of education, like analyses of child language, too often focus on language form when they should be concerned with language use. In arguing against oral language programs for teaching standard English to speakers of a non-standard dialect, Kochman says:

> My first quarrel with such a program is that it does not develop the ability of a person to use language, which I would further define as performance capability in a variety of social contexts on a variety of subject matter. . . . Underlying this approach seems to be a misapplication of Basil Bernstein's terms which falsely equate *restrictive code* and *elaborated code* with, respectively, non-standard dialect and standard dialect. It ought to be noted, as Bernstein uses the term, code is not to be equated with *langue*, but *parole*, not with *competence* but *performance*. What is restrictive or elaborated is not in fact the *code* as sociolinguists use the term, but the message (1969, p. 2).

To reject attempts to teach a single, socially prestigious language form is not to reject all attempts at change. Cultural differences in language use can result in deficiencies when children confront the demands of particular communicative situations.

> Cultural relativism, inferred from an enormous variety of existing cultures, remains a prerequisite of objective analysis. . . . But the moral corollary of cultural relativism – moral relativism – has been quietly discarded except as a form of intellectual indulgence among those who claim the privilege of non-involvement (Wolf, 1964, pp. 21–2).

Educators certainly cannot claim any privilege of non-involvement, and they must decide what goals they seek. Taking as his goal the education of a person who knows enough not to remain a victim, Olson says, 'A teacher must possess extraordinary knowledge and humanity if he is to distinguish what the school demands of children simply to symbolize its capacity for authority over them from what it legitimately "demands" or "woos out of them" to equip them for a niche in a technological society' (1967, p. 13).

Pieces of an answer can be suggested. On the basis of his experience as a teacher in a village school for Kwakiutl Indian children on Vancouver Island, Wolcott (1969) suggests teaching specific skills rather than trying to make over the child into one's own image. Marion Blank argues for education in the use of language for abstract thinking. Kochman (personal communication, 1969) recommends opportunity for the use of language in 'low-context' situations where speaker and listener do not share a common referent and where a greater burden of communication falls on the words alone; this requires a skill that thirty-three-month-old Gerald (Cazden, 1965) needs help in acquiring. Cazden and John (1969) argue for coordinate education for cultural pluralism in which patterns of language form and use (and beliefs and values as well) in the child's home community are maintained and valued alongside the introduction of forms of behavior required in a technological society.

In the end the goals of education are in large part matters of value, and decisions about them must be shared by educators and spokesmen for the child and his community. Such decisions, combined with knowledge of communicative competence and how it develops, will enable us to design more productive situations for oral language education in school.

References

AARONS, A. C., GORDON, B. Y., and STEWART, W. A. (eds.) (1970), 'Linguistic–cultural differences and American education', *Florida FL Reporter*, vol. 7, no. 1.

BARATZ, J. C. (1969a), 'A bi-dialectal task for determining language proficiency in economically disadvantaged Negro children', *Child Devel.*, pp. 889–901.

BARATZ, J. C. (1969b), 'Language and cognitive assessment of Negro children', ASHA, vol. 11, pp. 87–91.

BARKER, R. G. (1968), *Ecological Psychology*, Stanford University Press.

BERLYNE, D. E., and FROMMER, F. D. (1966), 'Some determinants of the incidence and content of children's questions', *Child Devel.*, vol. 37, pp. 177–89.

BERNAT, E. (1969), 'How speakers of different ages alter their speech when conversing with small children', unpublished term paper, Harvard Graduate School of Education.

BERNSTEIN, B. (1962), 'Social class, linguistic codes and grammatical elements', *Language and Speech*, vol. 5, pp. 221–40.

BERNSTEIN, B. (1972), 'A critique of the concept compensatory education', Introduction to Gahagan, D. M., and Gahagan, G. A., *Talk Reform: Explorations in Language for Infant School Children*, Routledge & Kegan Paul. Also in Cazden, C. B., Hymes, D., and John, V. (eds.) (in press), *Functions of Language in the Classroom*, Teachers College Press.

BRENT, S. B., and KATZ, E. W. (1967), 'A study of language deviations and cognitive processes', Progress Report no. 3, OEO Job Corps contract 1209, Wayne State University.

CAZDEN, C. B. (1965), 'Environmental assistance to the child's acquisition of grammar', unpublished doctoral dissertation, Harvard University.

CAZDEN, C. B. (1967), 'On individual differences in language competence and performance', *J. Spec. Educ.*, vol. 1, pp. 135–50.

CAZDEN, C. B. (in press), 'Language programs for young children: Views from England', in C. B. Lavatelli (ed.), *Preschool Language Training*, University of Illinois Press.

CAZDEN, C. B., and JOHN, V. P. (1969), 'Learning in American Indian children', in S. Ohannessian (ed.), *Styles of Learning Among American Indians: An Outline for Research*, Center for Applied Linguistics.

COWAN, P. A., WEBER, J., HODDINOTT, B. A., and KLEIN, J. (1967), 'Mean length of spoken response as a function of stimulus, experimenter, and subject', *Child Devel.*, vol. 33, pp. 199–203.

COWE, E. G. (1967), 'A study of kindergarten activities for language development', unpublished doctoral dissertation, Columbia University.

GOFFMAN, E. (1964), 'The neglected situation', *AmA* vol. 66, no. 6, part 2, pp. 133–6; reprinted in P. P. Giglioli (ed.), *Language and Social Context*, Penguin Books, 1972.

HEIDER, E. R., CAZDEN, C. B., and BROWN, R. (1968), 'Social class differences in the effectiveness and style of children's coding ability', Project Literacy Reports no. 9, Cornell University.

HERMAN, S. R. (1961), 'Explorations in the social psychology of language choice', *Hum. Rel.*, vol. 14, pp. 149–64.

HYMES, D. (1972), 'On communicative competence', (in this volume).

JENSEN, A. R. (1969), 'How much can we boost IQ and scholastic achievement?', *Harvard Educ. Rev.*, vol. 39, pp. 1–123.

KAGAN, J. (1967), 'On the need for relativism', *Amer. Psychol.*, vol. 22, pp. 131–42.

KAGAN, J. (1969), 'Inadequate evidence and illogical conclusions', *Harvard Educ. Rev.*, vol. 39, pp. 274–7.

KOCHMAN, T. (1969), 'Special factors in the consideration of teaching standard English', paper read at Convention of Teachers of English to Speakers of other Languages (TESOL), Chicago.

LABOV, W. (1969), *The Study of Non-Standard English*, Clearinghouse for Linguistics, Center for Applied Linguistics.

LABOV, W., COHEN, P., ROBINS, C., and LEWIS, J. (1968), *A Study of the Non-Standard English of Negro and Puerto Rican Speakers in New York City*, Final Report of Cooperative Research Project No. 3288, Columbia University, 2 vols.

LAWTON, D. (1968), *Social Class, Language and Education*, Routledge.

MACKAY, D., and THOMPSON, B. (1968), *The Initial Teaching of Reading and Writing: Some Notes Toward a Theory of Literacy*, program in linguistics and English teaching, Paper no. 3, University College, London and Longman.

MCNAMARA, J. (ed.) (1967), 'Problems of bilingualism', *J. of Soc. Iss.*, vol. 23, no. 2.

MOFFETT, J. (1968), *Teaching the Universe of Discourse*, Houghton Mifflin.

OLSON, P. A. (1967), 'Introduction: the craft of teaching and the school of teachers', report of the first national conference, US Office of Education Tri-University Project in Elementary Education, Denver.

PASAMANICK, B., and KNOBLOCH, H. (1955), 'Early language behavior in Negro children and the testing of intelligence', *J. Abnorm. and Soc. Psychol.*, vol. 50, pp. 401–402.

PLUMER, D. (1969), 'Parent–child verbal interaction: a naturalistic study of dialogue strategics', Interim Report, Harvard Graduate School of Education.

PSATHAS, G. (1968), 'Comment', *Amer. Psychol.*, vol. 23, pp. 135–7.

RESNICK, M. B., WELD, G. L., and LALLY, J. R. (1969), 'Verbalizations of environmentally deprived two-year-olds as a function of the presence of a tester in a standardized test situation', paper presented at the meeting of the American Educational Research Association, Los Angeles.

ROBINSON, W. P. (1965), 'The elaborated code in working-class language', *Language & Speech*, vol. 8, pp. 243–52.

ROBINSON, W. P. (1968), 'Restricted codes in sociolinguistics and the sociology of education', paper presented at Ninth International Seminar, University College, Dar-es-Salaam.

SHUY, R. W., WOLFRAM, W. A., and RILEY, W. K. (1967), *Linguistic Correlates of Social Stratification in Detroit Speech*, Final Report of Cooperative Research Project No. 6–1347. Wayne State University.

SMITH, M. E. (1935), 'A study of some factors influencing the development of the sentence in pre-school children', *J. Gen. Psychol.*, vol. 46, pp. 182–212.

STRANDBERG, T. E. (1969), 'An evaluation of three stimulus media for evoking verbalizations from preschool children.' Unpublished Master's thesis, Eastern Illinois University.

STRANDBERG, T. E., and GRIFFITH, J. (1968), 'A study of the effects of training in visual literacy on verbal language behavior. Unpublished manuscript, Eastern Ilinois University.

WILLIAMS, F., and NAREMORE, R. C. (1969a), 'On the functional analysis of social class differences in modes of speech. *Speech Monographs*, 36, 77–102.

WILLIAMS, F., and NAREMORE, R. C. (1969b), 'Social class differences in children's syntactic performance: A quantitative analysis of field study data. *Journal of Speech and Hearing Research*, 12, 777–93.

WOLCOTT, H. F. (1969), 'The teacher as an enemy.' Unpublished manuscript, University of Oregon,

WOLF, E. R. (1964), *Anthropology*, Englewood Cliffs, New Jersey: Prentice-Hall.

YURCHAK, M. J. (1969), 'Differences in speech of a three-year-old addressing mother and sister.' Unpublished term paper, Harvard Graduate School of Education.

20 D. Henderson

Contextual Specificity, Discretion and Cognitive Socialization: with Special Reference to Language

Excerpts from D. Henderson, 'Contextual specificity, discretion and cognitive socializations: with special reference to Language', *Primary Socialisation, Language and Education, Vol. 1: Social Class, Language and Communication*, Routledge & Keegan Paul.

The Sociological Research Unit of the Department of Sociology, University of London Institute of Education, has been engaged, for the past five years, upon a study of variations between and within social class in familial patterns of communication and control. These have been examined in relation to the socialization of the child considering particularly his response to school.[1] The theory which initially guided this research is set out in Bernstein (1962, 1970). This paper is concerned to examine social class differences in reported orientations in the emphasis on and the contextual usage of language in the socialization of the child.

The sample under discussion consists of 100 mothers who form a randomly selected sub-sample of 312 mothers who were interviewed when their children, who are also part of the inquiry, were seven years of age. [. . .]

One hundred and twenty of the mothers live in a MC (middle class) area of London and 192 live in a WC (working class) area. The variation between area and social class of the parents is 0·74. The index of social class was constructed by Walter Brandis of the Sociological Research Unit; it is based upon the terminal education and occupation of husband and wife. A full description of the index will be found in Brandis and Henderson (1970). Social class is measured on a ten-point scale, 0–9. In terms of the ten-point scale, the mean social class position of the MC group is 2·8, and the mean social class position of the WC group is 6·9. It was necessary to limit the sample of this study in order that a detailed analysis could be carried out, and in order to explore the data in depth. Before discussing the results of the analysis we shall state initially our expectation of the findings. [. . .]

1. We gratefully acknowledge the help we have received from the Department of Education and Science and The Ford Foundation. We are grateful to the Director of the Chaucer Publishing Co., Mr L. G. Grossman, for his interest and support. We should like to express further our gratitude to the two Local Education Authorities who gave permission for the research.

Mother–child communication

The following hypotheses were to be tested:

1. Both MC and WC would place greater emphasis upon the use of language in interpersonal aspects of socialization than the emphasis placed upon language in the socialization into basic skills.

2. The shift in emphasis in the use of language from the skill to the person area would be much greater in the MC group.

3. Within the skill area the MC group would place a greater emphasis upon language in the transmission of principles.

4. MC mothers would be more likely than WC mothers to take up the child's attempts to initiate verbal interaction.

5. There would be social class differences in the frequency with which questions were avoided or evaded. MC mothers would avoid answering less frequently than WC mothers.

6. There would be differences in response *between* types of questions. Some questions would elicit greater avoidance than others.

7. MC mothers would choose general definitions when explaining things to children more frequently than WC mothers.

8. MC mothers would choose exact, explicit concrete examples more frequently than WC mothers.

9. WC mothers would be more likely to choose concrete examples than MC mothers.

Four of the schedules were designed in order to examine the mothers' orientation towards the use of language with children, and to examine three aspects of the mother's pattern of verbal communication with her seven-year-old child.

Results
Schedule A

This schedule was designed to examine differences in the emphasis placed on the use of language in two areas of the socialization of pre-school children: inter-person relationships and the acquisition of basic skills. As these results have been extensively discussed in Bernstein and Henderson (1969), we shall only briefly summarize them here. This schedule was an attempt to discover the relative emphasis placed upon language in the socialization of the child into inter-person relationships and into elementary skill acquisition. Questions 5, 6, 8, 9 and 11 refer to the person area, questions 1, 2, 3 and 7 refer to the skill area, and questions 4 and 10 are dummy questions designed to move the mothers' responses towards the 'easy' point of the scale.

The overall difference in emphasis between the two areas, irrespective of the social class of the mothers, is highly significant ($F_{1,98} = 294\cdot53$, $p = 0\cdot001$). However, although greater emphasis was placed upon difficulty in the *person* area by *all* the mothers, the difference between the mean responses of the MC mothers, in relation to the two areas, was significantly greater than the difference between the mean responses of the WC mothers ($F_{1,98} = 73\cdot60$, $p = 0\cdot001$). MC mothers placed much *greater* emphasis upon the difficulty of doing the things described in the *person* area than the WC mothers, but much *less* emphasis upon the difficulty of doing the things described in the *skill* area. This highly significant interaction effect illustrates the polarization of the MC mothers' responses in relation to the two areas.

Table 1 sets out the mean scores for each social class within each area. The higher the score the greater the emphasis and the lower the score the less the emphasis. At the same time a highly significant interaction effect

Table 1

| | Statements | | |
	Skill areas	Person areas	Total $\bar{x}$
$\bar{x}$ Middle class	0·03	1·49	0·78
$\bar{x}$ Working class	0·33	0·80	0·56
Sample $\bar{x}$	0·20	1·14	

between the social class of the mothers and responses to the individual skill statements was found. MC mothers placed significantly greater emphasis on difficulty than the WC mothers in response to the statement 'Showing them how things work' ($F_{3,294} = 74\cdot88$, $p = 0\cdot001$). Table 2 shows the mean score of each social class for each of the statements in the skill area. Again, the higher the score the greater the emphasis, the lower the score the less the emphasis.

Table 2

Statement	1	2	3	4	Total $\bar{x}$
$\bar{x}$ Middle class	−0·48	0·12	0·04	0·62	0·30
$\bar{x}$ Working class	0·48	0·28	0·36	0·36	1·50
Sample $\bar{x}$	0·01	0·20	0·20	0·49	

We can summarize the results as follows:

1. MC mothers, relative to WC mothers, placed a greater emphasis upon the use of language in the socialization of the child into inter- and intra-personal relationships, whereas the WC placed a relatively greater emphasis upon language in the socialization of the child into elementary skills.

2. Without prejudice to the above, MC mothers placed greater emphasis on the use of language in the transmission of principles, i.e. 'Showing them how things work'. Here the MC, relative to the WC, appeared to find it necessary to explicate the principles *verbally*.

3. The MC mothers, relative to the WC mothers, more *sharply* discriminated between the skill and person areas as this is evidenced by the differential emphasis on the use of language.

Schedule B

This schedule was constructed in order to find out how the mother responded to her child's attempts to chat to her across a range of seven fairly typical contexts. Four different strategies were provided, and the mother was asked to place a tick against the one she was most likely to take up for each of the seven situations. The strategies were:

1. 'Tell him to stop' which was scored 1.
2. 'Tell him to wait' which was scored 2.
3. 'Answer him quickly' which was scored 3.
4. 'Chat to him' which scored 4.

A preliminary examination of the data revealed that there were minimal differences in response to particular contexts, so it was decided to analyse the differential frequency with which particular strategies were taken up. A Z × 4 experimental plan on repeated measures was therefore undertaken. The analysis revealed that MC mothers had significantly higher scores than WC mothers, thus showing that they were more likely to respond by chatting to the child ($F_{1,98} = 24.07$, p $= 0.001$). There was also a significant difference overall in the choice of strategies taken up ($F_{3,294} = 235.17$, p $= 0.001$). A second-order interaction effect due to the relationship between the social class of the mother and the strategy most frequently taken up was also significant ($F_{3,294} = 12.20$, p $= 0.001$). A further analysis of the simple main effects of social class on each of the strategies showed that there was a significant difference between the two social class groups on one strategy only – 'Chat to him'. MC mothers were more likely to take up this strategy than WC mothers ($F_{1,392} = 682.22$, p $= 0.01$). The analysis of simple main effects was extended to the differential choice of strategies *within* each social class. Both MC ($F_{3,294} = 166.42$, p $= 0.01$), and WC mothers ($F_{3,294} = 80.95$, p $= 0.01$) discriminated significantly between the frequency with which certain strategies were taken up. In both cases the strategy most frequently avoided was 'Tell him to stop', and in both cases the most frequent strategy was 'Chat to him'. There was little discrimination between 'Tell him to wait' and

'Answer him quickly', although discrimination between these two strategies tended to be greater in the WC than in the MC.

Schedule C

Here the mothers were presented with eight questions which a child was likely to ask, and they were invited to choose their initial response to each question from among six possible responses. Four of these responses indicated avoidance or evasion of the question on the part of the mother, whilst two were positive responses – 'Take the opportunity to discuss the matter with him' and 'Give him a brief answer and see if he's satisfied'. It was considered that the latter response allowed the child greater discretion in regulating the mother's flow of information than the former, and for this reason it was assigned the highest score, 2. 'Take the opportunity to discuss the matter with him' was assigned a score of 1, and any avoidance response was given a score of 0. The method of analysis was a 2×8 experimental plan, on repeated measures, the measures being the questions.

A significant main-order difference was found due to the social class of the mothers. WC mothers more frequently avoided or evaded answering questions than MC mothers ($F_{1,98} = 38\cdot40$, p $= 0\cdot001$). There was also a significant second-order difference due to an interaction effect between the social class of the mother and the particular question to which she responded ($F_{7,686} = 2\cdot92$, p $= 0\cdot01$). An analysis of the simple main effects of social class on the questions showed that there were significant differences in response *between* the questions within the WC but *not* within the MC ($F_{7,686} = 3\cdot74$, p $= 0\cdot01$). In other words, WC mothers were much more likely to avoid answering *particular* questions. A further analysis of simple main effects of social class on *each* of the questions was carried out, and we found that the questions which elicited the greatest incidence of avoidance among the mothers were:

1. Why there are wars.
2. Why boys are different from girls.
3. Why some people are mentally disturbed.
4. Daddy's part in making babies.

We then decided to carry out a secondary analysis of the data, because, not only were we interested in the relative incidence of avoidance responses, but also in the relative frequencies of the two positive responses within each social class. The percentage distributions of the total scores were examined, and are presented in Table 3.

We can clearly see from Table 3 that the maximum difference between MC and WC mothers is in the incidence of avoidance, despite the fact

Table 3 **Percentage distribution of total scores**

	Avoidance	Discussion	Brief answer	Total
MC (N = 400)	4·25	48·25	47·50	100·00
WC (N = 400)	23·00	55·75	21·25	100·00

that for both classes it is the most infrequent type of response. However, within the WC there is a very much greater incidence of 'discussion' responses relative to 'brief answer' responses, whilst the difference between these two types of response is minimal within the MC. Thus we find that when WC mothers do not avoid answering a question they are much more likely to take up the 'discussion' option than the 'brief answer' option. In order to test for the significance of these differences between the social class groups, t-tests were carried out. As we would expect, there was no significant difference between the two groups in the frequency with which the 'discussion' option was taken up. And, as we might expect, on the basis of the results of the initial analysis, WC mothers avoided answering questions more frequently than MC mothers (t = 11·97, df 98, p = 0·001). At the same time, MC mothers differed significantly from WC mothers in the frequency with which they took up the 'brief answers' option (t = 61·56, df 98, p = 0·001). However, we can see from the percentage distribution in the foregoing table that this was almost entirely due to the relative avoidance of 'brief answer' responses on the part of WC mothers in favour of 'discussion'.

Now, our findings showed that WC mothers discriminated between the questions in terms of avoidance–discussion responses on the whole. Examination of our data suggested that, whilst MC mothers did not discriminate in terms of avoidance, they might well be discriminating between the questions in terms of the *type* of positive response. The following table shows that MC mothers tended to respond with 'brief answers' to those statements which elicited avoidance responses from WC mothers.

Comment

In Bernstein and Henderson (1969), a full discussion was offered of the found differences in the use of language in the areas of the socialization of the pre-school child; inter-personal relationships and the acquisition of basic skills. Briefly, it was suggested that the MC are more concerned to make verbally explicit for the child the whole inter-personal area. Such explicitness provides for a greater reflexiveness on the part of the MC towards the area of experience. We note that MC mothers are more likely to take up attempts of the child to talk in a range of contexts.

Table 4

| Questions | Numbers of mothers | | | | | |
| | Avoidance | | 'Discussion' | | 'Brief answers' | |
	MC	WC	MC	WC	MC	WC
1	0	7	30	28	20	15
2	3	18	19	18	28	14
3	2	13	26	29	22	8
4	3	12	19	29	28	9
5	1	6	29	33	20	11
6	0	6	33	35	17	9
7	7	24	13	17	30	9
8	1	6	24	34	25	10

Further, that they report that they are less likely to avoid answering the child's questions in the inter-personal area. The MC mothers are more likely to give the response 'Give him a brief answer and see if he is satisfied' to what might be considered three very difficult questions to answer; whereas the WC tend to give 'avoidance' responses to the same questions. These results confirm all the hypotheses which relate to the schedules. The findings on the 'chat' and the 'avoidance' schedules repeat the results obtained from similar but less specific schedules put to the mother two years earlier (Brandis and Henderson, 1970).

We will now consider in rather more detail the analysis of schedule 'C' (the 'avoidance' schedule). We find that not only do MC mothers avoid or evade answering difficult questions *less* than the WC mothers, but also that the MC mothers discriminated between the questions. Within the WC discrimination only took the form of avoidance versus non-avoidance, whereas within the MC discrimination took the form of choosing between *different types of non-avoidance responses*. Questions which dealt with critical aspects of inter- or intra-personal relationships elicited the greatest avoidance among the WC mothers. These same questions elicited a particular type of response from MC mothers: they were more likely to elicit the response 'Give him a brief answer and see if he's satisfied' then 'Take the opportunity to discuss the matter with him'. It might be thought that such a response in the MC may have operated in lieu of an avoidance response. When this schedule was designed, it was considered that giving the child a brief answer and waiting to see if he was satisfied allowed the child greater discretion to regulate the amount of information.

It is a matter of considerable interest that the questions which called out the child-regulating strategy on the part of the MC mothers are all questions which on the whole elicit *avoidance* strategies from the WC mothers. These questions 'Why boys are different from girls', 'Daddy's part in making babies' and 'Why some people are mentally disturbed' were originally asked because it was thought that they refer to highly critical areas of experience which may form a taboo area. The MC mother's response indicates that firstly she is prepared to offer an explanation and secondly she may be conscious of not wanting to overload the child and so *gives* the child the initiative in seeking more information. We regard this as an important example of how these mothers will take into account the relationship between the explanatory style *and* the particular needs of the child. The MC mothers' explanatory styles appear to be *contingent* upon the problem, her explanations appear to be *context-specific*.

Whereas we feel confident in our interpretation of the contextual switch upon the part of the MC to 'Give him a brief answer and see if he's satisfied', we are not able to make strong inferences from the WC overall preference, when they do *not* avoid, for 'Take the opportunity to discuss it with him'. If the WC mother did not avoid the question, she was forced to choose one of the two explanatory strategies. It is conceivable that the *meaning* of the 'brief answer' strategy is *different* for the two social classes.

We have some evidence to suggest that this is indeed likely to be the case. When we examined, *within* the WC sample, the intercorrelation between mothers who choose 'Give him a brief answer etc.', and the mothers who opt for the 'Chat to him' strategy, we find that the correlation is significantly negative ($r = -0.29$, $p = 0.05$). On the other hand, the correlation between the 'discussion' response and the 'Chat to him' strategy is significantly positive ($r = 0.43$, $p = 0.01$). Therefore, within the WC sample the strategy 'Give him a brief answer etc.', is unlikely to be an index of a self-regulatory teaching style. It is more likely to be a minimal information strategy on the 'avoidance' dimension. We can strengthen this inference by giving the intercorrelation between the choice of the 'discussion' strategy and the frequency with which questions are avoided by the mother, which is significantly negative ($r = -0.28$, $p = 0.05$). The more verbally responsive the WC mother reports she is to her child, the more likely she is to give a 'discussion' response. We find *no* relationship between the choice of 'Give him a brief answer, etc.', and the choice of the 'Chat to him' strategy *within* the MC sample. Similarly, within the MC sample there is *no* relationship between 'Give him a brief answer' and avoidance of questions. Thus, MC mothers who choose 'Give him a brief answer' are not necessarily verbally unresponsive to their children. Minimally, we can say that 'Give him a brief answer' is an alternative response to 'discussion' in the MC. The MC mother's response is dependent upon the *question*, not upon the mother's general orientation to her child.

Schedule D

This schedule was constructed in order to find out how mothers explained the meanings of words to their children. We were particularly interested in finding out what *types* of definitions mothers were most likely to give. Four words were presented to them other – 'cool', 'mix', 'dangerous' and 'flexible' – and they were asked to choose *two* of four possible types of response for each of these words. The choices had to be ranked in terms of the *first* statement the mother would be most likely to choose and then the statement which she thought *second* best. Since there were four different types of statement given for each word, there was a possibility of the mother choosing any one of *six* possible combinations of statements in response to any one item. Thus it can be seen that, at first sight, the mothers' responses to this schedule promised to be rather difficult to analyse.

The four statements offered for each word were presented in the form of (*a*) a general definition, (*b*) an antonym, (*c*) a highly specific concrete example, and (*d*) a much less specific concrete example. The various possible combinations of first and second choices, then, were as follows:

1. General definition and highly specific concrete example.
2. General definition and an antonym.
3. General definition and least specific concrete example.
4. Highly specific concrete example and least specific concrete example.
5. Highly specific concrete example and antonym.
6. Least specific concrete example and antonym.

The various responses were not scored in any way, because this would have involved putting differential values on each of the combined choices. It was considered that this was unjustified. For example, how should one choose between the differential values of a general definition combined with a highly specific concrete example, and an antonym combined with a highly specific concrete example? Finally, it was decided to find:

1. The total number of each possible combinations for *each* word within each social class;

2. The total number of each possible combinations *across* the four words within each social class;

3. The *first* choice responses for *each* word within each social class;

4. The *first* choice responses *across* the four words within each social class.

First, a 2 × 4 chi-square was carried out in order to find out whether there was a significant social class difference in the incidence of *different* combined choices given across the four words. It was therefore possible for a mother to give one type of combined response for all four items, or for her to vary her response with each word, thus giving four different combinations. The result of this chi-square test showed that there was indeed a significant difference between the two social class groups on this measure. WC mothers were most likely to use only one or two different combinations across the four words, whilst MC mothers were most likely to use three or four different combinations across the words ($x^2 = 9\cdot94$, df 3, p = $0\cdot02$). We then tested for the significance of differences in the number of *first* choice responses across all four words, in a similar fashion, but no significant differences were found. It is important to stress that here we were concerned to examine *variation* in first choice response across the four words, *not* incidence of particular first choice responses.

Next, we were interested in differences between the social class groups in terms of the *first* choice response to *each* word. Four 2 × 4 chi-squares were carried out. This analysis revealed that there were significant differences in response to three of the words, as follows:

Mix. MC mothers were most likely to choose the highly specific concrete example first, whereas WC mothers were most likely to choose the least specific concrete example first ($x^2 = 21\cdot28$, df 3, p = $0\cdot001$).

Dangerous. MC mothers were most likely to choose the general definition first, whereas WC mothers were most likely to choose the least specific concrete example first ($x^2 = 20\cdot32$, df 3, p = $0\cdot001$).

Flexible. MC mothers were most likely to choose the general definition first, whereas WC mothers were more likely to choose the highly specific concrete example first ($x^2 = 14\cdot14$, df 3, p = $0\cdot01$).

To summarize briefly, MC mothers were found to be more likely than WC mothers to choose a general definition *first* in response to two of the words, 'dangerous' and 'flexible'. WC mothers were found to be more likely than MC mothers to choose the least specific concrete example *first* in response to two of the words, 'mix' and 'dangerous'.

The differences between MC and WC mothers in terms of the *combined* responses to each word were then examined. Four 2 × 6 chi-squares were carried out. Significant social class differences were found in relation to *two* of the words:

Dangerous. MC mothers were more likely to choose the general definition and the antonym, *or* the general definition and the highly specific concrete example, whereas WC mothers were more likely to choose the highly specific concrete example and the least specific concrete example ($x^2 = 20\cdot02$, df 5, p = $0\cdot01$).

Flexible. MC mothers were more likely to choose both the general definition and the highly specific concrete example, whereas WC mothers were more likely to choose both the highly specific and the least specific concrete examples ($x^2 = 11 \cdot 06$, df 5, p $= 0 \cdot 05$).

Again, we can briefly summarize these results. For both of the words which elicited significant differences in response, M C mothers were more likely to choose general definitions with highly specific concrete examples, whilst W C mothers, on the other hand, were more oriented to *both* varieties of concrete examples.

We can now examine the results of four 2×4 chi-squares which tested for significant differences in the *incidence* of particular *first* choices across the four words. No significant differences in the overall incidence of general definitions or least specific concrete examples were found. But there were significant differences in the incidence of highly specific concrete examples and in the incidence of antonyms.

Highly specific concrete examples. M C mothers were more likely than W C mothers to choose this type of statement when defining 'cool' and 'mix', and they were least likely to do this when defining 'dangerous' and 'flexible'. On the other hand, W C mothers were more likely than M C mothers to choose this type of statement when defining 'dangerous' and 'flexible' but least likely to do this when defining 'cool' and 'mix' ($x^2 = 13 \cdot 43$, df 3, p $= 0 \cdot 01$).

Antonyms. The overall incidence of the use of antonyms as first choices was low, but M C mothers were more likely to choose this type of statement than W C mothers. Antonyms were most likely to occur as first choices in the definition of 'cool' ($x^2 = 15 \cdot 99$, df 3, p $= 0 \cdot 01$).

Although these findings were extremely interesting, we found them somewhat difficult to summarize succinctly. It was therefore decided to examine the responses to each word in terms *only* of the *first* choices and these were to be summarized as either *abstract* in orientation (e.g. general definitions or antonyms) or *concrete* in orientation (e.g. highly specific and least specific concrete examples). Four 2×2 chi-squares were then carried out.

The M C and the W C mothers did not differ significantly when defining 'cool' and 'mix', although there was a tendency in both cases for M C mothers to be more abstract in orientation. There were significant differences in the cases of 'dangerous' and 'flexible':

Dangerous. M C mothers were most likely to give abstract definitions, whilst W C mothers were most likely to give concrete definitions ($x^2 = 13 \cdot 10$, df 1, p $= 0 \cdot 01$).

Flexible: MC mothers were again most likely to give abstract definitions, whilst WC mothers were most likely to give concrete definitions ($x^2 = 10 \cdot 20$, df 1, p $= 0 \cdot 01$).

Let us now summarize the findings of the analysis of this schedule, with the help of appropriate tables. M C mothers were found to be more consistent across the words than W C mothers in the type of statement which they chose first, as the following table clearly shows:

Table 5 **Number of different first choices used**

	MC	WC
1 or 2	36	24
3 or 4	14	26

The relevant first choice was most likely to be a general definition.

Table 6 **Incidence of first-choice definitions across words**

	MC	WC
General definition	118	76
Antonym	12	8
Highly specific concrete	51	60
Least specific concrete	19	56
Total	200	200

However, despite the consistency shown by the M C mothers in the type of first choices, there was greater variation within the M C in the number of different combinations used across the four words. This logically indicates that their second choice of definition was more likely to be contingent upon the particular word than was the case in the W C.

Table 7 **Number of different combined responses**

	MC	WC
1 or 2	18	28
3 or 4	32	22

Next, M C mothers were more likely than W C mothers to choose an abstract definition first, whereas W C mothers were more likely to choose a concrete definition first, overall.

Table 8

	MC	WC
Abstract	130	84
Concrete	70	116
Total	200	200

Finally, there were differences in the incidence of different types of combined first- and second-choice responses. MC mothers were more likely than WC mothers to choose a general definition with an antonym. WC mothers, on the other hand, were more likely than MC mothers to choose both a highly specific with a least specific concrete example, overall.

Table 9 Combined choices

	MC	WC
General definition + highly specific concrete	87	74
General definition + antonym	30	17
General definition + least specific concrete	38	36
Highly specific concrete + antonym	12	10
Highly specific concrete + least specific concrete	30	50
Least specific concrete + antonym	3	13

Comment

We find that MC mothers were not only more likely to aim primarily at a higher level of generality or abstraction when defining words for their children, but also that when they considered it necessary to give a concrete example, the example chosen was more *explicit* and *precise* than the examples chosen by WC mothers. MC mothers, at the same time, discriminated more frequently *between* the words requiring definition in terms of the response chosen as second-best. We find that, despite the relatively infrequent use of antonyms by all mothers, MC-mothers were more likely to use them than WC mothers, but their use of antonyms was *totally* avoided when defining 'mix', whilst their use was equally distributed when defining 'cool', 'dangerous' and 'flexible'. In other words, MC mothers were more likely to employ antonyms when defining *states* whereas the use of antonyms was avoided when defining a *process*. The WC mothers did not discriminate between the words in this way.

Whilst the data at our disposal from this schedule does not allow us to make any firm interpretation in terms of maternal teaching styles, we think the results here may reflect a tendency towards a *deductive* teaching style on the part of the MC mothers, and an *inductive* teaching style on the part of the WC mothers. Minimally, our justification for this hypothesis is based upon the overwhelming number of general definitions chosen by MC mothers as their primary response, and upon the much greater incidence of concrete examples among the primary responses of WC mothers. This is not to say that MC mothers do *not* give concrete examples, and that WC mothers do *not* give general definitions. MC mothers move from the general to the specific, whereas the WC mothers, when they use a general definition, rank it below a concrete example. They move from the specific to the general.

General discussion

First let us consider the questions of the contextual specificity of the verbal communications of the mothers *and* the emphasis upon language in different contexts. Contextual specificity of the communications refers to the extent that the mothers discriminate between contexts or to discrimination between verbal strategies within the *same* context. Emphasis refers to the extent to which a context evokes verbal communication.

Emphasis

[. . .]

1. MC mothers reported that they were more likely to chat to the child across a range of contexts. However, the most common strategies for *both* social classes were 'Tell him to stop' and 'Chat to him'.

2. MC mothers reported that they placed a relatively greater emphasis than did WC mothers upon the use of language in the socialization of the child into person relationships, whereas WC mothers reported that they placed a greater emphasis upon the use of language than did the MC mothers in the socialization of the child into elementary skills. However, the MC mothers emphasized language within the skill area in response to the question 'Showing him how things work'.

Contextual specificity

[. . .]

1. The analysis of schedule C (answering or evading questions put by the child to the mother) showed that the MC mothers alternated between *two* information-giving responses 'Take the opportunity to discuss the matter with him' and 'Give him a brief answer and see if he's satisfied', whereas the WC were more confined to the discussion strategy. We showed that in the WC, the 'brief answer' strategy was related to the avoidance dimension and also to mothers who were much less likely to take up the child's attempts to chat to the mother. Of more significance, the MC used the strategy 'Give him a brief answer and see if he's satisfied' in response to the statements 'Why boys are different from girls' 'Daddy's part in making babies' and 'Why some people are mentally disturbed'. Thus the explanatory style of the MC mother appears to be contingent upon the problem: her explanations appear to be contextually specific.

2. The analysis of the schedule concerned with word-defining strategies: we showed that despite the infrequent use of antonyms by all mothers,

M C mothers *totally* avoided their use when defining 'mix' but they distributed the use of this strategy across the other three words. They avoided the use of the antonym when defining *processes*. The W C mothers did not discriminate between the words in this way. M C mothers discriminated more between the words in terms of their second best choice of definitions.

3. The analysis of schedule *A* showed that although all mothers reported that they placed a greater emphasis upon the use of language in socializing the pre-school child into person-relationships rather than into elementary skills, the shift was five times as great in the M C from one area to the other, but only two and a half times in the case of the W C. It would appear then that the M C mothers made a much clearer differentiation between the use of language in the skill and person area than did the W C mothers. The M C mothers' responses were more context specific.

4. There is an interesting difference between the mothers of different social class background in the verbal realization of the inter-person area of discourse. On the one hand we have the M C mother who seems to be unwilling to talk to unspecified adults for inter-personal reasons[2] but who place a positive emphasis on talking to their children in this area. They also do not avoid or evade answering critical questions put by their children in the same area. On the other hand the W C mothers, who seem to be most willing to talk to other adults for inter-personal reasons, place less emphasis upon the use of language in this area when talking to their children, relative to the M C mothers. The W C also positively avoid answering critical questions in this area. This class difference in the contextual constraint upon talking in the inter-personal area may simply have arisen out of the *classification* we have introduced. On the other hand, it could point to the need for further inquiry into the relationships between role and topic as this is affected by social class.

Discretion

We will now go on to consider the discretion accorded to the child by the mother. By discretion we mean the range of alternatives the mother makes available to the child in different contexts. The data we have presented here does not allow us much room for comment. Other data the Sociological Research Unit has collected bears rather more pertinently on this area (Jones, 1966; Bernstein and Brandis, 1970). However, we can here point to the finding that M C mothers are more likely relatively to take up their child's attempts to *initiate* verbal interaction in a range of contexts. Further, that the M C relative to the W C use an information-giving strategy which, if we interpret it correctly, permits the child to regulate the

2. Data supporting this is given in material excluded due to space-limitations (Ed.)

amount of information he receives ('Give him a brief answer and see if he's satisfied').

Cognitive socialization

We have shown that according to the mothers' reports, MC mothers, relative to WC mothers:

1. Favour abstract definitions – the class-defining principle.

2. Favour *explicit* rather than implicit 'concrete' definitions.

3. Favour information giving strategies in answer to children's questions. They avoid or evade answering questions much less.

4. Favour emphasizing language in the transmission of moral principles and in the recognition of feeling.

5. Favour emphasizing language in the transmission of principles as these relate to objects ('Showing him how things work').

6. Favour talking frequently to unspecified other adults in the cognitive area. This leads us to assume that the MC mothers' cognitive world, relative to the WC mothers' cognitive world, is expanding, and the *consequences feed back to her child*.

We can summarize by suggesting that the MC child not only has access to a greater range of educationally relevant knowledge but that relative to the WC child he is oriented through language to *principles* as these relate to objects and persons. The MC child through the form of his linguistic socialization, relative to the WC child, is made aware of the meta-languages through which a certain form of knowledge is acquired. Our data strongly suggests that this is much less the case for the WC child.

It should be apparent that the linguistic socialization of the MC child is critically relevant to his ability to profit from the educational experience as this is *currently* defined. There is little discontinuity between the symbolic orders of the school and those to which he has been socialized through his family. Whereas for the working-class child there is a hiatus between the symbolic orders of the school and those of his family. He is less oriented towards the meta-languages of control and innovation and the pattern of social relationships through which they are transmitted. The genesis of educational failure, according to our findings, may well be found in the pattern of communication and control which are realizations and thus transmitters of specific subcultures.

It is important to emphasize and re-emphasize that these reported social class differences in forms of communication do *not* justify the inference that the WC communication forms are impoverished. Neither does it indicate that this group is linguistically deprived. It simply reveals that sub-cultures, or indeed, cultures, place a differential emphasis upon *language* in the context of socialization. The differences we have reported point to differences in the *social function* of linguistic communication. It is clearly the case that all cultures or sub-cultures are realized through communication forms which contain their own unique imaginative and aesthetic possibilities. Our schedules were *not* designed to reveal such possibilities. It must be borne in mind that this indicates that we have studied only a narrow range of competence and a narrow range of social relationships.

In conclusion, all but two of the hypotheses given in the introduction have been confirmed. The findings have also revealed certain unexpected fluctuations in patterns of communication within each social class, as well as directing our attention to differences in the degree of contextual-specificity. Thus, the analysis has enabled us to show that the patterning of verbal communication and, therefore, maternal definitions of the role of language in the socializing process, are dependent on and must be examined within, *contexts of use*. The behavioural setting and the topic under discussion are major determinants of *what* is said and *how* it is said (Hymes, 1962, 1967; Gumperz, 1968; Ervin-Tripp, 1964; Williams and Naremore, 1969). In later publications we hope to be able to show that these different forms of communication arise out of different orderings of roles within the family. We also hope to be able to show not only the variation in forms of communication *between* subcultural groups, but also the variations which are found *within* subcultural groups, together with their social antecedents. The communication system is itself a reflection of and transmitter of the underlying boundary maintenance procedures within the family. Perhaps the most important conclusion is one which has been stressed before: the need for small-scale naturalistic and experimental studies of the channels, codes and contexts which control processes of socialization. [. . .]

Schedule A

If parents could not speak, how much more difficult do you think it would be for them to do the following things with young children who had not yet started school?

	Very much more difficult	Much more difficult	More difficult	Not too difficult	Fairly easy	Easy
Teaching them everyday tasks, like dressing, and using a knife and fork.						
Helping them to make things						
Drawing their attention to different shapes						
Playing games with them						
Showing them what is right and wrong						
Letting them know what you're feeling						
Showing them how things work						
Helping them to work things out for themselves						
Disciplining them						
Showing them how pleased you are with their progress						
Dealing with them when they are unhappy						

Schedule B

Children often chatter quite a lot. Please say what you usually do if — starts chattering:

	Tell him to stop	Tell him to wait	Answer him quickly	Chat with him
1. When you are working around the house				
2. When you are walking along the street				
3. When you are trying to relax				
4. When you are talking to your husband				
5. When you are in a shop				
6. When you are in a bus or tube				
7. At meal-times				

Schedule C

Here are some more questions that — might ask. For each question, please say what you would be most likely to do *first*.

Questions

1. Why we have rules.
2. Why there are wars.
3. Why boys are different from girls.
4. Why some people are mentally disturbed.
5. Why some people are rich and others poor.
6. Why some people are physically disabled.
7. Daddy's part in making babies.
8. Why people die.

Strategies

(a) Make up something until he is older.
(b) Tell him to ask Daddy.
(c) Try and change the subject.
(d) Take the opportunity to discuss the matter with him.
(e) Tell him he's not old enough to understand.
(f) Give him a brief answer and see if he's satisfied.

Schedule D

If you were explaining the meaning of the following words to your child, which *two* of the four statements would you choose? Please put the figure 1 by the statement you would be most likely to choose, and a figure 2 by the statement you think is second best.

'Cool'
1. It's when something is no longer hot to touch.
2. It's the opposite of warm.
3. It's what you feel when the sun goes in.
4. It's a little bit warmer than 'cold'.

'Mix'
1. To put things together.
2. When I make a stew the food is all mixed up.
3. It's what you do when you put different paints together to make different colours.
4. It's the opposite of separate.

'Dangerous'
1. It's when you might get hurt.
2. A road where there are lots of accidents.
3. It's dangerous to play with fire.
4. It's the opposite of safe.

'Flexible'
1. Rubber is flexible.
2. It's the opposite of rigid or stiff.
3. Your shoes are flexible.
4. Something that will bend without breaking.

Schedule D was a particularly difficult schedule to design as it called for four distinct types of explanations which could be offered to a child of *seven years of age*. On the whole, we felt reasonably confident about the general definitions and antonyms.

	General	Antonyms
Cool	It's a little bit warmer than cold	It's the opposite of warm
Mix	To put things together	It's the opposite of separate
Dangerous	It's when you might get hurt	It's the opposite of safe
Flexible	Something that will bend without breaking	It's the opposite of rigid or or stiff

The major problem in the design was separating the concrete *explicit* from the concrete *implicit*.

Cool	It's when something is no longer warm to touch	It's what you feel when the sun goes in
Mix	It's what you do when you put different paints together to make different colours	When I make a stew the food is all mixed up
Dangerous	A road where there are lots of accidents	It's dangerous to play with fire
Flexible	Rubber is flexible	Your shoes are flexible

We think that when one considers *all* the 'explicit' statements and *all* the 'implicit' statements then one can see a difference in the type of explanation. Three of the 'implicit' statements mention the word to be defined in the explanation. The fourth contrasts 'it's what you feel when the sun goes in' (implicit) where the state is left open, with 'it's when something is no longer hot to touch' (explicit). In one case (the word 'flexible') the choice is between two explanations, both using the word 'flexible' in the statements: 'shoes are flexible' (implicit) and 'rubber is flexible' (explicit). We considered that the latter statement was a less limiting example than the former.

We found that despite the difficulty in clearly separating the concrete explanations into two unambiguous clauses, there was a greater incidence of implicit concrete choices with the WC and a greater incidence of explicit concrete choices witin the MC. We feel that this is a potentially useful approach which is worthy of greater development.

References

BERNSTEIN, B. (1962), 'Family role systems, communication and socialization', SRU manuscript.

BERNSTEIN, B. (1970), 'A sociolinguistic approach to socialization: with some reference to educability', in J. J. Gumperz and D. Hymes (eds.), *Directions in Sociolinguistics*, Holt, Rinehart & Winston (publ. 1971).

BERNSTEIN, B., and HENDERSON, D. (1969), 'Social class differences in the relevance of language to socialization', *Sociology*, vol. 3.

BERNSTEIN, B., and BRANDIS, W. (1970), 'Social class differences in communication and control', in *Primary Socialization, Language & Education, vol. 1: Social Class, Language and Communication*, University of London Institute of Education, Sociological Research Unit Monograph Series directed by Basil Bernstein, Routledge & Kegan Paul.

BRANDIS W., and HENDERSON, D. (1970), 'Primary Socialization, Language and Education,' Vol. 1: *Social Class, Language add Communication*, University of London Institute of Education, Sociological Research Unit Monograph Series, Routledge & Kegan Paul.

ERVIN-TRIPP, S. (1964), 'An analysis of the interaction of language, topic and listener', in J. J. Gumperz and D. Hymes (eds.), *The Ethnography of Communication, AmA*, vol. 66, no. 6, part 2.

GUMPERZ, J. J. (1968), 'On the ethnology of linguistic change', in J. J. Gumperz and D. Hymes (eds.), *Directions in Sociolinguistics*, Holt, Rinehart & Winston (published 1971).

HENDERSON, D. (1970), 'Social class differences in form-class usage among five-year-old children', in *Primary Socialisation, Language and Education, Vol. 1: Social Class, Language and Communication*, by W. Brandis and D. Henderson, University of London Institute of Education, Sociological Research Unit Monograph Series, Routledge & Kegan Paul.

HYMES, D. (1962), 'The ethnography of speaking', in Gladwin and Sturtevand (eds.), *Anthropology and Human Behaviour*, Anthropology Society of Washington.

HYMES, D. (1967), 'Models of the interaction of language and social setting', *J. Soc. Iss.*, vol. 23.

JONES, J. (1966), 'Social class and the under-fives', *New Society*, December 1966.

PARSONS, T., and SHILS, E. (1951), *Towards a General Theory of Action*, Harvard University Press, chapter 1.

WILLIAMS, F., and NAREMORE, R. C. (1969), 'On the functional analysis of social class differences in modes of speech', *Speech Monogrs,* vol. 35, no. 2.

WINER, B. (1962), *Statistical Principles in Experimental Design*, chapters 4 and 8, McGraw Hill.

21 W. E. Lambert

A Social Psychology of Bilingualism

Excerpts from W. E. Lambert, 'A social psychology of bilingualism',
Journal of Social Issues, vol. 23 (1967), no. w, pp. 91–108.

Other contributions in this series have drawn attention to various aspects of bilingualism, each of great importance for behavioral scientists. For instance, we have been introduced to the psychologist's interest in the bilingual switching process with its attendant mental and neurological implications, and his interest in the development of bilingual skill; to the linguist's interest in the bilingual's competence with his two linguistic systems and the way the systems interact; and to the social-anthropologist's concern with the socio-cultural settings of bilingualism and the role expectations involved. The purpose of the present paper is to extend and integrate certain of these interests by approaching bilingualism from a social-psychological perspective, one characterized not only by its interest in the reactions of the bilingual as an individual but also by the attention given to the social influences that affect the bilingual's behavior and to the social repercussions that follow from his behavior. From this perspective, a process such as language switching takes on a broader significance when its likely social and psychological consequences are contemplated, as, for example, when a language switch brings into play contrasting sets of stereotyped images of people who habitually use each of the languages involved in the switch. Similarly, the development of bilingual skill very likely involves something more than a special set of aptitudes because one would expect that various social attitudes and motives are intimately involved in learning a foreign language. Furthermore, the whole process of becoming bilingual can be expected to involve major conflicts of values and allegiances, and bilinguals could make various types of adjustments to the bicultural demands made on them. It is to these matters that I would like to direct attention. [...]

Dialect variations elicit stereotyped impressions

Over the past eight years, we have developed a research technique that makes use of language and dialect variations to elicit the stereotyped impressions or biased views which members of one social group hold of representative members of a contrasting group. Briefly, the procedure involves the reactions of listeners (referred to as judges) to the taped recordings of a number of perfectly bilingual speakers reading a two-minute passage at one time in one of their languages (e.g. French) and later a translation equivalent of the same passage in their second language (e.g. English). Groups of judges are asked to listen to this series of recording and evaluate the personality characteristics of each speaker as well as possible, using voice cues only. They are reminded of the common tendency to attempt to gauge the personalities of unfamiliar speakers heard over the phone or radio. Thus they are kept unaware that they will actually hear two readings by each of several bilinguals. In our experience no subjects have become aware of this fact. The judges are given practice trials, making them well acquainted with both versions of the message, copies of which are supplied in advance. They usually find the enterprise interesting, especially if they are promised, and receive, some feedback on how well they have done, for example, if the profiles for one or two speakers, based on the ratings of friends who know them well, are presented at the end of the series.

This procedure, referred to as the *matched-guise* technique, appears to reveal judges' more private reactions to the contrasting group than direct attitude questionnaires do (Lambert, Anisfeld and Yeni-Komshian, 1965), but much more research is needed to adequately assess its power in this regard. The technique is particularly valuable as a measure of *group* biases in evaluative reactions; it has very good reliability in the sense that essentially the same profile of traits for a particular group appear when different samples of judges, drawn from a particular subpopulation, are used. Differences between subpopulations are very marked, however, as will become apparent. On the other hand, the technique apparently has little reliability when measured by test-retest ratings produced by the same group of judges; we believe this type of unreliability is due in large part to the main statistic used, the difference between an individual's rating of a pair of guises on a single trait. Difference scores give notoriously low test-retest reliability coefficients although their use for comparing means is perfectly appropriate (Bereiter, 1963; Ferguson, 1959, pp. 285).

Several of our studies have been conducted since 1958 in greater Montreal, a setting that has a long history of tensions between English- and French-speaking Canadians. The conflict is currently so sharp that some French-Canadian (FC) political leaders in the Province of Quebec talk seriously about separating the Province from the rest of Canada, comprising a majority of English-Canadians (ECs). In 1958–9 (Lambert, Hodgson, Gardner and Fillenbaum, 1960), we asked a sizeable group of EC university students to evaluate the personalities of a series of speakers, actually the matched guises of male bilinguals speaking in Canadian-style

French and English. When their judgements were analysed it was found that their evaluations were strongly biased against the FC and in favor of the matched EC guises. They rated the speakers in their EC guises as being better looking, taller, more intelligent, more dependable, kinder, more ambitious and as having more character. This evaluational bias was just as apparent among judges who were bilingual as among monolinguals.

We presented the same set of taped voices to a group of FC students of equivalent age, social class and educational level. Here we were in for a surprise for they showed the same bias, evaluating the EC guises significantly *more* favorably than the FC guises on a whole series of traits, indicating, for example, that they viewed the EC guises as being more intelligent, dependable, likeable and as having more character! Only on two traits did they rate the FC guises more favorably, namely kindness and religiousness, and, considering the whole pattern of ratings, it could be that they interpreted too much religion as a questionable quality. Not only did the FC judges generally downgrade representatives of their own ethnic-linguistic group, they also rated the FC guises much more negatively than the EC judges had. We consider this pattern of results as a reflection of a community-wide stereotype of FCs as being relatively second-rate people, a view apparently fully shared by certain subgroups of FCs. Similar tendencies to downgrade one's own group have been reported in research with minority groups conducted in other parts of North America.

Extensions of the basic study
The follow-up study

Some of the questions left unanswered in the first study have been examined recently by Preston (1963). Using the same basic techniques, the following questions were asked:

1. Will female and male judges react similarly to language and accent variations of speakers?

2. Will judges react similarly to male and female speakers who change their pronunciation style or the language they speak?

3. Will there be systematic differences in reactions to FC and Continental French (CF) speakers?

For this study, eighty English Canadian and ninety-two French Canadian first-year college-age students from Montreal served as judges. The EC judges in this study were all Catholics since we wanted to determine if EC Catholics would be less biased in their views of FCs than the non-Catholic EC judges had been in the original study. Approximately the same number of males and females from both language groups were tested, making four groups of judges in all: an EC male group, an EC female, a FC male and a FC female group.

The eighteen personality traits used by the judges for expressing their reactions were grouped, for the purposes of interpretation, into three logically distinct categories of personality: (1) *competence* which included intelligence, ambition, self-confidence, leadership and courage; (2) *personal integrity* which included dependability, sincerity, character, conscientiousness and kindness; (3) *social attractiveness* which included sociability, likeability, entertainingness, sense of humor and affectionateness. Religiousness, good looks and height were not included in the above categories since they did not logically fit.

Results: *evaluative reactions of English-Canadian listeners*

In general it was found that the EC listeners viewed the female speakers more favorably in their French guises while they viewed the male speakers more favorably in their English guises. In particular, the EC men saw the FC lady speakers as more intelligent, ambitious, self-confident, dependable, courageous and sincere than their English counterparts. The EC ladies were not quite so gracious although they, too, rated the FC ladies as more intelligent, ambitious, self-confident (but shorter) than the EC women guises. Thus, ECs generally view FC females as more competent and the EC men see them as possessing more integrity and competence.

Several notions come to mind at this point. It may be that the attractiveness of the FC woman in the eyes of the EC male is partly a result of her inaccessibility. Perhaps also the EC women are cognizant of the EC men's latent preference for FC women and accordingly are themselves prompted to upgrade the FC female, even to the point of adopting the FC woman as a model of what a woman should be.

However, the thought that another group is better than their own should not be a comfortable one for members of any group, especially a group of young ladies! The realization, however latent, that men of their own cultural group prefer another type of woman might well be a very tender issue for the EC woman, one that could be easily exacerbated.

To examine this idea, we carried out a separate experiment. The Ss for the experiment were two groups of EC young women, one group serving as controls, the other as an experimental group. Both groups were asked to give their impressions of the personalities of a group of speakers, some using English-, some Canadian-style French. They were, of course, actually presented with female bilingual speakers using Canadian French and English guises. Just before they evaluated the speakers, the experimental group was given false information about FC women, information that was designed to upset them. They heard a tape recording of a man reading supposedly authentic statistical information about the increase in marriages between FC women and EC men. They were asked to listen to this loaded passage twice, for practice only, disregarding the content of the message and attending only to the personality of the speaker. We presumed, however, that they would not likely be able to disregard the content since it dealt with a matter that might well bother them – FC women, they were told, were competing for EC men, men who already had a tendency to prefer FC women, a preference that they possibly shared themselves. In contrast, the control group received quite neutral information which would not affect their ratings of FCs in any way. The results supported the prediction: The experimental Ss judged the FC women to be reliably more attractive but reliably less dependable and sincere than did the control Ss. That is, the favorable reactions toward FC women found previously were evident in the judgements of the control group, while the experimental Ss, who had been given false information designed to highlight the threat posed by the presumed greater competence and integrity of FC women, saw the FC women as men stealers – attractive but undependable and insincere. These findings support the general hypothesis we had developed and they serve as a first step in a series of experiments we are now planning to determine how judgements of personalities affect various types of social interaction.

Let us return again to the main investigation. It was found that FC men were not as favorably received as the women were by their EC judges, EC ladies liked EC men, rating them as taller, more likeable, affectionate sincere, and conscientious, and as possessing more character and a greater sense of humor than the FC versions of the same speakers. Furthermore, the EC male judges also favored EC male speakers, rating them as taller, more kind, dependable and entertaining. Thus, FC male speakers are viewed as lacking integrity and as being less socially attractive by both EC female, and, to a less marked extent, EC male judges. This tendency to downgrade the FC male, already noted in the basic study, may well be the expression of an unfavorable stereotyped and prejudiced attitude toward FCs, but, apparently, this prejudice is selectively directed toward FC males, possibly because they are better known than females as power figures who control local and regional governments and who thereby can be viewed as sources of threat or frustration (or as the guardians of FC women, keeping them all to themselves).

The reactions to Continental French (CF) speakers are generally more favorable although less marked. The EC male listeners viewed CF women as slightly more competent and CF men as equivalent to their EC controls except for height and religiousness. The EC female listeners upgraded CF women on sociability and self-confidence, but downgraded CF men on height, likeability and sincerity. Thus, EC judges appear to be less concerned about European French people in general than they are about the local French people; the European French are neither downgraded nor taken as potential social models to any great extent.

Evaluative reactions of French-Canadian listeners

Summarizing briefly, the FC listeners showed more significant guise differences than did their EC counterparts. FCs generally rated European French guises *more* favorably and Canadian French guises *less* favorably than they did their matched EC guises. One important exception was the FC women who viewed FC men as more competent and as more socially attractive than EC men.

The general pattern of evaluations presented by the FC judges, however, indicates that they view their own linguistic cultural group as *inferior* to both the English Canadian and the European French groups, suggesting that FCs are prone to take either of these other groups as models for changes in their own manners of behaving (including speech) and possibly in basic values. This tendency is more marked among FC men who definitely preferred male and female representatives of the EC and CF groups to those of their own group. The FC women, in contrast, appear to be guardians of FC culture at least in the sense that they favored male representatives of their own cultural group. We presume this reaction reflects something more than a preference for FC marriage partners. FC women may be particularly anxious to preserve FC values and to pass these on in their own families through language, religion and tradition.

Nevertheless, FC women apparently face a conflict of their own in that they favor characteristics of both CF and EC women. Thus, the FC female may be safeguarding the FC culture through a preference for FC values seen in FC men, at the same time as she is prone to change her own behavior and values in the direction of one of two foreign cultural models, those that the men in her group apparently favor. It is of interest that EC women are confronted with a similar conflict since they appear envious of FC women.

The developmental studies

Recently, we have been looking into the background of the inferiority reaction among FC youngsters, trying to determine at what age it starts and how it develops through the years. Anisfeld and I (1964) started by studying the reactions of ten-year-old RC children to the matched guises of bilingual youngsters of their own age reading French and English versions of *Little Red Riding Hood*, once in Canadian-style French and once in standard English. In this instance, half of the judges were bilingual in English and half were essentially monolingual in French. Stated briefly, it was found that FC guises were rated significantly *more* favorable on nearly all traits. (One exception was height; the EC speakers were judged as taller.) However, these favorable evaluations of the FC in contrast to the the EC guises were due almost entirely to the reactions of the monolingual children. The bilingual children saw very little difference between the two sets of guises, that is, on nearly all traits their ratings of the FC guises were essentially the same as their ratings of EC guises. The results, therefore, made it clear that, unlike college-age judges, FC children at the ten year age level do not have a negative bias against their own group.

The question then arises as to where the bias starts after age ten. A recent study (Lambert, Frankel and Tucker, 1966) was addressed to solving this puzzle. The investigation was conducted with 375 FC girls ranging in age from nine to eighteen, who gave their evaluations of three groups of matched guises, 1 of some girls about their own age, 2 of some adult women, and 3 of some adult men. Passages that were appropriate for each age level were read by the bilingual speakers once in English and once in Canadian-style French. In this study attention was given to the social class background of the judges (some were chosen from private schools, some from public schools, and to their knowledge of English (some were bilingual and some monolingual in French). It was found that definite preferences for EC guises appeared at about age twelve and were maintained through the late teen years. There was, however, a marked difference between the private and public school judges: the upper middle class girls were especially biased after age twelve, whereas the pattern for the working-class girls was less pronounced and less durable, suggesting that for them the bias is short-lived and fades out by the late teens. Note that we probably did not encounter girls from lower-class homes in our earlier studies using girls at FC *collèges* or *universités*.

The major implication of these findings is that the tendency for certain subgroups of college-age FCs to downgrade representatives of their own ethnic-linguistic group, noted in our earlier studies, seems to have its origin, at least with girls, at about age twelve, but the ultimate fate of this attitude depends to a great extent on social-class background. Girls who come from upper middle-class FC homes, and especially those who have become bilingual in English, are particularly likely to maintain this view, at least into the young adult years.

The pattern of results of these developmental studies can also be examined from a more psychodynamic perspective. If we assume that the adult female and male speakers in their FC guises represent parents or people like their own parents to the FC adolescent judges, just as the same-age speakers represent someone like themselves, then the findings suggest several possibilities that could be studied in more detail. First, the results are consistent with the notion that teen-age girls have a closer psychological relation with their fathers than with their mothers in the sense that the girls in the study rated FC female guises markedly inferior to EC ones, but generally favored or at least showed much less disfavor for the FC guises of male speakers. Considered in this light, social-class differences and bilingual skill apparently influence the degree of same-sex rejection and cross-sex identification: by the mid-teens the public school girls, both monolinguals and bilinguals, show essentially no rejection of either the FC female or male guises, whereas the private school girls, especially the bilinguals, show a rejection of both female and male FC guises through the late teens. These bilinguals might, because of their skill in English and their possible encouragement from home, be able to come in contact with the mothers of their EC associates and therefore may have developed stronger reasons to be envious of EC mothers and fathers than the monolingual girls would have.

Similarly, the reactions to 'same-age' speakers might reflect a tendency to accept or reject one's peer-group or one's self, at least for the monolinguals. From this point of view, the findings suggest that the public school monolinguals are generally satisfied with their FC image since they favor the FC guises of the same-age speakers at the sixteen year level. In contrast, the private school monolinguals may be expressing a marked rejection of themselves in the sense that they favor the EC guises. The bilinguals, of course, can consider themselves as being potential or actual members of both ethnic-linguistic groups represented by the guises. It is of interest, therefore, to note that both the public and particularly the private school bilinguals apparently favor the EC versions of themselves.

Two generalizations

This program of research, still far from complete, does permit us to make two important generalizations, both relevant to the main argument of this paper. First, a technique has been developed that rather effectively calls out the stereotyped impressions that members of one ethnic-linguistic group hold of another contrasting group. The type and strength of impression depends on characteristics of the speakers – their sex, age, the dialect they use, and, very likely, the social-class background as this is revealed in speech style. The impression also seems to depend on characteristics of the audience of *judges* – their age, sex, socio-economic background, their bilinguality and their own speech style. The type of reactions and adjustments listeners must make to those who reveal, through their speech style, their likely ethnic group allegiance is suggested by the traits that listeners use to indicate their impressions. Thus, EC male and female college students tend to look down on the FC male speaker, seeing him as less intelligent, less dependable and less interesting than he would be seen if he had presented himself in an EC guise. Imagine the types of role adjustment that would follow if the same person were first seen in the FC guise and then suddenly switched to a perfect EC guise. A group of EC listeners would probably be forced to perk up their ears, reconsider their original classification of the person and then either view him as becoming too intimate in 'their' language or decide otherwise and be pleasantly amazed that one of their own could manage the other group's language so well. Furthermore, since these comparative impressions are widespread throughout certain strata of each ethnic-linguistic community, they will probably have an enormous impact on young people who are either forced to learn the other group's language or who choose to do so.

The research findings outlined here have a second important message about the reactions of the bilingual who is able to convincingly switch languages or dialects. The bilingual can study the reactions of his audiences as he adopts one guise in certain settings and another in different settings, and receive a good deal of social feedback, permitting him to realize that he can be perceived in quite different ways, depending on how he presents himself. It could well be that his own self-concept takes two distinctive forms in the light of such feedback. He may also observe, with amusement or alarm, the role adjustments that follow when he suddenly switches guises with the same group of interlocutors. However, research is needed to document and examine these likely consequences of language or dialect switching from the perspective of the bilingual making the switches.

Although we have concentrated on a Canadian setting in these investigations, there is really nothing special about the Canadian scene with regard to the social effects of language or dialect switching. Equally instructive effects have been noted when the switch involves a change from standard American English to Jewish-accented English (Anisfeld, Bogo and Lambert, 1962); when the switch involves changing from Hebrew to Arabic for Israeli and Arab judges, or when the change is from Sephardic to Ashkenazic style Hebrew for Jewish listeners in Israel (Lambert, Anisfeld and Yeni-Komshian, 1965). Our most recent research, using a modified approach, has been conducted with American Negro speakers and listeners (Tucker and Lambert, 1967). The same type of social effects are inherent in this instance, too: Southern Negroes have more favorable impressions of people who use what the linguists call

Standard Network Style English than they do of those who speak with their own style, but they are more impressed with their own style than they are with the speech of educated, Southern whites, or of Negroes who become too 'white' in their speech by exaggerating the non-Negro features and over-correcting their verbal output. [. . .]

Instrumental and integrative motivation

When viewed from a social psychological perspective, the process of learning a second language takes on a special significance. From this viewpoint, one would expect that if the student is to be successful in his attempts to learn another social group's language he must be both able and willing to adopt various aspects of behavior, including verbal behavior, which characterize members of the other linguistic-cultural group. The learner's ethnocentric tendencies and his attitudes toward the other group are believed to determine his success in learning the new language. His motivation to learn is thought to be determined both by his attitudes and by the type of orientation he has toward learning a second language. The orientation is *instrumental* in form if, for example, the purposes of language study reflect the more utilitarian value of linguistic achievement, such as getting ahead in one's occupation, and is *integrative* if, for example, the student is oriented to learn more about the other cultural community, as if he desired to become a potential member of the other group. It is also argued that some may be anxious to learn another language as a means of being accepted in another cultural group because of dissatisfactions experienced in their own culture while other individuals may be as much interested in another culture as they are in their own. In either case, the more proficient one becomes in a second language the more he may find that his place in his original membership group is modified at the same time as the other linguistic-cultural group becomes something more than a reference group for him. It may, in fact, become a second membership group for him. Depending upon the compatibility of the two cultures, he may experience feelings of chagrin or regret as he loses ties in one group, mixed with the fearful anticipation of entering a relatively new group. The concept of *anomie* first proposed by Durkheim (1897) and more recently extended by Srole (1951) and Williams (1952), refers to such feelings of social uncertainty or dissatisfaction.

My studies with Gardner (1959) were carried out with English-speaking Montreal high-school students studying French who were evaluated for their language learning aptitude and verbal intelligence, as well as their attitudes and stereotypes toward members of the French community, and the intensity of their motivation to learn French. Our measure of motivation is conceptually similar to Jones' (1949 and 1950) index of interest in learning a language which he found to be important for success-ful learning among Welsh students. A factor analysis of scores on these various measures indicated that aptitude and intelligence formed a common factor which was independent of a second one comprising indices of motivation, type of orientation toward language and social attitudes toward FCs. Furthermore, a measure of achievement in French taken at the end of a year's study was reflected equally prominently in both factors. This statistical pattern meant that French achievement was dependent upon both aptitude and verbal intelligence as well as a sym-pathetic orientation toward the other group. This orientation was much less common among these students than was the instrumental one, as would be expected from the results of the matched-guise experiments. However, when sympathetic orientation was present it apparently sus-tained a strong motivation to learn the other group's language. Further-more, it was clear that students with an integrative orientation were more successful in learning French than were those with instrumental orient-ations.

A follow-up study (Gardner, 1960) confirmed and extended these findings. Using a larger sample of EC students and incorporating various measures of French achievement, the same two independent factors were revealed, and again both were related to French achievement. But whereas aptitude and achievement were especially important for those French skills stressed in school training, such as grammar, the development of such skills, skills that call for the active use of the language in communic-ational settings, such as pronunciation accuracy and auditory compre-hension, was determined in major part by measures of an integrative motivation to learn French. The aptitude variables were insignificant in this case. Further evidence from the intercorrelations indicated that this integrative motive was the converse of an authoritarian ideological syndrome, opening the possibility that basic personality dispositions may be involved in language learning efficiency.

In this same study information had been gathered from the parents of the students about their own orientations toward the French community. These data suggested that integrative or instrumental orientations toward the other group are developed within the family. That is, the minority of students with an integrative disposition to learn French had parents who also were integrative and sympathetic to the French community. However, students' orientations were not related to parents' skill in French nor to the number of French acquaintances the parents had, indicating that the integrative motive is not due to having more experience with French at home. Instead the integrative outlook more likely stems from a family-wide attitudinal disposition.

Language learning and anomie

Another feature of the language learning process came to light in an investigation of college and postgraduate students undergoing an intensive course in advanced French at McGill's French Summer School. We were interested here, among other matters, in changes in attitudes and feelings that might take place during the six-week study period (Lambert, et al., 1961). The majority of the students were Americans who oriented themselves mainly to the European-French rather than the American-French Community. We adjusted our attitude scales to make them appropriate for those learning European French. Certain results were of special interest. As the students progressed in French skill to the point that they said they 'thought' in French, and even dreamed in French, their feelings of anomie also increased markedly. At the same time, they began to seek out occasions to use English even though they had solemnly pledged to use only French for the six-week period. This pattern of results suggests to us that these already advanced students experienced a strong dose of anomie when they commenced to *really* master a second language. That is, when advanced students became so skilled that they begin to think and feel like Frenchmen, they then became so annoyed with feelings of anomie that they were prompted to develop strategies to minimize or control the annoyance. Reverting to English could be such a strategy. It should be emphasized however, that the chain of events just listed needs to be much more carefully explored.

Elizabeth Anisfeld and I took another look at this problem, experimenting with ten-year-old monolingual and bilingual students (Peal and Lambert, 1962). We found that the bilingual children (attending French schools in Montreal) were markedly more favorable towards the 'other' language group (i.e. the ECs) than the monolingual children were. Furthermore, the bilingual children reported that their parents held the same strongly sympathetic attitudes toward ECs, in contrast to the pro-FC attitudes reported for the parents of the monolingual children. Apparently, then, the development of second language skill to the point of balanced bilingualism is conditioned by family-shared attitudes toward the other linguistic-cultural group.

These findings are consistent and reliable enough to be of general interest. For example methods of language training could possibly be modified and strengthened by giving consideration to the social-psychological implications of language learning. Because of the possible practical as well as theoretical significance of this approach, it seemed appropriate to test its applicability in a cultural setting other than the bicultural Quebec scene. With measures of attitude and motivation modified for American students learning French, a large scale study, very similar in nature to those conducted in Montreal, was carried out in various settings in the United States with very similar general outcomes (Lamber, Gardener et al., 1962).

One further investigation indicated that these suggested social psychological principles are not restricted to English and French speakers in Canada. Moshe Anisfeld and I (1961) extended the same experimental procedure to samples of Jewish high-school students studying Hebrew at various parochial schools in different sectors of Montreal. They were questioned about their orientations toward learning Hebrew and their attitudes toward the Jewish culture and community, and tested for their verbal intelligence, language aptitude and achievement in the Hebrew language at the end of the school year. The results support the generalization that both intellectual capacity and attitudinal orientation affect success in learning Hebrew. However, whereas intelligence and linguistic aptitude were relatively stable predictors of success, the attitudinal measures varied from one Jewish community to another. For instance, the measure of a Jewish student's desire to become more acculturated in the Jewish tradition and culture was a sensitive indicator of progress in Hebrew for children from a particular district of Montreal, one where members of the Jewish sub-community were actually concerned with problems of integrating into the Jewish culture. In another district, made up mainly of Jews who recently arrived from central Europe and who were clearly of a lower socio-economic level, the measure of desire for Jewish acculturation did not correlate with achievement in Hebrew, whereas measures of pro-Semitic attitudes or pride in being Jewish did. [. . .]

References

ANISFELD, E. (1964), *A Comparison of the Cognitive Functioning of Monolinguals and Bilinguals*, unpublished Ph.D. thesis, Redpath Library, McGill University.

ANISFELD, M., BOGO, N., and LAMBERT, W. E. (1962), 'Evaluational reactions to accented English speech', *J. Abnorm. Soc. Psychology*, vol. 65, pp. 223–31.

ANISFELD, M., and LAMBERT, W. E. (1961), 'Social and psychological variables in learning Hebrew', *J. Abnorm. Soc. Psychol.*, vol. 63, pp. 524–29.

ANISFELD, E. and LAMBERT, W. E. (1964), 'Evaluational reactions of bilingual and monolingual children to spoken language', *J. Abnor. Soc. Psychol.*, vol. 69, pp. 89–97.

BEREITER, C. (1963), 'Some persisting dilemmas in the measurement of change', in C. W. Harris (ed.), *Problems in Measuring Change*, University of Wisconsin Press.

DURKHEIM, E. (1897), *Le Suicide*, Alcan.

FERGUSON, G. A. (1959), *Statistical Analysis in Psychology and Education*, McGraw-Hill.

GARDENER, R. C. and LAMBERT, W. E. (1959), 'Motivational variables in second-language acquisition', *Canad. J. Psychol.*, vol. 13, pp. 266–72.

GARDENER, R. C. (1960), *Motivational Variables in Second-Language Acquisition*, unpublished PhD thesis, McGill University.

JONES, W. R. (1949), 'Attitudes towards Welsh as a second language; a preliminary investigation', *Brit. J. Educ. Psychol.*, vol. 19, pp. 44–52.

JONES, W. R. (1950), 'Attitude towards Welsh as a second language; a further investigation', *Brit. J. Educ. Psychol.*, vol. 20, pp. 117–32.

LABOV, W. (1964), 'Hypercorrection by the lower middle class as a factor in linguistic change', Columbia University, mimeograph.

LAMBERT, W. E., HODGSON, R. C., GARDENER, R. C., and FILLENBAUM, S. (1960), 'Evaluational reactions to spoken languages', *J. Abnorm. Soc. Psychol.*, vol. 60, pp. 44–51.

LAMBERT, W. E., GARDENER, R. C., BARIK, H. E. and TUNSTALL, K. (1961), 'Attitudinal and cognitive aspects of intensive study of a second language', *J. Abnorm. Soc. Psychol.*, vol. 66, pp. 358–68.

LAMBERT, W. E., GARDENER, R. C., OLTON, R. and TUNSTALL, K. (1962), 'A study of the roles of attitudes and motivation in second-language learning', McGill University, 1962, mimeograph.

LAMBERT, W. E., ANISFELD, M., and YENI-KOMSHIAN, G. (1965), 'Evaluational reactions of Jewish and Arab adolescents to dialect and language variations', *J. Person. Soc. Psychol.*, vol. 2, pp. 84–90.

LAMBERT, W. E., FRANKEL, H., and TUCKER, G. R. (1966), 'Judging personality through speech: A French-Canadian example', *J. Communication*, vol. 16, pp. 305–21.

LAMBERT, W. E., and ANISFELD, E. (1966), 'A reply to John Macnamara'. Mimeographed and submitted to *Studies*.

LAMBERT, W. E., and MOORE, N. (1966), 'Word-association responses: Comparison of American and French monolinguals with Canadian monolinguals and bilinguals', *Journal of Personality and Social Psychology*, vol. 3, pp. 313–20.

MACNAMARA, J. (1964), 'The Commission on Irish: Psychological aspects', *Studies*, pp. 164–73.

McDAVID, R. I. (1958), 'The dialects of American English', in W. N. Francis (ed.), *The Structure of American English*, New York: Ronald.

PEAL, E., and LAMBERT, W. E. (1962), 'The relation of bilingualism to intelligence', *Psychol. Monogrs*, vol. 76, whole no. 546.

PRESTON, M. S. (1963), *Evaluational Reactions to English, Canadian French and European French Voices*, unpublished MA thesis, McGill University, Redpath Library.

SROLE, L. (1951), 'Social dysfunction, personality and social distance attitudes', paper read before American Sociological Society, mimeograph.

TUCKER, G. R., and LAMBERT, W. E. (1967), 'White and Negro listeners' reactions to various American–English dialects', McGill University, mimeograph.

WILLIAMS, R. N. (1952), *American Society*, Knopf.

22 J. Rubin

Acquisition and Proficiency

Excerpt from J. Rubin, *National Bilingualism in Paraguay*, Janua Linguarum, Series Practica, 60, Mouton, 1968.

The existence of two major languages in Paraguay – Spanish and Guaraní – results in speakers with three different linguistic capacities – a speaker may be monolingual in either Spanish or Guaraní, or he may be bilingual in both Spanish and Guaraní. The bilingual may have either learned both languages simultaneously as an infant or he may have learned them successively with either Spanish or Guaraní being the first language.

In order to understand the type of bilingual community which Paraguay has and to understand the importance of bilingualism to the entire community, we will discuss the social variables with which the acquisition and proficiency of both or either language relate. Among the many possible social variables are the following:

Social class	Family
Age	Locale
Sex	National origin
Occupation	School
Religious affiliation	Informal variables
Political affiliation	

By considering acquisition and proficiency in the light of these social variables, we may add to our understanding of the relation of the two languages to the political, economic, and legal structure of the country. An understanding of acquisition and proficiency will also contribute to our ability to predict the direction of linguistic change, if any.

We are concerned here with the most common patterns and means of achieving proficiency and not with individual variation resulting from differential intelligence or special linguistic aptitudes.

In addition to the description of the social variables with which acquisition and proficiency relate, it is important to describe the social conditions under which each language is achieved and which may facilitate or deter learning. Under what conditions is each language learned? Are the conditions formal or informal, forced or voluntary? Is exposure to either language frequent? In which order are the two languages of bilingualism generally learned and to what degree does this relate to linguistic prestige and pride?

Methodological considerations

General

The data for this chapter is taken principally from the random sample census made of Luque consisting of 299 individuals, five years and above, and from the house-to-house census made of Itapuami, consisting of 984 individuals, five years and above. Each individual in a household was interviewed, if present at the time of my visit. Additional data are from interviews with teachers and visits to schools in the area. In taking my census, I found that not all of the members of a household were at home and exact details were not obtainable from those members present. When this secondhand information was scanty or questionable, I excluded the individual from my results. Some informants were not sure of the details as to when and where they themselves had learned the second language. The last is to be expected, since in Luque, at least, one is often exposed informally to both languages.

Proficiency

Collecting data on bilingual proficiency in a large community is difficult. The investigator is faced with several problems:

1. '. . . no generally recognized scale exists for measuring accomplishment in language' (Haugen, 1956). The construction of such a scale would involve at least consideration of three factors:
(a) The skills one is measuring must first be defined. In speaking of proficiency is one referring to the speaker's ability to speak, read, write, translate, and/or understand aural material?
(b) The aspects of the language (phonological, lexical, or grammatical which one is measuring must be narrowly defined.
(c) The resulting scale of ability must constitute a reasonable combination of these two factors.

2. The measurement of bilingual capacity should take into account the speaker's relative proficiency, because, as Weinreich pointed out, not every individual has the same proficiency, even as a monolingual.

3. The test, while it should cover the above two considerations, should be short enough to administer in the field during an interview, because in dealing with community bilingualism, large groups of people are interviewed. It should usually be administered by the investigator himself to insure that the conditions for testing are equal for all participants.

In my field research, I did not find nor construct a test which met the above requirements or which solved the above-mentioned difficulties. Such a test is extremely difficult to construct and although attempts have begun to be made to do so, none to date seems to fulfill the above requirements. Diebold (1961) used a translation test consisting of words taken from the Swadesh basic word list to check the bilinguality of the Huave of Mexico. This test, although it satisfies the requirement of time, reveals only one skill – the speaker's ability to translate certain vocabulary items. A second test measuring bilingual dominance was constructed and used by Lambert (1955) in a controlled experiment testing relative ability to respond to word commands. The test measures, however, only a very limited part of the speaker's linguistic skills, namely relative understanding of vocabulary items. More recently, Carroll (1959) has constructed a test entitled 'Pictorial Auditory Comprehension Test'. This test is designed to measure only aural comprehension, not oral production.[1]

My proficiency data was based on subjective observation and judgement of the skill of an informant. I interviewed informants in both languages using a tripartite scale (none, so/so, good) to measure each informant's ability in speaking, understanding, and reading Spanish and Guaraní.[2] During an interview I might switch from one language to another observing the reaction of everyone present. In this way, I frequently discovered an incipient bilingual who, although unable to produce any utterances in the second language, might still indicate some understanding. In addition, I collected data by visits to schools where I interviewed children in different grades, checked their bilingual abilities and attended classes to see what percentage of the lesson was grasped and responded to.[3]

1. According to Carroll, the test takes about forty-five minutes to administer. (This period, as Carroll suggests, might be reduced by decreasing the number of items.) In addition to the time problem, there are two other problems. The first is that a wide range of linguistic structures is covered with the result that it is impossible to determine what structures or vocabulary are being measured. Secondly, although probably not as great a problem, there is the possible difficulty of picture interpretation. Nonetheless, the test might be used effectively in the field situation.
2. The author is quite fluent in Spanish, having studied it for six years in both high school and college, and has no difficulty in conversing with or in understanding native speakers of Spanish. Her ability in Guaraní is less proficient, having acquired it in the field. However, after three months in Paraguay, she had little difficulty in understanding a running conversation and could herself maintain a continued conversation in Guaraní after four months in Paraguay.
3. Another technique which I tried out but which I did not apply was to have different informants listen to a taped conversation in Guaraní and list which items they thought were not Guaraní. A definite correlation seemed to exist between the ability to recognize interference phenomena and bilingual proficiency. The person most monolingual in the sample, found that the text was 'pure' Guaraní. The most fluent and best

Fitting my impressionistic data into Diebold's useful tripartite scale of bilingualism, I established the following categories:

1. Coordinate bilingual – only those individuals who both spoke and understood both languages well. I included here persons who were fluent[4] but who had some accent in the second language, as well as individuals who were fluent but who made the standard sort of lexical interference error of loan translation from Guaraní into Spanish (for example: *Yo me asuste grande*, rather than *Yo me asuste mucho*).

2. Subordinate bilinguals – those individuals who were scored 'so/so' in speaking (able to speak but not fluently) and were 'good' or 'so/so' in understanding.

3. Incipient bilinguals – those individuals who could not speak one of the languages but who in understanding this second language scored 'so/so' or 'good'. This assignment of data while clearly based on the informant's ability to speak also represents some indication of his ability to understand (a factor which constitutes a strong potential in later bilingual development).

Results
Over-all

Table 1 **Percentage of linguistic proficiency for 984 Itapuami and 299 Luque speakers 5 years and above** (corrected to the nearest tenth)

	Itapuami (N=984)	*Luque* (N=299)
Monolingual	33·7	4·6[5]
Incipient	18·8	4·0
Subordinate	27·0	13·3[6]
Coordinate	20·4	77·9

Significant differences between the two areas can be seen in the higher percentage of coordinate bilinguals and the lower percentage of monolinguals in Luque and in the higher percentage of monolinguals and the much smaller percentage of coordinate bilinguals in the rural area.

---

educated of the sample found the greatest number of Spanish items. However, this test has difficulties when used in a normal field situation. It takes quite a bit of time to administer and it is difficult to insist on individual rather than group participation.
4. By fluent is meant the ability to carry on a continuous conversation without hesitating because of morphological or syntactic doubts.
5. Six were monolingual in Spanish.
6. For eight Spanish was the dominant language.

Relation to social variables

Age. The age of acquisition has a considerable part to play in the degree of proficiency in, and probably with the attitudes which people have toward, each language. I will use here a fourfold age classification suggested by Haugen (1956) infancy, childhood, adolescence, and adulthood, to indicate the approximate age of acquisition of each language.

Guaraní was the first language learned by the great majority living in the rural area of Itapuamí, whereas, Spanish was the first language of only two informants. Both Spanish and Guaraní were learned simultaneously as the first language of fourteen informants in Itapuamí.

In Itapuamí, the greatest number of informants, because of exposure to Spanish in the school system, said they began their bilingual career in childhood. Often this exposure begins late in childhood since many parents ignore the law prescribing seven years as the normal age for school entrance and do not enter their children until their eighth or ninth year. The following reasons were given for non-compliance with the law:

1. The children are needed at home to take care of smaller children.

2. Some parents feel that small children will be at a physical disadvantage at school and should wait until they get a bit bigger.

3. Some feel that small children should be more mature psychologically before they begin school. Although the majority of the rural children had entered by age ten, a small group began as late as their eleventh year. Of those bilinguals who did not attend school, only a small percentage had become bilingual as adolescents or as adults.

Guaraní was also the first language of a large proportion (approximately 55 per cent) of my sample in the town of Luque. A smaller but still sizeable percentage of the sample (approximately 35 per cent) had been exposed in their infancy to both languages simultaneously. The smallest percentage (approximately 10 per cent) had learned Spanish as their first language.

Because the school system also provided the first exposure to Spanish for many people in Luque, childhood bilingualism was the rule. Those for whom Guaraní was the second language usually learned it during their childhood and only a small percentage became bilingual during adolescence or adulthood.

As indicated above, most people have their first exposure to a second language in their childhood. As exposure increases through school, work, or home contact, one would expect increased bilingual proficiency. In addition, the number of bilinguals as a whole is increasing because of greater exposure of the younger generations to Spanish. This is due to the increasing number of persons who are able to attend school as well as the increasing number of years they are able to remain in school.

Sex. As we see in Table 2, in Itapuami, men have a greater bilingual proficiency than women. If we take a total of subordinate and coordinate bilinguals, we find a difference of 20 per cent. The explanation for the difference seems to lie in the greater amount of education for men, and the increased opportunities for exposure through travel, army service, and work experience.

Table 2 **Rural–urban contrast in proficiency by sex in percentages for those ten years of age and above** (corrected to nearest tenth)

	Itapuami		Luque	
	Male (N=353)	Female (N=464)	Male (N=112)	Female (N=160)
Monolingual	16·7	26·3	4·4	1·8
Incipient	15·5	26·5	4·4	4·3
Subordinate	40·5	25·8	12·5	12·5
Coordinate	27·3	21·3	78·5	81·2

In the town area, as indicated in Table 2, the difference between male and female bilingual ability does not seem very great. The difference between male and female coordinates is only 2·7 per cent.

We may note that in contrast to the findings of Diebold's study (1961), among the Huave where age and sex were the primary determinants of the degree of bilingualism of an individual, in Paraguay bilingualism in towns was limited neither to males nor to adults. In the rural area, bilingualism is more frequently a childhood skill with more men than women having high bilingual proficiency.

Additionally, in the rural area, among the women, it is the younger women who tend to be more bilingual than the older women, due probably to increased school opportunities.

Itapuami females	Relative linguistic ability in raw scores	
	17–40 (N=229)	41 plus (N=139)
Monolingual	40	64
Incipient	57	43
Subordinate	60	28
Coordinate	72	4

Social Class. My general experience in Paraguay indicated that upper class informants more frequently tended to learn Spanish first and Guaraní second and to be more proficient (at least in the amount of vocabulary) in

Spanish; whereas, lower-class or rural informants much more frequently tended to learn Guaraní first and to be more proficient in it. Since upper-class informants have greater access to schooling, they tend to have a more intensive exposure to Spanish. But by no means did all upper class informants learn Spanish first. Many learned Spanish and Guaraní simultaneously. The two informants in Itapuami who had learned Spanish as their first language were both born and educated in the town of Luque and came from higher status homes.

In Luque, informants whose first language was Spanish usually belonged to households generally classed as *la sociedad*, some having had this status for at least one or two generations or else they belonged to households in the indeterminate middle but nearer '*la sociedad*'.

In those cases in Luque where simultaneous exposure had occurred, it was often the case that there was a desire for social mobility.

Often some change in social status had taken place in the household.

Families presently in the middle range had formerly been poorer or had come from the rural area. While the heads of these households were more comfortable in Guaraní, they often spoke Spanish to their offspring and spouses to offer better opportunities to their children.

In some middle range homes, both languages were used indiscriminately with a great deal of code-switching. My impression was that in middle-range homes, in which parents had some degree of education, no particular attempt was made to control language.

In one upper-class household, several members said that in their infancy they had heard the servants use Guaraní and had thus been exposed to both languages. I suspect that among most of the upper class this is a frequent pattern so that simultaneous exposure is probably the rule.

Occupation. Most informants were not exposed to Spanish first through their job. The first exposure was through schooling. However, some did indicate that their knowledge of Spanish or an improvement of it came from their employment. Usually those living in the rural area who sought work worked in Luque or Asunción. Some even sought temporary work in Argentina and were thus exposed to Spanish. Many monolinguals learned Spanish in Argentina during the years immediately following the Revolution of 1947 when they had sought refuge there and had remained for two or three years. Other informants had travelled considerably throughout the country selling straw hats or other dry goods. In this way, they had had considerable exposure to Spanish. Some women travelled regularly to Luque or Asunción to sell vegetables or meats in the streets or in the markets. In this manner they acquired more Spanish. Others said they learned Spanish while in the army stationed in Asunción or through classes in Spanish which were provided for some army divisions.

Some children were exposed to Spanish while living in Luque or Asunción, serving as 'mother's helper', 'errand boy', or apprentice. They heard Spanish in the household and also learned Spanish because the families usually sent them to school.

For the rural area, as in Diebold's study (1961), it is not the occupation which correlates with bilingual ability, but the degree to which the occupation engages the individual in contact with the Spanish speaking town or city. The Paraguayan situation is different from the Huave because in many cases, even though he goes to Luque or Asunción, an individual may avoid using Spanish since so many people are bilingual. When an individual is not a coordinate bilingual he may prefer to use Guaraní.

In the case of speakers whose first language was Spanish, occupation played a role only to the extent that it obliged an individual to converse with monolingual Guaraní speakers. This, in fact, means that just about anyone in Luque would need Guaraní in his occupation. Both the medical doctor and the priest in Luque cited their daily need for Guaraní. Housewives also felt the need to converse in Guaraní with their maids and the greengrocer vendors.

In sum, while many Guaraní speakers learn Spanish because their occupation draws them to town and they may be required to learn Spanish, Spanish speakers in Luque must almost automatically learn some Guaraní because their employees or patients, clients, or parishioners are often monolingual Guaraní speakers.

Religious affiliation. Most Paraguayans are Catholic so this variable does not enter into consideration. The only indication of a possible relation between religious affiliation and bilingualism was the case of the family in Itapuami professing to be Seventh Day Adventists. These people made a conscious effort to use Spanish with their children.

Political affiliation. I did not feel it appropriate to inquire about the political affiliation of my informants. As a result, no evidence is available to demonstrate a relation between degree of bilingualism and political affiliation. My impression, however, was that it did not seem to be significant.

National origin. Informants whose parents had been born in other countries or who had themselves been born abroad always learned either Spanish first or both languages simultaneously. In Itapuami, there were two instances of this type. In both cases both languages were spoken in the home – one informant had a Brazilian mother and the other an Argentinian mother.

In Luque, I found two instances of individuals who had been born abroad or who had foreign parents and who insisted on using Spanish to their offspring, even though they themselves were fluent in Guaraní.

School. For most of my informants in the rural area, the first continuous exposure to Spanish was under the formal conditions of the classroom. Only a very small proportion of those who knew some Spanish had first been exposed to it outside the school system. A large portion of Itapuami had gone to the school in the area, but approximately 25 per cent had gone to Luque or Asunción for their schooling. Of these, a small group walked or rode to Luque daily, but most children were sent to live in the urban area to avoid the long trip. Many parents in their desire to provide an education for their children placed them in the home of a relative, a godparent or a person of means for several years. These children were frequently expected to help around the house and in return might receive some schooling, the amount depending upon the generosity and interest of the family concerned. Children were also sent to town to serve as apprentices. In these instances, they were usually sent to an accelerated evening school.

For those in Luque whose first language was Guarani, continuous exposure to Spanish also came most frequently in school.

Since Guaraní is never taught at the primary-school level and is only taught in one secondary school in Asunción, it is always learned informally and casually.

The single most important factor in making monolingual Guaraní speakers bilingual seems to be the number of grades completed. I found a high correlation between the number of school years and the degree of bilingual proficiency.

Table 3 **Degree of proficiency[7] and the number of school years completed for 817 Itapuami speakers, ten years and above** (in raw scores)

| | School years passed | | | | | | | | |
	None	1	2	3	4	5	6	7 plus	*Total*
Monolingual	143	27	13	2					185
Incipient	45	44	58	23	3				173
Subordinate	12	13	86	102	42	2	2		259
Coordinate	4	5	19	40	51	38	30	13	200

Several observations can be made from this chart:

7. Degree of proficiency was considered independently of a knowledge of the number of school years.

1. A large proportion (77 per cent) of monolingual Guarani speakers had never passed a single school grade. Almost all (92 per cent) of our monolingual speakers had passed no more than first grade.

2. Of those whose bilingual ability was considered incipient, the largest proportion (85 per cent) had never gone to school or had passed only the first or second grade.

3. Of those having subordinate bilingual ability, the largest proportion (88·8 per cent) had passed only the second, third, or fourth grades.

4. Of those whose bilingual ability was considered coordinate, the largest proportion (86 per cent) had passed the third grade or more in school.

Table 4 **Degree of proficiency and number of school years completed for 272 Luque speakers ten years and above** (in raw scores)

| | School years passed | | | | | | | | |
	None	1	2	3	4	5	6	7 plus	Total
Monolingual	3				1[8]		1[8]	3[8]	8
Incipient	4	6	2						12
Subordinate	5	7	5	10	3	1	1	2	34
Coordinate	5	6	25	31	20	31	49	51	218

Several observations can be made from this chart:

1. The number of monolinguals does not correlate to school grade passed because in Luque, 5 of the 8 monolinguals were Spanish speakers.

2. Of those who were incipient bilinguals, the great majority (83·3 per cent) had either not passed a single grade or had passed only the first grade.

3. Of those who were classified as subordinate bilinguals, a small majority (64·7 per cent) had passed the first, second, or third grade. It is interesting that a larger majority (64·7 per cent) had passed only the first, second, and third grades than had passed the second, third, and fourth grades (52·9 per cent). This differs from the finding for Itapuami where the amount of schooling relates directly to bilingual proficiency.

4. Of those who are coordinate bilinguals the large percentage (83·4 per cent) had had third grade or above education.

5. The opportunities for informal exposure to Spanish in Luque are much greater and would tend to make the direct effect of schooling less than in the rural areas where informal exposure to Spanish is much less.

The importance of the school system in the exposure to and acquisition of Spanish leads us to an examination of the methods used to teach Spanish, the motivations for learning which it creates, and the effectiveness of

8. Foreigner, whose only language was Spanish.

current methodology in teaching the language. Consideration will be given to the extent to which the teachers are conscious of the effectiveness of the methods which they employ.

It is important to recall that over the years the Ministry of Education has ignored the problem posed by trying to teach monolingual Guaraní speakers to read, write, and do arithmetic in Spanish without lessons in that language. Teachers are expected to use Spanish as early as possible. All of the teachers interviewed indicated that they had been given no special classes on how to cope with the language problem.

After interviewing school teachers in both areas, I found that although many were aware of the problem created by this monolingualism, most felt that it was not serious and felt that any difficulty encountered was a normal part of teaching. In most rural areas, the teachers were under the illusion that although their students could not speak Spanish, almost all of them could understand it. My classroom visits generally indicated this to be untrue. On occasion, I requested that a class be repeated in Guaraní after it had been given in Spanish. The difference in response was appreciable. Most teachers blame the students' inability to speak on lack of desire. Some teachers in Luque, recognizing the difficulty created by the linguistic problem, tried to use more Guaraní. Although linguistic problems are usually greater in the rural areas, the urban schools attract many rural students. The first and fourth grades often cause some difficulties, because it is at these two levels that new rural students generally enter urban schools. (One category of rural school has only the first three grades.)

Because of the general lack of awareness (Ministry, normal schools, teachers) of the urgency of this problem, the method used to teach Spanish is largely informal and subjective. In the first few grades, many teachers begin by using a certain amount of Spanish and gradually increase the amount during the year. The most frequent technique used to convey the meaning of the Spanish is through translation into Guaraní. The teacher says the sentence in Spanish, translates it into Guaraní, and then asks the student to repeat in Spanish. Another technique used is memorization of poems and stories in Spanish. For considerable time, the exercises are completely rote for the pupil. In a class observed in the Itapuami school the first grade teacher asked the students:

¿La escuela de Itapuami es cómo? (What is the school of Itapuami like?)

The students showed their lack of understanding by repeating the teacher's question instead of answering it.

¿La escuela de Itapuami es cómo?

In another instance a little girl read perfectly a selection of her first-grade reader. Upon questioning her, I found that she had understood very little of what she had read. In order to offset the monolinguals' silence in class, the teachers call on the bilingual students much more frequently.

In addition to reliance on the translation-repetition method used in the classroom, some teachers forbid the use of Guaraní in the classroom. This procedure, which used to be very common, has been considerably discouraged recently. Teachers have been requested to encourage use of Spanish but not to exercise sanctions against those using Guaraní. In some schools, teachers require the use of Spanish during the recreation period. They also attempt to put monolingual and bilingual students together. A third procedure is to encourage the use of Spanish in the homes of students.

Although students often did not understand the Spanish used in the classroom, insistence on Spanish made them conscious of its appropriateness in the schoolroom. So strong was this awareness that when I requested the use of Guaraní, both teachers and students broke into laughter.

In general, as might be expected, the linguistic ability and academic preparation of the teachers in Luque were higher than those of the teachers in Itapuami. Of the four teachers in Itapuami, the teacher who had had only seven years of schooling made grammatical and phonological errors in Spanish. Teachers in the rural areas have the additional problem of very little or no student exposure to Spanish outside the school. The result is that rural students are less skilled than their coequals in Luque. Recognizing this, some parents send their children to Luque or Asunción, particularly if they are serious about the children's progress in school.

Frequently students in the rural areas repeat the first two grades several times. Parents seem to accept this as a matter of course explaining that it is good for the child because he learns more. It is my impression that a high percentage of these repetitions is due to a lack of success in teaching Spanish to monolingual Guaraní speakers. If greater recognition were given to the student's need to learn Spanish as a foreign language and if more efficient procedures were followed, the number of repetitions would be dramatically reduced.

All school teachers seem to accept Spanish as *the* language of the schoolroom and of all culture. Many teachers are shocked by the thought of introducing Guaraní as a subject in school and feel it would be a waste of time. A few would accept it on an almost equal basis with Spanish while emphasizing the greater importance of Spanish as a cultural medium.

Family. In the rural area, there is no indication that family background affects either acquisition or proficiency. As indicated, for almost all informants acquisition came through schooling. As a result, proficiency was dependent on the amount of schooling an individual had.

In Luque, acquisition of Spanish depended mainly upon social class, national origin, and amount of schooling. Acquisition of Guaraní depended on social class, national origin, and the presence of relatives born or raised in rural areas (see below).

Proficiency in Guaraní depends upon informal exposure and in some families, Guaraní is played down and therefore the children do not have much opportunity in these cases to speak Guaraní at home. For boys, Guaraní is then learned in play groups. Upper class girls often do not learn Guaraní as well as their brothers in their childhood.

Location. Bilingual acquisition and proficiency may be correlated as in the study by Barker (1947), with the neighborhoods of a town or it may find some correlation with rural versus urban areas.

In Paraguay, the rural-urban contrast is extremely relevant in first language acquisition and proficiency. As indicated, in the rural area, Guaraní was the first language of the overwhelming majority living in the rural area. In the town of Luque, Guaraní was also the first language of a sizeable group (55 per cent), but a large group (35 per cent) were exposed simultaneously to both languages and a small group (10 per cent) had been exposed to Spanish first.

Again, while almost everyone (91·2 per cent) in my Luque sample was either a coordinate or a subordinate bilingual, in the rural area, Itapuami, the bilingual proficiency was almost equally divided with 52·5 per cent falling into the monolingual and incipient categories and 47·5 per cent falling into the subordinate and coordinate categories.

In Itapuami, those who had been exposed to both Spanish and Guaraní in their infancy, said they had spent some time in the urban area.

In the case of three informants, their early childhood had been spent in Asunción where most of the population is bilingual.[9]

The mother of three other informants was born and educated in Asunción and said she was from a 'good' family where Spanish was frequently spoken. This woman had married a man of *la gente* from Itapuami. Although he always spoke Guaraní to the children, she tried to inject a bit of her 'city breeding' into the children's education by speaking Spanish to them.

In the rural area, the relative linguistic isolation of the area, is achieved through inadequate school facilities, lack of informal opportunities to converse in Spanish and through endogamous marriages practices. In

9. The national census of 1951 indicated that of persons three years and older in Asunción, 76 per cent were bilingual.

Itapuami the majority of unions are between persons from the same rural area. In 177 unions, 146 males and 144 females were from the immediate area. Only 5 men and 4 women were born in Asunción.

In Luque the order of acquisition is largely determined by the individual household. The factors of social class and national origin are particularly relevant here. Also relevant are the place of birth of the ascending generation. If birthplace is rural, then the likelihood of either Guaraní or simultaneous acquisition is high. If urban, then only social class and national origin are relevant.

In two-upper class households, the wife had come from a rural area and both languages were used in the household although it is probable that Spanish was used more frequently.

In some middle-range households where a grandparent who had lived in the rural area most of his life was a permanent resident, he continued to use Guaraní while the parents used both languages.

In two cases, lower class household heads had been born in Asunción or in larger towns than Luque and, therefore, felt it important to expose their children to both languages. One informant himself had been born in Asunción and he had heard both languages at home.

Living in an urban area is sufficient to guarantee some exposure to both languages and usually sufficient to establish a reasonable degree of bilingualism (see post: informal variables).

In the urban area for those for whom Spanish was the first language, exposure to Guaraní came through contact either with servants or through residence in the country. Some informants indicated that they had spent their vacations in rural areas and learned Guaraní by speaking to the residents.

For those for whom Guaraní was the first language, exposure to Spanish came first from schooling, then from informal variables and lastly from occupational contact.

In rural areas students learn Spanish for purposes of reading and performing simple arithmetic operations. If a person remains in the rural area, he rarely feels any urgency about learning to speak Spanish. Motivation to learn to speak Spanish is greater in Luque. Spanish is often necessary for routine communication with some citizens and is also learned by some to attain greater social status.

Communication is always the motivation for learning Guaraní. In some instances Guaraní was needed to indicate intimacy with the addressee. It was never learned to achieve greater social status.

Informal variables. A number of means of exposure to both languages exists apart from the above-mentioned in Luque. Although continuous exposure came first from schooling for Guaraní monolinguals, additional exposure was available through informal means. In the rural area, little informal opportunity was available to learn Spanish. Informal variables include:

1. From friends or on the streets of the town. In Luque the opportunity to converse in Spanish informally was frequently due to the pattern of code-switching and that of frequent use of Spanish by upper-class persons.

2. Although not mentioned by informants, the mass media also represented another source of exposure to Spanish. This exposure probably provided some reinforcement of initial learning.

Guaraní is never learned under formal circumstances. Informants whose first language was Spanish indicated the following additional opportunities (besides contact with servants or residence in a rural area) which provided exposure to Guaraní:

1. In play groups. When children, particularly boys, play together they often use Guaraní. Some informants said they had picked up Guaraní in school, usually during recreation periods. The head doctor of the Luque hospital, who had been educated in Asunción, reported that his boyhood companions had ridiculed him into learning some Guaraní. Some conversations, particularly ones including jokes, are so much more spicy in Guaraní that if one does not want to be the butt of a joke, one learns Guaraní in self-defense.

2. From popular songs. Often people interested in popular songs will pick up Guaraní as a biproduct. In learning the words to the songs, many young people also learn considerable Guaraní vocabulary, pronunciation, and some grammar.

Conclusions

Of the three possible courses of action in linguistic acquisition – learning Guaraní first, learning Spanish first, or learning both simultaneously – I found that in both Luque and Itapuami, learning Guaraní first was the most common pattern. In the rural area, this was really the only pattern. In Luque, learning Guaraní first was common but some informants learned both languages simultaneously and a few learned Spanish first.

Haugen (1956) felt that the importance of a language in a bilingual area could be determined by asking: 'Who learns whose language?' In Paraguay, while more persons learn Spanish as a second language than learn Guaraní, this is generally attributable to the fact that the large percentage of the population learn Guaraní at home and Spanish in school as a second language. The learning often occurs only in this formal circumstance and usage is then often limited to formal situations. In the rural area, those who do not attend school do not usually learn much Spanish. On the other hand, most Paraguayans do learn some Guaraní during their life span. It would be almost impossible to reside outside Asunción and not learn Guaraní.

In both the rural and urban areas, some bilingual ability is acquired in childhood. In the interior rural areas, opportunity to learn Spanish is greatest during childhood and adolescence (the school years) and diminishes in adulthood. In the towns there are always opportunities to hear both languages.

In general, Spanish is acquired formally in Itapuami and both formally and informally in Luque where social and economic opportunities to use Spanish are greater. The opportunity to hear both languages in Luque is very high. As a result of this high degree and informal manner of exposure, the level of bilingual proficiency is higher in the town than in the rural area where contact with Spanish is on a formal level in schools, and where often the presentation is not very efficacious.

My description of the social variables which relate to acquisition and proficiency have shown the following:

1. Amount of schooling is the single most important factor in determining Spanish proficiency. In the rural areas, the actual number of years of school is extremely crucial.

2. Rural citizens tend to have less bilingual proficiency than urban citizens. Their need for Spanish is less than the urban areas. Rural people living in urban areas tend to use both languages.

3. Occupation does not correlate with acquisition or proficiency directly but the extent to which the occupation leads the individual to interact with monolingual speakers does. It exerts the most pressure in making Spanish speakers learn Guaraní.

4. In the urban area, social status exerts some influence on which language is learned first. Upper class members tend to learn Spanish first and lower class members learn Guarani first.

5. In the rural areas, we have seen that men attain higher bilingual proficiency than women. However, younger women seem to be attaining higher proficiency than older women. Bilingualism is usually attained or begun in childhood in both urban and rural areas. In the urban areas no difference between sexes in bilingual ability was found.

6. Informal variables in urban areas accounted for the principal way in which Guaraní was attained by monolingual Spanish speakers.

No important association was found between religious affiliation, political affiliation, or family and language. National origin played a role only in rare instances where the individuals were not Paraguayan.

Because Guarani is the first language of a large percentage of people in the district studied, the strong attitudes of language pride and loyalty become easier to understand. However, the strong pressures of the school system are largely responsible for the negative or ambivalent attitudes toward Guaraní. In the rural areas Guaraní is really the only important language and despite pressures to the contrary, continues to be so. In the urban areas, a significant number of factors have combined to make both languages equally important.

References

BARKER, G. C. (1947), 'Social functions of language in a Mexican-American community', *Acta Americana*, vol. 5, pp. 185–202.

CARROLL, J. B., and WAI-CHENG HO (1959), 'Pictorial auditory comprehension test', *Modern Language Association*, New York.

DIEBOLD, A. R. (1961), *Bilingualism and Biculturalism in a Huave Community*, unpublished doctoral dissertation, Department of Anthropology, Yale University.

HAUGEN, E. (1956), *Bilingualism in the Americas: A Bibliography and Research Guide*, The American Dialect Society, Alabama University.

LAMBERT, W. E. (1955), 'Measurement of the linguistic dominance of bilinguals', *J. Abnorm. & Soc. Psychol*, pp. 197–200.

Further Reading

F. Ardener (ed.), *Social Anthropology and Language*, Tavistock, 1971.

B. Bernstein and D. Henderson, 'Social class differences in the relevance of language to socialization', *Sociology*, vol. 3, 1969.

J.-P. Blom and J. J. Gumperz, 'Some social determinants of verbal behaviour', in J. J. Gumperz and D. Hymes (eds.), *Directions in Sociolinguistics* (see below).

W. Bandis and D. Henderson, *Social Class, Language and Communication*, Routledge & Kegan Paul, 1968.

W. Bright, *Sociolinguistics*, Mouton, 1966.

R. W. Brown and A. Gilman, 'The pronouns of power and solidarity', in T. Sebeok (ed.), *Style in Language*, MIT Press, Cambridge, Massachusetts, 1960.

C. B. Cazden, 'Subcultural differences in child language: an interdisciplinary review', *Merrill-Palmer Quarterly* vol. 12, pp. 185–218, 1966.

C. B. Cazden, 'On individual differences in language competence and performance', *Journal of Special Education*, vol. 1, pp. 135–50, 1967.

C. B. Cazden, 'Language programs for young children: views from England' in C. B. Lavatelli (ed.), *Preschool Language Training*, University of Illinois Press (in press).

N. Denison, 'Sauris – a trilingual community in dIatypic perspective', *Man* (N.S.), vol. 3, no. 4, pp. 578–94, 1968.

N. Denison, 'Sociolinguistics and plurilingualism', in *Acts of the Tenth International Congress of Linguists*, 1969.

S. Ervin-Tripp, 'Sociolinguistics', Working paper no. 3, Language Behavior Research Laboratory, Berkeley, 1967.

C. A. Ferguson, 'Diglossia', *Word*, vol. 15, pp. 325–40, 1959.

C. A. Ferguson and J. J. Gumperz, *Linguistic Diversity in South Asia*, Indiana University Research Center in Anthropology, Folklore, and Linguistics, Publication no. 13, 1960.

J. A. Fishman, 'Language maintenance and language shift as a field of inquiry', *Linguistics*, vol. 9, pp. 32–70, 1964.

J. A. Fishman, *Language Loyalty in the United States*, Mouton, 1966.

J. A. Fishman (ed.), *Readings in the Sociology of Language*, Mouton, 1968.

F. A. Fishman, *Bilingualism in the Barrio*, Final Report, Contract no. OEC-1-7-062817-0297. US Department of Health, Education and Welfare, 1968.

J. A. Fishman, C. A. Ferguson and J. Das Gupta, *Language Problems of Developing Nations*, Wiley, 1968.

R. Fox, 'Multilingualism in two communities', *Man* (N.S.), vol. 3, pp. 456–64, 1968.

J. J. Gumperz, 'Types of linguistic communities', *Anthropological Linguistics*, vol. 4, no. 1, pp. 28–40, 1962.

J. J. Gumperz, 'The speech community', in *International Encyclopedia of Social Sciences*, vol. 9, pp. 381–86, 1968.

J. J. Gumperz, 'Verbal strategies in multilingual communication', *Monograph Series on Languages and Linguistics*, Georgetown University, no. 23, pp. 129–48, 1970.

J. J. Gumperz and E. Hernandez, 'Cognitive aspects of bilingual communication', Working paper no. 28, Language Behavior Research Laboratory, Berkeley, 1969.

J. J. Gumperz and D. Hymes (eds.), *The Ethnography of Communication*, *AmA*, vol. 66, no. 6, part 2, 1964.

J. J. Gumperz and D. Hymes (eds.) *Directions in Sociolinguistics*, Holt, Rinehart & Winston (in press).

E. Haugen, *The Norwegian Language in America* (2 vols.), University of Pennsylvania Press, 1953.

E. Haugen, *Bilingualism in the Americas: a Bibliography and Research Guide*, American Dialect Society, no. 26, University of Alabama Press, 1956.

E. Haugen, *Language Conflict and Language Planning*, Massachusetts, 1966.

D. Hymes (ed.), *Language in Culture and Society, A Reader in Linguistics and Anthropology*, Harper & Row, 1964.

D. Hymes (ed.), *Pidginization and Creolization of Languages*, Cambridge University Press, 1971.

L. G. Kelly (ed.), *Description and Measurement of Bilingualism*, University of Toronto Press, 1969.

W. Labov, P. Cohen, C. Robins, and J. Lewis, *A Study of the Non-Standard English of Negro and Puerto Rican Speakers in New York City*, Final Report, Cooperative Research Project 3288, vols. 1 and 2, *Office of Education*, 1968.

W. Labov, *The Study of Non-Standard English*, Clearinghouse for Linguistics, Center for Applied Linguistics, 1969.

R. B. Le Page, *The National Language Question: Linguistic Problems of Newly Independent States*, Oxford University Press, 1964.

H. G. Lunt (ed.), *Proceedings of the Ninth International Congress of Linguists,* Janua Linguarum, Series Maior 12, Mouton, 1964.

J. McNamara, (ed.), *Problems of Bilingualism, Journal of Social Issues*, vol. 23, no. 2, 1967.

E. Schegloff, 'Sequencing in conversational openings', *AmA*, vol. 70, no. 6, pp. 1075–95, 1969.

R. W. Shuy, W. Wolfram, and W. K. Riley, *A Study of Social Dialects in Detroit*, Final Report, Project 6–1347, Office of Education, 1967.

U. Weinreich, *Languages in Contact*, Linguistic Circle of New York, 1953, 6th printing, Mouton, 1968.

W. H. Whiteley (ed.), *Language Use and Social Change*, Oxford University Press for the International African Institute, 1971.

Acknowledgements

Permission to reproduce the following readings in this volume
is acknowledged to the following sources:

1 *La Linguistique* and Professor J. A. Fishman
2 Professor Gillian Sankoff
3 *Anthropological Linguistics*
4 Tavistock Publications
5 American Anthropological Association
6 American Anthropological Association
7 Georgetown University Press
8 *Anthropological Linguistics*
9 Professor R. A. Hall
10 Mouton & Co.
11 The Free Press
12 Springer-Verlag
13 Language Behavior Research Laboratory and Professor J. J. Gumperz
14 Academic Press Inc.
15 *Durham University Journal* and Professor A. McIntosh
16 *New Society*
17 American Anthropological Association
18 Basic Books Inc.
19 *Journal of Social Issues*
20 Mouton & Co.
21 *Journal of Social Issues*
22 *Sociology*

Author Index

Aarons, A. C., 294
Abboud, P. F., 117
Abrahams, R. D., 284
Albert, E. M., 8, 276
Allen, W. F., 205
Andrzejewski, B. W., 115
Anisfeld, E., 341, 344, 347, 348
Anisfeld, M., 337, 344
Anshen, F., 184, 188, 190, 191

Bailey, C.-J. N., 195
Bales, R. F., 221
Baratz, J. C., 294
Barber, C., 19
Barik, H. E., 248
Barker, G. C., 19, 362
Barker, R. G., 294
Baugh, A. C., 147
Bender, B., 69
Bender, M. L., 123
Bereiter, C., 337
Bergmann, J., 66
Berlyne, D. E., 299
Bernat, E., 306
Bernstein, B., 107, 218, 289, 296, 303, 310, 314, 315, 328
Berry, P., 147
Blanc, H., 116, 117
Bloch, J., 160
Blom, J. P., 23, 28, 43, 239
Bloomfield, I., 82
Bloomfield, L., 98, 142, 195, 273, 274
Blount, B. G., 219
Bonhoffer, D., 272
Bott, E., 218
Brandis, W., 314, 319, 320, 328
Braunshausen, N., 20
Brent, S. B., 302, 303
Brigel, J., 161, 164
Bright, W., 105, 159, 286
Brown, L., 185

Brown, R. W., 129, 130, 231, 232
Brun, A., 99, 100
Bruniera, M., 65
Buck, C. D., 105, 144
Burke, K., 270, 278, 284
Burrow, T., 160
Butler, Samuel, 100

Capell, A., 142, 239
Carletti, E., 69
Carroll, J. B., 287, 352
Catford, J. C., 66
Cazden, C. B., 274, 278, 282
Chomsky, N., 91, 190, 204, 269, 271, 272, 273, 279, 280, 283, 286, 287
Cicourel, A., 217
Clivio, G., 100
Cohen, M., 147
Conklin, H. C., 260
Cooper, R. L., 30
Cooperman, O., 306, 307
Cowan, P. A., 299
Cowe, E. G., 307
Corgnali, G. B., 69

D'Ans, A.-M., 148
DeCamp, D., 36
Denison, M., 36
Denison, N., 47
Diebold, A. R., 352, 353, 355, 357
Dohrenwend, B. P., 19
Donicie, A., 145
Durkheim, E., 345

Edelman, M., 26, 27
Efron, E., 145
Ellis, J. O., 66
Ervin, S. M., 17, 21
Ervin-Tripp, S., 34, 35, 206, 215, 219, 330

Kernan, C., 219
Klein, J., 299
Kloss, H., 106
Knobloch, H., 307
Koch-Grünberg, T., 78
Kochman, T., 310
Kohl, H., 219
Kranzmayer, E., 65
Krishnamurti, B., 161
Kǔcera, H., 188

Labov, W., 36, 37, 50, 110, 210, 212,
 213, 219, 220, 222, 270, 277, 286, 287,
 288, 296, 300, 301, 305, 306, 308, 309,
 310
Lally, J. R., 307
Lambert, W. E., 196, 234, 235, 236,
 344, 345, 346, 348, 352
Langdon, M., 245
Lawton, D., 303, 305
Laycock, D. C., 47, 149
Leech, G. N., 66
Lennerberg, E., 204
Le Page, R. B., 66, 69, 105
Leslau, W., 118
Levine, L., 184, 191, 192, 193
Lieberson, S., 15
Lorenzoni, G., 65, 66
Lucchini, L., 65
Lukas, J., 124

Mackay, D., 302
Mackey, W. F., 17, 21
Magri, G., 65, 66, 69
Mak, W., 18
Malinowski, B., 34
Marchetti, G., 69
Markham, C., 88
Martin, S., 239
Martinet, A., 99, 100
Martius, K. F. P. von, 89
Mason, J. A., 81
Matthews, G., 160
McDavid, R. I., 349
McConnell, H. O., 148
McIntosh, A., 66

McNamara, J., 297
McNeill, D., 236
Meillet, A., 106
Mihalić, F., 148
Miller, G. A., 204
Mitchell, T. F., 117
Moerman, M., 217, 222
Moffett, J., 297, 301
Mohan, B., 223
Moore, N., 347
Morag, S., 106
Moser, B., 92
Murphy, J., 148

Nader, L., 122
Nahirny, V. C., 18
Naremore, R. C., 299, 300, 303, 304,
 305, 330
Neustupny, J., 85
Noble, G. K., 81

Oliver, D. L., 42
Olson, P. A., 297, 301
Olton, R., 337
Opler, M., 157

Parsons, T., 335
Parson, D., 242, 249
Pasamanick, B., 307
Peal, R., 347
Pirona, G. A., 69
Plumer, D., 307
Post, E., 228
Potter, R. J., 212
Poussaint, A. F., 225
Preston, M. S., 338
Psathas, G., 307

Quirk, R., 283

Ramanajun, A. K., 105
Ramaswamy Aiyar, L. V., 161
Ray, P. S., 144
Reichel-Dolmatoff, G., 80
Reid, T. B. W., 66
Reinecke, J. E., 145
Rens, L. L. E., 150

Subject Index

Abelam, Wosera dialect of, 47
Address system, as a social selector, 238, 239
  in socialization, 237, 238
  two-choice, 232
Alliteration, rules of, 253, 254
American address rules, 225, 226
  identity in, 228
  rank in, 227, 228
  social selector for race in, 229, 230
  status-marked situations in, 227
American language, 98
Amharic language, 115, 116, 120, 122
Anomie feelings, 347
Arabia, 252
Arabic in Ethiopia, as *lingua franca*, 112, 120, 121
  attitudes towards, 122
  as mother-tongue, 112
  in the national profile formula, 121, 122
  as religious language, 112, 119, 120
  as trade jargon, 112, 121
  Sudanese, 118, 119
  Yemeni, 118, 119
Arabic in Somali, 253
Arawakan language, 81
Armenian language, 107
Attic dialect, 98
Austrian Carinthia, 67

Background expectations in communication, 215, 216, 221
Bahasa Indonesia language, 128
Belgium, 104
Berber language, 275
Bernstein's study of London school children, 210, 211
Bidialectism, 157
Bilingual, coordinate, 353
  incipient, 353

proficiency, 351–3
subordinate, 353
switching process, 336
Bilingualism, guises switching in, 337–44
  manipulation of language in, 55
  relationship with high status, 59
Bilingualism in Paraguay, 350, 366
  informal variables relationship with, 363–6
  social variables relationship with, 354–63
Bisayan language, 231
Brazil, 90
Brazilian Indian people, 81
Buang case, the, 38–50
  code choice in, 39, 44, 49, 50
  language, 40, 41, 42, 43, 45, 47, 48
Bukawa language, 40
Bulolo goldfields, 38
Burundi of East Africa, 276

Cadorino dialect, 66
Canada, 104, 235
Canadian French language, 196
Child language research, 296–311
Chinese language, 177
Chinese Pidgin English, 142
Clans, 52
Class and ethnic identification in speech behavior, 36
Closed-role systems, 218
Code, as a component of speech, 35, 36
  elaborated, 218, 310
  restricted, 218, 219, 310
  use in Indonesia, 125–41
Code shifting, dynamics of, 131
Code-switching, 11, 37, 42, 43, 289, 356
  in terms of social function, 43
Colombia, 90

Malay language, 128, 137, 178
Mass media for the study of speech, 183
Mauritius, 149
Menomini language, 273, 274
Metaphors, understanding of, 220
Methodology in the study of language, 180
Monolingual proficiency, 351–3
Montreal, 235
 greater, 337
Morisseau-Leroy, Félix, 151
Mother-child communication, 315–34
Multilingual speech communities, 36
Muslims, 120

Negro English, 36
Neo-Melanesian, 38–40, 43, 45, 47–9
New Britain, 38
New Guinea, 38–63, 144, 145, 149–51
New Guinea Highlands, 52
 anthropological fieldwork in, 52
New York City, 182–4, 193, 194, 198, 199, 200
Nheenghatú, early non-Indian language of, 89–92
North American Standard English, 145
Northwest Amazon, inventory of tribes and languages in, 91, 92
 lineage in, 79
 linguistic groups in, 79, 80, 85
 the exogamy group in, 79, 80
 the longhouse group in, 79, 85, 86
 the nuclear family in, 79, 81
 the one-language-one-culture image, 90, 91
 the phratry in, 79, 80
 the sib, 79, 80
 the tribe, 79
Northwest Amazon culture, social units in, 79
Northwest Amazon Indians, 79
Northwest Amazon Indians' language learning, 89
Northwest Amazon Indians' multilingualism, 85, 87

Northwest Amazon Indians, repeating in translation, 84
Northwest Amazon Indians' Spanish, 83
Northwest Amazon Indian tribes, 80
Norway, 16
Norwegian, 104, 107

OED, 98, 100
Ono-keto dialect, 57
Open-role systems, 218
Oral language education, theory of, 309–11

Pakrit language, 108
Paradigmatic structure of speech, 212, 213
Paraguay, 289
 bilingualism in, 350, 355
Patois, 99, 100
Patois-dialect distinction, 100
Pidgin language, 54–7, 60, 61
 and creole vocabularies – shifts in meaning, 143
 as a lingua franca, 149
 definition of, 142
 in New Guinea, 144
 use of, 145, 148, 149
 status of, 150, 151
Piedmontese, as a dialect, 100
Pirituapuyo language, 82, 91
Plattdeutsh, 16
Port au Prince language, 145, 147
Portuguese language, 89–92
Pressoir, Charles-Fernand, 147
Puerto Rican address system, 234, 235
Puerto Rican bilingualism, 22–7
Puerto Rican language census in Jersey City, 25
Puerto Rican speech community, 22

Quebec, 235
 French speakers in, 196
Quechua language, 105
Quran, the, 252

Raleigh, Sir Walter, 98
Ramfau dialect, 53, 54, 57, 60
Relationship between participants as a
factor of speech behaviour, 36
Réunion, 149
Riksmaal, 16
Romance languages, 82, 98, 108
Romansch, 16, 67
Russian address system in nineteenth
century, 232, 233, 236, 237

St Pierre et Miquelon, 235
Sanskrit language, 108
Saurian German, Latin and Romance
loan-words in, 74
Sauris, 65–76
Sauris, German dialect of, 65, 66, 70,
73
Schizoglossia, 108
Schleswig, 16
Schwytzertütsh, 16
Second-language learning, 10, 289, 345
Second-language teaching, 10
Semantics, 291
Serbo-Croatian language, 107
Shakespeare, 247
Shifting, language, 289
second person pronoun, 289
Siane-Gahuku-Bena family of
languages, 53
Siane group of tribes, 52
ethnography of, 52
Siane language, 53–8, 63
as a factor in wife-selection, 60
dialects of, 53, 57
Siati dialect, 53
Siati villages, separation of, 61, 62
Slovene language, 67
Small group interaction, study of,
221–3
Social class differences, in relationship
with socialization of the child,
314–34
the situation as a source of, 309
Sociocultural variables, 277
Sociolinguistic description, domains

of language behaviour in, 290, 291
linguistic routines in, 290
verbal repertoire in, 290
Sociolinguistic elicitation techniques,
208–12, 219
Sociolinguistic interference, 287, 288,
289
Sociolinguistic markers, 188–200
Sociolinguistic relationship among
some constructs employed, 30
Sociolinguistic rules, role of, 41
Sociolinguistic structure, 188–96
problems of, 194–5
Sociolinguistic variable, 188, 189, 213,
214
Sociolinguistic variation in South
Asian Area, 157–65
Sociolinguistics, micro and macro, 28,
29, 31
Sociological Research Unit, University
of London, 314, 238
Somali culture, 252
Somali language, 252, 253
Somali Republic, 252
alliterative poetry in the, 253–8
dichotomy in the, 252
theatre in the, 258, 259
Somali vernacular, 115
South Asian area, 157
caste dialects in the, 158, 159
Spanish language, 22–7, 83, 90, 92,
289, 350–66
dialects of the, 92
Spanish–English bilinguals, 36
Speech, attention paid to, 180
formality in, 181
good data on, 181
social correction of, 195, 196
unsystematic observations on, 183
variation in, 208
Speech acts, repertoire of, 277
rules of, 278
Speech behaviour, structural aspects
of, 212–18
Standard Languages, 8, 105, 106–10
degree of standardization of, 106, 107